MARLENE DIETRICH

RANDOM HOUSE LARGE PRINT

LARGE PRINT - Paper

Riva, Maria
Marlene Dietrich
(Volume Two)

DATE DUE			
AP 22 '93			
AP 27 '93			
MY 7 '93			
MY 14 '93			
MY 27 '93			
JE 22 '93			
JY 6 '93			
JY 26 '93			
AG 27 '93			
NO 20 '93			
NO 14 '94			

VOLUME TWO

MARLENE DIETRICH

by her daughter

MARIA RIVA

Published by Random House Large Print
in association with Alfred A. Knopf
New York   1993

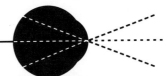

This Large Print Book carries the
Seal of Approval of N.A.V.H.

MARLENE DIETRICH

LONDON AND BEYOND

FROM FRENCH SUPER OPULENT to one of the hallmarks of British understatement was quite a contrast. The famous Claridge's hotel was so correct, so regal, so properly toned down, one felt compelled to sit very straight, hands primly folded, conversing in hushed Oxonian tones. My mother, her arms again laden with roses, marched straight to the master bedroom, exclaiming:

"Why can't they learn to cut the thorns off roses before they make up these funeral sprays? . . . But if they were not stupid, they wouldn't be working in a florist shop!" and threw the flowers into the bathtub, calling to me:

"Sweetheart, ring for the maid to clean the bathroom." It became one of my duties to cut thorns, as well as to see to the general care and maintenance of flowers. Although the great hotels employed "flower girls" to cut, trim, water, arrange, and oversee the floral displays of their hotel and its guests, my mother preferred her own staff to do it. It eliminated one more "outsider" having access to her suite. Except years later, when she stayed at the Savoy. That monarch of all London hotels employed very young ladies, of the debutante type, delicate as the flowers they were paid to cosset. Dietrich was always very cavalier when admitting them and their watering cans. She would pat their soft hands, smiling at their blush of confusion. When we remained at the Savoy for any extended time, I noticed that the flower girls assigned to our suite were rotated. The managers of the Savoy were very genteel diplomats as well as prudent ones.

As my father had already organized Claridge's, that left my mother only the toilets. While Tami and Nellie unpacked, I got rid of the fruit. Why did hotels always insist on filling our suites with baskets of fruit? Most arriving "goddesses" probably liked such juicy offerings—ours would have preferred pickled herring! Dietrich considered anything other than apples a waste of time.

I think the British press mentioned my height, and by their tone, questioned my supposed age of "just ten," for I was excluded from many Studio meetings and given orders to do "something constructive with Tami" instead. Once again, Tami became my official "governess," a solution to a ticklish situation I always profited from. Obediently, we rushed off to the British Museum and rediscovered each other as we discovered the Elgin Marbles. She seemed better than when I had seen her last in the Bel Air house. Thinner perhaps, her beautiful Slavic bone structure a bit more angular, too sharp in places, but her laugh was free of the faint note of hysteria I remembered, and she no longer picked at the skin of her fingers. Maybe the "cure" that my mother had said was so expensive had really done some good after all. We explored London together and I was reassured by Tami's new air of health. The slight tremor of her hands, the hesitancy before being able to swallow, that did not hit me until a few months later in Paris.

We usually met for breakfast in my mother's suite. My father made his appearance from the direction of his adjoining sitting room, Nellie from her room on a different floor, and Tami from her usual single down the hall. As was her lifelong custom, my mother carried her coffee cup while she walked and talked at us. Dietrich rarely talked with anyone. That would have required a certain interest in another's opinion. As my mother believed only her opinions worthwhile, she saw no reason for wasting time listening to those of others.

"Papilein, did you know that Robert Donat is married? On the screen, he doesn't look like that at all! . . . He is so beautiful! In this film, they won't know who to look at first—him or me. But when you talk to him, right away you know he *has* to be married. What a waste! A bourgeois mind with such a face! A little like Colman—you think something must be there—

but it isn't. . . . And his voice—like music! Can you imagine a voice like that talking about . . . hollyhocks? He told me all about how he has won prizes because of the special fertilizer he uses in his garden! It is not going to be easy in this film, making with the Grand Passion with a gardener!"

Poor Mr. Donat. He didn't have a chance of becoming a member of our exclusive "beef-tea club." I hoped my mother would find someone, though, she was easier when she was busy being "romantic" with someone. I needn't have worried. Soon, she donned superbly cut dresses that screamed, ever so understatedly, "woman." On entering a room, she flung her furs nonchalantly onto furniture, and left her trousers hanging in the closets. Browning replaced Goethe, paper-thin watercress sandwiches and Earl Grey tea, liverwurst and lager beer. She referred often to having played Hippolyta in *A Midsummer Night's Dream*. I wished it could all be for Brian's benefit but knew it wasn't.

Her voice took on the cadence of the BBC. She became a very, very "British" lady to the manner born. I expected at least a duke to make an appearance, but no crested invitations to Blenheim Palace arrived. No one surfaced until one day as we were once again crossing the English Channel on our way to Paris. We were making this trip frequently, to see the collections, fit, shop, and eat. This day, a dashing gentleman, complete with dark red carnation boutonniere, joined us, as though by merest chance. His eyes never left my mother's face. His hands touched, his immaculately tailored body bent toward her, at the slightest sway of the boat. Her girlish laugh trilled with "young love." They were definitely not strangers! I had recognized him immediately, his face was known—his name even more so. From then on, wherever Dietrich went, her swain was sure to go. She thought him "divine"! Alternated between being a Gainsborough maiden, an effervescent flirt, an irresistible siren, and a glamorous movie star. This did not stop her from making fun of him when discussing him with her husband:

"Papilein! He is really so funny—a real child! He wants to be knighted! Isn't that sweet? Being an American he thinks that having a title makes you a real gentleman . . . but isn't his father a Jew? You can't have a father who swings on ropes . . . and expect to become an aristocrat! But he is trying, and you know . . . he really *looks* the part. He may make it. If he does, he will have to stop using that stupid name. *That* really won't go with a Sir! He says he wants to 'present' me to Marina, the Duchess of Kent. He thinks I need him to do that. Isn't that sweet? But, of course, I let him think he is the only one who can do it . . . that *he* will be the one to give Royalty: DIETRICH! What is that American expression, Papi—means something like 'showing off'?"

My father, engrossed in the "London expenses" ledger, looked blank. Impatiently, my mother turned to me.

"You always know all those American things . . . what is it? It means being cocky."

"A feather in his cap?" I ventured.

"Yes, yes, that is it! 'A feather in his cap.' I am the shining feather in his nouveau-riche cap!" She laughed so hard she had to run and just made it to the bathroom. Her mood was "young bride" gay. Feeling desired by a handsome man always put her in an excellent mood, as it does most women. We all benefited from her joie de vivre and looked upon this new member of our family benignly. I never liked him as a person, but that had nothing to do with appreciating his effect on my mother's disposition.

Everything was such dedicated "hearts and flowers," such heavy breathing, such visions of walking hand in hand into the sunset, even to the exchanging of wedding rings, that Tami took hope.

For the first time, I too considered the possibility of my mother divorcing my father. I wouldn't mind a new father . . . if he was an American and the head of the house, then maybe I could go to school, have that lunch box, even be allowed to ride a bicycle, have child friends, have a birthday cake with real candles and sugar roses, have a family to celebrate Thanksgiving with, maybe even become a real American! I knew these wonderful things existed: I had seen them in the movies. But to have such a dream come true, it needed someone nice and settled . . . like a doctor or a lawyer. Even a businessman would do, but not a so-so actor trying to be a la-di-da titled Englishman and fooling no one but himself.

As Brian, Gilbert, Jo, and others had done before him, he too complained at times, expressing his hurts on paper, safer than confronting her face to face. True to her pattern, after reading his letters, my mother left them open for all to see. I read them before my father filed them for "posterity":

> Darling,
> . . . I thought your hugging Mrs. Edington and later your definite and outspoken flirtation with Gloria Vanderbilt was, to my banal, sophomoric *taste*, too much!
> I do not reproach you for your feelings in any way, sweetest—I can only wish I knew them earlier. . . .
> With all my love and God Bless you, my Dushka,

I could never decide if the "Dushka" was a suggestive reference to her trusty douche bag or the influence of the Russian theme of the picture she was making when they fell in love. Probably a bit of both. Everything he gave her had "Dushka" all over it. He gave her a gold cigarette case with it written across the lid. Years later, when he and the memory of this time were no longer important, she looked at it and said:

"You know—he wasn't bad. He knew how to dress and had very good manners. But he had no taste in presents. Look at this cigarette case! Stuck full of little charms that probably had special meanings to us then, and, of course, he *had* to write Dushka all over it—so now I can't even give it to someone for a present!"

My father played his roles of "husband when needed," "manager to famous movie-star wife," and confidant, while Dietrich filmed *Knight Without Armour* at the Denham Studios outside London, was in love, and enjoyed the heady novelty of being a big Hollywood star in a foreign land. Tami, Nellie, and I did our assigned duties efficiently and disappeared at the proper times.

An old friend from the di Frasso house days wrote and made my mother laugh. It didn't matter that Clifton Webb knew he was amusing, because he actually was. My mother often read his letters aloud, pointing out where she thought him especially clever or outrageous. Knowing how she hated *The Garden of Allah*, he addressed her by her name in the film:

The Lombardy
One Eleven East Fifty-Sixth Street
New York

August 25th, 1936

Dear sweet Miss Enfilden,

I was more than happy to get your post-card if for no other reason than to know that in all of that dizzy whirl you still remembered little me. . . . I arrived, en suite, last week, and the shrieks of "Le (or perhaps I should say "La") Webb" could have been heard in Laurel Canyon, the ex-abode of that vibrating raper Brian Aherne, or maybe I shouldn't have brought that up. On the train coming back was Granny Boyer, which practically made the trip perfect and filled with excitement as you can well imagine. . . .

Madame Dracula de Acosta came over to the house to go to dinner with us on the day of your departure. She was thrilled to the bone because you had sent her "eight dozen lilies" which she said was "The Old Sign," whatever that means. Well dear, I happened to be in the florist you had sent your flowers from and in a very nonchalant manner . . . inquired if you had sent eight dozen lilies to anyone. When the florist fainted dead away, I knew then and there that Mme. Dracula de A. had been lying just a teeny weeny bit. . . .

. . . N.Y. is grand, and I must say it is a relief to get back to people who do talk of something else but "my public, my long shots, my close-ups." . . . All one has to do is to get away from that self-etherized group to realize how little they mean outside of that glorious sunlit terrain.

My mother looked up:

"You see why I like him? He is one of the intelligent ones, like Noël Coward!" and went back to reading her letter aloud to us:

> I shall probably be crying for it this winter when I am up to my "whatsis" in snow and slush. . . .
>
> My days of "whoopie poo" are at an end. I go into rehearsal next week. Am doing a play with the Theatre Guild, about the grandest part one could wish for. I almost did *On Your Toes* in London. I had visions of being crowned along with dear David at the Coronation.

"Papi! I was right! Now we know! If Clifton Webb calls the King 'dear David,' he *must* be a *pansy*! I like them, but they can't be *kings*!" She lit another cigarette and continued:

> I also had visions of all the crowned heads of Europe at my feet—and spots North—and I must say I was greatly excited for a very short time at the outlook. . . .
>
> If you see Noël, just casually ask him what went on in Garbo's flat in Stockholm. My dear girl—I SAY NOTHING! . . .

By now you are probably palpitating over some illegitimate son of a frowsy old Earl. On the other hand, perhaps not. If I remember rightly, the English haven't got enough of that "zum, zip and zowie" for you, my puss.

My mother chuckled, and took a sip of her coffee. I noticed my father was in his "smoldering" mood and wondered why.

Do, if you have a chance, and even if you have not a chance, drop me a line and let me know a little bit what goes on. . . . I love you so very much, and even though you are the toy of London, being whoopsed off your feet (in more ways than one I HOPE!), shall be delighted to get any news. As you know, I am MAHD for you. Love to Maria and Rudi if he is with you. Bless you,

>Your, little mother
>CLIFTON
>(Public gentleman number 1)

Occasionally, my mother was back in time to join us at breakfast, then the conversation reverted to her special brand of noninterruptive monologues:

"They say that Edward will definitely marry that frightful Wallis Simpson, no matter what the old Queen says. I said, 'Then he has to abdicate!' . . . You can't have an American commoner on the throne of England! Impossible! But you know, Papi, that woman must be very clever to get a king so crazy about her. Or she is very good at 'doing' what he likes. You know what everyone says he is, and that kind always love their mothers! So, maybe he will listen to Queen Mary. We had dinner again last night with the Duke and Duchess of Kent. Now, that's a beautiful woman. Wasn't she a Greek princess once? Everyone made very polite conversations. No one dared to mention The Scandal, but of course, were dying to find out what the Kents knew! I think one of the things that attracted the King to this Simpson is that she is so flat. She looks like his favorite—young boys. But *why* does he want to *marry* her? He must be *very* stupid!''

To read newspapers was a waste of time when you had Dietrich as your very own town crier! I hoped she would give us further bulletins on the "scandal of the century." She did! A few weeks later, she strode into our suite and announced:

"I am going to see the King! I told the Duke of Kent last night: 'Send me! I can do it better than Wallis Simpson—and with *me*, you can be *sure* I won't try to be the Queen of England!' "

She was on her way to the Studio. Nellie and I collected the thermoses and usual paraphernalia. I opened the door and stood aside for

While shooting *Knight Without Armour* in England, my mother expected Robert Donat to be as romantic as he looked and was very disappointed when only his asthma attacks generated any kind of emotional upheaval. Halfway through the film, she decided she was making a flop.

We used to cross the English Channel to shop and eat in Paris. Although I always obeyed the order to step out of frame whenever a photographer materialized, this time I hadn't stepped back far enough.

A rare picture of Dietrich's daughter, husband, and dog together at lunch in Paris.

Young romance in London, 1937. Dietrich and her Knight looked so handsome together I sometimes thought that they kept up their relationship long after the emotion was gone because of that.

Our Knight joins his Lady's family and is costumed for a sojourn in Salzburg.

On one of her many transatlantic crossings, Dietrich finally got to meet someone whose work she admired and whom she, therefore, adored. Ernest Hemingway became a lifelong friend. They danced well together but preferred listening to each other being "brilliant."

my mother to precede me. Pulling on her gloves, she called back over her shoulder:

"Papi! When the Prime Minister calls, take the secret phone number of the King and call me immediately at the Studio."

The night that Dietrich's distinctive, one-of-a-kind Cadillac was discovered parked in the shadows by a side entrance of Buckingham Palace, the press went wild. My mother declared herself to be "thoroughly shocked at the stupid behavior of her chauffeur—for it undoubtedly was he who had taken her car, without her permission, in order to see the sights of London." It was amazing how quickly that rumor died and the press dropped the story.

It was one of my mother's favorite secrets, one of a few of her manufactured intrigues that, when mentioned, produced an immediate Mona Lisa smile, accompanied by a very wicked twinkle in the eyes. If Edward VIII had not given up his throne for the woman he loved, I am certain we would have heard much more of Dietrich's contribution to the preservation of the British Empire.

Knight Without Armour was filmed without my usual necessary presence. My father evacuated me for a time to Paris, where I lived with him and Tami. While Dietrich was busy, fleeing rapacious Bolsheviks, draped in diaphanous gowns copied from *The Garden of Allah*, protected by a too-too courageous Robert Donat in cossack disguise, I sat in my father's apartment reading *Mein Kampf* and trying to understand it. As I felt my mother would soon tire of allowing my father jurisdiction over me, I tried to make the most of this free time with my friends, Tami and Teddy. I hadn't realized how much I had missed my four-footed pal until he greeted me at my father's front door. His welcomes were not like other dogs'. No tail wagging, wriggling, standing on hind legs with excitement. If Teddy thought you were special, you rated "the look": Front paws planted firmly, hindquarters in respectful sitting position, head slightly cocked, ears perked—he would survey you. His eyes, doubtful, spoke volumes: "Are you really here? Finally? If you knew I missed you, would you care? If you hug me now, then I'll know!" and you would fling your arms around his strong little body and hold him tight. Then, only then, when he was sure of no rejection, would he give you a kiss and wag his stumpy tail. Teddy was a very special being.

So was my Tami. She tried so hard to please and nothing was ever good enough. My father, in his own domain, was terribly strict. He expected things to be done only according to his rules. If he suspected the slightest hesitancy in obeying an order, he shouted. His fury was usually out of context to the supposed misdeed. His rages frightened me, they galvanized Tami into frenzied panic.

"Tami—what is this? . . . I was speaking to you! Look at me! What do you call this? . . . Answer me! You call this a *steak*? . . . How much did you allow them to charge you for this? . . . Show me the bill! . . . Well, give it to me! . . . You can't, can you? 'Lost it' again? Like you do everything else? Can't remember anything? Careless and stupid? . . . YOU *never* do anything right. We know that, don't we? . . . You think you are now so much better? No, you are just the same—hopeless! You will now take this disgraceful piece of meat you bought back to the butcher, get my money back, then come back here and give it to me!" He slapped the meat into her shaking hands.

Her face was white, her eyes those of a hunted animal at bay.

"Rudilein, please, please, it's already COOKED . . . I can't . . ."

"Oh, now the excuses? You make mistakes— You have to pay for them! I said GO! . . . And don't try to come back here with any excuses!"

"I beg you . . . Rudi, please don't make me—"

"What do I have to do—DRAG YOU THERE MYSELF?"

Sobbing, Tami ran into the hall, clutching

the offensive piece of meat. I rose from the table, feeling sick—

"Sit! This is none of your business! Next *you* will be in trouble. Finish your lunch!" My father poured himself another glass of his excellent Bordeaux, leaned back in his special chair at the head of the table, sipped—watching me.

I tried to help. I went marketing with her, making sure that Tami got all the sales slips and that the centime count tallied. Checked the buttons on his shirts . . . if he found one missing, he might decide to kill her! Polished his shoes for her, brushed his clothes, filled his cigarette lighters, dusted his books, sharpened his pencils, filled his pens, ironed his handkerchiefs. I took over some of the cooking when Tami cut her hand. We both prayed we would get through each day without getting into trouble. At night, Tami took some of the new pills they had given her at the Spa and welcomed oblivion, while I read a madman's manifesto and wondered what made some people so ugly.

One of the things my mother learned during her time amongst the British aristocracy was their penchant for getting rid of their children as fast as possible. Starched and dedicated nannies received heirs wrapped in gossamer shawls and carried them off to the nursery wings, from where their charges later emerged, properly behaved and groomed, for special occasions only.

As soon as Beatrix Potter and her cute rabbit palled, nanny was pensioned off, her young ones fitted for knee pants or pleated skirts, blazer and cap, handed a lacrosse stick, and sent off to illustrious, ivy-covered establishments dedicated to "building character." These, in turn, were later exchanged for denser ivy at even more "Hallowed Halls," until the young were fully grown and properly "finished": girls to advantageous marriages and their own nursery wings, boys to inherited grandeur and heroic conduct on some battlefield.

Although I was too old for the nursery, I was not for the scholastic residency. My mother decided that, as a German aristocrat, her child too needed "finishing." Knowing the rather orthodox attitude the English have toward the process of education, my father must have convinced her that I would never be able to pass their entrance exams. So, saying that her decision was based solely on her wish that I learn French, she instructed him to find "the best boarding school in Europe where girls learn to speak beautiful French." My father, the consummate procurer, found it in Switzerland, convinced them to save Marlene Dietrich's daughter from the purgatory of utter ignorance, and I was inscribed as a paid-up pupil entering in September of 1936. Age: 11. Name: Maria Elizabeth Sieber, Hollywood.

I came to love Brillantmont. If I had known

then that they had put me down in their record books as being "Origin: Hollywood," I would have loved that school even more.

As Brillantmont required its pupils to supply their own linens, my mother arrived in Paris and bought me a trousseau; dozens of pure Irish linen sheets, heavy and slippery in their perfection, enormous napkins, of the same luxurious cloth. It was linen woven to last through generations of hopeful new brides. It was the only trousseau my mother ever bought me. She ordered my name to be hand-embroidered onto every article—none of those vulgar name tapes for a descendant of the Dietrichs! I was thrilled with my sumptuous hope chest and couldn't wait to make my first perfect bed at boarding school. I did not know that to be accepted by one's peers, it was better to conform to their standards, that to be different made one stand out and be judged, often unfairly. Never having lived in a real world, I had no guidelines to go by. I acquired those later, along with French. But I treasured my linens even after I learned to apologize for their ostentation.

My father delivered me to school; I thought perhaps my mother couldn't face the wrench of parting or was too busy with more important emotions. I was much too excited and scared to worry about why she wasn't there; to face things without the blinding glare of her presence was easier anyway. My father, very precise and informative, charmed the reserved headmistresses: this school was so elite, it had two of them—then told me, for what I hoped would be the last time:

"You are being given this opportunity to finally learn something. You will be watched. Here you will not be allowed to get away with anything. Remember, it is because of ME, not your mother, that you were accepted to this school. Here it will not be your usual Hollywood circus, where you can get away with everything because you have a famous mother. Only girls from the best families come to this school. I have given them my word that you will obey and behave yourself at all times. Your mother cannot protect you. Here a movie star's daughter does not count. Have you understood? . . . Then repeat it back to me. I want it word for word, so I know you have got it through your head!"

As this lecture was administered in front of my assigned roommates, I was dying of embarrassment. I hoped they couldn't understand German! He left me standing on a neat gravel path, bordered by decorative stone urns filled with matching flowers, below a Daphne du Maurier–type château that overlooked Lake Leman.

There were girls who cried and were miserable with loneliness, those came from "happy families," where people really loved them. Then there were those who, having grown up in boarding schools, were accustomed to the depersonalization, the uniformity of communal living. And there were us, the ones on vacation from being either hated or loved too much. We enjoyed boarding school, secretly envying those who had something to cry for.

At first, it was very difficult. We were allowed to speak only French, a language foreign to us all. This drastic method worked. It forced us to learn quickly in order to be able to communicate. For me, who had never learned how to be a real pupil, let alone most of the subjects required, the language barrier added to my panic of inadequacy. I didn't even know what "geography" was, suddenly I was expected to name the rivers of the world—in French! It didn't take Brillantmont long to find out that I couldn't spell in any language. That shook them a bit. I don't think they really knew what to do with me. I think they just gave up. But they were kind and let me stay, hoping that by some miracle I might catch up someday. If all else failed, at least I would be proficient in French and play an acceptable game of lacrosse.

My mother moved to 20 Grosvenor Square, the same address as her London lover. The girls at school talked a lot about "lovers." They too had mothers who had them. They even had fathers who kept something called a "mistress"—

who wore "vulgar" clothes, "shocking" black lace underwear, "took" money, cars, jewelry, furs, even houses from a father, in exchange for their "favors." I hated to show my ignorance by asking what that meant exactly, but as none of those requirements for "a mistress" fitted Tami, I rejected that category for her instantly. The girls were so vehemently convinced that those women of their fathers were evil, avaricious, and dirty, that I decided my tender, gentle Tami, who had never been anything but a loving wife to my father, was not a "mistress type" at all! My mother didn't fit the image of "mother with lover" either. She didn't "hide," go to "out-of-the-way-hotels-in-seaside-resorts out of season," make up lies to "fool" her husband. I had a mother who took a lover whenever she felt like it and it suited her—then told her husband all about him. I was a real misfit! Even my parents didn't conform to the accepted behavior of adultery. I stopped joining the secret "tell all" night sessions under the bed covers and missed a lot of valuable sex education that might have helped me a few years later.

My mother telephoned me constantly. Harried ladies would trot from the headmistress's office, knock hesitantly on classroom doors, requesting the urgent release of Mlle Sieber . . . to take an important phone call from Mme Dietrich, her mother. Even tests were interrupted.

It seemed that the unimpressionable Swiss were not movie star-proof after all. I would curtsey, excuse myself, embarrassed by the unsolicited attention, hurry to the *bureau*, apologize to whatever spinster happened to be in the seat of power, lift the waiting receiver to hear, not for the first time nor the last time that day, how miserable my mother was without me, how she missed me, nothing worked without me, the director was worse than our sick one on the last picture, that no one in England knew how to make films, that all the Kordas were "Hungarian Jews"—so what could one expect from "gypsies"—that Nellie had another cold and was useless with a nose that constantly dripped on the wigs, and, "Where did we pack the extra lashes?"

I listened and waited for her to hang up, without saying "good-bye," which was her custom. Then, curtseying, I did my apologizing act in reverse until I was once more behind my wooden flip-top desk—under the disapproving eye of the teacher. There was no escaping those calls. They hauled me in from hockey matches, even calisthenics! I tried hiding in the toilets—but those determined Swiss ladies would stand outside and wait, whispering urgently through the keyhole for me to hurry, to remember it was long-distance! If a scurrying lady dared to request that my mother call back, as her daughter was in the midst of attempting to conjugate Latin verbs, they were given such a tongue-lashing on the rights of motherhood and its priorities, that they flew, tore the chalk out of my hand, begging me with eyes gone pink and lips atremble to *please* get my *mère* off their backs. For more than sixty years, I tried to escape my mother's phone calls and never made it! She could find me anywhere! If Dietrich wanted you, you were doomed. Her private "homosexual fan Mafia," an adoring organization that circles the globe, were immediately alerted to "seek and find." As they also functioned as informants, lying to Dietrich as to one's whereabouts, in order to escape her, was useless. One year, my husband rented us an apartment in Madrid that had no phone. Ah! Bliss! Then cables began arriving every hour on the hour, until my mother remembered a fan in Barcelona and called him. He knew of a lovely antique dealer in Toledo who had just returned from a "divine" weekend in a gorgeous villa in Hammamet that belonged . . . the next day, we got a telephone! My mother was triumphant. In Spain in those days, people had to wait, sometimes for years, to get a phone. They didn't have Dietrich for a mother!

At school, I became the star of mail call. Other girls received letters, postcards, even small gifts. I got autographed pictures from my mother, but, best of all, the *Los Angeles Ex-*

aminer funny papers, rolled around a jar of peanut butter, from my favorite bodyguard. He never forgot, never missed a Sunday. The whole American contingent of Brillantmont was able to keep up with the adventures of Flash Gordon.

Although the school counted princesses, heiresses, and many prominent "blue bloods" among its pupils, I found, just like everyone else, they too regarded an autographed picture of a movie star a coveted trophy. One could even use it as barter: Two Dietrichs got you a Hershey bar, three, a lovely bottle of lavender toilet water, four, your neighbor's portion of roast beef on Sunday. It cost me three Dietrichs, the toilet water, Hershey bar, and two Sundays of my roast beef for a small autographed picture of Clark Gable! My mother would not have appreciated the rate of exchange.

I also found that I had the only parent whose profession was known to all. It fascinated them. The outside world wanted to know everything that concerned mine. I found that very interesting and a little heady. The bankers' daughters were never questioned on how their parent made his money. No one asked the Indian princess about her family. When my mother called, I asked for more autographs, but did not tell her about my wonderful American care packages from my bodyguard. She would have been jealous and spoiled it by saying something sarcastic about "funny papers" and the stupidity of Americans for reading them.

For my birthday, my mother sent me the contents of all the florist shops in Lausanne. A lot of the girls were jealous and made fun of me, and the headmistresses were shocked by such senseless extravagance. I apologized for being the cause of a "disturbance," donated the flowers to the infirmary, and hid in my room for the rest of the day.

At the beginning of Christmas vacation, I waited in the hall, next to my suitcase, for someone to pick me up. I hoped it wouldn't be my father. At the age of "just" twelve, I had taken my very first exams ever and done badly in everything but English Literature, and Religion. I prayed the latter would somehow placate my father's wrath but doubted that it would. My father strode through the big glass door, acknowledged my punctuality, and passed along the hall toward the inner sanctum of the headmistresses. I sat back down on the bench, wishing I could have spent Christmas at school. Looking as angry as I had feared, my father reappeared and signaled me to follow him out to the waiting taxi.

I think the sleeper we boarded was the Orient Express, but I was too frightened to notice if the marquetry was in patterns of overflowing fruit baskets or the plain geometric-chips-of-wood variety. I did get up the courage to ask where Tami was, was told she was visiting her brother and would not be with us for the holidays. Brother? I didn't even know she had a brother. I folded my hands and hoped my father's disposition would be improved by the usually impeccable lunch served before our arrival in Paris.

This time we were staying at the Hotel George V, in 1936, not quite as elite as the Plaza Athénée but a bit more famous. As I entered my mother's regency suite, she gasped:

"Oh! No! What has happened to you? What have they done to you in that place! . . . Papi! Didn't you notice? Look at her hair! . . . Call downstairs and tell them we want someone up here to cut Kater's hair. We also have to buy her clothes that fit! What do they give you to eat in that school? . . . Bread and potatoes?" She hustled me off to the bathroom to be weighed and washed.

From then on, whenever I reappeared from having been "away, together with a lot of strangers," I was disinfected along with the toilets. While my mother scrubbed, I ventured to ask her about Tami. She answered too fast, her voice high, a sure sign that she was lying without preparation:

"Oh, poor Tami! She had to have a little vacation. You know how hard she works to take care of Papi, so I told her: 'Go to Cannes and rest. I will pay the hotel—don't worry.' " She attacked my ears. I felt we were doing the washing scene from *Blonde Venus*! Could Tami's brother be living in Cannes? I doubted it—certainly not at a luxury hotel. Usually, my father and mother got their stories straight, very seldom did they not tally. Or, had I been just too young to notice? No, I decided, I had never been *that* young! They were both lying. Something was very wrong. I would have to be careful and find out the truth.

Although my mother had sent me away expressly to learn French, she was never actually convinced that I knew the language, and continued using it while discussing anything "that The Child mustn't know." She also considered that, as French was the recognized diplomatic language of aristocrats and monarchs, it must be beyond the capabilities of the mere masses. I could never figure out how she justified the population of France speaking it, but then, Dietrich had a way of ignoring realities whenever they didn't suit her that was phenomenal. She would say to me:

"Sweetheart. Call Hermès and tell them to send over scarves for me to choose from. You can speak to them in English—shop girls can't speak real French. Like maids and delivery boys, they all come from villages and are dumb. Most of them don't even know how to read."

I tried to tell her of my linguistic progress, but she looked dubious:

"Sweetheart. You—think—you—speak—French? No . . . no . . . it will take a long time before you are able to speak that beautiful language correctly. I learned my perfect French from my French governess. Girls from good families always learn to speak languages from their governesses."

I decided it was best to keep my knowledge of French to myself, and heard some interesting things that way.

Thinking that I was expected to talk about my life at school, I mentioned our lacrosse matches.

"You? Play that barbaric game? With those little nets on a stick? . . . You don't mean you run around in that Swiss cold, waving a pole!?"

Well, that hadn't worked, so I tried again:

"Mutti, I have a wonderful roommate. She is Norwegian and her family sends her big brown cheeses that—"

"Papi! Did you hear that? She has a roommate with cheese! No wonder she is so fat!"

I quickly tried to change the subject:

"Oh, Mutti. I told some of the girls about having a room—you know, that gets cleaned out every month for a baby someday? They thought it so nice—"

"What? What did you tell them? What

room? What baby? Papi!—*that's* a famous school for girls from fine families? They talk about *babies*! What *is* this place you put the child into? How old are those girls Kater is living with? Those homes they come from can't be so very *fine* if they talk about private things like having . . . periods. She is there to learn *French*—not vulgarities!''

This went on for days. When her outrage was finally over without dire consequences, I was so relieved. I had feared she might decide to remove me from my school. I never said another word about my new world, reverted to being completely engrossed in hers, and assured once again of my exclusive devotion, my mother stopped feeling threatened and was content.

One afternoon, she took me along to visit a lady for tea. Actually, there were two. One thin and ugly, the other roly-poly with sharp little eyes and a long thin mouth. They were as honored by my mother's presence as she seemed to be by their invitation. That intrigued me. Dietrich was rarely impressed by women, and unattractive ones even less. The apartment needed only velvet ropes used in museums to mark off exhibits. Many years later, this is exactly what was done to it. A fabulous collection of glass paperweights covered every surface, paintings adorned the walls, framed photographs and delicate bric-a-brac arranged on a large black marble mantelpiece. One could feel that the pudgy lady was the boss, that she gave the orders. She made my mother's eyes sparkle with her conversation, while the other carried in the tray, poured the tea, then stood by the large armchair . . . ready to be of further service. There was definitely something extra-special about our hostess. I couldn't understand her rapid French, but it sounded so eloquent, so fluid, one felt she was being brilliant without having to know what she said. She patted my mother's hand as punctuation and laughed with delight at some of my mother's rebuttals. Miss "Thin and Prim" remained silent and attentive. I caught her looking me over and I sat straighter, trying not to rattle my delicate blue cup. The thin-lipped lady's mouth had softened, her bushy red hair seemed to flame in the late afternoon sun. She rose from her deep chair and my mother followed her out of the room. The angular one remained watching me, her eyes strangely attentive, her body poised as though anticipating a summons. We waited for quite a long while. I didn't know where to place my empty cup.

It was dark when we returned to our hotel. As we entered our suite, my mother, full of enthusiasm, a spring in her decisive step, announced:

"Papilein, Colette was wonderful!"

. . .

The next lady to open her door to us looked like one of von Sternberg's specters from *The Scarlet Empress*. My mother brushed past this shadowed skeleton to greet an apparition in an austere sitting room. I had a feeling she might be a female but couldn't be quite sure. She was built like a truck—square, heavy, solid—above her man's shirt and tie emerged the head of a bulldog. I was shown to an antique piano stool and told to sit. My mother curled herself against the armchair containing the "Truck" and looked up reverently into the beaming face of the mastiff. The "Angel of Death" poured. She looked so ominous doing that, I decided not to drink the tea. The Venus flytrap next to my seat could have it! Again, the atmosphere seemed full of unleashed power, like an electric charge, it tingled. Very similar to the one that sparked whenever Marlene Dietrich materialized. Here, instead of visual beauty, it was generated by mental energy. I had felt this in the presence of Fitzgerald and the vibrant red-haired lady, and now, this one. She sounded American and very sure of her brilliance. I was so preoccupied trying to pour my tea into the flowerpot without getting caught, that I didn't concentrate on what she was saying. I wish I had—it was the only time I ever met Gertrude Stein. As with our other tea visit, my mother withdrew with our hostess, while I sat waiting politely, being observed by a strange woman gripping the back of an empty chair.

CHRISTMAS MUST HAVE BEEN MEMORABLE that year! I can't remember a thing about it, except that my mother didn't really like the scarf I made for her in knitting class. Crossing the English Channel the day after that I remember. That body of water is terrible at any time of the year and in December, it was worse. Even my mother felt queasy, but endured gallantly, saying to my father—in French:

"He wants me in London with him on my birthday. He says we will celebrate tomorrow all day in bed. Then go dancing all night at the Savoy. You must admit, Papi, he is much more romantic than Jaray was."

Well, if my mother was going to celebrate her birthday in bed with our Knight to Be, maybe I could dare ask permission to go to the Natural History Museum and see the dinosaurs.

Grosvenor Square was always posh, even before the American embassy dominated one side of it. My mother's apartment at Number 20 was nothing special, just convenient for getting back and forth from her swain's penthouse above us. The next morning, she appeared briefly, shrugged off birthday wishes, changed her clothes, approved of my father taking The Child to see all those "old bones," and vanished for the next few days.

My father was never mean in museums. Like churches, they brought out the best in him. It was a little like being in class, but he was an enthusiastic teacher, interested in his subject and, therefore, never boring—no matter how detailed his lectures got. I was sure my mother could not be having half as much fun staying in bed all day with her "knight" as I was, learning about the life cycle of the dung beetle.

NINETEEN THIRTY-SIX WAS NEARLY OVER. England had buried an old king, crowned his son—who deserted his country for "The Woman I Love," and replaced him with a much better one, his brother Bertie, George VI. Three kings—in one year. That must have been some historical record! Dietrich had made three films during the same time period that made no history whatsoever, lost the genius of von Sternberg, let John Gilbert die alone, picked up a few mediocre diversions along the way, and earned a great deal of money. *Gone with the Wind* was published, Monopoly was invented, MGM's genius Irving Thalberg died at the age of thirty-seven, Roosevelt was returned in a landslide election, our Fred Perry won his third Wimbledon title. Adolf Hitler took the Rhineland without being stopped by anyone, his friend Franco seized Spain, Mussolini slaughtered Ethiopians, Stalin his own countrymen. Fred Astaire and Ginger Rogers became the world's top box-office draws, and I welcomed 1937 by getting influenza!

When neither the charmed beef tea nor the "special" chicken soup cured her child, my mother panicked and called the Duchess of Kent for the private telephone number of the King's physician, saying to me:

"Rulers always have the best doctors. They have to be kept alive to rule. Look at that Queen Victoria . . . she went on forever! Even Roosevelt, with his Infantile Paralysis, runs America only because his doctors are brilliant!"

Sir Something-or-Other, very tall, long-fingered, immaculate in Savile Row gray pinstripe and stick pin, appeared as though sent over from central casting, shot me full of horse serum, and left (in those days, before penicillin and antibiotics, the only thing available). Everything would have been fine except that I was allergic. By the evening, I had swollen to twice my size, my lips looked like two eiderdowns sewn together, my eyes had turned "Chinese," my hands matched my lips. My mother, magnificent in black velvet and broadtail, stopped by my room to say good night, took one look, screamed, and ran to the phone.

Our eminent physician was tracked down

attending a royal banquet at Clarence House. Bridges was dispatched, with orders to haul him over to Grosvenor Square. As he came through the door, resplendent in orders and tails, my mother pounced, beating her fists against his starched shirtfront, yelling:

"What have you done to my child? What kind of a doctor are you? How dare you go to banquets while your patients are dying!" Her pummeling dislodged his pearl studs, they now popped out onto the floor. His heavily starched dickey snapped and, like a roller blind, ricocheted up under his chin. She kept right on punching his bared chest.

"Madam! . . . Please! . . . Do make an effort to contain yourself!" the royal physician murmured, backing off while trying to unroll his shirtfront. I lay there like a beached whale, enjoying the performance through my slits.

I recovered, although too slowly to suit my mother's medical timetable. What was missing? What was still necessary? Of course . . . sea air! So, I was bundled up in shetland and cashmere and shipped off to Bournemouth. In February, that was a real "seaside resort—out of season." Now I understood what the girls at school had meant when they spoke of mothers with lovers going to one. Deserted boardwalks drenched by pounding waves, barren cliffs, and empty tea shops damp and fogged from kettles kept constantly "on the boil" in case some lost mariner should wander in through the salty mist. Whenever I see Hitchcock's *Rebecca*, I remember the sea breaking against those cliffs, and when Trevor Howard meets Celia Johnson in that little "caff" in *Brief Encounter*, instantly I am back in Bournemouth, warming my hands around a steaming cup of milky tea, my fingers sticky from Banbury tarts.

The nurse who had taken me to the sea brought me back cured, and my mother was once again vindicated on the healing powers of salt air.

"You see, how much better the air is on this side? 'The air of the North Sea.' That's what my mother always said: 'That is the one that cures!' not that hot pond we have in California. What is it called, Papi? You know I never know such things . . ."

"The Pacific Ocean, Mutti."

"Why is *that* one called an ocean? What is the difference?"

I was very pleased to learn that my mother didn't know geography either.

I got an extra dose of curative air as we crossed the English Channel back to France, and Paris, where my mother discovered Schiaparelli. She had never paid any attention to this avant-garde designer, calling some of her outrageous designs "just cheap publicity getters." I do not know what decided her to visit this couturiere, perhaps it was the influence of her romance, the pretentiousness of her companion—whatever reason, we went to Schiaparelli, and my mother flipped. As my father's mouth got tighter and tighter, and I shuddered inwardly, she rhapsodized and *bought*. When my mother goofed, she did so on a royal scale! Astrological symbols in silver sequins on night-blue velvet. Brocade ropes that looked like writhing snakes appliquéd onto garish pink-figured damask, tight-waisted feminine suits with black fox overvests and matching powder-puff hats. Lots of odd fake jewelry, ornate buttons, decorations, bits and pieces—overdone, overstated, overworked. Everything startling, highly visible, and none of it Dietrich. Schiaparelli became a girlfriend-buddy. They traded secrets and gossip. My mother rarely wore any of her clothes more than once but kept on buying them nonetheless, the complete opposite to her relationship, years later, with Coco Chanel.

I returned to Brillantmont late, because of having been ill, to find that roommates had been changed around, as was the school's policy. It kept the pupils from learning each other's language instead of French. While I unpacked and stored my belongings according to the rules, a thin, dark-haired girl, with strange light-gray eyes, observed me. After a while, she asked, in very precise English:

"Did you inherit the legs of your mother?"

I was as startled by her courage to speak in English as by her question; I nearly dropped my sponge bag. That was the first time I was asked what would become a much too familiar question over the years. I always wondered why people would think it so vital that they abandoned all manners to ask it. If I had inherited Dietrich's legs, I might have been less embarrassed by the question, but as I didn't, I was. It took years before I stopped feeling guilty for having to disappoint them with a negative answer. I have even had people lift my skirt while inquiring about my legs. It is amazing how they are either pleased or disillusioned when they finally see them. I decided to keep out of the Gray-Eyed's way, which seemed to suit us both. The third girl in our room that term was an Indian princess, as delicate as a newborn butterfly and just as pretty. She smiled a lot, flitted about on silent feet, but did not mingle.

My mother's calls kept me abreast of her news:

Selznick had offered our Knight a starring part in a big swashbuckler. My mother had to convince him to take it—apparently he was a bit sensitive about playing anyone who flourished a sword. After he accepted the film, she began coaching him on "anti-Selznick" tactics, which included "how to handle that terrible man, who does nothing but write memos long enough to be books."

Lubitsch was preparing a new film for her that this time he would also direct. It had no title as yet but was "something about a wife of a titled Englishman who falls in love with a man in a Paris brothel, pretends to be someone else until they all meet and find out who is who." It was supposed to be very sophisticated comedy, she said, adding:

"It can be a real 'Lubitsch touch' film *if* he doesn't get too cute or vulgar."

As the Countess di Frasso was still in Italy, our favorite house would be available and wasn't it "a funny coincidence"—our Knight had rented one just down the street from us?

My mother managed to extricate me from school early, and I arrived in Paris in time to help pack the trunks. Tami was back, I hugged her with relief—then saw she had been crying. My mother was stuffing tissue paper into hats, holding court. She was in a good mood. My father made the lists and labeled the keys. Tami folded scarves, I bagged shoes, my mother packed and talked:

"Papilein, remember I told you how I liked Colette? Did you see what she wrote about *The Garden of Allah*? . . . all about my too-red lips

—terrible! Why would a great writer like that consent to do a film review? Graham Greene wrote one too. He said our desert looked like craters of Swiss cheese! But he isn't as good a writer as Colette—and probably needed the money."

We broke for lunch at my father's apartment. Tami had not had time to remove the butter from the refrigerator, so it was still too cold for easy spreading. My father gave her a biting lecture on her lack of memory, organization, and efficiency. She sat very still, head bent, submissive, letting the sarcasm wash over her, then broke and ran from the room. I followed. In the corridor, she shook her head, motioning me to return, not to get into trouble because of her. I was about to reenter the dining room when I heard my mother say:

"Papilein. You must not be so harsh with her. You must understand that Tamilein is only trying."

My mother defending Tami? How wonderful! I stood by the door, listening.

"But, Mutti. You can see that she is just impossible!"

"Papilein, why do you let her get that way? Haven't the pills helped? What did they say at that place we sent her to? Don't they know *any-thing*? They must know *something* about what makes a woman get pregnant all the time. I don't, because I get up and do something about it. Is she just too lazy to douche afterwards? There must be a reason? It isn't just the money for the abortions—you know I don't mind paying for them all the time, that is not the problem. But how she lets herself get that way, *that* we have to find a way to control. Can you imagine if that happened to *me* every time? Someday, someone is going to find out—no matter where we hide her. Can't you *talk* to her? Can't you force her to get up and go to the bathroom after? A little discipline, *that* she *has* to learn— Sh-sh . . . here is the child!"

I returned to my place at the table. They switched to French. I could not quite follow their rapid discussion, but I had already heard enough in German.

That afternoon, I looked up the word I had not understood. I knew very few grown-up words in any language. Now I learned what "abortion" meant. I sat, locked in the toilet, the dictionary open on my lap, wondering how a baby was first made, how one killed it, and why. I was absolutely certain that Tami could never do such a thing on her own. My mother and father—that was different. They were capable of anything.

WE SIPPED PERFECT BOUILLON while reclining in our reserved deck chairs, cozy under cashmere lap robes, walked the Promenade Deck, bet on the wooden horse races in the Solarium during afternoon tea, watched the skeet-shooting competitions. My mother, looking divine, danced every night in the Grill Room. I explored my beautiful *Normandie* and, except for having to leave Tami with my father, was happy.

In the opulent movie theater, I saw Norma Shearer in *Romeo and Juliet* and thought that Brian would have made a much better Romeo than Leslie Howard. When a lady's voice whispered urgently somewhere behind me in the dark, "Oh! I hope they are going to get together in the end," I turned and whispered back to her, "No . . . they don't, because it's Shakespeare!"

We steamed past Ambrose Light and—there she was! Constant and true. I waved and thanked her. I was back home!

BOX OFFICE POISON

WE TOOK OUR SUBTERRANEAN ESCAPE through the Waldorf kitchens while the press lay in wait for Dietrich above. My mother sniffed the pungent aroma of garlic and thyme, calling to me over her shoulder:

"They have Lamb Provençal today. We have to order that! Smells *good*!" and disappeared into the service elevator.

She removed her arrival costume and did her toilets, while I organized the waiting mail. A short cable from our Knight, who was about to follow us, she would like first, and a poetic effort from von Sternberg.

"Sweetheart, put a call in to 'the boys,' then ring for room service." She lit a cigarette, I handed her the two cables:

DIETRICH WALDORF ASTORIA NEW YORK
GETTING TERRIBLY EXCITED SHALL I PACK VINEGAR
OR DO THEY SELL IT THERE STOP BLESS YOU FOR
RESTING AND FOR BEING MINE

We had ordered our lamb by the time her Hollywood call came through:

"Sweethearts, did you get my list? Did you see Bridges when he arrived? And the car? Make sure he knows what time we get to Pasadena and tell him we'll go directly to Paramount, and to bring the thermoses. Order the crawfish to be delivered for Friday and don't forget to get the dill. I saw Colette in Paris. . . . Who? Colette. The great French writer! Being in Hollywood is no excuse for stupidity. Besides, you haven't been there that long! Even there, you can read good books! Call Travis—tell him I am bringing clothes from Paris that we can use in the film and not to tell anyone. . . . Are the bodyguards ordered for The Child? . . . I saw Jo in London. . . . Oh, yes—still making with the cow eyes . . . I just received a cable from him, listen: 'My heart is without rest I follow the clouds and the sunsets from which the color of your eyes and your hair drop from the sky stop if it were possible to forget or to sleep some place until one could wake to a new life and being called back from the forgetting sleep of death even then I would feel you stop you who are of my blood stop what is there when the rainbows lose themselves in eternity.' He could have said all that on the telephone! Probably not, looks better written out! . . . Don't forget to order the champagne and tell Nellie to make sure the water-cooler man puts in a fresh bottle in the dressing room."

My mother kept me so busy while we crossed America, I hardly had any time to visit with my porter friends. But when I was sure she was really asleep, I escaped to my magic balcony and breathed the rich air, marveling as always at the vastness and majesty of this country I loved.

Travis was waiting for us with open arms. I settled myself into the leather armchair by his desk, ready for a long session. I had a feeling they had missed each other.

"Travis! Wait till I tell you about the Korda film!"

"Well, I heard all about that bath scene! The papers here were full of it. Did you really do it, Marlene? You? Naked? With nothing but bubbles?"

"Of course not! You know me . . . but don't tell anyone! They think that scene will save the film at the box office—but I doubt it! It is all so booorring. But, what can you expect from an industry that stops shooting every afternoon at four so people can drink tea. I was told that they did that in England, but I didn't believe it until I saw it! Even their grips 'sip.' Can you see one of ours drinking—tea? . . . I saw Jo in London. He is going to do Robert Graves's *I, Claudius* with Charles Laughton and that Merle Oberon. Can you imagine . . . that Singapore streetwalker à la Roman poisoner? I am sure poor Jo *has* to take her because of Korda. He never used to do things like that, but *now*—he allows it. I don't know what has happened to him. Jo is much too good for them. They don't understand his genius. Laughton is a ham. You can imagine what is going to go on with *both* of them trying to be 'great' directors at the same time. Laughton should just listen and learn, but you know actors . . . they never know when to shut up!"

The coffee arrived. Travis poured, my mother lit another cigarette.

"I saw Cole Porter in Paris. He looks more and more like a hungry jockey. They say he can't live without cocaine. . . . I must say, his nose looks *very* peculiar. Strange little man. I don't like his music, but his words—they are brilliant! Is it true that he is madly in love with Cary Grant? What does Mae say about *that*? I went to his apartment—all black gloss and white pigskin, full of zebra skins scattered about. *Very* masculine, and *ever* so 'hired interior decorator chic.' Such bad taste! I thought he came from a good family?. . . I saw a picture of Lombard in something you did for her—in that black monkey fur . . . you want to give her a banana! Really, Travis! But in that film . . ." She turned to me. "What's the name of that film, where we saw the photographs and I said, 'Finally, Lombard looks beautiful!'?"

"*The Princess Comes Across*," I answered.

"Yes—a bad title—in that film, you finally did something for her. She looks just like Dietrich. I hear she calls you 'Teasie'—how very 'cutesy-poo'!" She had been riffling through some of the test stills on Travis's desk; now she held up one of Irene Dunne in a period ball gown, an exaggerated confection, its surface strewn with thousands of tiny sequins and enormous tulle bows.

"Travis . . . have you any tulle *left* in stock after making this dress? I know she must be 'the bow kind,' but haven't you exaggerated it just a *little* bit?"

Travis giggled.

"Oh, Marlene! How I have missed you! You are so right! Each bow we put on, I thought how *you* would hate it!"

"You were right! As long as you *know* that this sort of thing is terrible you are still all right. But when you start doing clothes like Orry-Kelly—*then* I start to worry. Did you see what Adrian poured on Crawford? I saw the pictures. The whole thing nothing but bugle beads—like a second skin! *What work!* Beautiful! But on her, with those hips, it just looks vulgar! But then, everything looks cheap on Crawford. Has Lubitsch told *you* what we have to make for this film . . . or is this going to be another one of those talked about but never written down pictures of his?"

"Marlene—didn't you get the script? It was supposed to be waiting for you when you arrived in New York."

"I gave it to Clifton Webb to read. I knew

by the time we arrived here, Lubitsch would have rewritten it, no matter whose name appears as the official writer. I know she is supposed to be the wife of an English lord. So, we do white chiffon blouse with ruffles along the neck and wrists, with a very simple black velvet suit and beautiful thin-heeled shoes . . . white kid gloves, very little jewelry, and a calm face. That's easy. I have all that. We don't even have to design it. What about the 'other man'? Who is he? Who's playing him?"

"Melvyn Douglas. He is a talented light comedian, but for my taste, not a romantic lead. He has no glamour—no sex appeal. Very unexciting to look at."

"Between Herbert Marshall and this Douglas, Dietrich is supposed to be elegantly sexy? Charming! At least the last time I was Marshall's wife I had Cary Grant to leave him for. Now I get a cold fish?"

She rose. I guessed she had decided it was time to read the script of her next film, *Angel*.

The exotic birds still perched on their silver branches, the mirrors sparkled, the panthers prowled, the gardenias bloomed, the di Frasso house was exactly as we had left it. Even the Afghan hound still posed in the shade of the magnolias, as though he hadn't moved in a year. Except for the change of lovers, we picked up where we had left off. Our Knight, ever the cha-

meleon, now took on the trappings that proclaimed: attractive Anglophile returned to his
origins of southern California. Flashed his famous inherited smile, bronzed his body, and
looked handsome by and in our pool. We made
beef tea for Herbert Marshall and George Raft,
goulash for Lubitsch, Anna May Wong got her
green tea piping hot at four, and John Barrymore
his whisky, smuggled to him in the thermoses on
the set by ten every morning. We designed hairpieces with Nellie and set up the dressing room.

It had been redecorated as a "welcome
back" gesture from the Paramount bosses. Massive Art Deco chairs and matching chaise longue
covered in a white fuzzy material that rested on
geranium red carpets. My mother loved it, calling the furniture her "white teddy bears," never
gave them up, took them with her when she
finally left Paramount for good, and kept them
in storage where they hibernated for the next
fifty years! Mae West never liked our "fuzzy
bears," saying that they made her behind itch,
but I think that was just jealousy. She continued
to snitch the flowers from our stoop: Life was
back to normal.

My mother, appalled at the pretentiousness
of Lubitsch's script, stopped going to see him for
weekends at his beach house, called Edington,
gave him hell, told him it was time he did something to save this latest disaster because she was

through being "nice" to an "ugly little man with a big nose and cigar"! When Clifton Webb wrote her that he liked the script, she got angry at him too.

410 PARK AVENUE

Sunday, March 28, 1937

My Pretty,

I read of your going to the Rathbone party in your tails and dancing with all the girls. Evidently spring is having a decided effect on your glands. I wish I could have seen it.

I have read your script *Angel*. It should be great for you and you should be divine in it. I feel however that you should have a good toss in the hay in Paris with the other man. That sitting-in-the-park scene might have been all right for Jeanette MacDonald. But not for you, Toots. Not if I know my Miss von Losch . . .

Suddenly, our pool was minus one tanned "knight" and my mother's bedroom remained unlocked.

Darling,

. . . I feel that you have taken our relationship and my stormy intense devotion to you too much for granted.

If one shares one's life to the extent of setting up, within certain necessary limits, a household and practices domesticity to the same degree that we have—then there are certain obligations. . . .

I believe that if you found it necessary to change your "one man woman" viewpoint then the proper thing to do would be to sit down and say to me that it was something you wished to do, and at least make a thoughtful attempt to make me understand. . . . I don't think it exactly respectful either to yourself, to me or to our relationship to treat me as though I were a gigolo —anxiously awaiting "milady's whim," i.e., if you feel like having me with you—then over I trot—if you have other plans then I'm expected to adjust myself accordingly and stay home until called for again. . . .

Between two people who are in love there must be concessions, respect and a coordination of heart and mind and soul. These cannot be demanded or asked for— it must come out of mutual or necessary desire. . . .

I'll not say anything more except . . . God bless you, dearest Dushka.

Their romance vacillated a great deal. When it was back "on," they kissed, held hands, dressed up, went to parties, did the night spots. The perfect couple—both beautiful and handsome at the same time. When "off," he prepared for his film, felt sorry for himself, blamed her for his unhappiness, and suffered. While she prepared her film, handed me his wedding ring to put away amongst the others, and managed, quite easily, to forget him without any emotional churning whatsoever. Although he did crop up in telephone conversations with my father and "the boys."

"Papilein. Tell me, why did I think he was so wonderful? Was it all *only* . . . London? The way he is there? Or could it have been because he was not working? Because now, here in Hollywood, he is behaving—suddenly—just like an actor! 'I–I–I, Me–Me–Me.' No wonder that father never sees him. I am even beginning to understand that terrible ex-wife of his. Do you think I maybe fell in love with him because he looked so wonderful in tails?"

The day the *Hindenburg* burst into flames while trying to dock in New Jersey, we heard it over the radio in the dressing room. The announcer broke down trying to describe the disaster. He was sobbing. My mother was jubilant:

"You see? Remember how I wouldn't let us take it? Even when Papi said we should? It must have been sabotage! Very good! Now the Nazis have to spend money to build another Zeppelin that nobody will go on because they will be too frightened after this!"

Somewhere along the preparation for *Angel*, my mother lost interest. For the first time since *The Blue Angel*, she allowed herself to get sloppy, and in the one category in which she had always been the most brilliant, the way she looked. Travis Banton, by now so confident to let Dietrich lead them, went right along, and together they made one error after another. It culminated in the only film they ever worked on that lacked their unique sense of style. Especially sad, as it was to be their last one together. The famous "jewel" dress from this film, an encrusted sheath of fake rubies and emeralds designed so she could wear her real ones, owed its notoriety more to its weight of fifty pounds and cost of four thousand dollars than to its photogenic perfection.

The whole film is slightly "off"—nothing works. Maybe my mother sensed this long before anyone else did, acknowledged the hopelessness of the situation, and just gave up. Of all the thousands of stills and portraits Dietrich kept of herself from every one of her films, she only saved a few from *Angel*, and those are mostly of her wearing her own "Tante Valli" velvet suit with the white ruffled blouse. By the time *Angel* was nearing completion, we no longer kept a supply of Lubitsch's favorite cigars in our dressing room; they were no longer on speaking terms.

ON THE 30TH OF MAY, 1937, the Independent Theater Owners of America took out an ad in all the motion-picture-industry trade papers:

The following stars are
BOX OFFICE *POISON*
Joan Crawford
Bette Davis
Marlene Dietrich
Greta Garbo
Katharine Hepburn

Suddenly these ladies supposedly had lost the ability to draw the paying public into the movie houses on the power of their name alone. Under pressure, Paramount canceled plans for Dietrich's next picture and put her out to pasture. Columbia, which had been after her to play George Sand, dropped the project.

For the first time since coming to America, my mother was unemployed. She called my father:

"Papi, we are leaving America. They say they can't sell Dietrich films anymore. Those idiots, *all idiots*, of course, they can't sell them . . . because they are *bad*—nothing to do with Dietrich. Even Garbo is on that list. The popeyed one, that is possible, who wants to pay money to look at her—but Hepburn? Yes, she is named too. Not to be believed! So now, who have they got left? Irene Dunne maybe? *That's a star?* A real madness."

We packed up the dressing room, stripped it of everything that wasn't nailed down. Storage vans drove it out through the Paramount gates

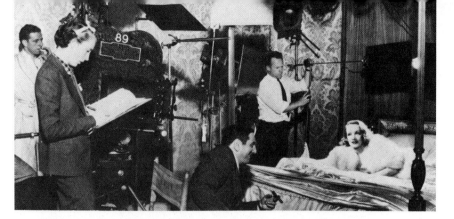

In 1937, filming *Angel*, a script she disliked, Dietrich hoped that with Ernst Lubitsch directing, the picture could be saved.

LEFT: Travis Banton and Dietrich—the magic pair. Between them, they designed some of the greatest clothes for a film star ever seen. *Angel* would be their last film together. BELOW: Dietrich, looking for a possible flaw in the reflection of the big mirror that was always stationed next to the camera. She knew she was in another flop, but that was no excuse for imperfections.

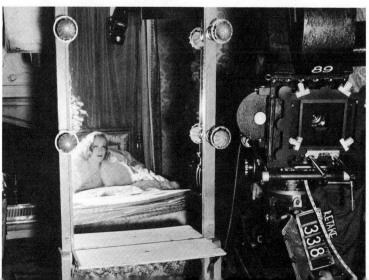

In *Angel.* Playing a "lady" always meant a black velvet suit with ruffled silk blouse.

In 1937, my mother was branded "Box Office Poison." We left America on the SS *Normandie*.

and that was that. No tearful good-byes, no "walks down memory lane." The battle won and somehow lost, our soldier left the field—unbowed. Next, we packed our things. We had always been gypsies anyway. Canceled the house, paid off the bodyguards, servants, and tennis teacher, stored the Cadillac, handed Bridges glowing references, and boarded the train, now called the Super Chief because it had acquired air-conditioning. I waved to Nellie long after the train had pulled out of Union Station. An era had come to an end.

I don't remember anything about that trip east, except for a feeling of loss, a hurting deep inside me. Even my little balcony was gone, replaced by streamlined chrome. Fast and cool, travel had become expedient—no longer an experience.

Once in New York, my mother enjoyed herself enormously. Being "box office poison" might damage her fame in the "nickel-and-dime" people category, but could not influence the rarefied circles she preferred to move in.

Someone must have alarmed my mother about my safety, even in Europe, for my head bodyguard was rehired and told to get east in time to accompany us to France, and why not go the whole hog, make it a really comfortable summer: my mother persuaded Paramount to give Nellie a leave of absence so she too could join us. Just before we were scheduled to leave, my mother called my father:

"Papi. Call Mutti. Tell her to call the doctor who cured The Child's legs—tell him she is growing too fast. Something must be wrong inside—she will be a giant. Every week nothing fits! Not only her fatness, but the bones are growing. He has to tell me what I should do—maybe he knows what is wrong. He can come to Paris to examine her."

Oh dear! I hadn't slouched enough! I hoped I wouldn't be locked away in one of those "spas" like Tami.

The day we all boarded the *Normandie*, I was in such despair, even that wonderful ship couldn't give me the usual euphoric lift of anticipation. I stood in the very back of the ship. I wanted to see the Lady as long as possible; the way my mother was behaving, it might be for the very last time. I made my wish but didn't really believe it had a chance of coming true. My grandmother cabled to the ship:

RADIO TELEGRAM
BERLIN
MARLENE DIETRICH
    S.S. NORMANDIE
DOCTOR NOT ALARMED SAYS CHILD COMPLETELY
NORMAL.
GROWING AS NATURE COMMANDS. ABSOLUTELY
WITHOUT DANGER
                           MUTTI

I knew my mother wasn't completely convinced—she still kept looking at me speculatively, though not as often. I hoped once we got to her precious Europe, she would stop worrying about my bones.

My father, ready at his post, met us in Le Havre, accepted the mighty luggage lists, and herded our expanded group onto the train for Paris.

What the *Normandie* was to ocean liners, the Hotel Lancaster was to hotels. Discreetly hidden down a side street off the Champs-Elysées, it functioned as one's own private château in Paris. Baccarat chandeliers, brocaded chairs, priceless antiques, beveled mirrors, Aubussons, ornate friezes, Versailles doors, swagged satin-taffeta-organdied French windows, flowers, flowers, flowers everywhere, dewy fresh in hues of perpetual spring, their perfume never allowed to intrude, only delight. In those days, there were other great hotels that could also boast such visual perfections. What the Lancaster achieved over and above its superb luxury was absolute privacy. For nearly three years, we lived there. It became our base, our European headquarters, and never, in all that time, did I meet or ever see another guest! How did they do that? How was it possible to run a hotel where every chambermaid, valet, porter, and waiter became one's personal servant?

Where rooms were cleaned and beds changed without one ever being disturbed or made to conform to anyone's timetable but one's own. How is it possible to run a hotel without a lobby? Without bells or bustle or elevators that never come. How can you maintain one without the sound of one vacuum cleaner at least being heard one time down some corridor? The Hotel Lancaster did! They didn't even expect you to register. After all, why should one be required to sign in on arriving at one's own château? Here we never entered by way of the kitchen. Although the French press and the adoring fans crowded the narrow side street, they parted like the Red Sea to let us pass. Once inside, nothing and no one could follow. Bribery of the Lancaster staff was unknown, unheard of, impossible—I am sure, if ever attempted, punishable by the guillotine.

My father had discovered this jewel but came to regret it, passionately. Fans and reporters kept their devoted vigil: night and day, rain or shine, the Rue de Berri was choked with people. Into this bottleneck, my father's big green Packard was expected to make its way whenever Madame Dietrich needed to be conveyed somewhere. This disturbed my father tremendously. After months of poring over paint samples, corresponding with Packard officials, he had repainted his precious car. Like a smitten youth, he was so enamored of his new, dark green patina, he glanced adoringly and fondled his fenders whenever near. He was also ferociously protective of his expensive paint job. We would emerge from our "château," the crowd surged forward:

"MARLÉNE! MARLÉNE!" excited voices shrieked. Flustered gendarmes, looking chic in little capes and spotless gloves, lifted their matching white truncheons in mild protest. Of course, *amour* triumphed over law and order! The crowd pushed forward to glimpse their idol, but my father's pride and joy blocked their way, so they pushed against it. Strange hands touched his glowing green metal and my father went berserk!

He bellowed: "My God! My sheen! My sheen! . . . Don't touch my *sheen*!" and Dietrich, this time, *didn't* make it to the toilet. She was laughing, peeing, crying. We had to cancel the fittings at Schiaparelli. From then on, the borscht and black bread story took second place to "Papi's paint."

"You should have seen it! People, hundreds of people, rushing toward me, and Papi? He wasn't worried about me—all he worried about was the paint on his precious car!"

In order to avoid Germany, we took the train via Switzerland to Austria and reached Salzburg in time for us all to be "costumed" for dinner. Nellie looked pretty in her patterned blue dirndl, with its dusty rose apron. She even got a jaunty straw hat with a bushy white feather that bobbed when she skipped. I was in cornflower blue that year, with a big, dark, dark blue apron that hid everything my mother had decided needed hiding. At first, my bodyguard, positioned outside the shop, refused to enter and be transformed, but when he saw my mother's disappointment, he relented and accepted a loden shooting hat sporting a big silver pin of a stag at bay. Tami and Teddy were spared as they were still being driven across borders by my father in Packard splendor.

My mother spent the evening talking to Jaray in Vienna and our lonely Knight in Beverly Hills. Nellie wrote postcards, my bodyguard oiled his revolver, I locked myself in the bathroom with its swan-shaped spigots and read *Gone with the Wind*, which I had "borrowed" from the Wardrobe Department. Its size made it terribly hard to hide. I kept my precious book in my knitting satchel from school, hoping no one would offer to carry it and feel how heavy it had become! Nellie knew, but she was my friend and wouldn't tell. *Gone with the Wind* became a sort of lodestone for me. Far from home, I read about a time in my country's history and felt less isolated.

. . .

My mother, looking like the most gorgeous milkmaid that ever was, my father, in leather shorts and Tyrolean knee socks, Tami and I in varying examples of flower-embroidered finery, got into the Packard, whose color matched our loden capes, and we were off. Nellie, bodyguard, and luggage followed by hired taxis. The road show of *Heidi* was about to begin!

Of course, he had found it! Exactly as his wife had ordered it. There it stood! Green shutters with cut-out hearts, gingham curtains swagged on six-pane windows, green bench sitting in the sun, bright red geraniums everywhere. A water pump, a wooden trough, red-and-white checkered tablecloths, feathered beds, working cuckoo clocks, even a pungent barn—courtesy of our very own living cow. Like a master set dresser, he had done it all! My mother stood before her ordered dream of an Austrian farmhouse and said:

"Papilein, are there enough closets for the clothes?" and without waiting for an answer, went to investigate for herself. But she couldn't fault him; she tried, but she couldn't. We stayed there for quite a while; that is, Teddy, I, and the cow stayed. My father was kept busy, chauffeuring and escorting my mother back and forth to nearby Salzburg and its famous festival attractions. Tami filled her usual role of "cover companion" to whoever was actually my mother's boyfriend for the evening. Those mornings when my mother was in residence, she rose early to keep an eye on the caretaker farmer as he milked her cow, warning him that should he hurt her in any way—he'd be *very* sorry. We would sit around the beautiful old farmhouse table, coffee and fresh bread keeping warm on a porcelain stove, while our group, resplendent in Knize silk, satin, and marabou, forgot our rules as "quaint peasants" and played sophisticates, reading the morning papers in Noël Coward style instead. Tami and I never read, we listened. We were always ready for the "breakfast" show.

"Papi! They finally are married! Now that awful Simpson woman is the Duchess of Windsor! The King has decreed that his brother can be addressed as 'Your Royal Highness,' but not she or any of their children. Well, they are never going to have any—*that* we know! But good, at least she can't call herself a 'Royal Highness'. 'Duchess' is already too good for a woman who is, after all, only an American divorcée!"

A few days later, we heard that the wonderful Jean Harlow had died at the age of twenty-six of uremic poisoning. My mother was livid:

"That mother of hers! That terrible Christian Science mother! She killed her! She wouldn't allow a doctor in the house. William Powell finally took Harlow to the hospital him-

self . . . but it was too late. They couldn't save
her. Somebody should kill that *mother*. Maybe
Powell will do it, but he is probably too heart-
broken. Louis B. Mayer might. She was a real
star. Wonderful body, wonderful hair. I never
liked her when she opened her mouth, too low-
class American, but . . . *silent*, she was beautiful.''

One of our side trips that summer of 1937
was to visit my father's parents in Aussig, on the
Czechoslovakian border. This time my mother
came along. Tami and the livestock were left
back on the farm. I tried not to run into my
grandmother's waiting arms. I knew this might
hurt her, but too much overt enthusiasm shown
by me toward my grandparents would only result
in my mother being jealous and becoming sarcastic with everyone. Dietrich stepped from the
Packard to greet her mother-in-law, who wiped
her hands quickly down her blue apron before
timidly shaking the gloved hand extended toward
her. When my mother turned to bow to her fa-
ther-in-law, I grabbed my sweet grandmother
and gave her a fast squeeze. The visit turned out
to be even more complex than I had anticipated.
It was so difficult to keep my grandmother from
hugging me, stroking my head as she talked,
showing her affection as loving warm people did
sometimes in "real life," I couldn't even try to
explain to her that my mother had to believe I

loved only her and no one else—for ever and ever, amen! It would have been incomprehensible to this simple, uncomplicated woman. My grandfather's way of dealing with "the star come to call" was interesting. He flirted with her and she fell for it! I had not realized what an intelligent man he was until then.

My father was pleased with his parents' proper deferential attitude toward his famous wife. Nevertheless, he remained constantly on guard in case they forgot themselves and spoke before being spoken to first.

We only stayed two days. I bent down to kiss her soft cheek and whispered:

"I love you, Grandmother. Next time, we will bake together and then you can teach me how to make your special chocolate cake. I promise! Please tell Grandfather I am sorry, but I just couldn't play checkers with him this time. Tell him I love him and that I still have my fox."

With my father watching my every move, I got into the car. Farewells were formal and very correct, and we drove away. I didn't even try to look back and wave. I would have cried and been told to control my emotions. I would be a grown woman before I saw them again, they—too old and war-worn to recognize me.

Back on the farm, our cow was giving birth and having a hard time of it. Immediately, my mother became the midwife, shouting instructions to the worried farmer trying his best to pull the calf from its resting place.

"Pull! Pull! Can't you see it's stuck in there?"

"Moo!" bellowed our frightened bovine.

"Listen to her! You are hurting her! Stop it! Stop!" shrieked the visiting movie star. Dripping with sweat, face red, the farmer wrapped burlap sacks around the two protruding hooves and pulled anew. Nothing budged except the laboring cow.

"It's stuck! We need oil!" Lifting her peach-satin dressing gown above her waist, Dietrich sprinted through the steaming manure toward the house and her supply cupboard, returning seconds later with the first lubricant at hand, a big bottle of Elizabeth Arden's Blue Grass Facial Oil, which she proceeded to pour into the heaving cow's behind. My mother took hold of one leg, handed the other to the farmer, and as though she were crewing a sculling race, counted:

"One—two—three. Pull!"

"One—two—three. Pull!" and out plopped the best-smelling calf ever born in the Austrian Tyrol. For weeks, the barn smelled of Arden's signature scent, while the poor cow tried to lick the stench off her newborn. My mother ordered a case of her oil to be sent from New York, so the farmer would have it handy for all his future "birthings."

Our breakfasts, as always, continued to be informative.

"Everybody says that *Othello* is a big success. Brian is in it. Can you imagine him playing Iago? Probably slinking around the scenery, looking ever so handsome. Ridiculous! First, he isn't a good enough actor to play that part, and second, he is too English to be a convincing Italian villain. . . . Noël Coward has another success—he just goes on and on! He is really brilliant! Remember when he cabled and asked me to come to his dress rehearsal to watch him? And how he said in that slightly affected English of his, 'Marlenah! I must not appear effeminate in any way. Do be a dear—watch for anything that could be considered less than "butch," if you see me being at all "queer," tell me immediately.' Now with him, I would do a play. Look what he has done for Gertrude Lawrence. A little, low-class soubrette. Now she is considered 'elegant' . . . all because of Coward. . . . Hitler has officially thrown Elisabeth Bergner out of Germany because she is Jewish. . . . Soon they won't have any talent left for their big 'cultural Reich'—except of course, that terrible Riefenstahl and Emil Jannings. *They* will stay, and those two 'well-poisoners'—the Nazis deserve!"

When I wrote to Brian, congratulating him on his success as Iago, I told him all about our new perfumed calf in our barn filled with the aura of Arden, and would he please send me a copy of *Othello*, so I could know what he was being so good in.

My mother was often away that summer. Besides the daily visits to Salzburg, she traveled to London, Paris, Venice, Cannes. On one of these "side trips" to England, she met George Bernard Shaw for the first time. She often told me *her* version of their meeting:

"There he was, that wonderful man . . . looking old even then, with that beard and parchment skin. Eating only vegetables always gives people a funny color. I sank down on my knees in front of him, and those light eyes of his just looked at me. He loved women at his feet. We talked all day . . . it was dark when I left. He said he would write a play for me, but he never did! You know he liked Hitler? Strange, how brilliant men can sometimes be so very stupid, but about the Russians, there Shaw was right! He loved them as much as I do. We recited our favorite poems to each other. He couldn't believe how many I knew by heart. You know, Shaw didn't look like a writer at all! More like an actor. He behaved like one too . . . very egotistical and full of himself!"

My father's version of this coming together

of these two "living legends" was somewhat different:

"During the time we had the farmhouse in Austria, Mutti found someone to take her to meet George Bernard Shaw. When she came back from spending the day at his house, she told me that when she sank down on her knees in front of him he unbuttoned his fly, took out his 'thing,' so she told me, 'Of course I had to do *it* before we could talk!' She never went back, but she always said that he was a brilliant man."

It was not unusual to be told varied versions of the same thing. As an adult, I was often used as a sounding board for the different scenarios constructed by my mother, her husband, lovers, friends, enemies, and "also-rans." After a while, one became quite expert at recognizing the lies from the truth. It became a sort of distasteful parlor game my family and I played with skill and a certain voyeurism. Dietrich "fell on her knees" a lot in front of famous men. Ever willing and proud to prove her absolute homage. She must have been very convincing. Once, after visiting the great sculptor Giacometti in his studio, she emerged a few hours later, her arms cradling one of his plaster statues, her knees only slightly red.

MY MOTHER STOOD in the doorway of our farm kitchen, pulling on her gloves:

"Papilein—if California calls, I am in Vienna for fittings. If Vienna calls, I am in Paris for fittings. If London calls, the same. And you don't know what hotel."

It seemed that our Knight, Hans Jaray, and someone in London were out of favor.

"Mutti, as your husband, I would be expected to know where my wife is staying!"

"Don't be ridiculous. Just tell them you don't know!" and she left for her supposed fitting in Salzburg.

My father's lips thinned. He never objected to lying to my mother's lovers—only being made to look a fool in their eyes. He was very vain as to their good opinion of him.

I never met the "Salzburg" boyfriend. He was, after all, only a summer replacement and didn't last long. But, while he did, Dietrich rhapsodized about *Faust*, good and evil, retold her "young girl's dream" of someday playing the devout Margarete, and did the famous prayer as an encore at breakfast.

My father was busy with his accounts and making sure that the hired couple didn't cheat Dietrich on the price of potatoes. My bodyguard was staking out the village, Nellie wrote postcards, Teddy quivered watching butterflies alight, Tami embroidered linen tablecloths with beautiful borders of Slavic design, and I read my "official" books sitting on the green bench. It was peaceful and sunny and calm. I was glad my mother had, once again, found someone to occupy her.

The peace didn't last long. My mother's mother arrived, accompanied by her elder daughter in dark brown wool. Neither one of them had changed, except to intensify their basic characteristics. My grandmother, cool, composed—commanding; my aunt, hesitant, fearful, and cowed. Tami and I were given the job of baby-sitters to this trembling dumpling of a woman, which the three of us thoroughly enjoyed, but were careful not to let show, except to each other. Discussions and arguments filled the house. My mother became more and more vehement:

"Mutti! You have no choice! You *have* to leave Berlin and come to America with us. If the Nazis now think they can bomb places as far away as Spain, there will *have* to be a war. The Americans are not going to do anything. As usual, they won't even know what is going on in the rest of the world. The English can't make up their minds—but the French won't allow such behavior and *will* go to war. My friend Hemingway, the great writer, told me so!"

"Lena, you do not understand. Franco is trying to liberate Spain from the oppression of the Loyalists! He is a good friend to Germany. All this talk of our new Luftwaffe being involved in a bombing of a small Basque village is nothing but anti-German propaganda. It never happened! Otto Dietrich is now the Party's press secretary, and I believe him!"

My aunt's hands clenched in her lap. All through this visit she had been trying so hard to stay out of discussions. Now she failed, could no longer remain silent—and plunged:

"No! It's not anti-German propaganda! It happened! Everything is true! Terrible, terrible things—and no one stops the evil . . . no one." Her hand flew to cover her mouth as the words left it, shocked at her own audacity.

"Liesel! *That* will suffice! You are only a woman neither intelligent enough, nor sufficiently informed, to consider yourself equipped to make moralistic judgments. Behave yourself, before you become an embarrassment to this house."

"Tante Liesel—let's go and pick some field flowers for your room," I chimed in, and led her quickly from the room. Tami followed in hurried pursuit.

We sat in the poppy field, making little bouquets, and listened to my aunt as she told us about a place called Guernica, as ever afraid to speak above a frightened whisper; even the flowers might be listening for the Gestapo.

When the time came for my mother's family to return to Berlin, I held my aunt close, wishing she could remain safely with us. My grandmother shook my hand, looked me in the eye and said:

"Maria—the world is about to change, for better or worse, only time will have the answer. But loyalty and duty, those will remain constant and never ending. It is *they* that set intelligent men apart from the rabble. Remember that!" She kissed my forehead, patted my shoulder, and stepped into the waiting car.

I never saw her again. She lived in her house in Berlin throughout the Second World War, dying shortly after the fall of Nazi Germany— whether in celebration or defeat, I was never sure. My mother stood watching the car wend its way down into the valley of St. Galgen, stepped back, and slammed the door. This time she did not cry.

I HAD PROBLEMS that summer. The "happy farmhouse" mood generated lots of cooking at the big iron stove, with me sitting at the kitchen table, being told to taste the copious results.

"Papi! I don't know why the child is getting so fat! She is beginning to look—ugly!" my mother would exclaim periodically, as she marched off to the kitchen to make me a four-egg omelette, followed by those special, just-baked-by-Tami vanilla cream puffs. When I hesitated to stuff myself, I was told:

"What is wrong? Are you sick? No? Then —*eat*! Eat. It is good for you—I made it just for you, sweetheart!"

So, I ballooned, split the cute bodices of my peasant finery, while my mother shook her head in consternation, and ordered ever-larger sizes to be sent out from Salzburg as she slapped a pound of butter into the pan for my daily ration of fried potatoes.

When they found my *Gone with the Wind*, that was the worst. All my English books, even my precious Shakespeare, were confiscated. I thought for a moment they were going to burn them in the village square! No one spoke to me for a week. Austria was never a lucky country for me.

Even the cow got into trouble. The summer evenings were so mild, the farmer had decided to house her in a slotted lean-to above the make-shift garage. She liked it there, relieved herself copiously, chewed her cud, while her highly acid urine seeped through the slats, splattered my father's precious Packard. The hot sun did the rest. The car acquired an interesting pattern of chartreuse polka dots burned into its dark green sheen. Our poor cow was presented to the local butcher without a chance of reprieve! The Austrian farmhouse had had it! We hung up our checkered aprons, changed into silk and gabardine, and left for Paris in the pockmarked Packard. It was the last time we were in Austria. By the next spring, Hitler had added it to his collection of shotless victories.

Maybe Hans Jaray had been told to follow her to Paris, maybe it was the Salzburg swain, or perhaps she had decided on a repeat performance with Chevalier or Colette—whoever or whatever was responsible, Dietrich went off on her supposed own and, as my father was immersed in negotiations for a new paint job, Tami and I were free to explore the great Exposition of 1937. The whole world had come to Paris that year to show off. Every country was represented by its own pavilion housing the finest examples of that country's achievements in every category imaginable. The architecture was very nationalistic. The Germans, ever faithful to Hitler's favorite Greco-Roman style, erected a skyscraper-type temple, on which they perched a twenty-foot eagle clutching a massive swastika in his vicious claws. Facing it was the U.S.S.R. pavilion. Looking like an Art Deco, off-center layer cake, it was topped by a twenty-foot statue of a charging comrade brandishing his lethal scythe. France electrified its Eiffel Tower for the occasion, built a lot of plush restaurants, displayed priceless art—even dedicated a building to the glories of my love, the SS *Normandie*. Siam represented itself in the shape of a golden temple bell, filled with jade Buddhas and delicate water lilies. Italy, a hodgepodge of da Vincis, Michelangelos, handmade fettucini drying on wooden trestles, interspersed by photographic proof of the glorious progress achieved by Mussolini's Fascism. Spain, still free, displayed its Cordoban leather, Valencian lace, toreador suits under glass, fountains in patio settings, and, in a special room off the main entrance, an enormous mural painted by someone called Pablo Ruiz Picasso. It was so ugly, it shocked. Gaping mouths, stretched in soundless screams, eyes that bulged, forever blinded by the horror they had seen, man and beast thrashing in the agony of violent death, crying their terror into hopeless silence. You felt it in color, yet it was done in black and white. Like death—colorless! I read the plaque: "Guernica, 1937," and I knew what my Aunt Liesel had been trying to tell us, understood what had happened in that Spanish town, what the Nazis had done.

Back at the Lancaster, I tried to tell my mother about what I had seen and felt that day. She wasn't interested:

"I don't like that Picasso. He paints only ugly faces. Crazy man. Hemingway thinks he is a great artist and a patriot. But then, anything to do with those people who keep fighting their civil war in the Spanish hills is *sacred* to Hemingway. . . . Tonight we are going to the Danish pavilion to eat their fish in dill sauce . . . then Papi wants to go over to the Turkish one to taste their baklava. I told Cocteau he and his friend can come and take me to the Yugoslavian pavilion to eat the little wild blueberries with sour cream instead. Sweetheart, you and Tami can go and have your favorite red pudding in Bulgaria—and we all meet in Java for coffee at eleven."

Tired and full of a thousand impressions, I sat, ate my flamed bananas à la Javanese, and listened to Cocteau gossiping. Elsa Maxwell and her party joined our table. A very elegant group. The ladies, their hair cropped close to their heads, evening dresses clinging against startlingly thin bodies, gloves to elbows, evening bags suspended from real diamond chains; their gentlemen, tuxedoed, exuding that aura of wealth, not necessarily worked for, but acquired with flair. When I heard Gertrude Stein mentioned, I paid extra attention. Finally, they were discussing someone I had met. .

"Oh—*that* bull dyke? She gives me a pain in the ass!" lisped Cocteau's friend, a fair-haired Dane with milk-white hands that fluttered. That expression confused me. Not the part about the "ass." I heard that one often—it was my father's favorite expression, but a "bull"? A bull was a bull and a dyke was a type of water barrier the Dutch were partial to. What had the coupling of these two words to do with describing a woman?

"Oh, look—quick! Over there!" Excitedly, my mother pointed to a beautiful woman drifting by in layers of lavender chiffon and Parma violets, trailing Guerlain's Shalimar.

"See her? The one done up like Irene Dunne? That's a *he*! Gorgeous!" My mother turned to Cocteau. "Do you know him? Introduce us!"

By the time the lovely lavender "lady," who wasn't a lady at all but a twenty-five-year-old apprentice to a pastry chef in Toulouse, had satisfied my mother's curiosity, been given tips on how to thin out his false eyelashes, and solicited numerous autographs for his many friends who filled éclairs back in the provinces, I was falling asleep in my carved teak chair.

It had been a long summer.

"PAPILEIN, *MUST* THE CHILD GO BACK to that school with all those strange girls? She has nothing more to learn there . . . she knows everything already. She spoke French to the overseas operator yesterday and they understood her."

Fortunately, my mother's pleas did not sway my father, and I arrived back at school for the 1937–38 winter term. It was nice to be back in solid Swiss reality. I hoped that this time I would be allowed to stay for the full semester.

No such luck! Two months later, Tami was sent to Switzerland with orders to haul me out of school. My mother *had* to see me in Paris. Those final exams? Not important—they could wait. Glad to escape having to translate Homer, I flung some clothes into my suitcase—they would all be considered too tight, old, or whatever, and be replaced anyway—curtsied to the disapproving headmistresses, wished them a breathless "Joyeux Noël," and jumped into the waiting taxi. We had a train to catch!

Tami seemed gay—nearly too much so. She spoke in rapid bursts, as though in a hurry to get the words out before others crowded her mind; her gestures were animated, unrelated to what she was saying; she fumbled with her wallet, paid the taxi too little, apologized profusely, then overpaid, searched frantically for our train tickets, found them, handed them over to the porter, dropped his tip, scrambled to retrieve it, took my hand, and hurried us after him and onto our waiting train.

"Water—didn't buy water? And newspapers? Passports? We have passports? Katerlein, you want chocolate? Yes! Yes! I will run and get some —is there time? When does the train leave? Do I have Swiss money? How much will it be? Will they take French francs? They don't, do they? . . . Maybe not enough time? Why didn't I think of the water—how stupid of me! Maybe they will have some on the train? Will they take French francs?" She hesitated by the door, at a loss, unable to decide what to do, where to hurry to.

I put my arms around her, turned her gently, sat her down, tried to assure her: We did not need papers; we each had a book; the train not only had a dining car, but vendors; water was easily accessible. All alone she had managed to travel from Paris to Lausanne, pick me up, then get back on the right train all by herself without a single mistake—all was well. She had done it. She could relax now—we would certainly make it back to Paris without any big trouble.

Like an exhausted child, she put her head on my shoulder and quietly fell asleep. My God, what was happening to her! I held this fragile, tormented soul and wondered what her demons looked like.

We were pulling into the Gare de Lyon. She tidied her hair, put on her hat, smiled shyly at me through the mirror. "Katerlein, you won't tell Mutti and Papi—anything about my being so silly? They are so good to me, have so much patience."

"Of course I am. I am going to walk into the Lancaster and say, 'What a trip! Nothing but her usual stupidities! Really, can't *that* woman learn a *little* discipline!' " I said in my very best Dietrich imitation, which made Tami laugh.

When our taxi pulled up to the hotel, my father was waiting on the curb. On ushering us into my mother's presence, he remarked:

"Mutti—they have arrived! And all in one piece! Amazing! The blind leading the blind!"

My mother was busy kissing my eyes.

MY MOTHER WAS ESPECIALLY BEAUTIFUL that winter. After I was disinfected, had my hair cut, been reclothed and reshod, she cried, kissed me good-bye, and left for America, stopping in New York to shop for hats and fall in love with a lady called Beth, before continuing on to Hollywood. *Knight Without Armour* had opened and flopped. *Angel*, opened the first week in November, also laid a rotten egg.

My billet was moved to a small, threadbare hotel just off the classy Place Vendôme, where from my window I could watch the comings and goings at the mighty Ritz; that is, when my new English governess permitted such "common" curiosity.

My mother, installed at the Beverly Wilshire Hotel, wrote my father her news:

> The Beverly Wilshire
> Beverly Hills, California
>
> November 30, 1937

Dearest,

I will try to write you a letter full of facts, because when I start to complain, it is hard for you to take.

First, the film that Paramount owes me won't start before February and may not be made at all because if they have to pay salaries while everyone waits, it will be too expensive. Maybe I will try to work someplace else and do the film for Paramount only in the New Year.

The trip was very bad. In the train suddenly Tauber stood in front of my door, singing his heart out. Then for days he poured his heart out to me. He is so unhappy. He sang here yesterday—so beautifully—better than ever. We all cried during *The Grenadiers* by Schumann. Reinhardt had such tears rolling down his face, that I wasn't embarrassed that I was crying. It was a marvelous success for him here and he was happy—for a few hours. In the train we sang together—all the old songs and Berlin was suddenly with us again—so near, so strong, that we were lost and forlorn when we arrived in Pasadena. Lang is looking after me. D. I have not seen. He wrote me this morning that he has found himself—and that his life is "calm" and purposeful! I am glad that everything has been solved so calmly. I wrote to Beth a farewell letter, because in New York I didn't have the courage to tell her that everything was finished between us. Edington is loyal and good, with him and Lang, I hope to get through this difficult time. I am so lost without The Child. In this country, that remains so for-

eign to me, as it always was, that only
through her joy I could feel close to, became
a home because of her—now makes me miss
her even more.

Adieu, my heart. I am lying here in
bed—and no door opens—from anywhere
—and that is frightening.

Always yours,

Mutti

For Christmas, Tami was sent to "pull herself together" in a mountain sanitarium. My father's plans were so obviously veiled, they had
to be clandestine, and I was delivered to an English country estate, with turrets, pomp, and circumstance, straight out of a Sir Walter Scott
novel. My room boasted a canopied bed, all
white ruffles and Elizabethan drapes, curved
window seat beneath Tudor windows, an Adam
fireplace whose ever-ready logs were lit by a uni-
formed lass each snowy morning before she
awakened me with: "Miss, Miss, the fire's lit,
your bath's run. Do hurry, the breakfast gong
will be sounded shortly." My hostess was the
model British lady, gracious, genteel, to the
"manor" born. Her husband, a younger version
of C. Aubrey Smith with a lot of Michael Redgrave thrown in, sat in a majestic, high-backed
chair, knitting argyle socks in rapid five-needle
perfection. He had become proficient in this
awesome skill while recovering from war injuries

to his hands. The picture he made, so elegantly nonchalant in that so-British chair, clicking away, his eyes never concerned with his sock in progress, is a treasured memory. Their daughter was very nice to me, it was not her doing that I felt alien in a world I wished I belonged to.

We took horse-drawn sleds to neighbors' stately homes for festive balls, were given real dance cards that kind Sirs, Lords, and Viscounts down from Eton and Harrow were kind enough to write their illustrious names in. On Christmas morning, the real one, I woke to discover a pillowcase at the foot of my pretty bed stuffed full of gaily colored gifts, and one incredible evening, guests in full-dress kilts, all black velvet, reds, greens, blues, and silver-buckled shoes, sat at our own banquet, given in our own ballroom, as pipers in tartan regalia marched around the laden table, piping their thrilling tunes welcoming in the New Year!

Never *ever* has one homeless child been handed such a perfect Christmas. It became my yardstick of what this holiday should and could be. Whenever I hear bagpipes, I see that lovely house, feel the warmth and security, and thank those kind strangers for giving a make-believe child her first taste of tradition.

Once back at school, my mother's calls continued their interruptive pattern. She had been

forced to go to a big gala opening and just had to tell me all about it! She didn't even give me a chance to thank her for letting me go to England for the holidays.

"Sweetheart! Listen! Listen! You won't believe this! I had to go to an opening. Klieg lights, fans, red carpet, everyone dressed to the teeth à la real glamour, radio interviews—everything. Like a real big movie premiere. I had to do the whole movie-star to-do! Hair, furs—even all the emeralds! The beautiful white chiffon didn't fit because you weren't here to tape the breasts. Anyway, all this glamour *to-do*—and you know for what? *Hopping rabbits!* Even you would have been too old for that! But you should have been there, just to hear the screaming when we stepped out of the car—box office poison or no box office poison, the people went wild—they pushed so hard against the barricades that some of them fainted from all the excitement and got stepped on!

"Afterwards in the car, I said: 'Now, tell me one thing! *Who* is going to go to see that? A full-length picture of nothing but "cutsey-poo"? . . . Except for the wonderful stepmother . . . it is for two year olds! And all those ugly little men, like midgets, and that Prince—looks queer. . . . You can't allow somebody who does Mickey Mouse to become a movie producer!' Sweetheart, you have to see it! [I couldn't wait!] They have a 'cleaning scene' . . . I nearly peed in my pants! Little 'birdies' and fluffy squirrels, all helping the village idiot! And terrible music. All sugary doodle-do. . . . They can't allow such things and then even have premieres for them. And for this abortion I had to dress up? . . . Sweetheart, I tell you one thing—it will never make money!"

The power of Disney's first full-length cartoon was such that when I finally did get to see *Snow White and the Seven Dwarfs*, even my mother hadn't been able to spoil it for me. I loved it—"birdies," "queer prince," and all!

Dietrich's old contract had until the end of February to run. Paramount, still owing her a picture, was now willing to pay her off. She wrote my father.

> I have already used up too much time and money hoping that the Studio would come up with something that could erase the "Box Office Poison" but they have nothing to offer. I have been advised, discreetly, that they are willing to pay and forget it, but that for appearances I must have a lawyer write to them, etc.
>
> The $250,000 will keep us going for a while. Something will come up eventually, and then things will be all right again. I have to believe that Hemingway was right when he said that it did not happen only by Jo's hand, that much came from inside me.
>
> Here it's very expensive but you know

the mentality around the studios. I don't
dare have the smell of "has been" or even
"out of work star." So, I'm spending what
I have in order to appear very glamorous,
when really I am lonely and bored and—to
you I can admit it—frightened.

Hitler marched into a welcoming Austria.
My mother moved out of the expensive hotel
into a little house in Beverly Hills.

My father delivered me into my mother's
arms for spring vacation. I hadn't been in school
long enough to deserve one, but the other pupils
had, and so, I got one too. Tami, I was told, was
once again "visiting her brother." I worried
where she had been hidden away this time and
if she had been forced, once again, to kill a baby.

My mother was beautiful that spring. Vibrant, talkative, and in command of her handsome Knight. He too seemed at his very best.
They laughed and played the "lovers" to perfection. But there must have been someone else,
for once or twice, I was told to say she was busy
discussing scripts, when I knew she wasn't—and
when he called early one morning, I had to pretend she was still in bed when, actually, it hadn't
been slept in.

We went to have tea with one of her old girl-
friends. I wondered if now Dorothy di Frasso
and my mother had something more in common

than just having rented her house. Our countess was about to rush off to Italy—to kill Mussolini. She had a foolproof plan. Sticking a fresh cigarette into her long ivory holder, she told us all about it: It seemed that tiger's whiskers, once ground and mixed into food, would perforate human intestines like a thousand fine needles, bring on agonizing death through peritonitis.

"Marlene—one's insides turn into a sieve, shit pours into the stomach—and *basta*! Stinking death!"

Once back in Rome, she was planning to throw a party, invite all of her titled Italian friends, hand each one tweezers, send them out on a scavenger hunt with orders to return with the whiskers of tigers.

"But, darling, once they're ground, how are you going to get them into Mussolini's food?" my mother asked, fascinated.

Our elegant assassin chuckled: "Silly girl— that's the *easy* part."

My mother threw back her head and roared.

We stayed the whole afternoon, going over the details, planning Mussolini's demise. It was agreed that as there were only two mangy tigers left in the Rome Zoo, di Frasso had to take airplanes to get there in time before they died and got carted away, so we would bring her Afghan hound over by ship when we came. Like two courageous legionnaires about to venture into dangers unknown, they kissed each other in gallant "farewell."

On entering our car, my mother exclaimed: "Oh! How I would love to be there! Watch her fuck and feed him to death!"; then realizing what she had said in front of me, tried to cover it up by quickly talking about our taking the dog to Europe, while I was desperately trying not to laugh.

With no other film offer on the horizon, her Paramount affiliation now severed, my mother became restless. Having put in her time on American soil required by law for those awaiting U.S. citizenship, she was ready to leave, anxious to get back to Europe. We joined my father, who had preferred to amuse himself in New York. He had a pretty redhead in tow and seemed very busy being shown the sights of the city. While my mother, with her friend who answered to "Beth" and clung, my father, and his Palm Beach debutante did the town, I got a chance to talk to Brian—told him all about his England being so special for Christmases, my worries about Tami, my constant incomplete marks at school because I was never really there, my mother being disturbed by my fat ugliness and growing bones. He listened. He was always ready to listen to my childhood woes, then tried to help—really couldn't, but just being able to talk to him was comfort enough.

I watched Rockefeller Center still being built, bought a secret copy of a new book, called *Rebecca*, with money I stole from the "tips," listened to the radio, learned all the words to "Flat Foot Floogie with the Floy Floy" so I would be the only one at school who could sing it, and wished, for the umpteenth time, I didn't have to leave.

Our rosé-beige apartment awaited us, the *Normandie* ever ready to enfold us in beauty, carry us to the opposite shore. The band played—horns blew. At "just thirteen," again, I was leaving "home." This time I had returned, but I doubted that I would ever be so lucky again! I prayed extra hard, hoping the Lady wouldn't mind if I thought of myself as one of those "homeless, tempest-tost" she was so willing to protect and love.

I tried to drown my sorrows in the *Normandie*'s ornate swimming pool, but my pining California spirit missed the sunlight. "Forgetting" at the movies was easier. Even my mother joined me. We saw *Marie Antoinette*. The *Normandie* was very partial to Norma Shearer films.

"She looks much better now than when that husband of hers, Thalberg, was alive," my mother's voice boomed out of the dark. The audience "ssshed" in unison the voice that had disturbed. Dietrich took no heed. As she considered films were shown for her benefit only, she believed movie houses the world over to be her private projection rooms.

"Sweetheart . . . look at that work! Best designs Adrian has ever done. Of course, they have nothing to do with the real Marie Antoinette, but nobody cares about that anyway—and Mayer wouldn't know the difference." Her comments came hot and heavy. The "shushing" increased. "The wigs! Look at those wigs! The work! That Sidney Guilleroff! Did he design all of them? . . . A bit overdone but . . ."

"Mais, alors!" muttered an exasperated gentleman behind us. My mother turned. He recognized her, apologized profusely for having disturbed her. She continued:

"Between the ostrich plumes, the cascading curls, the velvet bows, the jewelry . . . she looks ridiculous! Like a circus horse . . . but beautiful. You know, if Marie Antoinette had looked *that* good, they would never have cut off her head."

My father was occupied playing shuffleboard with a cute brunette. I often wondered if all those "cuties" really were interested in him or just wanted to sample what belonged to Dietrich. This holds true all the way down the genetic scale: If you can't get the queen, try the consort, or her princess. Fame and its aura are so desired, even grandchildren become coveted bed partners for no other reason than their illustrious genes. It is a real struggle of survival to exist within that spectrum. If the creator of this magical attraction is a Mme Curie or an Einstein, it is no less wearing, but at least a little easier to understand. If this sick obsession is generated by nothing more than physical beauty, it becomes, at times, unbearable.

"Sweetheart, I'm wearing the Alix with the satin flounce. Barbara Hutton is giving a party up in the Grill. Who do you think is her latest boyfriend? Our shirt salesman . . . from *Blonde Venus*! Amazing how these American heiresses go for pansies! . . . Cole Porter is probably furious and wishes he hadn't written 'Night and Day' for him!"

I was returned to boarding school just in time to prepare for exams before the summer break. I didn't even know what had been taught. My new roommate was a girl whose father had once spent a weekend at the Hotel Ambassador with my mother, so we were practically related! Sometime during that very short term, my official family came to visit me. My mother, my father, a resurrected Tami, and Teddy stopped off in Switzerland from Somewhere to Somewhere, signed me out for a sumptuous lunch in Lausanne, then delivered me back to school, where my mother signed autograph books, patted youthful cheeks, was gracious, regal, impressed everyone with her perfection, and cried as she bade me a Chekhovian farewell. Despite the moving scenes of a "mother's farewell," she seemed in a dewy haze, utterly in the throes of some new "perfect" love. It was very "Anna Karenina." I waved good-bye, had time to feel sorry for our Knight and Beth before reporting to "French Lit—Room B," where we were deep into Proust. The interruptive telephone calls came hot and heavy, but this didn't get me into trouble anymore. Brillantmont had given up trying to fight my mother. I didn't blame them, I knew the feeling!

Her voice soft, she spoke in lyrical German, her best "à la Heine": "Jo is here. They are showing his films in this festival. He is very famous here—being feted, so is never around. Sweetheart! Venice must be seen only at twilight or dawn—in the light of Tintoretto. We drink Dom Pérignon as the golden light paints the sky, silhouetting the domes of a thousand churches! We walk over little curved bridges and listen to the gondoliers sing—they all sound like Caruso!"

I wondered who the other half of the "we" was . . . he knew his painters.

"Oh, sweetheart! If you could see it! We are in a small fishing village—little boats on a blue-blue sea, white sails billowing, fishermen repairing their nets in the golden evening sun, beautiful barefoot women carrying their water jugs on one hip to the village well. We eat little fish roasted over coals with fresh thyme from the Provence and breathe in the perfume of pine trees that grow right down to the sea. At night, we listen to their beautiful Italian songs of love and the sea makes little wave sounds onto the soft sand."

I was dying to meet the other half of that "we."

"Sweetheart—the grapes! Everywhere you look, little sturdy vines. Today, we are driving to drink white Burgundy in a little country inn . . ."

She sounded more and more fairy-tale happy, with overtones of "German breathless"! I decided her new lover must be German, a wine connoisseur, an artist, a true romantic worthy of her, certainly someone very special.

I NEVER KNEW why my mother ordered me back to Paris, for when I arrived at the Hotel Lancaster, she wasn't there. But the lilacs were! Someone must have bought out France in white lilac. You couldn't see the furniture for the flowers, and breathing was definitely difficult. Suddenly, my father materialized from behind the vases, said hello, and introduced me to my new governess, who inspected me without enthusiasm. I curtsied, removed my train gloves, we shook hands, I was told to put my gloves back on as we were leaving, I was being moved to another hotel, where I would henceforth reside with "Mademoiselle" as guardian and chaperone. This was the beginning of sometimes being billeted apart from my mother when she had a new lover in residence. Suddenly, at the age of "just thirteen" in my mother's mind, I had attained the age of perception.

The Hotel Windsor was brown. Furniture, walls, carpeting—even the dried flower arrangements looked like baked mud. Our "special wing" boasted a pretty bay window, otherwise it was just as somber as the rest of the establishment. Except for my memories of the time spent in a perfect little park nearby, the Hotel Windsor had nothing to recommend it. In the square, Rodin's huge statue of a depressed Balzac brooding on top of a massive pedestal set the tone of the area.

My father, having installed his charges, left. While my governess unpacked us, I observed her. She was not easy to cast. She was not a Zasu Pitts, certainly not a spinster version of Claudette Colbert—if there ever was such a thing as a Colbert with overtones of spinsterhood. What made this woman interesting was that her lack of personality—such a necessary requirement in a proper governess—was there, but in her case seemed purposely acquired. Her costume was right: prim navy serge suit, immaculate white

Meeting and loving von Sternberg in Venice.

A rare candid picture of my mother having a good time in the golden sun of Italy.

The moment Erich Maria Remarque lit her cigarette, my mother knew she was in love with him.

The Mediterranean, the pool, the cliffs below the Hôtel du Cap d'Antibes—the summer of 1938 was luxury in high gear.

blouse, cameo at throat, sensible black leather shoes, very proper, unattractive, out-of-fashion hair in serviceable bun at nape of neck—all correct, and yet, completely false. She looked the colorless spinster lady, but wasn't—her walk was wrong; it undulated, enticed—she wouldn't have gotten past my friend Mae West with her camouflage! She might have fooled a casting director. Certainly my usually sharp father must have been taken in, but I wondered . . . had he seen that walk? Noticed the way her shoulders followed the lift of each hip, how she glanced furtively at herself whenever she passed a reflective surface? Perhaps he hadn't been hoodwinked at all—had been so intrigued by her too-carefully hidden attributes and decided to engage her for future inspection? I had noticed that whenever Tami was put away somewhere, he had a certain type of woman ready at hand. I hoped this one wouldn't be one of them. Being the girlfriend of the boss might give her airs. This one had enough of those already. Trusting someone who played a lie so cleverly could be dangerous. She must really need this thankless job to have gone to such lengths to get it. I decided to find out why.

My new life became rather structured. In the morning, waiting for my mother's summons to report to her at her hotel, I did my homework while my governess caught up on her "hidden beauty" sleep. Promptly before lunch, refreshed

and accurately prim, she delivered me into my
mother's waiting arms and disappeared. I did the
mail, helped my mother dress for whatever
luncheon rendezvous was scheduled, listened to
her, saw her off, tidied her bathroom and
makeup, put away and filed her evening clothes
from the night before, did the flowers and cards,
was told by my father not to dawdle, gave Teddy
a fast hug, tried constantly to find out where
Tami had been hidden this time, then helped my
mother change for dinner, tidied and refiled her
day wear before "Mademoiselle" reappeared to
collect her charge, conduct us back to our somber abode and our usual room-service dinner of
Poached Sole Jardiniere. I was left to finish my
fruit and cheese course by myself as Mademoiselle needed time to prepare for our nightly "outing." Her long hair looked so pretty, all combed
out, curling down to her shoulders; I thought the
lipstick she wore was a bit too crimson, but the
lip gloss was effective; the floral silk clung, molding her body, very high heels accentuated the
walk that had first given her away. Swiftly, we
made our way through the empty lobby and to
an already waiting taxi. We would sit silently in
our respective corners, the lady of the evening
and her young charge, until the lights of Mont-
martre and the dome of the Basilica of the Sacré-
Coeur heralded our arrival at her destination.
She would pay the taxi fare from her little purse

that swung jauntily from its silken cords, push
me ahead of her through a small hidden door,
sit me down in the remotest corner of the candle-
lit bar, vanish up a flight of creaking stairs, trailing a scent of cheap musk. I learned to like the
taste of cherry brandy that June of '38! A sullen
woman with dirty hair kept replenishing my glass
with the sticky elixir. As the hours passed, I, the
child of censored movies, whose only concept of
human relationships was lyrical, adoring romance, or cruelty, sat obediently, waiting for my
governess to return from wherever she was and
take me home. If someone had told me then I
was sipping brandy in a brothel, I wouldn't have
known what they meant, and as my school
friends' descriptions did not really fit my governess, the label "prostitute" never entered my
mind. I had been told by my father's appointed
authority to *sit* and *wait*, and like Teddy, I did;
behaved myself until Mademoiselle, all smiles
and tangled hair, reappeared and took me home.
As she was especially lenient and permissive
after these clandestine soirees, I quickly learned
to keep silent and reaped the benefits of her
approval of my cooperation of her "little secret."

In the daytime, I continued shuttling between the airy white-and-gold beauty of the Hotel Lancaster, returning to the brown gloom of
the Windsor whenever my mother and her new
lover resided in Paris. It never occurred to me

that the year of "The Child might discover" had begun. My mother's behavior did not change, just where I was housed, and even this was so erratic that I never could figure out when I could be "viewable" and when not. Finally, I gave up trying to understand the elaborate attempts at subterfuge and continued to play dumb as far as my mother's romances were concerned. It had always worked in the past, it surely would keep everyone reassured in the present. I had my father's slick example: Befriend and charm all who enter here, wait them out until they and their accompanying rules were replaced by others.

The white lilacs kept arriving in unparalleled abundance, accompanied by cases of Dom Pérignon and some of the sweetest love letters I had ever seen. I had yet to meet the man responsible for them and the retraining of Dietrich's palate for champagne. Whoever he was, his influence over her was complete. Goethe had been replaced by Rainer Maria Rilke, all the Hemingway books by one entitled *All Quiet on the Western Front* in multiple languages by someone called Erich Maria Remarque. I never could understand this strange German penchant for calling boys by my name.

My mother swept through the lilacs, pulling a reluctant man behind her:

"Sweetheart! Come here. I want you to meet the most brilliant writer of our time—the

man who wrote *All Quiet on the Western Front*
—Mr. Remarque!"

I curtsied and looked up into the face of an
intriguing man. The eyes veiled, giving nothing
away, mouth as vulnerable as a woman's, a face
to be sculpted.

"Kater? Is that what you like to be called?
I am known as Boni to friends. How do you do?"
he said in a soft, aristocratic German, as though
reading good poetry.

"No, no—my heart! The Child must only
address you as *Mister* Remarque," my mother
cooed, melting herself into his side. She locked
her arm in his and strolled him out of the lilac
bower. I went back to unpacking *Mr.* Remarque's books, thinking—this one might really
be worth mooning over!

Remarque and I became close friends. I always thought that he had the look of a debonair
fox, like an illustration out of the *Fables* of La
Fontaine, even the tops of his ears pointed
slightly. He had an innate theatricality—an actor
in a heroic production standing perpetually in
the wings, waiting for the right cue; in the in-
terim, he wrote books in which all the male roles
represented the powers within him; in life never
placed together to form one whole character,
just the most intriguing parts of himself, doomed
never to meld into one complete man. Not because he didn't know how to, but because he felt

himself undeserving of such exemplary completion.

My mother used to describe her first meeting with this charming, complex depressive. The scene went like this:

She was having lunch with von Sternberg on the Lido in Venice, when a man approached their table.

"Herr von Sternberg? Madame?"

Although my mother resented strangers approaching her, his deep voice, with its cultured tone, intrigued her. She looked up into the finely chiseled face, the sensitive mouth; his falcon eyes softened as he bent toward her.

"May I introduce myself? I am Erich Maria Remarque."

My mother held out her hand, he raised it to his lips in homage. Von Sternberg motioned to the waiter for another chair, saying: "Won't you join us?"

"Thank you. May I, Madame?"

My mother, enchanted by his impeccable manners, smiled faintly, inclined her head, giving him permission to sit.

"You look much too young to have written one of the greatest books of our time." Her eyes had not left his face.

"I may have written it solely to hear your enchanting voice tell me so." He flicked his gold lighter, extending it to light her cigarette, she cupped her pale hands around his bronzed ones, inhaled, the tip of her tongue dislodged a speck of tobacco from her lower lip. Von Sternberg, the consummate cameraman, left quietly. He knew a great two-shot when he saw one.

"Remarque and I talked until dawn! It was wonderful! Then he looked at me and said, 'I must tell you—I am impotent!' and I looked up at him and said: 'Oh, how wonderful!' With such relief! You know how I hate to do 'it'—I was so happy! It meant we could just talk and sleep, love each other, all nice and cozy!"

I always imagined Remarque's reaction to her enthusiasm at his supplicant confession and wished I could have seen his face when he heard her utter it.

They looked very strange, all that blackness against the white and gold of our Lancaster ante-room. I had arrived to help my mother dress for lunch and been told she was busy, to wait until summoned. So I sat, watching the two men guarding our living-room door, behaving as though they belonged there. Both were young, thick-necked, square-jawed, steely-eyed, and very blond. They could have been twins. Even without all those silver eagles and swastikas all over their uniforms, they would have looked menacing. They scared me. I sat very still, hoping the "Siegfrieds" wouldn't deign to notice a mere "Aryan" child. I wondered who they were there to guard and why my mother would consent to a meeting with a Nazi! The door opened, expert clicking of heels, lips brushed elegantly across my mother's extended hand, a clipped "Heil Hitler," and a tall German strode out of our suite, followed by his henchmen.

"Papi—have you ever seen such a thing? How can such a well-educated man like Ribbentrop believe in Hitler! He is an intelligent man, from one of the best families in Germany, so you can't tell me that he doesn't *know* any better. I had to hide Remarque in the bathroom! After they burned all his books, I was afraid if those 'well poisoners' saw him—a ridiculous situation! *I* have to be careful—just because Mutti and Liesel refuse to leave Germany? Next time you talk to them, just tell Mutti they *have* to leave —so I don't have to go through things like this. But . . . did you *see* that uniform? How those shoulders fit? That's where all the Jewish tailors have disappeared to! They have taken them to make their costumes! Sweetheart, get Mr. Remarque—he can come out of the bathroom now."

Remarque didn't like being locked away, even if it was for his own safety; he stormed into the living room:

"Marlene—never, never dare to lock me away again! Do you hear me? I am not an errant child nor an irresponsible idiot bent on defying reality for the sake of irrational bravura!"

"Oh, my only love! I was only frightened for you! You know how they hate you because you, a non-Jew, left Germany. They might have been sent here just to find *you*! All that story about Hitler wanting me to be the "Great Star" of his German Reich . . . that is all not true! The only reason he keeps sending his 'so important' officers to get me to come back is because he saw me in *The Blue Angel* garter belt and wants to get into those lace panties!"

Remarque threw back his head and roared. He, who so rarely found life amusing, laughed with complete abandon on those rare occasions when he did.

My flighty governess was given excellent references from my father. Her services were no longer required. Tami had returned, restored once again to surface health, clutching a handful of new prescriptions guaranteed to keep her happy, at least through the summer. My mother, on seeing her, had commented:

"Well—all the money was finally worth it. You look human!" and we left to vacation in the south of France, *en famille*.

The Hôtel du Cap d'Antibes, perched white opulence overlooking the Mediterranean, in 1938 still sapphire blue and crystal clear, its water so clean one swallowed it without fear while swimming in its cool beauty. As one of the most famous hotels along the Côte d'Azur, the so-called "beautiful people" of the thirties gathered there to observe each other and exchange their privileged gossip. They were different from those of today. Maybe it was the silks and linens they wore, the Patous, Lanvins, Molineuxs, Schiaparellis—the absence of jeans, sneakers, and unisex—that gave them such an aura of real chic. Just as the movie stars of the silver screen were visually unique, they too had special individuality seldom seen today, even on the most luxurious yachts anchored in Monte Carlo's harbor. The men, whose business acumen or inherited wealth made all this effervescent luxury possible, they haven't changed as much, although their 1930s prototypes had a bit more style, looked classier, were better mannered.

Our summer palace was, and still is, a truly great hotel, one of those rare few in the world that have defied change of any kind. The Dietrich entourage had connecting suites, Remarque, my mother, my father, and the luggage. Tami down the hall, I, up the hall. Teddy divided his loyalties like the diplomat he was.

There is a special summer light along this part of the French coast. Stark, intense, hot, and white, making all color come into its own. That first summer in Antibes, Dietrich forsook her beiges and blacks, wore flowing beach robes in Schiaparelli's invention, "shocking pink," and looked divine.

A nondescript woman and her secret machine became the latest discovery in the never-ending quest of the rich and famous for "eternal youth." This clever ex-postmistress from Manchester had built a contraption that was rumored to possess the powers of immortality. A black box, the size of my mother's portable gramophone, it was festooned with Frankenstein-like filament tubes, lots of serious-looking knobs and dials, above which stretched a wide band of milky rubber—the type used in surgical gloves.

"Now, Miss Dietrich, give me your finger. Just a little prick of this pin, a tiny squeeze— and observe, we have a lovely sample of your bright red blood. That did not hurt at all, now did it? . . . Now, onto the magnetic surface it will go," and she would grasp the bleeding finger, rubbing it and its blood onto the rubber surface. This done, the "patient" was asked which one of her organs was giving her the most discomfort. My mother, who was always sick to her stomach because of her enormous consumption of Epsom salts, said in dead earnest:

"My liver—I am sure it is the liver why I feel carsick all the time."

"Aha! I thought so! The moment I came in through the door, I felt it! I said to myself, 'There is a peakish liver!' I shall now set my machine to the frequency generated by this organ, and through this drop of your living blood, treat your sluggish liver magnetically back to health!" and fiddling with the dials, making her radio tubes glow, she rubbed, spreading my mother's blood back and forth along the strip until the rubber squeaked. My mother, fascinated, watched, felt the surge of electricity course through her afflicted organ, and announced:

"Wonderful! I feel better—let's go eat!"

Over the years, that clever lady was paid enormous sums. As she claimed her machine could cure "in absentia," drops of blood were continually drawn, soaked into pieces of white blotting paper, then sent on to her by mail. While she rubbed her rubber and cashed checks, my mother was convinced she felt ever so much better. Of course, Tami was the first of us who was made to try it. When the woman asked Tami which organ needed magnetic attention, my mother answered for her: "Her head!"

Because of her "liver" cure and no scheduled film, my mother, for the first time, embraced the process of acquiring a tan. Of course, all this new exposure was possible by another, much more extraordinary invention: the "built-in bra." We had found a jewel, a French seamstress who made brassieres cut on the bias, darted underneath. The first really perfect support for Dietrich's breasts. When this genius suggested incorporating her idea into bathing suits, the first ever exposure of Dietrich's body to summer was born, and the admiring glances were legion!

First thing every morning, it was my job to mix and distribute the sun oil, guaranteed to bronze and hold, a mixture of the finest olive oil and iodine, with just a hint of red wine vinegar. This was funneled into glass bottles, corked, and handed out to those ready to brave the herculean task of acquiring an even tan. That summer, everyone smelled like a salad! Laden down with books, bottles, makeup cases, sun hats, and beach robes, we commenced our descent to the rocks below, on which perched our candy-stripe cabanas, like something left over from the Charge of the Light Brigade. We also had stick huts, little houses like those in *The Three Little Pigs*. I think I once counted a hundred and fifty steps from the hotel to the beginning of its sloping, formal, mile-long esplanade that finally brought one down to our boulders along the sea and—collapse!

We had to descend those never-ending stairs before the sun could heat them to "frying an egg" temperature. God forbid if anyone forgot something. It took an hour to get back up to our rooms and then back down again, if you survived sunstroke! The hotel, aware that no one would ever make it up to lunch in their beautiful dining room, compensated for those distances by building a superb restaurant that overlooked both the sapphire-blue pool as well as the equally blue sea, and called it the Eden Roc Pavilion.

Remarque had his own table, at which his newly acquired family ate and enjoyed his superb choice of champagnes and wines; where my father, for the first time displaced as table authority, took out his frustration on the only things still under his jurisdiction: Tami, Teddy, and my lemonade. At the age of "just thirteen," I had arrived at an astounding conclusion: All those years of shaking in my "sensible" shoes over the possible unfreshness of my lemonade could so easily have been avoided had I only had the sense to order mineral water instead! I was amazed at myself. How could I have been so stupid not to do that long ago? With this new-found intelligence, I decided to switch beverages, and at one momentous luncheon, announced that henceforth I would prefer Vittel with my meals, "Please," to which my father replied:

"What? Expensive mineral water for a child? Certainly not! You are having fresh lemonade, Maria!" and so ended my teenage rebellion.

I remember most vividly the sparkle of those lunches. Everything in shimmering Technicolor

—the tall fluted goblets, the ornate silver, the elaborate ice sculptures, changed every day, of leaping dolphins, Neptune rising from foaming seas, reclining mermaids, majestic swans— amidst flame red lobsters, pink shrimp, orange salmon, purple sea urchins, midnight blue mussels, silvery fishes, primrose langoustines, and pearly gray oysters. Luncheons lasted the required three hours, followed by rest periods in louvered, darkened suites to ensure the energy necessary for the nightly balls, galas, and intimate dinners of fifty in nearby Cannes and its summer mansions sprawled along the Mediterranean coast, or public "slumming" in Juan-les-Pins, a nearby village where the artists' colony camped out.

Remarque began working on *The Arch of Triumph* that summer. He wrote in German, on lined yellow pads. His script small, neat, precise, the sharp tips of his pencils never breaking under exaggerated pressure. The large tub of meticulously sharpened pencils he kept forever ready wherever he was, ever hoping for inspiration, was one of the most revealing things about him. Of course, he modeled his heroine, Joan Madou, after my mother. His "hero," Ravic—on himself. He even used that name in some of the many letters he kept writing to my mother, whether they were together or not. He also invented a little boy, who would talk for him whenever my mother withdrew herself from their relationship. Little "Alfred" was such a touching child—I grew very fond of him. He called my mother Aunt Lena, always wrote in German, and was highly articulate for an eight-year-old! Sometimes, when I read one of his many letters that kept being pushed under her door, I wished he were real—I would have liked to talk to him.

While our "famous author" labored in his shadowed room high above the sea, his lady, sexy in fitted white bathing suit, befriended the sexy Irish politician on the cliffs below. The American Ambassador to the Court of St. James was kind of rakish. For a man with such a patient little wife, who had borne him so many children, I thought he flirted a bit too much, but outside of that, Mr. Kennedy was a very nice man, and I thought his nine children were—wonderful! And I would have gladly given up my right arm, the left, and any remaining limb, to be one of them. They looked, and were, so American. All had smiles that never ended, with such perfect teeth each of them could have advertised toothpaste.

Big Joe, the heir, broad and chunky, a handsome football player with an Irish grin and kind eyes. Kathleen, a lovely girl who assumed the role of the official eldest daughter, although she wasn't and seemed to have matured too soon because of it. Eunice, opinionated, not to be crossed, the sharp mind of an intellectual achiever—her constant identity. John, affectionately known as Jack, the glamour boy, the charmer of the wicked grin and the "come hither" look—every maiden's dream, my secret hero. Pat, nearest my age, but not gawky, nor fat, with not a pimple in sight, a vivacious girl already on her way to womanhood. Bobby, the "fixer," the one who knew everything and never minded being asked to share his information. Jean, a quiet, gentle girl who picked up forgotten tennis rackets and wet towels—a concerned mother in the making, and then came Teddy, on his chubby little legs, always running, always eager to show you love, trying to keep up with his long-legged siblings. Rosemary, the eldest daughter, the damaged child amidst these effervescent and quick-witted children, was my friend. Perhaps being two misfits, we felt comfortable in each other's company. We would sit in the shade, watching the calm sea, holding hands.

Mrs. Kennedy was always nice to me. She even invited me to lunch at their private villa adjacent to our hotel. Tami told me not to be nervous. Nevertheless, I changed my sundress four times before I was satisfied that I didn't look dressed too "aristocratic European," could pass for just a normal child coming to lunch. Their table was so long! We, the younger children, listened while the older ones discussed topics and issues proposed by their father, while Mrs. Kennedy supervised the serving of lunch by her staff and the table manners of her youngests. Never once was a critical comment made without corroborating evaluation. No sarcasms. No one "starred" and yet, all had a starlike quality. After Ambassador Kennedy became a regular visitor to our beach cabana, I stopped going. I didn't want any one of his family to feel uncomfortable. Although I had heard a spindly lady in nautical linen say, in one of my mother's type of whispers: "That's the American Ambassador over there . . . the one with all those children, who is Gloria Swanson's lover!" So maybe they were as used to their father disappearing as I was my mother.

My father was very angry about something. With Tami and Teddy in the back seat, he drove his Packard out of the hotel gates and left for somewhere. Remarque stayed, continued to write his book by day and drank by night. My mother told everyone how she searched for him in every bar between Monte Carlo and Cannes—afraid he would be arrested and news of his disgraceful conduct hit the world headlines.

"Everyone already knows that Fitzgerald is a drunkard, and Hemingway drinks only because he is a Real man, but Boni—he is a *sensitive* writer. Sensitive writers are poets, so they are delicate, they can't lie in gutters and get sick!"

That summer, I was reassigned my dresser duties. I would wait in my mother's suite for her return from the many parties, help her undress, file away the clothes, then leave. I was putting away the cooled shoes when he strolled in. Remarque was in favor, so was permitted entrance to the suite unannounced.

"Boni, why is Somerset Maugham so dirty? I mean dirty vulgar, not dirty unwashed. Does he do that just to be clever and shock, or is that him really?" my mother called from the bathroom.

"Like most gifted homosexuals, he mistrusts normalcy to such an extent, he has to embarrass those that practice it." My mother laughed. "Like women who see a rival in every woman they meet and must discredit them, so Maugham plays the vindictive bitch. Thank God, when he writes this leaves him—most of the time."

"He is a *wonderful* writer!" my mother retorted, annoyed by what she considered Remarque's criticism of Maugham. "*The Letter*—what a script that is. Now *that* woman, I could play—and right!" She squirted paste onto her toothbrush. Remarque removed his cigarette case from his dressing gown, extracted a cigarette, lit it, leaned back in the armchair, crossed his pajamaed leg, and said:

"My beautiful Puma, most roles of deceiving women you could play magnificently."

My mother gave him one of her "looks," spat into the decorated sink, noticed I was still in the room, told me that was all—to go to bed. I kissed her, Remarque, and left them to their heated discussion that I knew was brewing.

At lunch the next day, my mother repeated Remarque's assessment of Somerset Maugham to their guests as though it were her own, adding:

"It is only those young boys he keeps surrounding himself with that gets too much. Where does he pick them up? On Moroccan beaches? Noël does that too, but at least he does it politely, sotto voce. That's what is such a relief when you are with Hemingway, finally a *real* man—who writes!"

I quickly looked at Remarque and caught the slightest wince.

I was delivering something forgotten back down to the Rocks when a dowager, in orange toweling turban and matching robe, stopped my descent.

"Do you know where Marlene Dietrich's little girl could be?"

"Why? Are you looking for her?"

"Oh, I've got to see her. I've read so much about her. Do you know she is her mother's whole life—her only reason for living? She makes all those films, is a star, only for that little girl of hers?" gushed the plump lady, flashing diamond rings too tight for her pudgy fingers.

I had the feeling that if I said "Here I am —it's me!" she would be terribly disappointed. No angelic smallness, no porcelain delicacy— no miniature replica of the star she obviously admired—so I pointed down the walk and said helpfully:

"Madame, I think I just saw her skipping down toward the cliffs."

The orange lady went in search of me.

My father and his "family" had returned for Elsa Maxwell's summer ball, being paid for, as usual, by someone else. Elsa Maxwell was shrewd, coarse, an opportunist—and ruthless. But, once your friend, she never stabbed you in the back, never tried to hurt and had a sense of pity for the "Followers" of this world of which she was one. She recognized my position and often was very kind. I was taken to a lot of her parties. She always made sure I sat next to "nice" people, who rarely asked me to tell them all about my mother, even made sure my assigned table was far removed from my famous parent. Being ugly herself, she recognized the insecurities of those who knew they were unattractive in the midst of the beautiful and never forced me into the lime- light. As I remember every single person who was ever kind to me, I remember that often ma- ligned woman very well.

Everyone had been sent an invitation on

gold-edged cards, printed in thick raised letters by Cartier and, because the teenage Kennedys were going, I was allowed to go too. My mother even bought me my very own first ever evening dress, stiffened white net with a wide, inset cummerbund encrusted with chips of multicolored glass. I looked like a mosquito tent with sparkle. I wanted to hide in a very dark closet, preferably die! Newly tanned, my mother in floating white chiffon, looking like silky butterscotch poured into whipped cream, slapped some calamine lotion onto my peeling nose, pinned a net bow on my head, and pushed me into the waiting car. The huge ballroom looked like Aladdin's cave à la humans—the whole place a travel poster perfection. Miss Maxwell had assigned me a seat at a table amidst the potted ferns, with people who were kind, who didn't pay any attention to me. She placed my mother, my father, Tami, and Remarque miles away across the room. It turned out to be a very special evening, for Jack hiked all the way across the ballroom and asked me to dance the latest rage, the Lambeth Walk! A breathtaking dream who, at the age of just twenty-one, has the kindness to ask a net tent to dance, you must admit is truly wonderful!

I don't remember who started the rumor that Mars was scheduled to collide with the Earth that summer of 1938. True, every evening, the red glow from that ominous planet seemed to be getting closer and closer! Beatrice Lillie kept eyeing it, shaking her head, murmuring, "Doomed, my dears—doomed!" while the Sitwells prayed; the historian Will Durant, very disturbed, packed, ordered his car, and drove off at top speed—my mother always maintained—in the direction of Maugham's villa. The more curious gentlemen ordered powerful binoculars, telescopes, and books on astronomy to be sent down from Paris by car and train, then busied themselves calculating when Armageddon was certain to occur, while their ladies made beauty appointments and wondered which of their many evening gowns would be most suitable to enter eternity in. Lying on rocks roasting, observing the calm waters of the Mediterranean, wondering if it was time yet for lunch, or time to begin dressing for dinner, had begun to pall a little, and so, the movements of the flaming planet became an exciting and appreciated diversion. Evelyn Walsh McLean, who owned the infamous Hope diamond, rumored to strike dead anyone who dared touch it, decided to throw caution to the wind, removed her lethal gem from the hotel vault, and let people fondle it if they dared. We all agreed that it was a most appropriate jewel to wear for the first party to be given to celebrate the annihilation of the world.

On the designated fatal night, everyone threw each other a gala. The gentlemen, resplendent in white mess jackets or full dress tails, their ladies trailing satin, chiffon, lace, organza, and piqué, everyone was truly breathtaking. Huge crystal bowls of caviar nestled amongst mountains of shaved ice on ornate silver platters; Dom Pérignon, Taittinger, Veuve Clicquot in their tulip-shaped Baccarat, bubbled pale gold in the moonlight. Some preferred Black Velvets, considering Guinness mixed with "bubbly" more suitable for the last toast; others chose Pink Ladies or Stinger cocktails in delicately frosted Lalique. It was a gorgeous farewell party! It lasted until the pink dawn shimmered across the surface of the silvery sea, when everyone suddenly realized that their world had not come to an end after all—and went to bed, just a little disappointed. The next summer, not Mars, but a little man in Berlin changed the course of human history.

I WAS RETURNED to my brown Paris exile, where a new governess awaited me. Gray of hair and vestments, she smelled of lavender sachets and spinster purity. English tea, brewed correctly in a pot, replaced cherry brandy, clandestine junkets by bedtime at eight and Milton's *Paradise Lost*. I wondered why I wasn't being sent back to school.

Dietrich on a schooner, posing in a real bathing suit
—and tanned. Very unusual. But then, the summer
of 1939 was special for many reasons.

A gala evening with Dietrich's "family" in attendance. Remarque, who never did get used to the
constant snapping of pictures, tried to shield his
face, as though the whole world didn't know he
was one of Dietrich's lovers.

ABOVE: Our cabanas above the sea. My friends the Kennedy children had theirs next to ours. Jack, Pat, Bobby, Eunice—I thought them all wonderful and yearned to be part of such a joyous family. BELOW: My father took this picture. He wanted to prove to my mother that the outfit she had donned for her rendezvous with Ambassador Kennedy was a little overdone, even for Antibes. She retorted that her latest, the Pirate, loved it.

"That stupid man, Chamberlain, thinks he can persuade Hitler?" My mother paced, the morning newspapers in one hand, her coffee cup in the other. Her family listened while buttering their croissants.

"What does he think? That the Prime Minister of England going to Berchtesgaden, *that* will impress the "Führer"? Always the British behave as though they are an empire!"

"That may be the attitude that will save them in the end," Remarque said in his soft voice.

My mother whirled:

"Boni! You of all people! You, the great authority on the suffering of war, how can you think this stupid trip of Chamberlain's to Hitler is going to do any good?"

"Marlene, I did not make a judgment on a political maneuver but an observation of a national characteristic."

"Papi," my mother turned her attention from my latest father to my primary one:

"What do *you* think? When Boni uses that 'professor' tone of his . . . Kater, sit up straight. Finish your egg. Tami—don't fidget, and watch The Child. Papi? Well? Boni and I agree if war is inevitable . . . The Child must be evacuated! She must be saved. . . . Boni, you too. . . . I am safe, they won't dare touch a Dietrich! Anyway, Hitler, with this thing for garter belts . . . do you know he kept a print of *The Blue Angel* for himself when they burned all the films? . . . Kater, get ready—*you are leaving*! Papi will tell us where you have to go to be safe from danger!"

Remarque placed his napkin by his plate, rose, and said:

"I would recommend Holland. They have ports. Ships will be able to leave from there for the safety of America and the Dutch will not capitulate."

"You see," my mother was triumphant. "Only a man who knows real war thinks correctly when one is about to happen. Papi: Holland! Tonight! The Child goes to Holland tonight! Tami can take her!" and she left for her fitting at Schiaparelli. My father called Thomas Cook.

I wondered what one packed to flee a war. My mother returned in time, said refugees must be unhampered by baggage, and gave me one of her special overnight cases. Handmade especially for her by Hermès, it was of such delicate pigskin, it boasted its own canvas slipcover to protect it. The interior of cream suede was fitted with cut-crystal bottles, jars and tubes for creams, face powders, soap, and toothbrushes. The lids to all this glass splendor were of inlaid enamel of geometric design, in shades of petal pink and lapis lazuli. Empty, this small overnight case weighed a ton—which is why my mother never used it. With the added weight of pajamas, shoes, skirt, blouse, sweater, and book—if I had had to flee across borders, I wouldn't have made it. My mother removed our hats, tied woolen scarves around our heads, with big safety pins pinned dollar bills into our underpants, saying, "You never know, said the widow," cried, kissed us good-bye, handed her refugees over to her "train-taking" husband, and, cradled in the arms of her lover, sobbed:

"To safety—to safety—go! Quickly!"

Tami was shaking like a leaf. With nothing but her very dubious Nansen passport, a true museum piece of glued-together permits that looked like a hastily constructed tail of a child's kite to cross Slavic frontiers, I with my German eagle-festooned one, we boarded a sleeper in the dead of night—to The Hague. I don't know who was more scared. Probably Tami, who was not only reliving her original flight from Russia, but was being separated from the man who had, for some inexplicable reason, become her whole life. She looked so forlorn, huddled in the corner of the faded plush seat, I took her into my arms, held her as the train sped through the night. At the border, we got the works. The inspectors took one look at the swastika on my passport and my mother's elegant case was torn apart: every jar opened, her face powder left over from when she had once used the cases, dumped, sifted through with the tip of a pencil, hems were squeezed; heels were tapped for possible hollow sounds. They were calm, cool, silent, and extremely thorough. I felt completely guilty, just for being the focal point of their precise attention. Funny feeling, being afraid—though innocent. Later, one remembers the sense of utter helplessness, more than the fear.

Neville Chamberlain returned from signing the Munich Agreement, proclaimed to the world that he had achieved "Peace in our time," and my mother's "refugees" were recalled from Holland. I didn't want a terrible war, but I had so looked forward to going home to America, I returned to Paris a little disappointed. In anticipation of war, my governess had been let go, so I was housed with my father. The tongue-lashings of Tami recommenced, so did my efforts to shield her from their cruelty. My mother, who had returned to Hollywood, called me to tell me about what had happened for Halloween:

"Sweetheart! The whole country has gone crazy! A radio show did it! Unbelievable? Yes, yes, all over America—panic! Real panic! Something to do with little green men from Mars landing in spaceships in—New Jersey? And they believed it! Just a man's voice doing all this through the radio! *Him*—I've got to meet!"

Orson Welles became a true buddy of hers. They fed each other's fame, recognized and respected their manufactured flamboyance, and never, ever, tattled on each other.

Finally, I was allowed to return to school, had my fourteenth birthday amongst my mother's floral extravagance, labored over exams that I had no hope in hell of passing, watched as happy girls left for Christmas at home with families. Reported to my father's penitentiary in Paris, smuggled an exhausted Teddy into my bed, listened to him snore contentedly, while waiting for the lectures and subsequent sobs to die down in my father's bedroom.

After the Christmas holidays, instead of being returned to school, I was moved back to the Hotel Vendôme. Maybe I had been expelled? For never being there on time and doing badly? I wanted to ask but didn't—I was too scared to hear the answer. My new, very British governess was strict and noncommittal, considered it a comedown looking after a mere movie star's offspring, while informing everyone in the park she was employed by the famous "Miss Marlene Dietrich."

I wondered when I would be called to report and where and why I had been put back into a hotel, when my father had an apartment in the same town. On January 30, 1939, my mother cabled him what I have always considered to be one of the prize examples of a true Dietrich cable.

HOW ARE YOU DOING STOP WHEN IS WAR STOP
CABLED TAMI FOR DAY AND CLEANSING CREME
ETTINGER CHEEK ROUGE OLD COLOR CYCLAMEN
ARDEN POLISH RECEIVED NOTHING KISSES LOVE

In February, ready to leave America, my mother cabled that she was not allowed to leave the country because her English earnings were being investigated by American tax authorities, that she now would only receive her first American passport on the 6th of June. That the sum in question was one hundred eighty thousand dollars, to kiss me, then quoted a favorite line: "It was not meant to be because it was too wonderful."

In March, Hitler took Czechoslovakia, and I worried so—my sweet grandparents, what would happen to them? Why hadn't my father brought them to Paris long ago? So many questions can sit in the heart of a child that are never answered, even if asked.

Suddenly, I was taken back to school. I didn't know whether to be grateful or repentant, so concentrated on being invisible, cause no one any trouble.

In June, I was sent into my school's summer "holding tank." A mountain chalet amidst Swiss buttercups. I stored my things at Brillantmont, curtsied, said my good-byes—not knowing it would be thirty-four years before I would see that lovely school again.

ON A SWELTERING JUNE DAY in 1939, the world press ran the picture of Dietrich becoming a U.S. citizen. Eyes downcast, looking bored, she is leaning nonchalantly on the desk of the magistrate administering the Oath of Allegiance. He in vest and shirtsleeves, she in a winter suit complete with felt hat and gloves. A very strange pose for such a momentous occasion. In Berlin, *Der Stürmer*, Dr. Goebbels's preferred newspaper, ran the photograph with the caption:

> The German film actress Marlene Dietrich spent so many years amongst Hollywood's film Jews that she has now become an American citizen. Here we have a picture in which she is receiving her papers in Los Angeles. What a Jewish judge thinks of the occasion can be seen from his attitude as he stands in his shirtsleeves. He is taking from Dietrich the oath with which she betrays her Fatherland.

My father called me in Switzerland, told me that I also had been made a citizen of the United States—not to let it go to my head—asked about my algebra, and hearing the answer, hung up.

Was I really? It seemed too good to be

true. Was I finally—actually—a *real American*? No more vicious eagles, no more German? I ran to my room, from under the bed pulled out my shoe box of hidden treasures, found the little American flag I kept to celebrate the Fourth of July, set it on my marble-topped night table, saluted it—and cried my heart out!

My father must have gone to America to try and help with the tax situation, for he was supposedly there to star in yet another famous Dietrich script that played on the day the *Normandie* was scheduled to sail from New York to France. As I have absolutely no memory of this supposed drama, except through my mother, her often performed scenario will have to do; be it altered truth or pure fiction, it has enough Dietrich flavor to warrant repeating. It is entitled "The Day the Tax Gangsters Seized Papi!"

Certain that no one would ever see the cable she had sent back in February proving she knew this was all going on long before boarding the ship, her story goes like this: Dietrich arrived at Pier 88, boarded the SS *Normandie*, entered her Deauville suite, and found it empty. Her eight steamer trunks, thirty pieces of assorted luggage, and one husband had been seized—were now back on the pier being guarded by agents of the Treasury Department.

She rushed off the ship, clasped her husband to her beautifully tailored bosom, and in tones that could have curdled milk in Jersey, demanded:

"What are you doing with my husband?" and was told she owed the United States government three hundred thousand dollars in back taxes for monies earned for the film *Knight Without Armour.*

"Why do I have to declare in America what I earned in England?" was her dumbfounded retort. My mother always told this next part in a voice filled with rage, became speechless for just a second, then continued: "I had to leave poor Papi there between those American gangsters and ran back up the gangplank to plead with the captain of the *Normandie* to hold the ship until I could call Roosevelt. Of course, he held the ship, but said something about 'the tide.' Anyway, I got through to Washington—the President was out, but Joe Kennedy's friend, the Secretary of the Treasury, Henry Morgenthau, I got, and he said he was shocked that I should be treated like this right after becoming an American citizen and maybe the tax people had received an anonymous tip that I was leaving America forever, taking all my money with me. I said, 'What money?' 'Well, maybe,' he said, 'the tip came from the American Nazis as revenge?' *That* would have been just like them! But *he* was no help—So you know what I did? I hung up, rushed back down the gangplank, handed the tax gangsters all my beautiful emeralds, and they gave me back Papi and the trunks, and the *Normandie* could sail!"

At other times, my mother claimed that as a distraught supplicant, she had gone to Washington clutching her jewel case, handed her emeralds personally over to Secretary Morgenthau—sometimes President Roosevelt, depending on who was listening. In 1945, she told everyone that she was forced to sell her precious emeralds to have money to live on, because she had sacrificed her earnings to serve in the war!

When she arrived in Paris, I was called back, this time to live with her at the Lancaster. Remarque was at his home in Porto Ronco, overseeing the packing of his many treasures for shipment through Holland to America. I did my usual chores, wondered why there was no one new on my mother's romantic horizon, and was happy that Boni had managed to last out the year.

Jack Kennedy called, said he would be coming through Paris and asked me out to tea. I was in seventh heaven! I had three days to work at getting thin and disguise my pimples. My mother was not pleased. She considered it bad manners for a "schoolboy" to invite a "child" to tea. She called Remarque, who saw nothing sinister in such an invitation, and suggested she buy me a pretty dress for the occasion. She relented, took me to a fancy children's store where they did not go up to my size, stormed out, took me to another where I tried on whatever she flung at me; finally bought me a dark green crinkly silk with huge white and red daisies printed all over it; a green cummerbund encircled my thick waist, puffed sleeves completed this vision. Even with the blended camomile lotion all over my face, I thought I looked better than usual, almost okay.

"Your governess will accompany you," my mother announced, and my bubble burst.

"Oh, Mutti! Please, no. He will think I am a baby!" I gasped.

"You will be chaperoned or you will not be allowed to go." My mother was adamant.

I secretly called Jack: "I have to tell you something—I have to come with a chaperone, so if you want to cancel, I'll understand, really!"

"Don't worry—we'll stuff her so full of éclairs, she won't have the time to be nosy!" Jack always made everything seem easy.

We met upstairs in the glass-enclosed tea room of the Café de Triomphe on the Champs-Elysées. First, Jack kissed my cheek, which made my knees wobble, seated my governess at one of the small marble-topped tables, ordered her a tray of French pastries, then guided me to a table of our own. He answered all my eager questions, told me all the latest goings and com-

ings of his big family. We had a wonderful afternoon.

Our summer exodus to the Cap d'Antibes began.
Remarque called from Switzerland to say he
would drive his Lancia down to the south of
France and meet us later in Antibes. Our suites
were waiting, the hotel as serene and opulent as
always. Nothing had changed. I always loved it
when places stayed the same. It felt so comfortable being sure of something.

Even the Kennedys were back, vacationing
from all their official posts and important
schools. For the first time in my life I had friends
to greet. Quickly, I put on my bathing suit and
robe and, before anyone could call me to perform some service, I escaped down the esplanade
toward the cliffs.

None of my friends had changed, except to
enhance their special individualities. All, except
Teddy, he was even cuddlier. Some rare children
can do that, retain their cherubic sweetness, un-
affected by having to grow up. Bobby caught my
arm:

"Rosemary has to take her nap—come, we
are going to dive for octopus. Joe has a terrific
new gun—it shoots under water, like a harpoon.
He wants to try it out. The President gave it to
him!"

The Kennedys always had the most fasci-

While Nazi Germany gnashed its teeth,
Marlene Dietrich became a U.S. citizen in 1939.

Accompanied by the Countess di Frasso's
Afghan hound, she returned to Europe on the
SS *Normandie* and was met by Tami.

Looking every inch Marlene Dietrich, she exits her hat designer's atelier in Paris, waiting for her chauffeur.

Tami, who was also ordered to always step out of frame whenever the press pounced, was next to me but not seen in this candid photo of "Dietrich and her husband and child."

nating new inventions that they wanted to test. If no one had ever seen it, if it couldn't be bought yet, if something was hot off the drawing board, they already had it.

"Octopus? They'll grab our ankles and pull us down! I'll watch you from the rocks!"

"Ah, come on! These are Mediterranean, they are small! They don't attack! They hide between the rocks. All you have to do is dive, pry them loose, and bring them up. When they squirt their ink at you, just close your eyes and surface. They wrap themselves around your arm—so it's easy!"

"Bobby, is everybody diving for octopus, even Jack?" I asked, hoping he would say no.

"Sure, come on. Nothing to be scared of. We do it all the time. If we catch enough, we can have them for supper."

It worked just as he said. Following Bobby's instructions usually did.

Remarque's Lancia, just as he described it in *Three Comrades*, purred to a halt. He had called ahead from Cannes and my mother was waiting for him. He took her face between his slender hands, cradling it, just looking down at her. Without heels, my mother always appeared so small, although she really wasn't. They kissed; then, taking her hand, he introduced her to his best friend, his car. He was anxious that his "gray puma" would understand his love for the golden puma and not be raked by jealousy. My mother loved the imagery of being presented as a rival to a car. Remarque took them both for a drive along the coast to get acquainted.

That evening he arrived in my mother's suite, especially handsome in his white dinner jacket, carrying a German schoolbag, just like the one I always wanted when I was little. He removed some yellowed papers. While waiting for the carpenters to crate his paintings, he had found stories he had worked on in 1920 but never finished.

"They were good then and they'd be good today, but I couldn't finish them now. I no longer have that wonderful bold immaturity." As he leafed through the pages, his golden eyes dulled. "Twenty years ago, when there was a war and I wrote this, I thought only of saving the world. In Porto Ronco a few weeks ago, I saw that another war looms, and I thought only of saving my collections."

My mother moved over to kiss him, saying: "My love—how ridiculous. You are a *great* writer—what else do you need? Look at Hemingway. *He* never worries about how *he* feels or what *he* felt long ago. It just comes flowing out of him, all that beauty!"

I was wakened by: "Papi, Papi—are you awake?" My mother's voice was shrill as she shouted at my father over the house phone. I looked at my travel clock: four a.m. Something was wrong! I put on my dressing gown and crossed the hall to my mother's suite.

"Papi! Wake up! And listen to me. Boni and I had a fight. You remember how strangely he behaved at dinner. Well, later he accused me of sleeping with Hemingway. Of course, he wouldn't believe me when I said I didn't. He said terrible things to me, then stormed out. Probably he went to gamble at the casino and get drunk. Get dressed—take the car and find him! Maybe he is lying somewhere and strangers will find him! Call me the moment you know something!" She hung up, noticed me, told me to order coffee from room service, and began pacing the floor.

Two hours passed, then the phone rang. My father had found Remarque in a bar in Juan-les-Pins, drunk, desperate, but unharmed.

That summer, our blood and rubber lady was absent, but we had another medical sensation that my mother had discovered. This one came in a tiny tube, all the way from Russia, and was guaranteed to cure the common cold. My mother was explaining the application procedure to Beatrice Lillie when I happened on the scene.

"Bea, sweetheart! It is absolutely amazing! Never has been seen before—give me your arm. No, no, turn it, this stuff has to be rubbed inside of your arm, where the pulsing vein is." The cap clamped between her teeth, she squeezed a big glob of yellow grease onto the skin, screwed the top back on, began rubbing the ointment savagely into Bea's arm. The spot reddened, a slight swelling appeared where the "pulse pulsed."

"Marlene, did I say I had a cold?"

"Of course you did—you said you were 'stopped up.' "

"Oh, is this good for constipation as well?"

By now, the spot is nice and red, and Bea Lillie is trying to get her arm back from my mother.

"Marlene—what is this goo made from?"

"Snake venom. It inflames the tissues, then dries them up, and suddenly, you can *breathe* again!"

I never saw anyone get down our walk that fast! My mother stood watching Bea Lillie sprint toward the pool, a confused look on her face:

"What is the matter with that woman? Noël always said she was so funny—but I thought funny 'ha-ha,' not funny 'strange.' "

One day, everyone was "a-twitter." They congregated along the rocks like hungry sea gulls, searching the surface of the sea. A strange ship had been sighted making for our private cove. A magnificent three-masted schooner, its black hull skimming through the glassy water, its teak decks gleaming in the morning sun, at

the helm, a beautiful boy. Bronzed and sleek—
even from a distance, one sensed the power of
the rippling muscles of his tight chest and
haunches. He waved at his appreciative audience, flashed a rakish white-toothed smile, and
gave the command to drop anchor among the
white yachts. If he had run up the Jolly Roger,
no one would have been surprised. The first
thought on seeing him had been Pirate—followed by Pillage and Plunder.

My mother touched Remarque's arm:
"Boni—isn't he beautiful? He must be coming
here for lunch. Who is he?" She watched him
being rowed ashore. Dressed in skin-tight ducks
and striped sailor's jersey, he climbed the steps
leading up to the Eden Roc and turned from a
sexy boy into a sexy, flat-chested woman. At a
time when "madcap" heiresses were a dime a
dozen, this one was a dedicated adventurer and
explorer—owned ships, developed and gov-
erned her own islands, was known as "Jo" to
her intimates, became my mother's summer of
'39 interlude, and was the only one who ever
called Dietrich "Babe" and got away with it. Her
majordomo was a two-ton truck. Although she
wore her tailored suits with a skirt and painted
the nails of her sausage fingers deep red, this
made absolutely no difference to the general effect of—ugly male. With close-set eyes, bulk that
overshadowed her pylon legs and very small feet,

her resemblance to a rhinoceros was startling. I expected any second her ears to wiggle and a pilot bird to pick insects off her hide.

While Remarque labored in his shuttered rooms over his yellow pads, and drank himself senseless at night, my father checked hotel expenses and improved his already perfect tan, and Tami swallowed any new pill guaranteed to bring on instant happiness given to her by solicitous dilettantes, I swam, watched the Kennedys being a happy family, and helped to dress my mother for her daily rendezvous on her "Pirate's" ship, hoping she would return before Boni emerged from his day's entombment to be with her.

We were having breakfast in my mother's suite, when my father answered the telephone and announced that a call from Hollywood was coming through. My mother frowned.

"At this hour? You take it, Papi—must be something stupid."

My father handed her the receiver.

"It is person-to-person from Joseph Pasternak."

My mother was definitely annoyed.

"Who?"

"Remember? He used to be around Ufa during *The Blue Angel*. He is an important producer now at Universal. You better talk to him."

My mother gave my father a dirty look and took the receiver.

"This is Marlene Dietrich. Why are you calling me in the south of France?"

I remember my mother's eyebrows as they arched even higher in utter surprise and her glacial good-bye before she slammed the receiver and said:

"Now *that* is a real Hungarian idiot! Do you know what he said? He wants me to be in a Western! Starring Jimmy Stewart! Ridiculous. They get more stupid every day out there in Hollywood!" and with that, dismissed the topic for the rest of the morning until she told it as a joke to Kennedy over lunch.

"Papa Joe . . ."

We had so many "Joes," she had begun to refer to Ambassador Kennedy as "Papa Joe" to avoid confusion between his oldest son, von Sternberg, and the Pirate.

"Papa Joe, you must admit—it's too funny. Dietrich and that mumbling baby-faced beanpole? And trying to be ever so 'real American'?"

"How much are they offering you?"

"I didn't even ask. You think it's not such a crazy idea?"

"Marlene, if you want me to, I'll talk to Universal. Pasternak may just have hit on a brilliant combination."

My mother turned to my father: "Papi. Put a call in to Jo. Tell *him* about Pasternak. Ask him what he thinks and to call me back before seven o'clock tonight, our time, then book a call to Pasternak for eight." She turned to Kennedy: "Are you free then?" She rose. "I want to ask Boni about this," and left the table. By seven p.m., everyone had been consulted. Von Sternberg had said that in his opinion Stewart was like another Cooper, only with more acting ability, and that playing a Western "dance-hall floozie" was simply taking "Lola" out of Berlin and plunking her down in Virginia City, and that she was insane if she turned it down. Kennedy told her the money offered was too good to refuse and gave her the name of Charles Feldman, who became my mother's most trusted and beloved agent of her professional life.

The Pirate loved the idea so much, she promised to rent a mansion in Beverly Hills—to be near her "Babe." She was already planning to give my mother her island in the Caribbean, population included! Even Remarque liked the idea of Dietrich going "Western."

Still, she hesitated: "Papa Joe—what will happen if there is a war? Do I have to take everyone with me to America, or can I leave them here? You are the Ambassador to England, you must know that that gaga Chamberlain with his pretty boy Eden, they are not going to be able to stop Hitler. So what will happen? I can't be away making a stupid film if anything happens!"

Kennedy assured her that if and when he felt the danger of war was imminent, he would evacuate his family back to England and safety and that her family would be given the same protection as his.

My father ordered up the trunks, made the travel arrangements; my mother, Tami, and I packed. Before being driven to Paris, my mother took my hand and laid it into Remarque's:

"My only love—I give you my child. Protect her, keep her safe—for me!" Calling over her shoulder to my father: "Don't forget to call Paramount. They have to release Nellie to do my hair at Universal." She stepped into the limousine.

Between costume meetings, flirting with Pasternak, and song-writing sessions with her *Blue Angel* composer, Frederick Hollander, and a "sweet" man she called "a fresh, but talented lyricist," Frank Loesser, my mother kept in constant touch by phone.

Vera West wasn't Travis, but it didn't matter. She was designing the clothes herself anyway, making a dance-hall dress in the "nightgown cut" that Travis always loved so, but with her built-in bra so she could move in it, and in short, that would be the "look" of the film. Stockings made of a new invention called nylon were amazing; they lasted through a whole day without laddering! Her name was "Frenchy," to justify her far-from-Western American accent. She and Nellie were working on a "honky-tonk saloon tart" hairdo, all fake curls, like big corkscrews—"like Shirley Temple, only sexy," is how she described it; and the director, George Marshall, was sweet; Pasternak was tricky, like all Hungarians, just as she had expected, but sweet; her dressing room was a house—"Yes, a real little house, not like our cupboard rooms at Paramount"; and Jimmy Stewart was not at all "cowboy boring" but "very sweet." She was practically bubbling, and with everyone so "sweet," I figured she was having a ball and wondered which sugared individual would win out.

Hitler and Stalin signed a nonaggression pact, and the Kennedys left sooner than anyone had expected. The moment had come that everyone had been waiting for, praying that somehow it wouldn't happen. The message ran through the hotel like a flash fire:

"Go, get out. Leave France—fast!"

From across the world, my mother pulled her mighty strings and secured passage on the *Queen Mary*, scheduled to sail from Cherbourg on September 2, 1939. We left Antibes in convoy. Remarque and I, in his splendid Lancia leading the way, my father, our luggage, Tami, and Teddy in his Packard, trying to keep up, following behind. Nobody had said, "The Germans are an hour away," but that's how we evacuated Antibes. We stopped only to refuel, but we were slowed by long columns of mules and horses that were being mobilized.

"Kater, remember this," Remarque urged, "memorize it so you will always have it! The feeling of despair, the anger of these French farmers, their hopeless faces, the shadowed colors as they herd their black mules off to war in twilight. Mules and horses—against the Wehrmacht and the Luftwaffe."

As we passed through the French countryside, there was a sense of defeat before the war had even begun. No patriotic fervor to join up, no heads held high singing the "Marseillaise." Those farmers were not marching to war with their animals, they were trudging as though to defeat, stopping on the way to sit dejected by the wayside.

"Boni? They already know they're going to lose?"

"Yes. They are old enough to remember the last war. Look at the faces, Kater. Remember—war has no glory—only the sound of mothers weeping."

I was a young girl witnessing a new war in the making, with a man who had known, had lived through the old one, captured its horror for the whole world to read, to bear witness. I felt very privileged being with such a man as another war was about to begin.

The Lancia began to overheat. We stopped at a garage. It was abandoned. Boni let the radiator cool, there was no time to fix it. We had to get to Paris in time to take the boat train to Cherbourg. He folded the hood up on his side for ventilation. It blocked his view, so he drove holding his door ajar, leaning out the side in order to see the road. He cursed his beloved car for deserting him, berated his Puma for being a coward in the face of danger. His fury had nothing to do with his car. I wished I could share in his sense of loss. I had never felt I belonged to Europe, but knew that for Boni this time was immense, that he was about to confront a profound leave-taking, convinced he could never return—for he believed that Hitler had the power of evil, would win the war and become the master of all Europe.

Paris was dark, we drove slowly. I looked for the Eiffel Tower, which had just been illuminated the year before, and saw only its somber outline against the night sky.

"Paris—the City of Lights!" Remarque whispered. "Beautiful Paris, suffering her first blackout. Never in modern history has she been forced to extinguish her brilliance. We must toast her and wish her well. Come, while Papi says good-bye to his furniture, you and I will go to

Fouquet's, sit on the Champs-Elysées one more summer evening, and say good-bye to Paris."

We drove to his garage. He gave his keys to the owner, instructing him to guard his friend from the Boche, adding:

"But, if you must flee the city with your family, take my car. Pumas are good at escaping." One last look, then he took my hand and we walked away in the direction of Fouquet's.

The great Burgundies, the 1911 cognacs, the special champagne, Fouquet's famous cellar was emptied that night. The citizens of Paris crowded the Champs-Elysées, everyone drank—no one was drunk.

"Monsieur," Remarque's favorite sommelier bent low, offering a dusty bottle cradled lovingly in his arms, "we don't want the Boche to find this—do we?"

Remarque agreed. He filled a small glass for me.

"Kater, this you will never forget—neither the taste of this wine, nor the occasion for it being uncorked." He was right on both counts.

That night, Boni and I became friends, not a girl and a man, a child and an adult, the daughter of the woman he loved, nothing to do with that. We were comrades, experiencing something tragic together.

In New York, under the cover of darkness, the *Bremen*, her lights dimmed, with only her

German crew aboard, slipped stealthily into the Hudson on the night tide. She had been ordered to get back home to the Fatherland with all speed and at all cost.

Hitler bombed Warsaw and invaded Poland.

My father, Tami, and, thank God, Teddy, met us in Cherbourg. I was so happy to see that sturdy little fellow in his black-and-white fur. I don't know why, but I had been afraid my father would leave him behind to be captured by the Nazis.

The *Queen Mary*, so regal "empire" elegant, felt like a disappointed hostess whose party has somehow gone awry. No band, no gay abandon, hundreds of people scurrying about with tense faces and worried looks. My father told me that the swimming pool might have to be drained to accommodate cots, sections of the main dining room had beds in it. Some people had suggested that the billiard tables could be slept on. This was destined to be the last crossing of the *Queen Mary* as a luxury liner until after the war. Immediately on arrival in America, she would be painted gray and converted into a troop ship.

One day out at sea, the ship's loudspeakers announced that Great Britain and France were now at war with Germany. The *Queen Mary* was committed to making the dash across the Atlantic. There was fear that German submarines might now take action against our English ship. We watched the sea for telltale periscopes; at night we imagined U-boats stalking in the depths.

Daily lifeboat drills were ordered. I asked our steward if he would help me sew extra-long ties onto my life vest, so if we were torpedoed, I could hold Teddy inside. He was so nice he did, even helped when I practiced. At first, Teddy was very uncooperative. He didn't like being clutched, but after a few tries, he understood I wasn't being "dramatic," just "prepared," and curled against me real small.

Gentlemen expounded their theories on how to win a war around crowded card tables enveloped in rich cigar smoke. Jewish families huddled in groups, prayed, wept for those left behind, unable to escape in time. There were those who, never having lost freedom, considered it their permanent right and behaved as though this were a normal crossing. The children played, dowagers wore their life vests to dinner and carted their jewel cases wherever they went.

Our captain announced radio silence for the remainder of the crossing. We sailed alone, out of touch with the rest of the world. There were rumors that we were changing course, that the *Queen Mary* had received orders to avoid an American port and would make her way to a

Canadian one instead. When my mother was informed by the British consul in Los Angeles that the ship might be rerouted, she sent Studio representatives and lawyers to Canada to await our arrival there, but told those waiting in New York to stay put until further notice. Between issuing orders to Immigration lawyers and shipping agents, my mother began filming *Destry Rides Again.*

The top decks were crowded; we rounded Ambrose Light and—there She was! Such a cheer welled up, I'm sure it could be heard all the way in New York City. We had made it— We were safe— We were home! Of course, I cried, but this time I had so much company, I didn't feel silly at all.

We were such a motley group the Immigration officials had a hard time sorting us out. Remarque, with his special refugee passport from Panama, my father with his German one, Tami with her Nansen, which, of course, was a never-seen-before curiosity. Finally, thanks to the lawyers my mother had sent, after a long day of discussions and waiting, we passed through Immigration. I, as a minor, offspring of a legal American citizen, Teddy as an accompanying disease-free canine, the others as "pink card" aliens. At times like these, the power of fame becomes very acceptable.

WARTIME

WE CHECKED INTO Remarque's favorite American hotel, the Sherry Netherland on Fifth Avenue, and my mother's refugees called her on the set at Universal. We took turns talking to her; she insisted on hearing each voice to be certain we were all there. Of course, I was delirious with joy. Secretly, I couldn't help thinking that with a war raging in Europe, my mother would be stuck in America and I would be spared having to go back there all the time. So, when my turn came to speak to her, she got no regrets from my having been forced to leave the Old World behind:

"Mutti, it's wonderful! Everything is wonderful! Do you know they have a World's Fair here, right here in New York City? May we stay and see it—please?"

"Angel—you can *all* stay. Nobody has to rush. The film is difficult. This little studio is not Paramount. The director, George Marshall, is sweet, so that is all right. Some of the songs are good, and Stewart has something, I don't know exactly what it is, but there is something so sweet about him."

She paused, then continued, softly:

"Don't tell Boni, you know how he gets jealous about everything, like Jo. Put Papi on the phone. I want to tell him where to get money so you all can stay there."

Tami and I spent days at the fair. Like the Paris one the year before, it had absolutely everything—this time, with added American razzmatazz. I even got Boni to come with us. He was so sad, for so many legitimate reasons, I kept coming up with all sorts of excursions, hoping to distract him a little. My father was just as depressed. Of course, Tami believed she must be the cause of his unhappiness and shook.

When we finally arrived at the Beverly Hills Hotel, my mother had our assigned quarters ready for us. She had her private bungalow, Remarque had his next door across the way, my father had a suite in the main hotel, Tami a single down the hall from him, I a single next to her.

There was a hand-delivered letter waiting for me from Brian, telling me he had married a lovely woman who was sure to make him eternally happy, that he was so sorry I couldn't be there for the wedding, that he loved me, welcomed me home, would try to see me soon. I looked at the letter again for her name . . . oh! Joan Fontaine. She *must* be nice because her sister was playing Melanie in *Gone with the Wind*.

Dietrich was news again. *Destry* was rumored to be a Box Office Smash in the making. The chemistry between its costars was described as "sizzling," and "See What the Boys in the Back Room Will Have," a song written for the film, was certain to be a hit. The Studio Publicity Department was ecstatic. Pasternak, the genius innovator at Universal, had done it again! This renewed glare of the limelight bothered my mother. She had become used to the Europeans' nonchalant attitude toward "unconventional" households, but America was different. Trying to keep secrets from the diligent American press was always dangerous—especially ones that had anything to do with moral behavior.

"Those terrible Puritans," my mother used to say. "America is full of them. Is that because of those awful people who came over on those ships? The ones who started that Thanksgiving thing you love so?"

As she now had a few too many "husbands" about, she tried to convince Remarque that New York was the place for "brilliant authors," not this cultural wasteland known as Hollywood, and got nowhere. So, she concentrated on the one she could order around and sent my father with his dog and Tami back east to live. I was allowed to stay. I was happy I had escaped the purge.

I and my new bodyguard took them to Union Station. My father had given me his lecture on behavior, loyalty, and filial duty in the car, so there was little left to say. He kissed my cheek, patted my shoulder, told Teddy to precede him, and boarded the train in deep discussion with the porters. Tami and I hugged each other good-bye.

"Please, please—be more careful with yourself, Tamilein! If he ever hurts you, if you need help, promise you will call me right away. Promise!" I whispered, foolishly believing she would ever do so or that I could really help if she did. I waved long after the train had left, hoping Tami and Teddy could still see me. It would be four years and an emotional lifetime before I saw them again.

That took care of one problem. Next, my mother called her Pirate, acquired the services of her Rhinoceros, then housed this "woman" and her "beloved Child," just the two of us alone, in the back of the hotel in one of the apartments above the garages in the alley. Now began a time when I saw my mother by appointment only. My days were spent finishing whatever grade I was supposedly in. My tutor was a lady who arrived at ten, chatted, drank her coffee, opened a few books on the subjects I liked best and excelled in, then departed, having had a nice visit—with pay.

Remarque remained, by day a virtual recluse, forcing himself to write, only to tear up each day's work before my mother returned home from the Studio in the evening. He lived for the sound of her car pulling up in front of her bungalow, the ring of the telephone telling him that she was alone and he was now permitted to steal across the path, and take her in his arms. Sometimes, when she was very late coming home, especially Saturday nights, when she usually didn't appear until the evening of the next day, I sat with him, keeping him company during his sad vigil. Of all the people I knew during my youth, Remarque was the only one who ever understood that where my mother was concerned, I was not a child, probably had stopped being one at the age of six. My mother's current passion, one could not really fault her for. Half the women in America would have given their eyeteeth to be where Dietrich was on those Saturday nights. Remarque not only suffered from utter rejection, but like Jo, from self-hate, because he loved her too much to leave her. He needed to be close to her, just see her, hear her voice, even listen to her telling him about her new love, which she did, asking his advice on how she could make the moments spent in her new lover's arms even more wonderful than they already were.

"She expects me to write her 'love scenes,' phrases to enchant. Sometimes I do, then she bestows on me her wonderfully romantic smile and goes to make me dinner. Kater, it is such heaven to please her," he would say, looking out the window, watching for his Puma's return. This lovely man had become a pathetic voyeur, a Beverly Hills Cyrano.

The Studio released a rumor that Dietrich, having found out that Stewart was a fan of the comic-strip hero Flash Gordon, had ordered a life-size doll to be made for him. She giggled when she heard it and didn't get angry. She had changed. She was still the dedicated perfectionist, the professional tyrant, but in *Destry*, when she had achieved acceptability in those categories she believed her duty, she allowed herself to relax, have fun. Of course, it helped that Jimmy Stewart was the designated box-office star. If the film failed to pull in the money, he would be the one blamed—not she. This had not happened to her since *The Blue Angel* and Jannings. Now she found it wonderfully relaxing, once again having another carry the burden of stardom. This letting go of responsibility resulted in Dietrich giving a very good performance.

She tried to persuade the director, George Marshall, to let her do her own stunt work for the saloon fight. He said no! The stuntwomen had been hired, rehearsed, and would deliver on film a wild and rowdy brawl with their usual expertise. Dietrich and Una Merkel, properly bloodied and disheveled, would then take their places for the medium shots and close-ups. She might have gotten Pasternak to agree to her scheme, but the possibility of both performers being injured was just too great a risk. The fight had been choreographed for professionals. But the prospect of the enormous publicity that would be generated from Marlene Dietrich brawling in a saloon finally outweighed any objections the worried Studio could come up with. To my knowledge, Miss Una Merkel, the other contestant in this grudge match, was never given a chance to withdraw.

I had never seen so much press crowding a movie set. *Life*, *Look*, all the wire services and fan magazines, photographers everywhere. Dietrich doing a Western had sparked excitement in the first place, now she was fanning the flames, playing it raucous and rowdy all the way—no holds barred.

A first-aid station had been set up outside the soundstage, just in case. The stuntwomen, ready to take over, watched from the sideline. Una Merkel and Dietrich took their places, the cameras rolled, my mother whispered, "Una, don't hold back—kick me, hit me, tear my hair. You can punch me too—because I am going to punch you!" and with a snarl, jumped on Merkel's back, knocking her to the floor. They kicked each other, screamed, grabbed handfuls of hair and yanked, slapped, scratched, rolled on the dirty floor—were oblivious to everything except trying to kill each other, until Stewart stepped into the fray and dumped a bucket of water over them.

Marshall yelled "Cut!" and the set exploded in applause. The press called it the best "slug-fest since Tunney and Dempsey." My mother was stronger than Una, that nice lady suffered a lot of ugly bruises, but that fight and the fantastic press coverage it received resulted in turning *Destry Rides Again* into a Dietrich film at the box office.

I had just helped her dress for a date with her romantic "beanpole" when Remarque wandered in, unannounced. He stood looking at her in wonder, her body molded in black silk jersey that pedestaled into a thick flounce of absinthe green satin, her black turban repeating this color in a crown of minute, closely laid bird feathers —a Juno balanced on green fire.

"Well, why did you come over?" she asked impatiently. I handed her the evening bag with the emerald clasp, packed with her diamond compact from Gilbert and the Knight's cigarette case.

"Did you know when Sigmund Freud died in London, it was of cancer?"

"Good! All he did was talk about sex and got people all mixed up," she threw over her shoulder as she ran out of the door. Her "date" had honked his horn.

Dietrich had utter disdain for all forms of psychiatry and those who needed such "talking to on couches by strangers." Instinctively, she probably feared this science—it delved, discovered, invaded, exposed, all very dangerous words within my mother's private universe.

My special friend had become a star—a real, MGM star! I had told her she would. I was so proud of her. I was sorry, though, her breasts had to be tied flat, and hoped it hadn't hurt. It wasn't easy pretending to be twelve when you are sixteen. I identified with the Dorothy of *The Wizard of Oz*: Toto was like Teddy, the Bad Witch I knew, the Good Witch I would like to meet, a home I would also like to come back to, and Oz I lived in. Only the magic shoes I couldn't imagine ever escaping in.

Winston Churchill became First Lord of the Admiralty. The French waited, secure in their belief in the Maginot Line, winter rolled in over the Atlantic, nothing happened. American war correspondents had no war as such, dubbed it "the phony war," and Marlene Dietrich, the new citizen, voted, for the first time, on the set of *Destry*. She hadn't a clue who, what, or why, but she looked so glamorous contemplating her decision, the Publicity Department, which had set it up to remind the paying public that Dietrich was no longer a foreigner, milked it for all its worth. The Americanization of Lola was complete.

Destry opened in New York City in November 1939 and was a smash hit. Russia invaded Finland, everyone went to see Garbo actually laugh in *Ninotchka*, although some felt a grimace of painful embarrassment could hardly qualify for mirth.

On my mother's thirty-eighth birthday, she attended the West Coast gala opening of *Gone with the Wind*. It had already been acclaimed at its first premiere in Atlanta, and so everyone knew they were about to see a motion-picture masterpiece. I listened to it all on the radio, the screams as Gable and Lombard arrived, the oohs and aahs as gorgeous stars appeared in never-ending cavalcade—the Kings and Queens of America on parade! My mother's comments on this milestone of motion-picture history?

"Now I have seen everything! Leslie Howard, with orange hair!" She stepped out of her velvet evening dress. I began soaking the adhesive tape off her breasts. "That girl who plays the lead, the one who is so in love with Noël's old boyfriend who is so handsome and a good actor, *she* is very good, but the one who plays the saint? Not to be believed! *That's* Brian's sister-in-law? *That*—he doesn't deserve!"

Dietrich had many monologues on *Gone with the Wind*, but that was the first.

Rationing began in Britain. Hitler was about to overrun Norway and Denmark, Russia took Finland, and I dreamed of one day being allowed to have a black dress. Cautiously, I asked my mother, and got a "What? *Children* don't wear black!" I was very sad. A few days later, a big elegant box was delivered to the alley apartment, bearing my name. I cut the fancy string, lifted the deep lid, grabbed thick hunks of silky tissue paper and, there it was! A real, honest-to-goodness black dress! It was so grown up, Deanna Durbin could have worn it! And, when I tried it on, it fit! Not since my Indian suit had I felt so smart. For the first time in my whole life, I thought I looked terrific! I showed myself to the Rhinoceros, who said:

"I *am* pleased that you like it so much. I was a bit worried I wouldn't choose the exact style you wanted," and I realized it was she who had bought me the lovely dress.

Confused why she would give me such a big present, I thanked her very, very much, adding:

"How did you ever get my mother to allow it?"

She chuckled.

"If you want a black dress so much, why shouldn't you have one? And you look so nice in it. We just won't tell your mother you have it, shall we? It will be our special secret." Not since my lemonade stand had anyone employed by my mother hidden anything from her for me. A week later, I received my first pair of stockings—nylon ones! Then, a pair of shoes, in black—with two-inch wedges! Never had I dreamed of ever owning a pair of real "wedgies." After a while, I had so many "secret" treasures, all I needed now was a secret occasion to wear them. I was so terribly innocent—I didn't know I was being courted.

When I voiced a desire to become an actress, the gift-giving Rhinoceros, whose one aim it seemed was to grant me whatever my little heart desired, presented my wish diplomatically to my mother, who called one of "the boys" and arranged for him to give me acting lessons to keep her child "happy." Every afternoon I had to report to her empty bungalow to be coached by a know-nothing actor with a thick German accent in the "art of enunciating Shakespeare."

While he preened and I gnashed my teeth listening to him doing Juliet's soliloquies à la Weber and Fields, my mother began preparing her second film for Pasternak. She brought in her favorite designer, Irene, and both, thinking they were being truly inventive, had fun. The white tails from *Blonde Venus* were turned into a white naval officer's uniform; the striped, white-tipped-feathered negligee from *The Scar-*

let Empress, into a concoction slightly more vulgar but still as effective.

The same team that had given her "See What the Boys in the Back Room Will Have" for *Destry* did not do so well for *Seven Sinners* —although "The Man's in the Navy" came close. She always wanted Noël Coward to sing it— which he never did, because he hadn't written it, but mostly because that tasteless a homosexual he was not!

She enjoyed her resurrected fame, was still "in love" with one "cowboy" while eyeing another, clowned on the set, was very American, calling the crew "Honey!," munched sticky doughnuts, drank coffee out of Commissary urns without making any sarcastic comments, palled around with Broderick Crawford, charmed the ever-so-pretty Anna Lee, flirted outrageously with her new leading man, brought him beef tea, tried to ply him with gifts—and got nowhere!

John Wayne and Dietrich made three films together over three years, and each time out came the beef-tea jars, gold watches, silk dressing gowns—and each time Dietrich struck out. Wayne became such a frustrating thorn in her side that she began concocting stories about him, told so often and to so many that they found their way into the Dietrich lore and were believed by all as gospel truths. One of her favorites: that John Wayne was such a complete un-known that, after she spied him entering the Studio Commissary, she had to persuade Universal to hire him for *Seven Sinners*. She embellished this by further stating that after the first day of shooting, it was so evident that Wayne was such an "ungifted amateur" that she had to call her agent, Charles Feldman, and instruct him to hire an acting coach for her new "so untalented" leading man. The fact that Wayne had been superb in John Ford's brilliant film *Stagecoach*, released in 1939, a year before *Seven Sinners*, seemed to vanish from everyone's memory when Dietrich was telling *her* version of things. Somewhere, sometime, John Wayne must have made Dietrich really mad about something to get her that riled.

Many years later, in London, Wayne and I had dinner together with mutual friends, and I finally got my chance to ask him what magic spell had so protected him against the siren's onslaught. He laughed with his eyes, took a slug, shifted his big frame on the too small chair, and grunted: "Never liked being part of a stable—never did!"

In *public*, Dietrich claimed to have no great love for "screen cowboys" in general.

"Those long drinks of water, like Cooper and Wayne, they are all alike. All they do is clink their spurs, mumble 'Howdy, Ma'am,' and fuck their horses!'' and people believed her—of course.

I had always wanted to go to Catalina, that little island off the coast, where big abalone shells, all iridescent shimmer, were sold as souvenirs. My mother refused. It was just a day trip there and back, but "No!"

The Rhinoceros spoke: "I do think that as Maria has worked so diligently, her behavior has been so exemplary, she deserves an outing—she has earned it, Miss Dietrich"—and lo and behold I got to go to Catalina. This strange woman really wanted to be my friend, even lied for me. Grown-ups didn't behave that way for children of "important people"! But this ugly woman was ready and somehow prepared to do battle for me, stand up to the all-powerful, omnipotent Marlene Dietrich, Star of the Silver Screen. I had never had a friend like *that* before. It felt sort of—nice. She even bought me a beautiful abalone—"To remember our day," as she put it.

Remarque finally had enough, moved out of his bungalow into a rented house in Brentwood. It was a temporary place, a nice one but not what Boni would have chosen for himself as a permanent frame. Only one of his paintings was hung, van Gogh's *Yellow Bridge*. The rest were stacked against the walls. To me, it was amazing that all these priceless treasures had safely crossed the ocean, the American continent, to finally arrive in that nondescript house in sunny California. He bought himself two dogs, proud Kerry blues, that kept him company. I visited him often. Even with his passionate "affliction," he was saner than anyone I knew.

Remarque owned Daumier's *Don Quixote*. It was my favorite. I loved the texture of its untreated canvas, its unconventional size to accommodate Quixote's long lance. Remarque enjoyed watching me; I could sit for hours feasting my eyes.

"One day it will be yours. I will leave it to you in my will, Miss Sancho Panza. But your taste is sometimes too emotional." He would shuffle through those hundreds of canvases, looking for what he thought I should learn to appreciate on any given day. He'd say, "Let's have a van Gogh day."

I was very courageous with Remarque. Sometimes, I'd say:

"No, I really don't feel like a van Gogh day."

"Then what kind of day do you feel like?"

"How about Cézanne?"

He'd smile, nod, flip through his paintings.

"Watercolor or oil Cézanne?"

Most of the time, I'd ask him for El Greco. His somber style suited my worries. I think Boni knew something was very wrong, but he was afraid to ask for fear he couldn't help me after he knew. It would have shattered him to be impotent in friendship as well.

I asked him why he didn't hang his paintings, he said that it was a foreign house, that it was not his friend. He hoped his home in Switzerland would wait for him. Remarque kept busy unpacking his museum crates, placing his Tang dynasty treasures around the empty rooms without joy, kept his priceless carpets rolled along the walls—his treasures were his only friends, his dogs his only companions, and writing to my mother his only release. As always, he wrote to her in German most often, referring to himself as Ravic:

> Look at Ravic, scratched all over, caressed, kissed and spat upon. . . . I, Ravic, have seen many wolves that know how to change their appearances, but I have only seen one Puma of this kind. A wonderful animal. It is capable of manifold transformations when the moonlight sweeps over the birches, I have seen it as a child kneeling over a pond, speaking with frogs, and while she spoke, the frogs grew golden crowns on their heads, and because she put such will into her eyes, they became little kings. I have seen her in a house wearing a white apron, scrambling eggs. . . . I have seen the Puma as a panting Tiger-Cat, even as the shrew Xanthippe, close to my face with fairly long nails. . . .

I have seen the Puma go away and I wanted to shout out to it, to warn—but had to hold my tongue. . . . My friends, have you ever noticed how the Puma walks like a flame, dancing to and away from me? How's that? You say I'm not feeling well? That on my forehead there is an open wound and that I have lost a tuft of my hair? That's what happens when one lives with a Puma, my friends. They scratch sometimes when they mean to caress, and even when asleep, one is never certain when they might attack.

Each time he wrote to her, she called him, swore she loved *only* him, sometimes allowed him to love her, then in the early morning sent him packing again before going to the Studio. This turning on and off of emotion played havoc with his creativity. After a while, the yellow pads remained empty; the ever-ready pencils waited —unused.

THE FIRST THOUGHT that comes when disturbing a secret grave is—Did I really have to bury it *that* deep to feel safe? Once opened and exposed, milky sensations float to the surface like specters from some Halloween greeting card. . . . The weight of her huge body, pushing me down. A hand probing into places that had been mine alone. The sudden revulsion, without understanding what was being done to me. The cold—that terrible, terrible cold—that started the trembling, that nearly stopped the heart beating, that choked the silent scream I thought I heard aloud.

I did not know I was being raped—that word only took on meaning long after the fact, when I learned that what had been done to me *had* a name. Nighttime became a soundless crying and I thought I had learned what sex was and shuddered at its approach. When she was through with me, I pulled down my nightgown, curled up small, pretended she didn't exist, and escaped into sleep, convinced I was being punished for something unspeakable I had no knowledge of.

In some ways, I was trained for rape. Always obedient, always trying to please those in charge of me, pliable, an owned object, conditioned to usage. If you don't have an identity and someone helps themselves to you, you respond more passively, you're so unaccustomed to the right of question. Oh, I ran. In my own way I ran, but I had nowhere to go, no one to listen and be kind—even if I could have found the right words. So I went to the only place I knew, thought was safe, the inside of me. Hid it—let it fester, become my private hell. Becoming damaged through the instigated negligence of the one nature and society recognize as your "loving" parent begets a special hell.

Why had my mother chosen that woman, then put me with her—all alone? Did she want it to happen to me? What had I done to deserve that? Mothers were supposed to love their children, protect them from hurt. I had been a good girl. Why did she want me punished? Why did she want me hurt? What had I done? Was I *that* bad?

These searing questions stayed deep inside me, and despair was born to lie beside the damage already done. I was convinced that my dream of someday being allowed to have a real home with a husband who loved me was lost forever, and that it must be my fault because I had allowed such a terrible thing to happen to me.

Yet, I must have still believed in miracles, for I asked for an audience with my mother. I don't know why I did. All my life, I have wondered what I thought I would get to comfort me—probably simply instinctive, to run to one's mother when hurt. Stupid, just the same. Desperate need often begets such stupidity.

I was told my mother was ill but that if I had to see her, I could come over to her bungalow if I made my visit very short and undisturbing.

The blinds were drawn, the room lay in cool shadows. Wan and strangely listless, she lay amongst the cushions of the deep couch, one slim hand clutching a soft woolen shawl to her chest.

"Sweetheart," she sighed, as though even this small expulsion of air cost her too much effort. I thought she might be dying. I knelt by her side, her hand fell gently onto my head, like a benediction. Nellie hovered close.

"Your mother needs a little sleep now, honey. Come back again tomorrow—okay? She'll call you, I promise."

With a last look at my mother's fluttering lids, I left. . . . Maybe she knew? Didn't want me around anymore? . . . No, just bad timing. Never turn to your mother for help when she has just had an abortion.

My mother played Camille for the next four days, and by that time, my desperation had turned onto itself. It was too late for miracles.

God was kind, and my time was safer. No angel dust, no ice, no crack, no street-corner pushers, no needle parks. The drug of my youth was alcohol, one that takes a little longer to achieve one's need for self-destruction. It deadens the done-to-hurt, to hurt oneself voluntarily: It beguiles you into thinking that for *this* degradation, *you* are in control. So you hurt yourself more than others can and feel safe—an insane self-delusion; and are truly lost.

I stayed within my self-punishment, kept my famous owner satisfied, kept my despicable owner at bay when I could—kept myself? Not at all. I wasn't worth that much effort. Booze

nullified what was left. Life went on. It has a
way of doing that, despite everything.

TO KEEP ME "HAPPY," I was enrolled in the
Max Reinhardt Academy, now housed in a nondescript building next to a filling station on the
corner of Fairfax and Wilshire Boulevard. Why
Dr. Reinhardt, now one of the illustrious refugees, thought that his elite drama school had a
chance always astounded me. No one, in those
days anyway, came to Hollywood to "act."
Handsome boys and pretty girls flocked to California to be seen, be discovered sipping ice
cream sodas at Schwab's drugstore, their pointed
breasts sticking way out in too-tight sweaters.
Lana Turner had been—why not they? The
boys, they stuck out all sorts of things on Santa
Monica beaches, hoping for the same magic results of instant stardom. Who needed to act?
And learning it in the laid-down rules of a strict
Germanic curriculum? Who was kidding who?
So pupils in the once-renowned academy were
few, the Herr Doktor mostly absent, the teaching chores left in the hands of his wife, Helene
Thimig—a fine actress, mostly out of work, except when Warner Brothers needed another Nazi
landlady or Gestapo informant. She became my
champion, taught me her craft with dedication,
patience, and skill. Dietrich could now proclaim,

"My daughter is a theater student at the Max Reinhardt Academy—just like I was as 'a very young girl,' " and everyone was impressed and "happy."

A gallant armada of little ships chugged bravely out onto the night sea, lifted off three hundred thousand trapped men, and brought them home to England. Dunkirk became the first symbol of what this "tight little island" and its courageous people were capable of. Glued to our radios, the still-free world listened and cheered.

Winston Churchill became Prime Minister, Roosevelt ran for an unprecedented third term, France fell, Hermann Göring vowed to bring England to its knees, and the Battle of Britain began. Many of the British colony left Hollywood to stand by their countrymen in their hour of need.

Smoking and pacing, my mother was arguing with Remarque when I entered her bungalow to deliver the mail.

"Sweetheart—I just got back from taking Noël to the station! Boni, it was so touching. He looked so proud going off to war to fight for his beloved England. We stood there together, like two old soldiers, not knowing how to say goodbye. He nearly missed the train, when the whistles blew he had to rush. I stood and waved until the train was gone—and cried!" Her voice conjured up two exhausted comrades intrepidly wending their desperate way to the last evacuation train. Remarque was smiling.

"You know, Aunt Lena, it's a touching scene, seeing a dear friend off to war, but it would play better if you had taken him to the troop ship in Canada. Saying good-bye in Pasadena . . . it misses something!"

She whirled: "You're the one who's 'missing something'!" Sympathy for a patriot who does his duty, puts on the uniform of his country, goes to face the enemy . . . like a real *man*! And, for Noël, that is something already!"

"Well, for bayonets in no-man's-land, I could empathize, but today it was still Pasadena and a chauffeured limousine—and he wore a pin-striped suit with a red carnation, he had two chorus boys with him, was armed with an alligator briefcase, and arrived safely in his drawing room on the Super Chief without a shot being fired. Also, there was no fog."

"I said nothing about fog!"

"You were thinking it."

Unable to compete with Boni in this type of repartee, my mother turned up the radio. She had developed the habit of keeping a radio on, to hear the latest news from Europe, complaining that there never was any, that the Americans, in their usual way, knew nothing of what was going on in any part of the world but their own.

"Just look at them. War is raging and the Americans, what do they do? Make pictures, play gin rummy, and stay neutral!"

Remarque answered her in English:

"Give them time. The future of the world rests on their shoulders. It is a burden that requires all the time they can get."

"Well, if you are suddenly so pro-American, you better do something about your German accent. You sound like a Berlin butcher trying to be a gentleman! After all, you are supposed to be a "famous" refugee!" In the "European days," she would never have treated him with such disdain, but those days were over—he was no longer her "sublime love." White lilacs had lost their magic. Remarque sighed, started to leave.

"Puma, do you know what Robert Graves wrote when the Spanish Civil War forced him to abandon his home? 'Never be a refugee if you can possibly avoid it. Stay exactly where you are, kiss the rod, and, if very hungry, eat grass or bark off the trees . . . but never be a refugee.' Of course, he only had Franco to contend with, not Adolf Hitler."

Determined to break England's morale, Hitler ordered nightly bombing raids on its civilian population. How we waited by our radios for that wonderful voice, that deep, honest growl that announced: 'This is London,' that led us, made us see, feel the terrible struggle, the devastation, the astounding bravery of its besieged people. So vividly did Edward R. Murrow bring the London Blitz into the consciousness of the American people that they began feeling slightly guilty for being still neutral. As Murrow set the scene vocally, Hollywood began to do it visually.

We packed Bundles for Britain, loved everything that was English; Mrs. Miniver became our symbolic heroine, were proud when American flyers left to join the glorious RAF and formed their own Eagle Squadron, worked full-time, around the clock, to send England whatever she needed to hold Hitler at bay; unconsciously were being emotionally conditioned to be willing, once again, to fight a war far from home.

MY MOTHER WAS SO FROUFROU FRENCH in *The Flame of New Orleans*—like meringue, its sticky sweetness hurt your back teeth. Nothing could be that overdone "ooh-la-la" and be a success at the box office. It deserved to flop, which it did. This film screamed "give me Lubitsch," was directed by a famous French refugee, René Clair, who should have known better. Still, the only thing Dietrich hated about this film was her leading man. She called my father in New York.

"Papilein, I have another dance teacher!"

Considering she meant Bruce Cabot, she had a legitimate beef. "Why would Pasternak give me a gigolo? With von Sternberg we know why. After Cooper, he only gave me leading men he was *sure* I wouldn't like—but Pasternak? He can't be jealous already—I haven't slept with him yet! I told him 'No! Not until after Hitler loses the war!' "

Charles de Gaulle escaped to England, and my mother fell madly in love with him, began wearing the Cross of Lorraine with Free French fervor. The Nazis goose-stepped down the Champs-Elysées and 20th Century Fox announced that they had signed France's reigning male star, Jean Gabin.

"Boni, that unbelievable actor from that magnificent film, *Grand Illusion*—They are bringing him over to be in cheap American films? He probably can't even speak English. They will ruin him! He is perfect the way he is—and there will be no one to protect him. Can one still call France? Isn't Michèle Morgan in love with him? I could call her and find out where to reach him?" my mother asked, not mentioning that as far back as 1938, she had cabled my father from Hollywood:

I HEAR GABIN MAY BE COMING HERE. FIND OUT. I SHOULD GET HIM FIRST.

Using his American contract to get out of Occupied France, Jean Gabin was on his way—

Dietrich's arms were waiting, ready to enfold him. He didn't know it yet, but his doom for the next few years was sealed.

Remarque decided to move to New York. I helped him pack.

"You really have to leave her?"

"The dock cannot leave the ship that sailed the night before."

"Must you, Boni?"

"Yes, Sadness. If I could turn you to happiness I would stay, but I am short of my former powers."

"You call me 'Sadness.' Why?"

"I call you many tender things, a gasp for breath because your mother breathes up all the oxygen around you."

"I don't love her, you know." It felt so good saying it!

"You must. She loves you as she perceives love. But her rpm's are a thousand a minute, whereas ours are a normal hundred a minute. We need an hour to love her, she loves us as well in six minutes and is on to everything else she must do, while we are wondering why she isn't loving us as we are loving her. We are mistaken, she already has."

His Studio installed Gabin in the bungalow Remarque had vacated. A chauffeured Rolls-Royce and a yacht were at his disposal. Anything he

New start, new Studio, new image, new love. Dietrich as Frenchy in *Destry Rides Again*, with Jimmy Stewart. They enjoyed each other.

On the set of *Seven Sinners*, with costar John Wayne, director Tay Garnett, and Broderick Crawford.

In her favorite costume from that film, the naval officer's uniform, designed for the Hollander-Loesser song "The Man's in the Navy."

The froufrou French look of *The Flame of New Orleans*, with René Clair and Joseph Pasternak.

RIGHT: The wonderful hooker look of *Manpower*.

The French cowboy look of her new consuming passion, Jean Gabin.

Lunching with two of her pals, Ann Warner, a confidante, and Noël Coward, a devoted friend who knew all, kept her secrets, and stood by with compassion.

Gabin and his *Grande*. Still "happy times" in 1943.

wanted, Zanuck was prepared to give his new star. He was the new king of Hollywood. Poor Gabin! All he knew, was comfortable with, left behind, his beloved country lost. He, who hated all pretense, assumed glitter and ostentation, was now expected to behave like an Important Star within an insular foreign community, in a language he hardly knew. Jean was such a simple soul, a little boy in a gruff man's body, easy to love, easy to hurt. Over the many years, we became distant friends, rarely were together, never really talked—yet, somehow, felt a kinship. In Jean's concept of things, a man did not involve his mistress's child in his adult passion. I always thought Jean Gabin was the most instinctive gentleman of all my mother's lovers.

His waiting "general" prepared the field for combat. All he had to do was surrender himself into her loving hands—and lose the battle. Holding on to her bungalow, but to escape prying hotel eyes, my mother rented a little house up in the hills of Brentwood and transformed it into a bit of France. Called Gabin at the hotel, said in her beautiful French:

"Jean, c'est Marléne!" and one of the great romances of the 1940s was born. Their love affair was to be one of the most enduring, most passionate, and most painful of both their lives, and of course, Gabin suffered the most.

But now he ran into my mother's arms like

a floundering ship finding its home port. She reveled in his dependence on her. For his home-sickness for his country that he felt he was des-erting in its time of need, she recreated France for him in sunny California. She wore striped jerseys, knotted a jaunty kerchief around her neck, and took to wearing berets over one eye. Chevalier would have been proud, had he not been busy entertaining the Nazi occupation forces in Paris.

This French cocoon my mother enveloped Gabin in was not constructive. He had to earn his living in America, work with American actors and crews; making no effort to meet them half-way did not help him. Jean Gabin, the man of the people, through Dietrich's influence became the aloof foreigner, and this affected his work and popularity.

One day before the anniversary of Napo-leon's try in 1812, Hitler invaded—Russia.

My mother was making *Manpower* at War-ner Brothers with her old pal George Raft, and one she had no liking for: "Ugly little man—why is *he* a star?" Edward G. Robinson. She did her job, achieved one "look" in a raincoat and beret that was superb, hated the film as it was "just for money" and took her away from being with the "love of her life."

Manpower was such an easy film, there were many days Dietrich was not on call. She had time to devote herself to taking care of her "man." When he came home in the evenings, she greeted him at the door of "their" house, enveloped in her big apron, the pungent perfume of her cassoulet filling the air. On Sundays, she cooked crawfish and pot-au-feu for Hollywood's French refugees. The directors, René Clair, Jean Renoir, Duvivier, Gabin's friend from *Grand Illusion* Dalio, and many more. Feeling far from home, they reveled in this Gallic sanctuary. She allowed no foreign intrusion into the safety of their little French household. Only Jean's inner male clique were welcome. It was "bistro" time in Brentwood.

Gabin called her *"Ma grande,"* one of those wonderfully romantic expressions that are so difficult to translate. Literally "My big one," it really means "My woman," "My pride," "My world." The way my mother looked at him when she said "Jean, *mon amour*" needed no translation. She loved everything about him—especially his hips: "The most beautiful hips I have seen on a man." The only part of him that she had the slightest reservation about was his intelligence. His background and education lacked the sophisticated polish that attracted her so to Remarque.

She set to work on Gabin's English pronunciation. His French accent did not have the

lilt of Chevalier's, nor the sexy softness of Boyer.
Gabin growled; in French his voice could give a
dead fish goose pimples, but in English, he
sounded like an angry headwaiter. She fought
for him at his studio and made enemies for him
in absentia. She even persuaded someone to as-
sign her old lover, Fritz Lang, to direct Gabin's
film. Fortunately, he was replaced in the first
four days of shooting. As it was, the film turned
out to be such a nonentity, it wouldn't have mattered who directed it! Still, Lang must have had
enough time to have a man-to-man talk with
Gabin, for he came home one day and accused
her of having had an affair with Lang, to which
she replied, utterly amazed:

"*That* ugly Jew? You must be joking, *mon
amour*," and enclosed him in her embrace.

Throughout her life, Dietrich did that
constantly—erased lovers from her memory as
though they had never existed. Not just a convenient trick to get out of a sticky situation, but
true mental erasure. She could do it with other
things too, a frightening trait.

MY APPRENTICESHIP DONE, I graduated to
being permitted to perform on stage, and chose
a professional name for myself—"Maria Manton." I thought it sounded strong and un-
European. I was given the leading role of Lavinia
in *Mourning Becomes Electra*, a Greek tragedy

set in New England, that our director had switched to the Deep South, revolving around the hatred between a daughter and a mother. Interesting choice! My mother came to the opening night with "the boys" and de Acosta, didn't understand what that "depressing" O'Neill was talking about, thought me superb except my hair was too curly, and the rented antebellum gown should have been made especially by Irene, and why didn't I tell her I had to wear "period"?

Her agent, now a producer, offered her a picture to be called *The Lady Is Willing*, at Columbia. She accepted without knowing the director, full script, or leading man. Charlie Feldman was pleased, though a bit surprised. I wasn't, she trusted him, and, for the first time in her life, was so in love—work had taken second place.

Once installed in her dressing room at Columbia, reality hit a little, but unfortunately, not strongly enough. The director, Mitchell Leisen, worshiped her, had been, was, and would be her fan forever, so she was in the driver's seat, and between them, they managed a production that can only be described as high camp. In the forties, this took real, concentrated effort to achieve, not as easy as it is today. Of course, everyone was convinced they were shooting a marvelous picture with the even more marvelous Marlene.

Poor Fred MacMurray. Ever the dependable workhorse of Hollywood's leading men, found himself in the midst of this gay extravaganza, and in his unflappable way, never said a word, did his job, took his paycheck, and like any normal breadwinner, went home to his little woman. No love was lost between the stars. Actually, the way everyone behaved, there was only one Star in this film—Dietrich.

A baby figured prominently in the story. One day, carrying it in her arms, she tripped, stumbled, and fell. As she couldn't very well toss the child like a forward pass, she twisted her body to avoid squashing it and broke her ankle. I was called, told to get to Columbia fast—my mother had been in a terrible accident! I found her looking gorgeous, reclining on a gurney waiting to be taken to the hospital.

"Sweetheart," her voice registered unconditional awe, "you know what that astrologer said about today? 'Beware of accidents'! Unbelievable! This morning I called him and he said I shouldn't go to the Studio until after lunch, but of course, I went—and see!"

From that moment, Carroll Righter became her all-seeing, all-knowing guru. That very skilled and very sweet man often regretted having warned her that day. He had to cast the horoscopes of all potential as well as accepted lovers, family members, coworkers, acquaintances, servants, decide travel dates and contract signings. Over the years, day or night, he was "on call"—interrogated, asked for advice and magic solutions. She rarely followed his counsel, but blamed him if things didn't work out to her satisfaction. Carroll Righter became my lifelong friend, one of the fathers I would have wished.

One of Dietrich's famous gams being injured while "saving the life of a little baby" knocked the war off the front pages.

She refused to hold up the film until the ankle was healed and the cast could be removed, insisted on a walking cast, very unusual in those days, and with all long shots eliminated from the shooting script, was back at work within days. Her only problem: appearing natural in medium shots without her upper body reflecting the restricted movements caused by the heavy cast and obvious limp.

"What did Marshall use to do? Remember —with his wooden leg? He had all those little tricks to look normal in scenes?"

We ordered a Herbert Marshall film and did our homework. She got his timing, his subtle distractions so down pat, few people on seeing *The Lady Is Willing* can catch the point in the film where the break happened and the cast begins. This accident gave Dietrich "heroine" status, both privately and professionally, paid off at the box office, and allowed her to use a very elegant walking stick when wearing her male attire, without being criticized for this added, overly masculine accessory. Dietrich couldn't even break a simple ankle without profiting from it. After a while, this talent of hers to turn everything to her advantage took on the faintest diabolical overtones.

Finished at Columbia, she went immediately into another film with John Wayne at Universal, even finding a part in it for her old flame, Richard Barthelmess. Gabin, still uninitiated to my mother's emotional life-style, basked in the intense celestial fire of her all-encompassing love and was innocently happy. *Moontide*, his first American film, began shooting in November.

AT FIRST, when I heard it on the radio I thought it must be another one of those scary Orson Welles shows, but then, it sounded much too real to be just a script. I called my mother. Being Sunday, she was busy organizing a crawfish dinner, angry I had not arrived yet to scrub their bellies.

"What? They bombed ships? Finally! So, it took the *Japanese* to bring the Americans to their senses? Good! *Now* they will fight! Now it will all be over soon—like when they came into the war the last time, before I was born. I need more butter when you come. Oh . . . where *is* this Pearl Harbor?"

Overnight, every gardener disappeared. Flowers drooped, lawns withered in the hot sun. This marked the end of the era of manicured horticultural splendors of movie-star estates. For the landscapes of the Hollywood mighty of today, Mexican gentlemen labor diligently among the bougainvillea, but somehow, the sublime magic is gone—a little like the stars themselves.

A sign in a barber shop read:

Japs Shaved
Not Responsible for Accidents!

California, now so close to the enemy, panicked. A six p.m. curfew was ordered for all Japanese, their radios confiscated. All were potential spies, undoubtedly loyal to their Emperor Hirohito, whether American-born or not. All Oriental-theme pictures were shelved. The Studios geared up for "heroic propaganda" and "morale boosters," upgraded anti-Nazi scripts. Hollywood went to war its way and did a magnificent job.

Under the auspices of the Hollywood Victory Committee, stars volunteered their time and fame to help with the war effort. For once, my mother joined her peers. Mystery and aloofness were no longer prerequisites for glamour. This was 1942 and "realness" was in. Her early Berlin cabaret days now paid off. She went everywhere—did anything—cracked saucy jokes with

Charlie McCarthy, joined impromptu chorus lines, broke into song whenever called on. As the wounded arrived from Pearl Harbor, she joined the hospital shows hastily organized, was a "good sport," a "regular guy," a "real trooper," and had a ball. She was in rehearsal for the biggest role of her life—"the gallant war entertainer"—but didn't know it yet.

Carole Lombard was killed when her plane crashed returning from a war bond drive. My mother's fear of flying was again vindicated.

"See? What do I always say? Never fly! Airplanes are dangerous. I never really liked her, but she could be beautiful when someone dressed her right. I wonder who Gable will find next?"

The *Normandie*, confined to her New York berth since 1939, being stripped of her finery to be converted into a troop ship, caught fire, rolled over on her side, and died. For us, who loved her, it was like a death in the family.

I now played leads, was mildly successful, began teaching, directing, and getting paid for it. I was coasting in the afternoons, drunk at night, hung-over in the mornings. Rot-gut bourbon had taken over from brandy; Stingers, Sidecars, and Alexanders I used as chasers.

The perfect lovers must have had a fight. Maybe over John Wayne, or Remarque's love letters were arriving too often . . . whatever, or whoever, when Gabin left to go on location, my mother was convinced that he was angry with her and would therefore have an immediate torrid affair with his costar, Ida Lupino. Poor Jean, he was being judged by Dietrich's rule of thumb, not his. She canceled a bond tour to devote herself to "pining" and recorded her yearning into a navy blue diary—as with all of her written outpourings, with an eye to posterity, later leaving it in a conspicuous place so Jean could find it, read of her magnificent love for him, "if" he returned. In later years, when Jean was no more, she would haul it out whenever she wanted to impress a famous author swain of her talent for lyrical French prose, inspired by her great love for "the one man who knew not what he gave up."

15th February. He has gone.

16th February. I am thinking in French. It's funny! 10 A.M. I am thinking about him—thinking about him I could sleep for years if only I could see him for one second.
He is with me like a blazing fire.
Jean, *je t'aime.*
All that I plan to give you is my love. If you don't want it my life is finished, forever. And I realize saying that does not prove anything—even saying "I will love you all my life long and afterwards too"—because even when I am dead, I will still love you. I love you—it feels good saying it without

you having to answer: "I don't believe you."
However, if you were here I could kiss you
and lay my head on your shoulder and I
believe that you love me. Because if you
don't, all is finished for me—because if you
don't want me anymore I intend to die.
I am in bed. My body is cold and I look at
myself, don't find myself attractive, not attractive enough—I would like to be very
beautiful for you. For you I would like to
be the best woman in the world and I'm not.
But I love you. You are all my heart, all my
soul. I never knew what soul was. Now I
do. Tomorrow I will sleep in your bed. It is
going to hurt. But I will be nearer to you.
I love you—I love you.

February 17th—I haven't slept. I took some
pills at 3 A.M. but I was too cold to be able
to sleep. I worked in the afternoon. I wait
for you as though you were going to come
back any time from the studio.
Please, my adored one, come back, please.

18th February—I slept so well in his bed.
At first it hurt to be there without him—but
I pretended he was there and went to sleep.
Time passes so slowly! It is because I count
the hours—even the minutes! I had lunch
with George Raft and talked about him!
Raft asked me how could he look at another
woman?
I can't believe that only three days have
passed since he went away. It seems an
eternity to me, or a lost life. I am breathing,

but that's all. I realize I am only thinking about myself. Maybe that is what one does when one really loves. I always thought that real love was not to think about oneself but it can't be true. I love him with every drop of my blood and I think only about one thing: Being next to him—to listen to his voice—feel his lips—his arms around me—and I think that I want to give myself to him for life.

Most nights I stayed in the theater, passed out on one of the prop couches stored in the loft above the stage. It was dark and cool up there, and much safer than where I was expected to be.

21st February—I still have the fever. My head is burning and so are my hands—this book I touch feels cold. I write slowly, my heart beats quickly. It's a good thing he doesn't know I'm sick.

Sunday, 22nd February—He called me. I am very ill. The doctor is coming at lunch-time. All those injections! What are they doing to the baby which I think is inside of me? But I can't have it if he is not free. And to have the child and say it is not from him, no, I don't want to think about that.

Sunday evening—If I only could touch his heart, however lightly, for him to see me as I am. If he said he loved me and wants me,

that he needs me in his life just as much as
he is necessary to mine—only this could end
this misery which shrouds me like an eternal
night.

Every day she wrote, page after page of her love
and longing.

Thursday, 26th February. I sent him a telegram with the number of La Quinta. I'm
going to wait for him there.

Like Garbo, my mother often went to La
Quinta, then a hideaway oasis way out beyond
Palm Springs. I sometimes felt this lush com-
pound of discreet bungalows had been built for
the sole purpose of movie stars' secret assigna-
tions. If someone was having a blazing affair with
someone that was either illegal, scandalous, bad
box office, or against their Studio's orders, off
they flitted to the desert and "hidden" La
Quinta.

Friday, 27th February, La Quinta—I woke
up with the sound of his voice in my ears.
He keeps me alive with his voice, to take
the place of his arms and his shoulders. He
gives it back to me with such a sweetness
which touches me deeply. He knows he
keeps me alive that way. Therefore he calls
me and talks to me sweetly. There is no
sunshine in this place which is usually so
sunny. Maybe the sun is jealous of you. I
think that prisoners must feel what I feel.
They exist without really living. They wait

for the day when they will get out of this misery to go on living again. I feel cold, my love. But if you were here, I would be clinging to your warm body and love the rain because it would be reason to go to bed. And you would ask: "Are you all right, my face?" Oh Jean, my love!

Saturday, 28th February—I didn't sleep at all. I kept thinking, thinking. Thinking . . . If I have his child, I am going to ask him to decide what we are going to do. I don't want to hide myself the last five months. If he wants, I'll have the child as though we were married. I don't give a damn what people think. I wouldn't be able to kill that child. But if he wants to, I'll do it. I could get my divorce a lot sooner than he, but that is not important. I hope that this time I am not pregnant because I am afraid he would stay with me for that reason and not because he loves me. In the future, when he is completely certain he wants to live with me, then I will want a child—but only if he wants it —and not because it happened without him wanting to. Oh, Jean, come— Come to cure all my pain.

The Battle of the Java Sea was lost. The triumphant Japanese were through to the Indian Ocean.

Sunday, 1st of March. I have a small tummy but no symptoms. Another Sunday without him. My body feels warm because I was in the sun and had a bath. I would like to go to bed but if I do, I'll be thinking too much about him.

Thursday, 5th March. He comes tomorrow. Oh, Jean—I love you. This is the last day I write in this little book which holds my deepest feelings—my sufferings, my tears—my hopes.

Reunited, they stayed locked in each other's arms for weeks. They came back to town dressed as sexy cowboys, both handsome, vibrant, and tanned all over.

Only one flaw in this idyllic picture—she told my father on the phone:

"And, Papi, after all the joy, Jean really loving me, something terrible has happened. I'm not carrying his child after all. How is that? I didn't douche on purpose. Funny, no?"

My mother decided the back-and-forth from Beverly Hills to Brentwood took too much time, let her hotel bungalow go, rented herself a hacienda near her man, and moved me and my "constant" companion from the alley to a house of our own down the hill in the next village of Westwood.

"The Child—since she has that woman to look after her and is learning to act—is so quiet. No problem at all. At least, I don't have to worry about her all the time on top of work and cooking for Jean," my mother told my father on one of her frequent calls to New York.

Singapore had fallen. After a desperate struggle, Bataan surrendered in April.

Jean's film was going badly, and he knew it. Trying too hard to be "Gabin," he became stilted, lost that enchanting actorless ease that reminded one of how much he resembled Spencer Tracy. In later years, their style of just being wonderful without the least apparent effort was so similar, they even began to resemble each other physically, at times.

Jean had not only found my mother's planted love pourings, but also letters from Remarque, Pasternak, Beth, even ones from the Pirate to her Babe. Normal jealousy consumed him. He accused her of having an affair with Wayne.

"Between selling bonds, retakes that won't help another disaster, and cooking for your buddy-buddies, I haven't got time . . . ," she snapped.

If he could be jealous, he must love her. She was once more sure of her hold over him and became abusive, accused him of being "bourgeois," "possessive," and "jealous beyond reason."

She would return to her house, summon me from mine, and let off steam:

"A peasant—and French! The worst kind,

after Hungarians . . . but he can be so sweet.
. . . What is the matter with him? I love only
him. I die for him. He is my whole world! He
does nothing but talk about 'poor France.' Only
the war? Is that why he behaves so strangely?"

Between fights, they went dancing. Orchestra leaders seeing them arrive would break into
the "Marseillaise" in Gabin's honor. He sat
down quickly, embarrassed, while Dietrich stood
at attention, singing fervently until the last note.

"I hate it when you do that French patriot
act," Jean would growl.

"Have you noticed that you are the only
one?" she retorted, saluting the band, bowing
low to the leader, "and 'act'? What gives you
that idea?"

Colonel Doolittle led sixteen B-25s off the
deck of the mighty *Hornet* and bombed Tokyo!
All ran out of fuel, crashed, some taken prisoner,
three executed by the Japanese, but we had
bombed Hirohito's hometown and morale was
high.

I was in the midst of a "dramatic" speech in some
play, my mother and her date George Raft were
in the audience, so was the new rival to the
mighty Louella Parsons, Hedda Hopper, when
suddenly the air-raid sirens recently installed on
the street corners went off! Everyone knew it
couldn't be an actual raid, so sat listening to the

play as best they could, waiting for the din to stop. Not my mother! She wriggled out of her row, sprinted outside, grabbed the filling-station attendant, made him haul his ladder to the lamp-post, climbed up it, and stuffed her mink into the offending horn that had dared to interrupt her "brilliant" daughter's monologue. The show outside was so entertaining, the audience left us and traipsed outside to see it. Hedda Hopper was the only one who ever told this story with any sympathy for the rejected actors left stranded while Dietrich, her skirt hiked up to her hips, was performing *her* act in the parking lot. Everyone else took it as yet another proof of Dietrich's great devotion to her child. The siren silenced, she climbed down, lowered her tight skirt to the deep disappointment of the on-lookers, herded them back into the theater, calling to us, rooted in our positions on stage:

"Go back to where he says, 'Darling—what is this all about?' so Maria can start her speech again." Turning to her adoring herd she instructed them: "Everyone—sit down! They are going to do it over again from the top. Okay! Dim the lights—you can start!"

Hedda became my champion. Whenever she wrote about anything involving my mother's "goodness," there was just a hint of tongue-in-cheek sarcasm, a flash of censure. The first columnist ever to buck the tide of "perfect motherhood." Over the years, she was very kind to me. Whether she really liked me or just disliked my mother wasn't really important. Anyone who questioned my mother's "sainthood" was okay by me.

AT A STRANGE COCKTAIL PARTY of dislikable people, a gentle, likable man took my arm, walked me out of there to his car, drove me to the beach—let the sharp sea air clean away the impressions of that unsavory gathering. He fell in love with me, this oh-so-good man with the lovely talent to make people laugh, and resurrected my spirit in the process—made life seem, once more, livable. Of course, I adored him, and not only because he wouldn't let "that woman" get near me from then on.

Very properly, we became engaged. I was walking on air. My mother was furious, hid it gallantly, and called my father to come "immediately" to California to help with the "craziness of The Child!" Their combined efforts of dissuasion hit a stone wall of British determination. My fiancé presented me with a beautiful amethyst ring, and complete with "smiling" golden-haired parents, we were photographed celebrating our official engagement.

The Rhino pawed the ground, breathed fire, and quit. My mother was so shocked at her sud-

My mother loved going out with Gabin,
showing the world she belonged to him.
He, missing France and worried about the
war raging in Europe, went out only to
please her.

Her insistence on showing off her one-time skill on the violin in public places embarrassed Gabin, but he accepted it
all with quiet charm.

Whenever she was in New York, Remarque was there, ready to listen to and love her. My mother always had old loves ever waiting to embrace her.

At Universal, on the set of *Pittsburgh*. Although John Wayne was Dietrich's leading man in three films, his refusal to become one of her many conquests absolutely infuriated her.

ABOVE: **Dietrich joined the many stars who toured the States selling war bonds.**

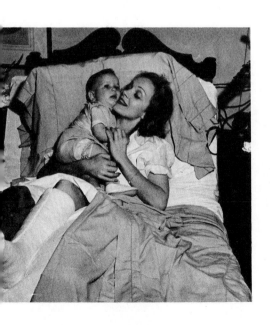

Filming a scene in *The Lady Is Willing*, she tripped while carrying a baby. To avoid injuring it, she twisted her body and broke an ankle. The Columbia Studios Publicity Department rejoiced! They brought the baby to the hospital, photographed it with the "heroine star," and knocked the war off the front pages.

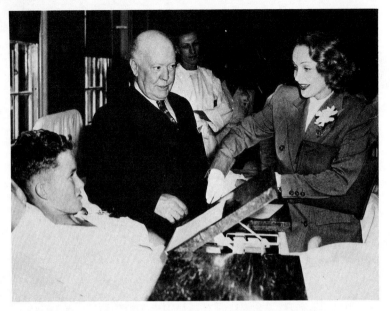

In 1943, organized military hospital visits by stars were a must. Guy Kibbee thought my mother's bedside manner was delightful. She loved cheering up "her boys," as she called them.

Gabin in uniform, about to leave the United States to join the Free French Forces overseas, danced one last dance with the woman he loved. She swore to follow him to war, then kissed him farewell.

den departure, she told my father to check for some ulterior motive. When he informed her some checks could—might—seemed likely to have been tampered with, she said:

"I knew it! I had a feeling she was stealing something—that's why she left so suddenly." Henceforth, always referred to her as "that woman—the one we had for The Child—the forger." Even after my father discovered that others had embezzled huge sums of Dietrich's earnings, her moniker was not reassessed.

Strange, I never really blamed that woman. She frightened me, disgusted me, harmed me, but "blame"? Why? Lock an alcoholic into a liquor store and he helps himself—who's to blame? The one who takes what is made available or the one who put him there? Even an innocent parent would not have put a young girl into an unsupervised, wholly private environment with such a visually obvious lesbian. My mother was certainly not an innocent.

All was suddenly such a real B-picture script, so "hearts and flowers" perfect, I should have been more on my guard. But I was in such a daze of "normal people" fairy tale, I was delirious; visions of wedding dress, veil, and bridesmaids played tag with rice, honeymoon, and happy-ever-after. I was once more an "untarnished" virgin, in the first throes of idyllic love. That poor sweet man, loving me as he did, seeing this raw need gathering momentum, rolling toward him out of control.

We walked along the sand, the early morning cool and still. Hesitantly, he told me he was leaving, was returning to England to enlist, our wedding would have to be postponed. He said he loved me, promised he would come back, to wait for him. He meant it all. He could not know the extent of my fears, that believing myself to be so rejectable made it impossible for me to accept that anyone would ever want to return and love me still.

I think I begged a little. That day has taken on the cataract haze that seems to appear to envelop such hurts and subsequent foolish actions. I saw him off—kissed him good-bye, convinced he had left for more reasons than the love of his country and turned my back on his precious gift of salvation.

My mother was very pleased.

"Good for him! He knew what he was doing. Don't be so la-di-da romantic. He was twenty years older than you and a comic actor! No—no! Good you are out of that—without any *big* problems!" and called my father to tell him The Child was saved and back to normal. The Rhino was also pleased and waited patiently, hoping.

My mother decided I needed further "curing." As undoubtedly it had to be my misfunctioning glands that were at the root of my inexplicable stupidity of falling in love, she put me into a hospital for metabolic disorders in La Jolla. There I was given lettuce, gained weight, was accused of bribing the staff to smuggle in candy bars, drank a bottle of milk of magnesia the night before every Friday's weighing, made friends with a nice lady who shared our adjoining bathroom, or she would have, had she been able to walk, which she couldn't because her legs were black from diabetic gangrene; and concluded that I had always known I would be put away into a "spa" like Tami someday. I was discharged at the same overweight I had entered with but wiser in the agony of gangrene, and resumed my quiet self-destruction.

The Reinhardt Academy failed—was taken over by a drama school run on expedient lines: "Got the money? Want to act? Be a star? Here you can— No waiting— No heavy classes— No classics— Only modern plays you can be seen in by talent scouts— An instant showcase— Learn while doing." A natural for Hollywood. I stayed on as one of the directors.

A breathless young student timidly interrupted one of my multiple rehearsals of *The Women*.

"Miss Manton? Please excuse me but," here she took a deep breath as though oxygen had become imperative, "there is a young officer in the front office asking for you." Her eyes shone, her slight bosom fluttered, "He is waiting for you in the lobby."

I was sure there must be a mistake, no one with that effect on women could be coming to see me!

There he stood, in that dingy lobby, looking like an ad for what joining the navy could do for a young man. His officer's whites immaculate, his cap set at an angle even my mother would envy, that rakish white-toothed grin—so handsome, so young, so alive, so American! Jack Kennedy said:

"Hi, Maria," and my knees went just as wobbly as they had so long ago.

At the drive-in next door, he bought me a cheeseburger, answered all my eager questions about his wonderful brothers and sisters, was kind, attentive, and a joy to be with. He never changed. When we said good-bye, he kissed my cheek, then walked away to his red convertible. As he drove off, we waved to each other, mouthing, "See you soon! Take care of yourself!" We never saw each other again. As to taking care of ourselves, we didn't do that very well either.

SUGAR AND COFFEE were rationed. The use of klieg lights that shone their long beams into the night sky were banned for the duration, and fancy movie premieres were no more. A hundred stars went to Washington, D.C., to launch the first billion-dollar war bond drive. Tyrone Power became a marine, Henry Fonda joined the navy, and Bette Davis, with John Garfield as cofounder, had begged, borrowed, and finagled enough money to open the Hollywood Canteen. In the first six months, six hundred thousand men passed through its doors—seven nights a week, volunteers welcomed the boys far from home, showed them they cared. Where else would a young man waiting to be shipped out to the Pacific be served a cup of coffee by Ann Sheridan, get a ham sandwich from Alice Faye, a doughnut from Betty Grable, hold Lana Turner in his arms to the strains of Tommy Dorsey's orchestra, jitterbug with Ginger Rogers to Glenn Miller's band, twirl Rita Hayworth to the beat of Benny Goodman, while Woody Herman joined in on his "licorice stick"? Chew the fat with Bogart, Tracy, and Cagney, have an egg plucked from their nose by Orson Welles, finally find out that Veronica Lake DID have a second eye under that peekaboo bob?

The European contingent preferred the kitchen detail. Hedy Lamarr made hundreds of sandwiches, Dietrich scrubbed pots in clinging dress and attractive snood, up to her elbows in dirty dishwater—it drove Bette Davis crazy. I once heard that wonderful four-octave-range voice of hers declare: "If I find those dames back there one more time . . . I'll brain them! What is it with those hausfraus? Show them a kitchen and they're off! Like a horse to water! I need glamour out *here* for the boys—not in there with the pots! Oh, God! What I couldn't do with a dozen Grables!"

At the Canteen, those unreachable "gods" stepped down from the silver screen and turned into flesh-and-blood people, suddenly touchable. It had a profound effect on those young men, and, eventually, on the entire industry that supplied their entertainment. Once exposed, made human, stars lost their divinity and became "lovable"! When a Betty Grable film was shown in some tent behind the lines on some Jap-infested island, they knew her—they had actually held her a time-stop moment on a crowded dance floor. All the stars, both male and female, that made that bridge from make-believe to reality gained that special place—when an audience replaces awe with genuine affection. Garbo never appeared at the Canteen. A shame, it might have saved her from extinction. Again that incredible, completely intuitive weather vane of Dietrich's pointed her in the direction that would eventually prolong her visual fame by thirty years.

Gabin didn't resent my mother's giving her time to any cause that helped the war effort. It was my mother's all-consuming pleasure, the emotional high that her "war work," as she called it, gave her that made him feel even more the outsider, the ineffectual foreigner. When she came home brimming over with stories of how the GIs had held her very, very close, how she could feel their rising excitement, how sweet they were with those freshly washed faces, those innocent young boys about to be heroes, how she knew their last dance with "Marlene" would remain with them through the terrors of war, Gabin was jealous of her enthusiasm and emotional satisfaction that excluded him. She, never aware of such subtleties of another's sensitivity, was annoyed by what she called "his moods," accused him of being jealous of "her boys" because all he was doing for the war was "making a stupid picture."

My ever-devoted mother must have bribed someone, for I was given my final high school exams and *passed*. Amazing! For years I expected the California Department of Education would wake up one day and haul me off to jail. Now, after fifty years, I figure the statute of limitations is on my side.

Rumors of a massacre in a Warsaw ghetto were faint but there, still few believed them. The Allies landed in Sicily, bombings of Germany intensified.

I found someone who was willing to marry me and thought salvation was at hand. The day

I packed my few belongings for this sad and foolish teenage marriage, my mother, her face frozen, stood watching me, walked out, returned, handed me my wedding present: a brand-new douche bag.

"At least, make sure he doesn't get you pregnant!" With that sage and loving counsel, I left my mother's house. I was married in a summer dress of gray, printed with purple violets— funeral colors, unplanned, but very appropriate. That poor boy, neither old enough nor trained to cope with the neurotic mess he acquired. Our "legal cohabitation" lasted just long enough to gain yet another gold star on my mother's "martyred mother" tally board. She searched and found a small apartment, a real feat in wartime, cleaned and furnished it. Created a little love nest of marital bliss for the ungrateful daughter that everyone knew had "deserted" her.

Of course, this desperate attempt at escape, this pathetic self-delusion of normalcy, was doomed from the start. The so-called "marriage" was finished before it ever began. I was left with three choices, besides an obvious fourth of working the corner of Hollywood and Vine, which in my drunken state I probably would have tried had I believed I could earn enough to survive on; the way I looked, I had my doubts. So, it was either returning to my mother or the ever-waiting Rhinoceros, or hitchhiking across America to my father's punitive asylum. I chose the lesser of those evils . . . my mother. I wasn't very bright. Maybe reading all that *Hamlet* at an impressionable age had gotten to me and so opted for the "ills" I knew. With her, at least, I knew all that awaited me, knew what to expect, including giving her the divine satisfaction of having "the love of her life" return, tail properly clamped between her legs.

And how she enjoyed it, for more than fifty years reminding everyone—me included—how she took me in, welcomed the penitent home, the "ever-forgiving mother." She even added a touching scene of how in the dead of night, I crawled into her bed, whispered pitifully, "Mutti, I am back—please can I sleep here with you tonight?"

I returned at high noon, downed a slug of bourbon, and, gritting my teeth, went to do penance. But my mother wasn't home, she was still in Gabin's house. But her version is a much better script for a prodigal's return. And by this time, I didn't care what anyone did to me— worse, what I did to myself.

Gabin had had enough. His country defeated, his American film career going nowhere, he began pulling diplomatic strings to join up with the Free French Forces formed by de Gaulle out of England. Zanuck assured him he would not stand in his way. Not only did he sympathize with Gabin's loyalties, it would also relieve him of having to honor his contract—finding vehicles for an actor whose American box-office appeal was proving a dud. My mother wept, but was brave. Her man was doing what he *had* to do: "going off to war to do his duty." Somehow, she would find a way to follow him into the field. The impossibility of travel during wartime without official orders and her Universal contract kept her tied down in Hollywood for the time being. Still, she resolved to find a way. I was not present at their leave-taking, but it must have been a lulu! Probably fog and all!

Papilein,
    Jean went tonight to New York. You will see it in the papers when he arrives.
    My great love seems too much for him, and too sudden for him, after all that time when he thought that my love was not enough in comparison with his which included everything. I have promised him to eat and to take care of myself until he comes back.
    I will not work, have canceled the Camp Tour because in my misery I could not take all that.
    I only know one thing: that I have loved without being selfish, without any thoughts at the back of my mind, and I have always tried to give happiness even though I did not succeed always. After this, I will be

more able to do it and I will try not to clutch myself to him, but I would like to have, finally, the chance to be a real woman and not to strive toward ideals that are in the moon and do not bring any happiness because one can keep them only for a while. Kisses and love,

Mutti

Still, she couldn't let him go without a last lingering farewell and actually got into a plane and flew to New York, saw Gabin one more time, danced in his arms—she, ethereal in clinging black and feathered hat, he, wonderfully handsome in his French uniform.

"Sweetheart," she called on her return as she strode through the door, the chauffeur following lugging her cases, "flying is so easy! No different arrival clothes to pack, no endless cornfields, no lists, no tipping—not even that heat! Why did we always take trains? Next time, we must try it instead of boats!" Planes had arrived! Flying, given the Dietrich stamp of approval.

Now that I was once more housed with her, mail was again my duty. The flood of love letters from Gabin was never-ending. Wartime V-mail, opened first by French-speaking censors before being sent on microfilm, then printed in the States before reaching my mother's trembling hands, and she could sigh, cry, yearn while devouring the contents.

11th Febr. 1944

. . . Ma grande, my love, my life! You are here before me, I look at you: La Quinta, you, me. I've nothing but that in my head. I'm alone, like a kid lost in a crowd. Is it possible to love this much? Do you think that one day we will be together again and will live together, the two of us, only the two of us! Will you wait for me. . . . Will God want me to find you again, you, the greatest of all? . . . You are in my veins, in my blood, I hear you inside of me. . . . For the first time, I tell you: I need you, I need you for all my life or I'm lost.

J.

After a few months of this, Gabin's letters outnumbered hers. She was very busy adoring Orson Welles. They spent days together discussing his brilliance. As with anyone of higher intellect, she was his fan, and Orson, being Orson, saw no reason why he shouldn't agree with her assessment of his genius. As recompense, he taught her to perform as his assistant in his magic act. They did camp shows and appeared together in a big morale booster, *Follow the Boys*, that featured an array of stars. As I had worked for Orson on his Mercury Theatre of the Air, my mother was always a little jealous of my actor's association with him, became very possessive whenever discussing "*my* friend Orson Welles" with me. When Orson fell in love with Rita

Hayworth, my mother had been shocked.

"An intelligent man like that? Falls for a Mexican hoofer? You, who think you know him, will *you* tell me why? Does he maybe like hair under arms?" She was very disappointed in him but forgave her pal, as she did all his future disastrous amours, by saying: "Orson needs it. Don't ask me why. He just needs to love somebody all the time—poor man!"

Leslie Howard, rumored to be a valuable British spy, was killed in a mysterious plane crash, and Hollywood was buzzing. The most believed story was that his plane had been purposely shot down by the British because they had discovered he was a double agent for the Nazis.

"See? What did I tell you. Such a terrible actor, he *had* to do something else. After that orange hair—anything was possible!"

I often wondered about my grandmother and Liesel. What had happened to them? My mother never mentioned them, never said a word, behaved as though they didn't exist. Ever so slowly, rumors of unbelievable horrors began filtering back, unknown names of places where Nazi cruelties and actions lost plausibility in the sheer magnitude of their evil. Still, no one had yet seen the visual proof of hell and, therefore, could not be expected to believe such things were possible. Over the next two years, my mother, ever so gently, let drop that her mother was safe in Berlin and that her sister was in Belsen. As horrific rumors became heinous reality, it was automatically assumed that Liesel was in *the* Belsen—the only Belsen in everyone's mind at the time. That concentration camps were simply given the name of the town they belonged to was not a concept that even seemed plausible. Just too normal, for geography to designate the placement of hell. I, too, had no reason to think otherwise, accepted my mother's tragic version, and worried about the fate of that tender little woman.

In New York, Teddy died. Strange to think of a world without him. Many years later, his spirit settled into a glossy black cat who appeared one day at my door, and stayed to be my friend. So like him to have no animosity toward felines.

My mother found out Gabin was in Algiers. How she got that information is one of those mysteries so often associated with Dietrich. This now galvanized her need to follow her man into battle. She began her campaigns at the top. Abe Lastfogel, of the mighty William Morris Agency, had been put in charge of camp shows for the USO—the civilian organization responsible for sending entertainers to lift the morale of America's fighting men wherever they might happen to be. Lastfogel and his power became my mother's primary target. The daily "Oh, Abe—sweetheart" phone calls came hot and heavy. He was impressed, promised to keep her in mind, do everything possible to grant her ardent request, adding his respect for her courage and patriotism. Jack Benny was already overseas, so were Danny Kaye, Paulette Goddard, and others. Ingrid Bergman was scheduled to spend New Year's with the troops stationed in Alaska. While waiting for her assignment, Dietrich signed to do a picture at MGM.

THE SKY WAS JUST TURNING PINK as we drove through the imposing gates of Metro-Goldwyn-Mayer. After fourteen years of envy, Dietrich had finally made it to Garbo's studio—three years after her leaving it. She smoothed her hands over her legs—it was the fifth time she had checked to make sure that the seams of her nylons were straight. She was nervous. She had much to be apprehensive about. She thought the script of *Kismet* was hackneyed and MGM an enemy lot, and her leading man, a former lover now married to a very sharp lady, might be difficult to handle.

"Sweetheart, remember how we all hated *Song of Songs* and that other stupid one I did for Korda in England? We thought those were awful, but at least they were made *before* the war! But this picture! Who will go to see Ronald Colman making cow eyes at Dietrich 'à la Baghdad'? You know him—he will be ever so British, no matter how many turbans they plunk on his head. Besides, why isn't he in England fighting? The only thing that will save this picture is, maybe, Dietrich looking unbelievably glamorous. Thank God Irene is here for the costumes and Guilleroff for the wigs."

Although Irene and she had been working on her secret foundation for years, using it for her private wardrobe as well as the costumes she wore in *The Lady Is Willing*, they now perfected its basic structure. In 1944, they still had to use thick silk. It was only after the war, when the great Italian fabric houses, like Birannccini, were able once more to manufacture their renowned materials, that my mother found the "soufflé." Aptly named, it *was* a "breath" of silk, delicate and weightless, a spider's web with the retaining strength of canvas, which she used from then on for her foundations for Las Vegas and throughout the rest of her career. The ritual of getting into her foundation never varied, always in secret, never taken lightly, always regarded as the most important duty, requiring her inner circle's absolute concentration.

First, she stepped into the garment, we fastened its thin inner belt around her waist, then she secured the triangular piece of elastic between her legs, adjusting its fit between the sides of her vulva to minimize the pain of the tension that would be necessary. Bending over until her breasts hung clear of her body, she slipped one arm into one capelet armhole, then the other. Next, she scooped up her drooping breasts and placed each one into the bias bralike structure, carefully positioning each nipple into its proper slot. Once they were placed to her satisfaction, she cupped her breasts from underneath, holding them and the foundation in place, quickly straightened up, and we zipped her in from the back. If a breast shifted, a nipple was just a hairline off, the whole procedure had to be repeated. If the specially made, incredibly delicate metal zipper snapped under the extreme tension, it was like a death in the family, although three dozen backup foundations hung, waiting, hidden under their silk covers, ever ready and willing to do their magic act of giving Dietrich the sublime body she craved all her life. Once she was in her gossamer harness, only two places could give her secret away to any probing eyes: the line that circled the base of her neck where the foundation stopped and the line of the zipper that extended from the back of her neck all the way down to the end of her spine. The neck she camouflaged with embroidery or necklaces, the other by managing to align the appliquéd zipper of the covering garment exactly with that of the foundation. Once placed, positioned, and zipped into her most treasured secret, my mother became a statue; breathing was a conscious effort, movement a calculated and limited luxury. For the film *Kismet*, she was placed amongst satin harem cushions and just froze herself into positions. Dietrich always admired soldiers who could endure long periods of "standing at attention," and so she welcomed such tests of physical discipline.

Irene's genius, the fabulous execution of Karinska, and tireless dedication to perfection resulted in some of the most flamboyant costumes Dietrich ever wore on film. Now they needed only equally inventive wigs to complete the exaggerated look. The genius of Sidney Guilleroff was up to the task. In the process of designing ornate wigs and hairpieces, he too discovered Dietrich's amazing ability and willingness to endure physical pain in order to achieve a look she felt impossible to capture otherwise. As Irene and she had pulled her body in to simulated perfection, so now she and Guilleroff pulled her face. The fact that she was tampering with a face that was already perfect did not seem to cross her mind. It was not a conscious decision. Dietrich simply did what she believed was necessary, never wasting time on the process of thought or evaluation. The instant that she had seen her face in *The Devil Is a Woman*, she had fallen madly in love with its perfection. From then on, no other image of herself ever satisfied her mind's eye completely. As von Sternberg was no longer there to create that face for her, she attempted to do it herself whenever she could and by any means at her command. Now, she and Guilleroff took minute strands of her wispy hair all along her hairline, braided them into tight little ropes, pushed straight hairpins, whose ends had been bent into miniature fishhooks, into them and twisted the little ropes of hair until the skin of her scalp could take no more. The pain was excruciating. The "instant face-lift": Now it is done often, then it was a very new process. During the lunch break, this procedure had to be repeated, as the tension of the little braids slackened, causing my mother's face to resume its normal beauty. She did a lot of crazy things in *Kismet*. She tried for any effect she thought was necessary. Perhaps it was her inner fury at shooting a preordained flop on Garbo's lot, or an impatience to get to war—probably a mixture of both. She kept trying to "save" the picture, at least make it into a "Dietrich" one. She and Irene designed trousers of tiny gold chains, looped like Victorian curtains that encircled her legs for the "harem dance" sequence in the film. My mother, who had never actually danced before on the screen, was very apprehensive. That day, she found herself in a hairdo that made her scalp bleed and her back teeth ache, breathing carefully for fear of cracking the zipper of her foundation, her body covered in barbarian embroidery of metallic thread that pricked her propped-up breasts like a thousand fine needles, her legs aching under twenty pounds of looped chains, expected to undulate her seductive form down the ornate staircase of the sultan's palace. I will say she tried—she looked like a desperate ostrich with a migraine trying to be a sexy snake, but she tried. The sound man finally saved her. Every time she moved her legs, the chains bounced, causing such a racket that it drowned out the musical playback. Everyone agreed that the chain idea had to go! She pretended to be upset at the loss of what everyone had thought was such a terrific idea, until we got back to the dressing room. There she opened a bottle of champagne, heaved a sigh of relief as we cut the chains off her legs, and smiled:

"Thank god, that's over! But what are we going to do now? That ridiculous dance—did you see me? 'Theda Bara à la Arabia'! Ridiculous! But now we have to think of something! They want that dance. But everything that moves makes a noise . . . so? What is exciting—that hasn't been seen before, that we can put on the legs—that doesn't move?"

Everyone had an idea that was rejected. Finally, Dietrich ordered brushes and cans of paint from the Art Department and painted her legs gold! The dressing room reeked of toxic fumes, the skin of her legs turned green under the thick

At the end of 1943, finally having made it to Garbo's studio, MGM, Dietrich prepares for her role in *Kismet*.

RIGHT: Sidney Guilleroff creating a hair design.

Dietrich's idea of having her legs painted gold is the only thing anyone remembers from this Arabian disaster!

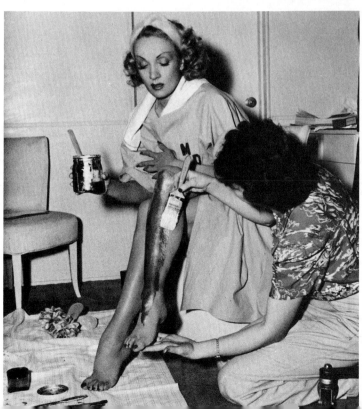

The golden legs looked great, but they weren't worth the possibility of lead poisoning.

coats of metal paint, her stomach heaved, she became dizzy for days, on the brink of lead poisoning, but: Dietrich's golden legs knocked the battle of Monte Cassino off the front pages! It is the only "look" remembered from that awful film.

My great treat during the preparation of this disaster was being on my friend's home lot at a time when she was working. Whenever I could, I escaped my mother's imperious eye and sneaked onto the set of *Meet Me in St. Louis*, a world of ruffled charm and sparkling talent. There is a feeling on the set of a hit picture in the making that cannot be explained. It's something in the air, like an energy field, that gives off an electrical current, that feeds, charges all talents to ever higher output. It is a rare phenomenon. It can happen within any artistic union, but when this force pervades an enormous soundstage, it is truly magical.

"Hi," said the Voice—now so famous, so instantly recognizable.

"Hi—god, you look fabulous! Can you breathe in that corset?"

"Enough," she took a breath to prove it. "But this wig is so heavy, my neck's breaking."

"It'll photograph wonderfully. And it *moves*! Just terrific. Guilleroff knows what he's doing. You should see what he and my mother have concocted for *our* picture! Real crazy! But that's how she wants it. We're doing a flop anyway."

The giggle still sounded like little pebbles rolling under water. One of her many attendants came to investigate who was monopolizing The Star.

"We are ready for you now, Miss Garland."

She got her "trooper" look. She always had that capacity to call up the discipline of her working childhood. Even when she was so sick, so finally broken, that tough vaudeville training kept her going. I wish it hadn't. It prolonged her suffering.

Halfway through our picture, MGM received security inquiries from the FBI for a Dietrich clearance as a loyal American. The Studio, happy to oblige, gave her the green light. She might be scheduled to leave before a second film could be put into production—they too had seen the rushes!

The day finally came when my mother received notice that her wish had been granted. She and a selected accompanying group were scheduled to go overseas to entertain the troops as soon as she had completed her present assignment at MGM. She took her first series of required inoculations the day before she had to shoot a love scene with our "Ronnie." Off the set they avoided each other so, it had become comical. No love was lost between them. She covered this up by telling everyone that Colman was so frightened of her, that was why he never dared to touch her, even avoided looking her way whenever possible.

"You know, he is frightened stiff of me! Probably his wife told him, before he started this picture, that if he went *near* me . . ."

She always allowed her listening audience to supply their own version of the dire punishment that Benita Hume might have threatened her husband with should he stray into Dietrich's clutches. The day my mother's upper arms were swollen, throbbing with the reaction to the tetanus-paratyphoid injections, Ronald Colman "forgot" himself, grabbed her violently in a fit of unleashed passion; she screamed, he recoiled!

Later, in the dressing room, we applied ice packs. She was laughing:

"Through this whole terrible film, he never dared to touch me! Then suddenly today, when my arms are inflamed from the shots, he gets 'dramatic'! Typically English! You can never tell with them—when suddenly they will decide to let themselves go and get passionate. Stupid man."

I always felt our "Ronnie" knew exactly what he was doing, but kept that thought to myself.

Kismet ended as it had begun, a vacuum of nonexpectation. My mother was ready to follow her man to war. She did not go quite as far as the high-heeled shoes and silk dress from the last shot of *Morocco*, but the feeling was the same.

Her orders were to report to USO headquarters in New York for rehearsals in preparation to being shipped overseas. She was triumphant.

> Papilein,
> My cholera-typhus shot is still swollen and red but does not hurt anymore. I have, I think, packed everything except the hand things I need for traveling. Please write to Jean and do not forget that mail is being opened so allude to me as "La Grande" or "Louise." Jean Gabin, French Liaison Office APO 512 c/o Postmaster New York City.

Spies were everywhere, all troop movements highly secret. Posters proclaimed, "Loose Lips Sink Ships." Fighting men never knew where they were being shipped to until after they had left U.S. shores. One even had to have FBI clearance to serve coffee at the Canteen! But Dietrich, the born German, knew she was being sent to the European theater of war and not the Pacific one. Amazing! Her letter continues:

> I am eating tonight with Gable—with the purest intentions. But the choice is difficult—because Sinatra hangs on the phone and he is small and shy. I'll send you his records, they are not for sale yet. Gable says he hasn't got lights or heat on his ranch, because of the storm, so it sounds as though it might get "difficult"—but I didn't want to cancel.

I want to give this letter to the postman.
It is almost ten o'clock. I hope to fly away
on Tuesday but I will send you a telegram.
Adieu my love,
Mutti

All her belongings stored at a Bekins warehouse, my mother cried, put a check in my hand,
and left to win the war.

I remained, teaching people who had the
money to pursue their dream even if they had
no talent, directed play after play, on the same
level of mediocrity, drank, slept with anyone
who said I was pretty or "loved" me, woke not
knowing where I was or with whom, sought for
ever deeper degrees of oblivion, ran, and ran—
while standing still.

In a woodland shack in one of the canyons,
I spent a weekend amongst the coterie of Henry
Miller. One of his *Tropics* was then hot and
shocking, and young girls flung themselves into
his burly arms with rebel abandon. He considered such juicy offerings his due and took whatever he fancied, regardless of their, at times, very
tender age. I did not sleep with him. Considering
the fogged state I was usually in, quite an interesting achievement. Everyone *else* did. He liked
multiple numbers and communal appreciation of
his sexual prowess. Afterwards, instead of smoking a cigarette, he read from his banned book
as though delivering the Sermon on the Mount.

GONE A' SOLDIERING

IN NEW YORK, my mother went into rehearsals. Her troupe consisted of an accordionist, a male vocalist, a comedienne—who would be her handmaiden and female companion, and a recently successful young comic, who would function as master of ceremonies, entertainer, and jack-of-all-trades. Lastfogel knew his business; Danny Thomas was the perfect choice for Dietrich. His humor clean, very American, he was also wise in the art of handling large, sometimes unruly, crowds. His youth and respectful attitude made him immediately acceptable to my mother. She listened to him, did what he told her, and learned invaluable lessons from a master. He taught her American comedy timing, not too far removed from her own Berlin humor, but more structured, less rapid, less sardonic. Routines were polished, an overall show constructed. Thanks to Danny's skill, the Dietrich troupe became a tight, highly effective unit.

Between rehearsals, she got her uniform. Irene and she had already made the gold sequin sheath that would become her real wartime uniform, and later, the basis for her stage costumes. Now, at Saks Fifth Avenue, she fitted her reg-

ulation one—not the army, air force, paratrooper ones that she was to be photographed
in, only two months later and forever after visually associated with, but the civilian uniform of
the USO, a sort of cross between World War I
Red Cross and very early airline hostess. A little
stodgy but quite adequate for riding in jeeps and
doing one's job. Once overseas, my mother got
rid of it quickly, acquired "proper" military attire, kept only her required USO arm patch,
although she hated it, later even letting that
somehow disappear, replacing it by the one of
the 82nd Airborne, her favorite division. Everyone was so busy trying to win a war, no one had
time to stop and reprimand a glamorous movie
star for disregarding her civilian organization's
dress code. Besides, Dietrich looked so very
right in military garb that soon the Eisenhower
jackets, complete with service ribbons and hash
marks, tailored trousers, combat boots, and GI
Joe helmet became her accepted, rightful costume of the day.

It was the best part she was ever given, the
role she loved the most, the one that was to bring
her the greatest success. She collected laurels for
her heroic bravery, medals, citations, devotion,
and respect. Worked her way through the enlisted ranks up to five-star generals, had a glorious time being a true "hero," and then got
decorated for it. In her own words, "I never felt

so happy as in the army." The Prussian was in her element; her German soul embraced the tragedy of war with all of its macabre sentimentality and—she had it both ways.

To hear Dietrich describe her tour of duty, one would believe that she was actually *in* the army, overseas for at least the full four years under constant fire, in imminent danger of death, or worse, capture by vengeful Nazis. Anyone listening to her became convinced of this, for she had convinced herself that this was so. Actually, on and off, she worked from April 1944 to July 1945, in between returning to New York City, Hollywood, and, later on, remaining either in Paris or at the headquarters of her favorite general in Berlin. Dietrich's laudable civilian contribution to the war effort is not to be downgraded by this, only put into its proper perspective. She was fearless, heroic, and dedicated. But so were many civilian women and many entertainers who were not given the Legion of Honor in three escalated grades or the Medal of Freedom. It is just that Dietrich was so much better at playing the valiant soldier and had the fame and beauty to be noticed doing so.

She spoke of her days "in the army" with reverence. Wrote her version of that time repeatedly. As with anything concerning her life, truth and fiction interlaced, in the end becoming accepted history even for those who had been there and should have known better. Legend and logic don't mix too well.

On the 14th of April, 1944, her USO troupe left in a hailstorm from La Guardia Airport, their destination "officially" unknown until after they were airborne, when they were told they were on their way to the African theater of war, and not the Pacific theater, as everyone had believed. Except my mother, of course. Her goal was Gabin, not Hirohito.

They stopped to refuel in Greenland and again in the Azores, finally landing in Casablanca, then went on to Algiers. Considering this was before jets and taking into account the different time zones, they could not have arrived there until at least the 17th of April. All this, while some biographers and, on occasion, Dietrich herself, have her searching through mounds of corpses, looking for her sister's at the concentration camp of Bergen-Belsen. As Belsen was liberated by the British on April 15th one year later, this does not seem likely, somehow.

The Dietrich troupe did their first show in Algiers. Danny Thomas opened the show, won the boys over with his special humor, then the comedienne did her act, she was followed by the male vocalist—then it was time for the main attraction. Danny announced:

"Fellahs! I've got bad news! We were expecting Marlene Dietrich—but she went out for dinner with a general and she hasn't shown up . . ."

This planned "tease" got the anticipated groans, the boos. Suddenly, from the back of the theater, the unmistakable voice called:

"No! No! I'm here! . . . I'm here!" in uniform, carrying a small suitcase, she appeared, running down the aisle toward the stage. By the time she reached the microphone, she had pulled off her tie, was beginning to unbutton her khaki shirt.

"I'm not with any general—I'm here! I've just got to change into . . ." She was down to the last button and the GIs howled. She "suddenly" remembered that she was not alone.

"Ooh! Sorry, boys, I'll just be a second," and disappeared into the wings.

Danny called after her: "That'll be a tough act for you to follow, Miss Dietrich. Let's save that for the end. I think they'll wait!"

That got the desired foot stomping and whistles. In a flash, Dietrich reappeared in her sequined sheath and *wow*! It really was Marlene, the screen goddess, who could be enjoying the luxuries of Hollywood but had come all the way to North Africa to entertain them, and the boys were on their feet cheering! She sang her famous songs. They loved her. She chose a boy from the audience to be the subject of Orson's mind-reading act. The boy stood there, gazing at her in the shimmering dress, she looked at him, then out at her audience:

"When a GI looks at me, it's not hard to read his mind!"

That was a sure laugh-getter. At the close of her act, she hiked up her dress, sat on a chair, put her musical saw between her legs, and played it! Pandemonium!

As was the custom between shows, she toured hospital wards, singing or just visiting. Raising morale was the primary goal of the USO entertainers. She loved to tell how the doctors would take her to dying German prisoners, would ask her to speak to them in German. How these suffering boys would look up at her and ask in their whispers, "Are you really, the real Marlene Dietrich?" How, "like to children," she would croon "Lili Marlene" in German, comfort them as much as she could, they had so "little time." My mother wrote scenes for herself that were worth believing.

There was a rumor that the front had been reinforced by an armored division of the Free French. She commandeered a Jeep and a driver from the motor pool, went searching for a tank division, and, before dark, found it. Tanks, spread out under trees, their hatches open, their crews resting on top.

"I ran from tank to tank—crying his name. Suddenly, I saw that wonderful salt-and-pepper hair! He had his back to me—'Jean, Jean, *mon amour!*' He spun around, exclaimed, *'Merde!'*, jumped to the ground and took me in his arms."

They stood in their passionate embrace, oblivious to all those longing eyes, envying the gray-haired man holding a dream. The kiss went on—they doffed their corps berets, and cheered their approval, tinged with jealousy.

The sound of tanks starting up their engines finally broke them apart. He kissed her once more—"We go, *Ma grande, Ma grande, Ma vie* . . ." Held her to him for one timeless moment, then let go and leaped back onto his tank and down into its belly. Tanks began moving into formation. She stood in the clouds of dust they churned up, shielding her eyes, trying to catch one last glimpse of him, afraid she might never see him again.

I drifted—ketchup and hot water made a great soup and left money for the more important nourishment of bourbon. I remember a limbo time in San Francisco. How did I get there and why? I spent my time in bars and transvestite nightclubs. Earned booze money doing odd jobs. A trained-by-Dietrich dresser can function very nicely as handmaiden to a female impersonator of Sophie Tucker. His name was Walter, his fame quite legitimate and deserved. He kept his many sumptuous evening gowns, like museum pieces, in ventilated cedar-lined closets, his huge collection of accessories in catalogued archival boxes, let me bunk down in his boudoir, fed me, worried about me, protected me by his patronage, and very probably kept me from really being hurt. Why I have always remembered him—that bald, Rubenesque, outrageously flamboyant drag queen who took the time to—care.

After playing North Africa, Dietrich's troupe was flown to Italy and assigned to travel with a Texas division. She sent snapshots: she in khaki, sleeves rolled up, washing in her upturned helmet; on the back was written: "To the sweetheart of the American Army. A swell G.I., Hqrts. 34th Inf. Div. Italy, 1944." She was laughing, the soldier's daughter had found "home." Other pictures followed: Holding her mess kit, she stood in chow lines, and whenever she was asked, "Can I have a picture taken with you, Marlene?" she put her arm around the boy's shoulder and smiled for his folks back home. Anything they wanted was theirs. If a boy was about to go into battle and she could make him happy one last time, why not? Dietrich considered the morale of all fighting men her sacred responsibility. To send a brave man into battle, his spirit renewed from having spent his last hours in the arms of a beautiful woman, had always been one of my mother's most romantic fantasies. Now she had the whole Fifth Army to inspire. There was one "tall drink of water" from Iowa who called her "Chicken" and was loved; another gangly kid from Missouri named her "Lammie Pie"; to a brash kid from Chicago, she was "Toots"; to another, "Princess," but whatever they called her, she was their dream come true amidst the hell of killing.

She had crabs often—looked upon them as part of being a real soldier and insisted one did not, absolutely *not*, get those from intimate physical contact. Years later, a member of one of my mother's troupes told me that it was their job to stand guard outside her billet, be it tent, bombed-out hotel, or Quonset hut, making sure the "traffic" ran smoothly. She wrote to her Brentwood neighbor and pal, Evie Wynne, secretly letting her know where she was by saying "Frankie's country is wonderful."

Still in Italy, my mother came down with pneumonia and was hospitalized in Bari. She always maintained that it was there her life was saved by the new miracle drug penicillin, and its discoverer, Alexander Fleming, became one of her medical heroes.

For me, life lost its color. Became a sameness. Meaningless hours—to meaningless days that ended in empty weeks that became meaningless hours on their way to infinity.

On the 6th of June, 1944, Dietrich announced the news of the Normandy invasion to an audience of nearly four thousand GIs. Soon after, her troupe was sent Stateside and disbanded. She came home dissatisfied. Being a restricted USO entertainer did not fulfill her need to go a' soldiering. A month later, on the 25th of August, my mother was still in New York when Paris was liberated. It galled her that she was not there to march at the head of the "victorious troops." Years later, she had her revenge when she did march in the anniversary parade commemorating this glorious day, was photographed and her war fame was such that whenever this picture was printed, it was assumed it had been taken on the actual day of the Paris liberation in 1944. Somehow, no one noticed that in the photograph she is wearing her medals—only received after the war.

I began hoarding sleeping pills. Never ever waking had become nearly a necessity. Jumping from a high place—that scared me, so did the thought of pulling a trigger. Strange, how one can still be frightened when killing oneself.

In September, with a new troupe that again included her Texas handmaiden com-pal, Dietrich was on her way to France. Whatever official travel orders or carefully worked out and correlated military itineraries by the USO and the Special Services Division now vanished. Through her connections, she managed to be brought to the personal attention of one of her heroes, the flamboyant, pistol-packing Patton. It was one of Dietrich's most treasured stories, one she would haul out at the drop of a military hat:

"Oh! He was so wonderful! A real soldier! Tall, strong! Powerful! A leader! He looked at me and asked if I really had the courage to face the danger of going to the front: 'Could I take it? Was I brave enough?' Of course, I told him I was ready to do anything he wanted for his boys—only I was a little afraid of what the Nazis would do if they captured me. When I told him that, you know what he said to me? 'They wouldn't waste you. If you're captured, it is more likely that you would be utilized for propaganda, forced to make radio broadcasts like you did for us.' Then he took a small gun from the pocket of his windbreaker and said: 'Here. Shoot some of the bastards before you surrender.' Oh, he was wonderful!"

Dietrich now had the war she wanted. They were billeted in France in a town she referred to in her letters as "Sinatra's wife." From their *Nancy* headquarters, they drove to different installations near the front, did their shows with orders to return before nightfall.

From this point, my mother's often-told "War Stories" take on the texture of film. The poignant drama of scenes augmented by her consummate skill as scenarist, director, and cameraman:

She who had always feared flying now flew. War-time made everything acceptable.

Wherever she went, she played her musical saw and GIs cheered.

No mere war could stop Dietrich. She found Gabin in Algiers just as she had planned.

Strutting a routine with Danny Thomas somewhere in Italy, 1944.

ABOVE, LEFT: My mother in her element, feeding someone. RIGHT: One of her favorites from her huge collection of wartime snapshots.

BELOW, LEFT: Anything and everything could become a stage when moving with the troops. RIGHT: She sent me this. On the back was written: "My tent is cosy."

Dietrich always looked so right in military garb.

"That day, we did our show in an old barn—it was cold, bitter cold and dark—the noise of war was very close. In my gold sequin dress, they could see me with their flashlights—" and as she conjures up this moment, one is there—her memory's captive. . . .

Like a beacon, she stands. The sequins of her golden dress reflecting beams of flashlights trained on her body. The sounds of war mingle with the strains of a single guitar like an accompanying beat of hell. Softly, she sings. The makeshift microphone cupped between caressing hands, she is to those war-weary men the half-forgotten dream of all women longed for. A shell bursts too near— Old timbers groan—wood dust cascades, catching the faint light. The repetitive click of Zippos sounds like crickets who have lost their way from sun-filled places. She sings of "Boys in the Back Room" and young faces grin. "I Can't Give You Anything But Love"— Home may be Mom and Apple Pie—but here —now—is raw desire. "Move out!" A barked command, its heightened pitch betrays an edge of fear. Curses, as men return to their reality— prepare to leave her golden aura.

"See you, Marlene!" "You take real good care of yourself now, you hear?" "Hey, Babe— Adios!" "Bye, Sugar!" as they shuffle out to give death or receive it.

My mother's voice drops to a hollow sigh:

"I stood there, cold and forlorn—and watched them go. . . . Sometimes . . ." Her voice lifts in anticipation of a lighter memory. "We played far behind the lines—then the hills were full of men—wherever you looked, just a sea of young faces . . . hundreds . . . of them. I, on a little stage far below and their whistles floated down to me—like adolescent kisses and the war seemed far away."

And so it went, day in, day out—one scene better than the other.

Dietrich stayed attached to Patton's Third Army. He hinted that he had no intention of stopping for the Russians—that his job was to beat Germans, not play Roosevelt-Stalin politics. Of course, she loved this brash soldier, his bravado, his military arrogance, and supported anything he felt it his duty to do. He, in turn, basked in her utter devotion and kept her close to him as long as possible, until orders separated them in December of '44.

Dietrich says she was in the Ardennes, at Bastogne, when the Germans surrounded the American forces to which she was attached, among them the 101st Airborne Division with its commanding general, Anthony McAuliffe. She knew they were surrounded. Everyone did. She expected to be captured. She wondered what would happen to her. She waited. What she had done with her civilian troupe is a Dietrich legend no-no! She does not say, nor ever knew, that General Sepp Dietrich, probably a cousin, was one of the commanders of the Panzer armies surrounding her. Neither did she know that when General Luttwitz asked for the Americans to surrender, he got back the now-famous reply of McAuliffe's—"Nuts!"—an expression impossible to translate into German. As a matter of fact, it took the translators and interpreters two hours before they delivered McAuliffe's meaning to the Nazi general, who didn't really understand its implication even then. But the American troops had, and its effect on their morale was cataclysmic—it gave them renewed courage in the face of what they had only a short time before believed was a certain defeat.

My personal favorite Dietrich war story now takes center stage:

In the midst of what was to be known in the history books as the Battle of the Bulge, one concerned American general is supposed to have had the time to request, of another general, that Marlene Dietrich, being in danger, needed to be evacuated immediately. At once, a major jump was mounted. A whole planeload of the 82nd Airborne Division fell from the skies, so that their general could rescue one heroic movie star! It seems unlikely that a division of paratroopers would be ordered, in the midst of one of the fiercest battles of World War II, to risk their lives making such a jump. If the wives and mothers of those boys had heard that! But the legend actually brazenly upholds that the mass jump occurred and that the general was the first to find his quest. My mother loved to tell of how she sat on the ground, coughing, waiting in the snow-hushed stillness, when a mighty hum from above became the sound of an airplane, and looking up, she saw an American Flying Fortress, from whose hatch parachutes opened against the bleak gray sky, that the first paratrooper to land was the 82nd Airborne Division commander, General James M. Gavin himself, and the first thing he did—was find her. Isn't that lovely? "Jumping Jim Gavin" became my mother's favorite hero general, after Patton. Tall, handsome, young, and brave, he gained the devotion and respect of his heroic paratroopers by asking as much of himself as he did of his men.

Dietrich says that Gavin brought her safely back to Paris in his Jeep—not on a white horse—then left her. How this was done under USO regulations was never checked too carefully, but it's *so* romantic, who cares? She was billeted at the Ritz, which had been commandeered for the use of American officers, VIPs, and dashing war correspondents. I never did find out what happened to the accordionist, Texas comedienne, and comic—but I'm sure they were safe too.

.   .   .

I WAS A TWENTY-YEAR-OLD DRUNK living with a man who balanced on the hairline edge of true insanity. To prove that he was perfectly sane, he memorized the complete works of Freud and Jung, devoured the writings of any who deciphered the secrets of the human mind. His own schizophrenic brilliance was such that, when undergoing psychiatric examinations, he could answer whatever questions were asked him correctly within the accepted guidelines of normalcy and passed every test with flying colors. Some doctors sensed the virulent madness, but could not prove it by the rules laid down. Others were not skilled enough to even know they were being duped. One day, this "madman" handed me a book and ordered me to read it. Its title, *The Neurotic Personality of Our Time*, written for the first time in laymen's terms by a very (then) modern psychoanalyst, Karen Horney, and there I was—on every page! It was me—the Me of Me! She knew me. A startling revelation to find one's innermost wounds exposed, explained, known by a total stranger and without censure. That's the greatest discovery, that's what opens the door to salvation—that sudden realization that you are *not* alone. If your desperation can be written about, there must be others like you. Being one of many makes you feel so much less dislikable. One's self-hate becomes tempered by this sudden loss of uniqueness. I carried that book within me and its teachings saved me. Quite literally, saved me. Without it, I would have eliminated myself eventually—I am certain of it—and missed all the loving that was just waiting for me down the road. It took a long time before I could walk that road, but now I had a surface to balance on.

My mother continued fighting the war with songs, sequins, sex, and sympathy. Suddenly, she was ordered back to "Forward 10," the code name of the commanding general, Omar Bradley. She says she arrived at his trailer in the Heortgene Forest. He looked pale and tired.

"Tomorrow, we are going to enter Germany," she says he told her. "The outfit you are attached to is going in first. I've discussed this with General Eisenhower and we both agree that it is better for you to stay back. Playing hospitals and such."

She wanted to march with her soldiers into Berlin. She pleaded, but Bradley was adamant.

"We're afraid of you going into Germany. If the Germans were to get their hands on you, all hell might break loose. We could not stand the criticism if anything happened to you."

She wrote my father of this meeting:

He seemed distant, thoroughly uninterested in how much I cared to go in with the first troops. I must tell you one very important thing, all Generals are lonely. G.I.s go into the bushes with the local girls, but Generals can't do such things. They have guards around the clock, with machine guns strapped to their sides; they are surrounded wherever they go. They can never, never have a "kiss and tumble" in the hay or out of the hay. They are all desperately alone ever since the war began.

Dietrich never liked Eisenhower, like with John Wayne, always had stinging stories about him. I often wondered why. After the war, when Eisenhower's private wartime romance was exposed, then I knew. But General Bradley had no "lady driver" to stand between him and Dietrich, and so, lo-and-behold, she entered Germany, schlepping her troupe willy-nilly along with her on the way to Berlin. In Aachen, they took over the movie theater for a performance. With no fuel for heat, the building was like ice. The German caretaker brought his thermos, poured a cup of his precious coffee for Dietrich. The members of her troupe warned her not to drink it, it might be poisoned.

"No," she said, "they wouldn't do that to me," and she drank, thanking the man in German, asking him why he had wanted to share something so precious as coffee when, "You know I am on the other side."

"Yes, yes, but *The Blue Angel*—ah! I can forget what you are, but *The Blue Angel*? Never!"

There were no threats on her life, few insults. As they moved through the bombed towns, the German population paid her homage and genuine affection, so she maintained. Being such a good scriptwriter, all her scenes involving her one-time countrymen play well. Full of human pathos, adoration for her and respect, with none of the hatred that one would expect, considering all the ingredients of this human tragedy.

On the 19th of February, 1945, my mother was again in Paris. Why she was suddenly there and how she got there three whole months *before* the end of hostilities is another one of those "legendary no-nos." She sent my father this menu:

It is headed by her observations: "You can imagine how the poor eat if *this* is what you get in a deluxe restaurant!" and "To have dinner you walk half an hour only to find this! My stomach is bad from the phenol in Army food and I have to eat 'fresh food.' This is it! 200 for the wine which is about the only good food you can find. Around 680—together, which is $13.50. So, if you read that Paris is gay and there are terrific Black Market restaurants, don't believe it." The "luxury tax" gets a dig too: "What luxury?" The margin is my favorite: "Jean has been out on the tanks all day, came all the way here to see

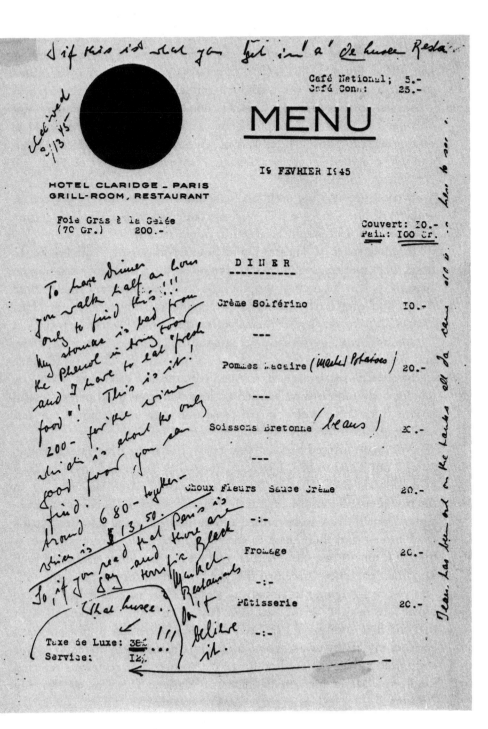

[handwritten across top] if this is what you get in a' de luxe Resta...

[handwritten, left] received 2/13 45

Café National; 5.-
Café Conc: 25.-

MENU

HOTEL CLARIDGE – PARIS
GRILL-ROOM, RESTAURANT

16 FÉVRIER 1945

Foie Gras à la Gelée
(70 Gr.)   200.-

Couvert: 10.-
Pain: 100 Gr.

D I N E R

Crème Solférino   10.-

Pommes Macaire *(mashed Potatoes)*   20.-

Soissons Bretonne *(beans)*   x.-

Choux Fleurs Sauce Crème   20.-

-:-

Fromage   20.-

-:-

Pâtisserie   20.-

-:-

Taxe de Luxe: 30%
Service: 12%

[handwritten notes, left side] To have dinner you walk half an hour only to find this !!! My stomach is bad from the phenol in tap water and I have to eat "fresh food"! This is it! 200.- for the wine which is about the only good food you can find. around 680- together which is $ 13.50. So, if you read that Paris is gay and there are terrific Black Market Restaurants don't believe it. that luxee. !!! ...

[handwritten, right side, vertical] Jean has been at on the banks all the way old G. ... has to see .

me again and washes and eats his rations and hates it.''

NEARLY FULL-TIME SOBER, I traveled to New York—hoping to find a job in the theater. Little money forced me to stay in my father's apartment. Between auditions, I took care of Tami. Her condition had deteriorated alarmingly. Shuttled from one psychiatrist to another by my "long-suffering" father, ordered and paid for by my equally "long-suffering" mother, she had been diagnosed as schizophrenic by some, a manic-depressive by others, a paranoid, an obsessive-compulsive, a hysteric, given other equally extreme labels for want of one correct diagnosis.

While she suffered her torments, my father, who had always believed that all she needed to come to her senses was stringently applied discipline, behaved according to his beliefs, thereby reducing this already damaged soul further, until she was a trapped animal that quivered in abject fear whenever he was near. My mother, who believed that psychiatry was only for the weak and unintelligent of this world, shook her head in disapproval of "Tami's stupid lack of self-control," paid the doctors' bills, and told everybody about her burden, "having to take care of Tami and her 'illness,' for poor Papi!"

I tried out at a big audition for a showcase

part any young actress would kill for—and got it! I was now an employed actress and getting sober to boot. Life might be worth trying after all!

Foolish Notion, a Theatre Guild production starring Tallulah Bankhead, went on the usual weeks of tryouts on the road before opening on Broadway. It was exciting, and not only on stage. Our star, usually blind drunk and completely naked, liked chasing me down hotel corridors. Poor Tallulah, she hadn't managed to get "into Dietrich's pants" at Paramount, now figured she'd get into the daughter's in Columbus, Ohio, and points west. Trying to hold onto a job can get dicey under such circumstances, particularly if you don't let the star catch you. I did my job, kept my mouth shut, learned a great deal from good people, useful lessons from those skilled in self-projection, also understudied our star and disappointed her greatly with my agility for flight.

We finally arrived back in New York prior to the Broadway opening. After I put Tami to bed, I went to Forty-fifth Street and stood in front of the Martin Beck Theater. The theater was still dark, the lettering on the marquee still unfinished, but the giant blowups of Bankhead and her costar Donald Cook were framed and positioned on the columns outside the theater— and there, next to theirs, eight feet tall, was one of me, as though I, too, were a star. Neither my part nor my talent warranted such important exposure. It seemed that the fascination for the "daughter of" was just as intriguing to Broadway audiences in 1945 as it had been to movie fans in 1931. Seeing that huge poster, I had the disturbing thought that the first audition I had been so proud of getting might not have been on my ability as an actress after all! Changing my name to escape identification had achieved nothing. We opened. The reviewers referred kindly to "Maria Manton daughter of Marlene Dietrich" as showing "promise."

In April, President Roosevelt died at the beginning of his fourth term in office. In New York, we stood silent and shaken as Tallulah announced his death to the audience before our performance. To me, Roosevelt had been *the* President—the only one I had ever known, like a protective father, always there, and I mourned him as such. It felt so strange without him.

Hitler supposedly committed suicide in his bunker the end of that April, but no one really believed it until a week later, when we all went crazy celebrating VE Day. I couldn't help wishing Roosevelt had lived just a little longer to witness the end of the European war. Now the men, who had fought and survived one terrible conflict, waited to be shipped, not back home but to the other half of the war, still raging in the Pacific. When the play closed, I applied to the USO for a part in one of the many plays they were now sending overseas to entertain the occupation forces and those waiting to be shipped out. My mother wrote that she was back in Paris, I never did find out where her poor troupe was, nor did she elaborate—she was busy asking everyone who had travel orders to enter Berlin to deliver packages of food to her mother. Almost invariably the officers doing the errand of mercy were able to acquire extra items to augment her packages, their attitude being, "It's the least we can do for our gallant Marlene." Aware her accompanying, hand-carried letters would be read by censors, she wrote in English, using American wording:

28 June 1945

I hope the package reaches you all right.
I am doing all I can to come to see you or to have you come out if you want to.
I am worried about you and I am sending messages by everyone who goes there.

Please keep well until I can come. I am in Paris now. Maria and Rudi are in New York, but Maria will come here soon to play for the troops and might also come to see you later.

I pray that I can see you soon. In the meantime I will send all my friends to see you, who go there where you are.

All my love.
God Bless you always.
Your daughter,

Marlene

On the 13th of July, 1945, Dietrich and her trusty and trusting troupe were shipped back Stateside. Her famous script starts with their lonely return on a rainy night when no one met them at La Guardia because "security" had not permitted their arrival to be announced. Hand weapons given her as souvenirs by adoring GIs as well as generals, she *says*, were confiscated by Customs. Outside the terminal, a surly taxi driver wouldn't open the door to his cab for them. It seems he was not impressed by their uniforms—he was too used to returning GIs who did not have American currency to pay for their ride. No one in the troupe had anything but French francs. Accustomed to army life, they had forgotten that civilians have to pay for transportation.

She asked the driver if he recognized her, and he did. She promised that if he took them to the St. Regis Hotel, he would get the biggest tip of his life. At the hotel, she cashed a blank check for a hundred dollars, paid the taxi lavishly, and split the rest of the money with the troupe so that they could get home. She said they stood in the lobby of the hotel with her, none of them wanting to make the transition back into this once familiar, "now so strange civilian society." My mother had them all go upstairs to her suite, where they took baths, ate, and talked. Apparently, no loved ones awaited them. Her story continues:

"I called Feldman in Hollywood, and you know what he said? 'Don't write any more checks—they'll bounce.' 'You must be crazy,' I said. 'No!' I was in the war too long not making pictures! So I was broke. So I said: 'Get me a picture!' That wasn't going to be so easy either, he said, because I had been off the screen for all those years."

This established once and for all her great sacrifice for the war and supported the "second" selling of the emeralds. After that, she called my father, said that she was going to move in with us in the morning, it was cheaper, that she had called Remarque and we were all going to the Stork Club to celebrate "a soldier's return."

In the heat of a New York July, my USO play, *The Front Page*, rehearsed in the dingy rooms of a dance studio on Forty-sixth Street. When everything was ready, we received our stage costumes, papers, uniform purchase orders, and inoculations. As I was playing the whore, my costume was easy—I just copied my one-time governess and looked very authentic. I got my heavy uniform, brogues, ties, shirts, waterproof overcoat, lined gloves, olive-drab wool hat, and wondered where in the hell we were being shipped to in August in long johns.

My mother had a confidential talk with me—to prepare me for war.

"Oh, those wonderful boys—they want to give you everything, Lugers, Mausers, Nazi daggers—you won't have enough room in your valpack to carry them all." She inspected my ready-and-waiting musette bag. "Soap, tooth things, shower cap, shampoo, makeup, towel . . . where is your douche bag?"

"I . . ."

"And your diaphragms?"

"I don't have one—I really don't think . . . I . . ."

She grabbed me, pushed me into the elevator, into a cab, into the gynecologist's office. An hour later, I was the owner of half a dozen little compacts containing what my mother called "the greatest invention since Pan-Cake makeup," adding, "How did you imagine you could go overseas to entertain soldiers without one? You never know . . . said the widow . . ."

She left for Hollywood before I was shipped out, wept, said we would meet again, didn't know where, didn't know when . . . but we would meet again. Sounded very familiar, like a lyric.

My company reported to Camp Patrick Henry in Maryland. We stayed at that big training camp for a while, waiting for our troop ship. I got very nervous around there. A lot of clenched-jawed men, with very blond hair and big POWs written across their backs, kept tidying up the manicured parade grounds. I had nightmares of one of them turning around one day and, on seeing me, yell: "Ach! If it isn't little

Heidede, our Marlene's little girl!'"

Our Victory Ship entered the Bay of Naples, trucks deposited *The Front Page* company in our billets in Caserta, where we were issued regulation summer uniforms in tall stacks, like jumbo loaves of sandwich bread, and I wondered how my mother, at the height of the war, had managed to have hers so beautifully tailored and all for the correct climate. Allen Jones and his operetta troupe were in Caserta on their way home. We exchanged news, got our PX cards, were lectured on the evils and precautions of VD, accompanied by colored slide shows and prophylactic demonstrations—and we were ready to move out.

For the next six months, we made our way through Italy, up and into Germany.

On the 6th of August, America unleashed the nuclear age and, in a flash, reduced eighty thousand living beings to powdered bonemeal. And those were the lucky ones. On the 8th, Russia declared war on Japan and invaded Manchuria. On the 9th, to make sure it would work a second time, we added another thirty-five thousand to the dust pile, in Nagasaki. America no longer needed the Russians to help conquer Japan, and the war was over.

In a quiet Italian town, we interrupted the performance, and I was given the honor of telling the boys the great news: Instead of being shipped out to the Pacific, they were now going—*home*! Their joy exploded, and those little milky balloons filled the summer air. This was not new, this had happened often. Whenever I made my first entrance in black-net stockings, four-inch ankle-strap shoes, and clinging dress, they usually floated in to greet me, a sign of yearning, intended vulgarity, anger, protest toward stupid actors who could come, make with the brave patriotic gesture, then be flown home, while they, having miraculously survived one war, sat waiting to be shipped out to fight the other half of it, this time surely to die. But this time was quite different. On this lovely summer evening, those little balloons looked like soft white blossoms swaying in the warm Italian air, were signs of gaiety, a naughty prank from men who suddenly knew they had the time to be the children they thought had been lost forever. Condoms afloat can be very pretty.

The Second World War was officially over. America had lost 300,000 of her youth, 600,000 wounded. This was a low count, for she was the only country whose civilian population did not need to be counted amongst the casualties. France lost a quarter of a million men, 30,000 of her civilians had been shot by firing squads. Britain counted her dead at 250,000, her wounded and missing at half a million, her civilian casualties at over hundreds of thousands.

Russia lost 7 million men, another 14 million were wounded, her civilian deaths—a staggering 14 million. Germany counted three and a quarter million dead, 7 million wounded, and 3 million of her civilians killed. Japan lost 1½ million, a million of her civilians dead, another 500,000 wounded.

Behind the lines, the Master Race had starved, frozen, mass murdered, gassed, incinerated, mutilated, exterminated 6 million human beings for being Jews. Seventy thousand "race-defilers," the sick, retarded, crippled, homosexuals, and gypsies, were also eliminated in these ways, for contaminating the purity of the Aryan bloodstream. For this, German generations to come would carry the mark of Cain, and should. But, in all probability, will not. As with all such man-made hells, they will be forgiven for creating it for some convenient reasons, then forgotten. Remembered only in books and through the pain of its survivors, who too will fade in time and their wails of outrage with them.

Gabin, now back in Paris, begged my mother to come, make a film with him, maybe even marry him? She answered by cable that she would do both. He cabled his delirious joy. She began working on getting the necessary postwar permission to get back to Europe. The USO needed entertainers to relieve the boredom of the thousands of men in the Army of Occupation, and Dietrich's request was welcomed with open arms. She also asked to be sent to Berlin. She had two reasons for wanting to go: her mother, and her handsome general now stationed there.

August 13, 1945

Angel—

You are completely crazy—and you drive me insane with your doubts. In *my* last letter, I spoke of *my* divorce of course. I think, after the film, will be the best time to do it. Rudi will try for a job in Paris. He naturally is completely in accord with the divorce—it is more the idea of it that shocks him—I have to admit me too. Just the idea of it, nothing more. We are both really such bourgeois, we have decided, if it is possible, not to be present but make the lawyers do it all. Please find out what are the most dignified reasons for getting a divorce in France.

The Claridge is fine if you move my things from the Ritz, because when I get there I must have warm clothes right away as I must go to my mother first. I hope you understand this—after that, I am all yours. If you are sweet to me, I will stay with you for the rest of my life—married or not married however you want it. But, if you want a child, then it is better if we marry. —

I hope you got some of the things I sent

from O'Hara. There are not too many planes now and one is not allowed to send things like clothes to France. Unbelievable but true. It is allowed to Holland though. I am bringing enough clothes for a regiment and boots for the winter. André, instead of bringing your make-up, mailed it direct. That was before I knew that one is allowed to send only food to France. So I told him to bring a new set here, so I can bring it. Jack Pierce from Universal brought me all the make-up I will need also I am bringing the oil for us to take off our make-up. Also I bring soap and for laundry, pens, razor blades and olive oil. I have been packing all day and if all these cost duty, I don't care. They are necessary for the film. Do you still love me, my angel? What is with your apartment? If you don't get it, maybe I don't need to bring all the sheets and linen. I am worried about my Visa—It said "Not for Work" on the form. If all goes well I leave on the 10th of September by *plane*. I'll cable before.

I kiss you as always my angel—I love you.

Your Grande

The news of her planned return to Europe preceded her. She received a cable that interested her very much indeed—from the man who was soon to be the supreme commander of Berlin's American Zone:

HAD A VERY PLEASANT VISIT WITH YOUR MOTHER.
SHE IS FINE. THE 82ND IS LOOKING FORWARD TO
SEEING YOU SOON.

GENERAL GAVIN

By September, she was back in Paris, the romantic vision of marriage and babies already dimmed. She wrote my father, who had been put in charge of shipping Gabin's belongings, stored in Hollywood during the war, to him in Paris.

Hotel Claridge
Avenue des Champs-Elysées
Paris

Sunday, Sept 16, 1945

Papi sweetheart,

I miss you terribly! Takes me so long to get used to the ways of Jean. Why his nerves are in such a state I can't explain. The town is full of French soldiers walking on crutches without legs—he came out of the war all in one piece and is not happy about anything. I make all the effort I can but it wears me out because I cannot pull him out of his depth. Finally, yesterday he received his car. A Citroën 2-seat coupe, used, $4,000. I was told that he sat in his room all day— only went out after dark—because he had a car and is ashamed. He has the Presidential Citation and does not wear it. I ask you if that's not definitely a complex! He hides out like Garbo. Those two should have been married!

We have had a fight every night. About what, you ask? For instance: He took one bedroom with salon for both of us. I said that it would be better to have two adjoining bedrooms so we have two little girls' rooms, because that is one thing that is uncomfortable and I tried to explain to him that sometimes one wants "Privacy!" Whereupon he got up and dressed and left. He took his shaving things and went back to his apartment to shave, saying he did not want to disturb me. Instead of phoning downstairs and taking two rooms with bathrooms. How can I live during the winter with one bathroom making a film? Where one has to wait for the other in the morning!! Is that insane? Last night we had another scene because a couple we passed in the restaurant said "Bravo." He flew into a rage. I said that wasn't so bad, as we had been the only couple on the dance floor, that it was meant nicely and could happen anywhere. That ended the evening in ice cold silence.

The enclosed letter came just now, Sunday evening. So you see, it is always the same.

It was a sweet note of apology from Gabin, asking her to forgive his behavior. He admitted being "unbearable," and he understood that she must be very bored with him. He felt miserable because it was his fault that she was in Paris and unhappy. He told her not to worry about anything except her mother and to forgive him.

She continued her letter to my father:

Monday morning

His trunks arrived. Thank God!

I am still waiting to go to Berlin. Promises, promises! It is impossible to telegraph Private Messages to Berlin from here! Easier from New York. Here the red tape is unbelievable.

Please go to Bloomingdale's and pay for the next four months, each month one package to the same addresses: Coffee, olive oil (if possible), chocolate, good honey, rice, canned meat (if possible). Tell the saleslady to change the contents from month to month depending on what she gets in. The things needed are fats, meat, chocolate, rice, coffee, sardines. As it takes two months for the packages to arrive, tell them to send one every two weeks, so that they have the food during winter.

Please send me books. I am starving for mental food. I will write more soon.

All my love
Mutti

As we had been overseas for several months, our company was given a few days off and I was able to get travel orders to France; and on a clear autumn day, I saw Paris again. Without the intense emotion of the last time with Remarque, or the effervescent elegance of when

I had known it as a child—now a little shabby, a little worn, perhaps even a little self-conscious at being so very well preserved after such a devastating war.

I climbed the stairs to my mother's hotel room. She was waiting for me. She looked strained, a soldier without a "front," suddenly at loose ends. I took off my army overcoat.

"So why are you still wearing your skirt? How can you wear skirts when you have to ride around in Jeeps dodging shells?" she asked.

No use explaining that the bombings had stopped. My mother never did get used to the idea of Peace Time when there were still troops to entertain.

I had expected to see Jean and asked where he was.

"He's in the country, as usual fixing his house."

Perhaps, if I hadn't come, she could have gone to the country with him?

"No, sweetheart, I was waiting just for you!" She plugged in her hot plate to boil water for our coffee. There was a can of Nestlé's condensed milk and an open army ration of butter on the ledge outside her window. I looked around the small room, remembering all those opulent suites we had lived in with extra bedrooms just for the trunks. Yet, somehow, this Spartan atmosphere suited her more.

"You know, Jean is still a rich man, but for some reason, he feels out of place in a place like the Lancaster, even if one could get a suite there, which is impossible. Jean likes living like the peasant he is. Now he is suddenly so guilty about everything—why?"

I wanted to answer but thought better of it. To try and explain Jean's sensitivity was hopeless, to defend him would only set her against him more—as a reaction to what she would see as my disloyalty to her.

"At least, here we have hot water on Saturday and Sunday, a real shower, and a real bed to sleep in—no rats running over your face with their ice-cold feet, like in the war. Last time I was here, I stayed at the Ritz. . . . Oh, it was wonderful, Papa was there. . . ." She stirred the coffee grounds. For a moment I thought, which Papa? Kennedy or Hemingway? Then knew it had to be the latter:

"He was there looking so beautiful in one of those war-correspondent trench coats. When he saw me, he roared, 'My Kraut!,' threw his big arms around me. He was so happy to see me . . . everyone just stared." She sounded wistful, as though wishing herself back to that day. "He has a new woman, a reporter called Mary something, who works for Luce, that awful man that that woman who wrote that awful play, *The Women*—remember, how Clifton hated it?—

married. She was at the Ritz too, now a hoity-toity congresswoman. How can you write plays and then be in the government?" She got the can of milk from the window sill. "The Ritz gave me a double bed. It was wonderful, but I gave it to Papa and Mary—I was alone." Another sigh.

"One night they had a terrible fight. He was drunk, and of course, his cronies were too, and for some reason he shot her toilet! Don't ask me why. She got so angry, she screamed at him, called him terrible things, and he hit her—and, you know what she did? She hit him back! Can you believe it! And Papa was like a little boy—all upset! I sat on the bidet while he shaved and he told me he 'killed her toilet' and asked me to go and talk to her. 'Daughter, talk to Miss Mary. You know how,' he pleaded. A wonderful man like that, putty in that woman's hands. Amazing! He wants to marry her, and she has the chutzpah to tell him he has to learn to behave himself first! I told her: 'So—he shoots a toilet! So what? He is Hemingway!' But this woman insists on flushing it, and of course, the water gushes through the holes like an Italian fountain—and she stands there pointing and says, 'See?' I tell her: 'But he *loves* you! He is a *great* man! What more do you want?' That's what I mean about women—their brains are too small, they can't think straight. I went back to Papa's room and told him his 'Miss Mary' would forgive him. We drank a scotch together and just talked, about the war, what we did, what we saw, all the tragedy, the bravery . . . It was wonderful! Then he left, went upstairs to her where my bed was." Again, that wistfulness. She lit a cigarette, flicking her Zippo like a true soldier. "Did you know I saw Jean-Pierre Aumont? We met in a mine field. We had to get across because his Jeep was on the other side. You know what a 'perfect' gentleman he always *has* to be, so—he steps aside ever so politely and says, 'Marléne, you first.' Then suddenly remembers where we are and screams: 'No! No! No! Marléne—*I* go first!' and I say, 'No, No, No, Jean-Pierre, me!' By the time we got through 'No-no-ing,' we were across without stepping on a mine. But it was funnn-eee!" She began slicing the butt end of a hard salami.

"I got some bread for you. Not like before the war, sour and just right, but bread anyway! The concierge had to stand in line for it. When he finally came back, he was so proud that he had been able to find some for me to give to my daughter who wanted some." She smiled. "Remember the night when Papi ordered his borscht and got so angry because they didn't have his black bread? . . . Another world! We worried about having the right bread to eat with what, and I designed evening bags so that we could carry it with us."

One of her favorite heroes, General George S. Patton, Jr. He liked her spunk. She loved his daring audacity. They got along like "jam on bread."

General Omar Bradley was so scared of her, he usually granted anything she wanted, just to get her out of his headquarters.

ABOVE: Meeting up with General Gavin on some
lonely country road. The look says it all.
BELOW: France, 1944. War or no war, whenever
she appeared, crowds gathered.

In Berlin, in 1945, Dietrich, carrying her trusty musical saw, was met by her mother, who had survived the war.

Dancing with Gabin or Hemingway was delightful, but dancing with her very favorite general— the dashing James Gavin, commander of the 82nd Airborne Division—*that* was sublime.

My mother cried when she saw the burnt-out shell of the church where she had been married.

In the winter of 1945, she entertained the occupation forces stationed in and around Berlin.

We drank our milky coffee, dunking our precious bread.

"Oh! I haven't shown you my lucky 'short-snorter'!" and jumped up to get it, held it out proudly for me to inspect. It was as thick as a roll of toilet paper. She unrolled it for me—all that paper money glued with Scotch tape, end to end, bearing the signatures, messages, names of boys she had known, played to, loved, sent out to fight. "See, that's Russian money. I got that when we met up with one of their units— wonderful peasant faces, angry and strong! . . . That's British, I have a lot of those. Sweet boys—always so polite . . . but the dollars the GIs gave me are the best. When I met Irving Berlin, I think it was somewhere in France, we compared our short-snorters. Of course, mine was much longer than his. He, the 'big army song writer,' didn't like that at all!"

I asked when she thought she would get permission to travel to Berlin to see her mother.

"General Gavin is doing everything! He is a *sweet* man, and then I can see him again. Naturally, Jean is jealous. He is sure I had an affair with him during the war. But I didn't—he didn't ask me. Of course, Jean doesn't believe me when I tell him I only have a fan-type crush on my general. Where are you being sent after this?"

"I have to report to Special Services in Frankfurt," I answered.

"Oh, what a terrible place *that* is! Like a

giant PX! They have everything! Because it is Eisenhower's 'supreme' headquarters! Very hoity-toity! Even in the war, he always had all the comforts of home, no matter where he was. Terrible man, the whole war he stayed so far back, he never heard a shot!''

I left for Frankfurt, where I worked for the Armed Forces Radio with a very talented GI Joe—freckle-faced grin, bouncy charm, loaded with charisma, by the name of Mickey Rooney, then rejoined *The Front Page* on our continued tour through Germany.

My mother, smart in her uniform, now all army, even to service ribbons, no sign of a USO insignia anywhere, carrying the special patent-leather case containing her musical saw, was met at Berlin's airport by an elegant woman in a gray-tailored suit, tie, veiled hat, and silver fox—her mother. They embraced. Her mother had serious news for her. My father's parents had been thrown out of their house, interned in a refugee camp in the Russian sector. They had sent a pitiable letter to her in Berlin, begging for permission to come and stay with her. My mother immediately asked General Gavin to issue her travel orders through restricted occupied zones to find them. While waiting, she did her two shows a day and wrote to my father, as always in German:

Berlin–Chalottenburg
Thursday, 27 Sept. '45

My Darling,

Sometimes life is very hard—even for me. Was supposed to have travel orders for Thuringen from the Russians early this morning—but didn't get them. So I went home (How many "Homes" have I had already? This one is Klopstockstrasse—15A in Zehlendorf West), and am now waiting if at 3 p.m. the orders come and can leave early tomorrow morning! Time against human life! I should have been a nurse. They never have to explain why they help people regardless of their nationality. Remember how I used to say one day I'll cry my eyes out because I can't speak Russian? So now I will stand there and try to put all my pleas into my eyes—but I am afraid that they have so often been prostituted by film—they will not be able to communicate what my heart is saying. My mother answered your parents' postcard of Aug. 23 immediately— where they told her they could come to her—which is still allowed until the 30th. Since the 6th of August they have been in the Refugee Camp.

Papilein, how sad this world is—our house at 54 still stands and although it is full of shell holes, there are red geraniums on our balcony. No. 135 only has walls left— is completely gutted—its balcony just hangs there and every day my mother searched in the ruins, and on top of the rubble and ashes, there lay that bronze mask of my face completely intact—for a long time she sat there and cried! I take her everything to eat I can find. Since I've been here, I've only eaten bread. Look like an old soup-chicken—with a shriveled neck. All the people we knew are in Vienna. Heinrich George (Big Nazi) shovels coal for the Russians! The Three-Penny Opera with Kate Kühl and Hupsi is playing. As I have two shows a day, I can't go. Femina Theatre on the Mollendorf Platz has *My Sister Eileen*. The Kaiser Wilhelm Memorial Church is bombed out, Bahnhof Zoo, Joachimthaler, Taumentzinnstrasse—all in ashes. Friedenau and here outside the city, everything still stands, nearly all. The Felsing store still stands. The Russians stole all the watches. For 5 days, they broke in and rifled the safe. Now Mutti repairs clocks and my old glass beads lie on a counter in the window. The big clock outside was stolen, too, and Mutti put up a wood one—that she painted! Claire Waldorf, who was not allowed to perform by the Nazis, is still in Reichenhall and doesn't have an apartment any more. All day long it thunders—like in the war. They are dynamiting to level the ruins—I haven't had the courage yet to go to my school in the Nürenbergerstrasse. One is already sad enough about one's lost youth when seeing old places again—without seeing this, this is just too terrible.

The Berliners love me, bring me every-
thing from photos to their rations of herring.
The language sounds familiar when I walk
through the streets and the children play
"Heaven and Hell" amongst the rubble.
The Marmonhaus still stands and because it
is in the English Sector, they are showing
Rembrandt with Charles Laughton.

My Heart—I hope by the time you get
this letter, you will already have good news
from me by cable. I will stop at nothing—
absolutely nothing (Don't tell Jean this!)—
to get your parents out.

With all my love, Your Mutti

Paris, October 9, 1945

Papilein,

Don't know where to start. You must
have by now your parents' letter that I
mailed from Berlin. When Mutti received
the card from them in Martinroda, I immediately started to contact the Russians for
permission to go there. That took three
days. When I finally had the travel orders,
which *nobody* else could get, I left at five
in the morning, went to Leipzig, Jena, Weimar, Erfurt, and down to Martinroda. It
took six hours as the autobahn stops all the
time because of bomb craters. Had blankets, food, clothes in the car, jumped out,
ran for barrack 3 and there was told they
had left! You can imagine my despair. Went
to Arisbadt, Amstrat, but as it was Saturday

afternoon, all offices with the files where they might have gone were closed until Monday! I was told that they had been evacuated to families around the district. I went to the Russian Commander and arranged that Monday morning the information would be phoned to Berlin. That was all I could do as my travel pass was only for one day—and I had a show to do that night! I cannot describe to you the trip back, the disappointment, the helplessness, and the racing through rain against time.

We made it in time for the show. I stood as shaking and dirty on the stage as I will ever be. That night I had another car to take me home and the driver said that he thought your parents were at my mother's house, as he had brought my breakfast rations there as usual and had seen them. I nearly fell out of the car. I found them there! They had traveled all the way to Berlin just on that one postcard from Mutti. Now they were in another misery! They had gone to the police to register, where they were told they could not get a ration card and would have to go to another refugee camp if they wanted to be fed in the winter. They were shaking with fright and said that now they would have to die. They told me how terrible the camp had been—bad enough for them to walk from Czechoslovakia all the way to Berlin without a penny, and they asked only that I explain to you that they have no other way out. I told them to sit tight and raced to do my two shows. Then I went to Gavin. It was he who had made that rule, because Berlin is so overcrowded and they have not enough food for the winter! By the next morning, I had heavy labor ration cards which give much more than the normal ones, and an apartment! I did not take the apartment as Mutti wants to take care of them, but later, if they want it, they can get it. At two p.m. that day, I left by plane. OK?

I was so exhausted mentally, seeing, hearing all those horrible things they had to tell—the nerves, afraid I would not succeed, no food for two weeks (I took everything from the table in a shower cap in my bag for them and Mutti before that), that I nearly collapsed. Besides, I had other emotional troubles about my private life.

OI YOI YOI is my life messed up! I wish I could stay with the Army—There everything is clear and easy.

Gavin could be Abelard, you know!

I love you
Mutti

Of course, my mother adored the legend of Heloise and her undying love for her Abelard.

On the 11th of October, General Gavin wrote to her from Berlin, signing his letter, "Your Jimmie." Some widows are very protective of their dear departed. Especially where love letters to other women are concerned. So, the

General's outpourings must be longingly imagined instead of read. Don't blame me—blame the laws of copyright.

During this time, my mother continued her life with Gabin, convincing him, when necessary, of her "true" love, half-heartedly prepared their French film she was really not interested in, while yearning for the organized life of the army and the commanding strength of compassionate generals.

> Papilein,
> . . . I wish you were here to tell me if I am doing right in thinking that I could not live like this forever. He has no friends except sports people and people who work for him. There is no mental food around anymore. If you were here I would not need anybody. . . . But when are you going to come?
>
> I am living in a tiny hotel, cramped in, without a maid, I do the washing, ironing, sewing because I don't make any money.
>
> Hollywood is decent compared to the business people here. The Jewish film producers are not back yet and the "goys" just don't understand how to make good pictures and treat artists.
>
> I am stuck on the Army I guess. Hemingway is expected here for the Nürnberg trials. Hope I can spend some time with him.
>
> What do you think I should do? Abelard flies in here today to see me. This has be-

come quite serious. He is a wonderful man. Wrote me yesterday about having to go to England—to thank the villages where his men trained before Normandy. Sweet—no? Also worried about the 36,000 troops stationed in Berlin, said potential dynamite there and wants to stay—until British general can take over, that he would personally talk to the Commander of the 78th Division when they take over Berlin to take care of your parents. They are asking the War Department to give me the Legion of Merit.

Thank God I can work for the Army, otherwise I would go nuts.

I am still at the Claridge, hoping through the Embassy or the French to get a room somewhere else. That's why I feel a bit better now. Jean had wrecked my nerves for good when I returned from America. If one has a little hope around the corner, it is easier. He is coming to Paris Tuesday for one day. I called him Abelard in my last letter, you know who I mean, don't you? The 82nd? His name is very close to Jean's. Said he loves me too!

Gabin wrote her:

. . . I know that you are in love,
What you don't know is how much I suffer,
                                                J.

On the 6th of November, my mother's mother died in her sleep. Through military channels, my mother got a message through to me in Stuttgart. I immediately requested permission to leave the play in order to travel the three hundred miles to Berlin. I thought my mother might need me, that I should be by her side when she buried her mother.

As USO plays were produced under Equity rules, I was under union contract to perform, and my request to leave the play was denied. When the company manager gasped: "You can't leave! The show must go on!" I had the once-in-a-lifetime chance to reply "Why?" and left. I had no travel orders, no papers to move from one city to another—a very serious offense in occupied Germany in the winter of '45, but I was determined to make it to Berlin in time for my grandmother's funeral. I finally reached Berlin late at night, only to find that I had missed the funeral by a few hours. I asked General Gavin's aide-de-camp where I could find Miss Dietrich's billet and realized that he was choosing his words very carefully indeed. Suddenly, it dawned on me that my mother was already being comforted and that my overly dramatic dash to her side had not been necessary. So I inquired of the embarrassed colonel if he could possibly requisition a billet for me for the night. He did immediately, repeating all the while in a voice full of exaggerated sincerity that the only reason why he hadn't rushed me to my dear mother's side had been orders issued that "no one was allowed to disturb Miss Dietrich" that night! I assured him that I had no intention of demanding to see my mother, that I understood "the situation" perfectly, which relieved him enormously. He saluted and marched smartly into the night, his watchdog duty done. I went to bed, decided that as long as I had defied my union, my profession, and the laws of the army of occupation to get to Berlin, I could at least see my grandparents; I might even try to acquire a Jeep and driver to take me to my Aunt Liesel in Belsen. Why a former inmate would remain in such a place was beyond my comprehension.

My mother had not appeared by the time I walked through Berlin that cold winter morning. A shell of a town, ugly and scarred, filled with seemingly beaten people who shuffled amongst the ruins, their heads low to hide the hatred that burned behind their eyes. Everywhere women were clearing, piling brick upon brick, neatly organizing the rubble. I had seen this often through Italy. There it was done as haphazard clearing of roads, whereas in Germany, one had the distinct impression each brick was being saved for the future—to build another Reich.

My American uniform marked me; they mumbled in their Berlin slang that they had no way of knowing I understood. Some bowed to my uniform as they passed me, making sure their mask of deference was set in place. It was quite obvious that the Russian soldier with his ever-ready carbine was feared and therefore merited respect, while the American soldier, handing out his ever-ready Hershey bars, was beneath contempt.

I broke the law, traded my army ration of American cigarettes for cuts of fresh meat on the black market by the Brandenburg Gate, my officer's liquor allowance for precious carrots, onions, and a whole loaf of real German bread. By the time I arrived at the apartment where my grandparents lived, I had the makings of a sumptuous stew stowed in my musette bag. Cautiously, my grandmother opened the door. How small she was! Seeing a uniform, she shrank back, eyes wide.

"It's me . . . Grandmother, Heidede—Really! It's me, Rudi's child," I said softly, not wanting to startle her. She just looked at me, clutching the doorknob. Her hair was all white.

"Grandmother, may I come in? I have fresh vegetables and meat." The door opened wider, I stepped into the dark hall. It smelled of furniture wax, just like I remembered, the special one my other grandmother had taught me how to properly polish with.

"Rosa? Who was that at the door?" my grandfather limped into view, no longer tall, no longer strong—a bent man whose age had become unfathomable.

"Who are you? What are you doing in this house?" he growled.

"She says she is Rudi's child," my grand-mother whispered.

"I am, Grandfather. Really I am! See—I have brought you fresh food, all I could get . . ." I rattled on, not knowing what to say to make them accept me.

A little hand reached up, touched the insignia on my sleeve

"I have to wear a uniform because I act in a play for the soldiers . . ." I caught her hand. "It's me, Heidede. I love you, Grandmother—like I always did, remember?"

She reached up, pulled my face down to her, searched my eyes, and burst into tears. I held her smallness in my arms and cried for all the years of loving lost, the childhood that could have been, that never was. My grandfather moved beside us, I felt his big hand on my hand, and I was a little girl again in a sky-blue dirndl come to visit.

I told them about their son. Happy, good things, what they wanted to hear, making up what would please them, imbuing my father with a goodness I wished he had. They told me of their gratitude to my wonderful mother, of her goodness, and I shattered none of their necessary illusions. I could not stay long. My last memory is of them framed in that big oak door, a man and a woman grown old with a love as young as when I first knew them. They died the next winter within hours of each other. They never did like being separated for long.

In my best beguiling "daughter of" manner, I asked the general's aide for a Jeep and driver to take me to Belsen. It was cold, we drove fast. My driver, fully armed, didn't like being on a deserted Nazi autobahn amidst a dense pine forest. He only broke speed when bomb craters necessitated detours. I fully agreed with him— the metallic winter sky, the ominous silence, that dark forest, the memories so new of what this joyless place had been witness to and where we were headed, all made me shudder and want to have it over with.

Up a flight of stairs in a cozy apartment above a movie house, I found my aunt installed in a deep armchair. I bent down, held her close, and felt her healthy plumpness. Her eyes were fearful but they had been so since I could remember. Her attitude still timid and hesitant. She had not changed! This startling continuity of her so normal state shook me. This woman was intact. No concentration camp cadaver here, no still-breathing leftover skeleton. This had never been one of Jo's specters! What twisted script had my mother written now—to evade yet another truth from being known? This time, aided and abetted by the British as well as the American military? I gave my aunt the precious rations I had brought. No longer life-giving, now simply luxuries. Answered her usual fluttering questions about her beloved Pussy Cat in the context she wanted to hear them, shared her tea and cakes and loved her still. It was not her fault that I was angry. She was the victim she had always been, just not the one I had expected. I kissed her good-bye, my time was up and I had to leave.

We drove fast, it was cold. My fury burned deep inside me. I wanted to scream, bellow my rage, ask forgiveness of all those tortured souls whose misery still clung in that evil air, whose suffering had somehow been desecrated by an outrageous lie for personal convenience by one I was related to. You can't take the agony of a people and use it for your own aggrandizement and be allowed to get away with it I cried, knowing that Dietrich already had. My aunt lived in the town of Belsen until the day she died—it was her home.

My mother never changed her story. The power of "the legend" was such that whenever Dietrich dramatically announced that she had found her sister in Belsen, the listener had an instantaneous vision of gas ovens and cyanide showers—and she let them.

This time I had official travel orders to rejoin my company. My mother complained that as I had arrived too late for the funeral, I should at least be allowed to stay with her now, cried as she kissed me good-bye. Neither one of us mentioned her sister. I left, knowing she was very well looked after by her Abelard. A few weeks later, her letter caught up with me somewhere in Germany:

Paris, Thanksgiving 45

My Angel,

After you left I was so terribly miserable there that I couldn't get away fast enough. Three nice colonels from China-Burma drove me to Frankfurt. Then the train to Paris at six p.m. Without those three nice men I would not have been able to do it, but they took care of me like a baby.

Once back in my miserable room, the entire weight of all that had happened fell suddenly on me. I don't think that I was quite aware that my mother had died.

If you could only get out of the show and live with me. I need your advice for so many things.

Two days after I arrived, at five in the morning, Jean knocked at my door. He sat down and said, "Let me have it. I am prepared to hear everything." I couldn't tell him. Didn't have the courage, maybe.

Abelard arrived yesterday and was so sweet and tender and terribly kind and quite different from in Berlin, where he had to be so discreet and correct and impersonal in front of all his staff to whom his loving me would be misconstrued as a love affair.

And there I stood and was in love with him all over again. He is leaving middle

December—and my wish came true. Their big parade on Fifth Avenue beginning in January. He was so happy about it—like a child. They'll all get new scarves and caps and they'll be "the best-looking soldiers of any army" when they march down Fifth Avenue. This all is still very confidential.

Then I thought of poor Jean while I was having dinner with Abelard at Korniloff's (remember?) and wished you were there to help me make order in my head and heart.

All my love. I love you terribly.

Mutti

She enclosed her note from Gabin:

My Grande—

I have just left you. I realize I have lost you forever. . . . I know that this letter is stupid and ridiculous in such a moment when you have such a deep grief. Please forgive me. I am deeply sad too. I don't know what to do next. I hurt, I hurt so much. I feel alone. I don't know what's going to happen. Doesn't matter! Adieu. I will never come back.

J.

She wrote my father:

Paris, December 1, '45

Papilein,

I have moved to the Elysées-Park. I sent this new address to you with a pilot who flew back to America three days ago.

Gavin goes home Christmas for the big parade. I have trouble here. Have no idea what to do. Where to live—and with whom. You never answered my September letters so I don't know what you think.

Love.

M.

Paris, December 5, '45

Beloved Papi,

Thank God your letter arrived. I was almost going crazy.

I have never been so alone and lost. Paris without you was from the beginning a strange town, but now it is worse than China. You can't even begin to realize how I live. True, I have lived in worse places during the war. But that was different. For one thing, everybody was young around you and one laughed about the misery of it all. And then one is not alone. But alone I have no more sense of humor.

It looks as if we fought the war for nothing. The people have changed so terribly, the great spirit that was there during the war has gone or maybe was never there in civilians. In Germany it is the same. Hitler has left his mark. Everyone still denounces his friends, only now to the other side, to get some good out of it. Nobody needs business and everyone is impolite. I mean the hotels in particular. Finally, through Adi Hollander who knows someone at the Préfecture, I have this two-room, unheated suite at the Elysées-Park. It is charming and cozy and I overlook the Champs-Elysées. I have, with a lot of tips, a wood fire burning in one room. The other one is ice cold. Most French people still have their apartments with black-market coal heat and their "pied à terre" and the swanky cars drive around.

Taxis are there only for deported and wounded although the people who ride in them don't look it. A carriage takes ages and costs: Fouquet's to Lanvin 200 Fr. 4$, which is coming and going too much. This is just to tell you how I live. I found no mention in your letter of Abelard. Maybe you are being careful, which I appreciate as Lin was not and wrote: "I was happy that Jim was with you," which is the letter Jean found, behind Kater's picture and he tore up everything in my miserable room as he had a suspicion about my staying in Berlin so long. And we have been parted ever since. And I was really behaving very well. Had no idea of anything else but, as you know, to live with him for good. But it was quite impossible. Scenes all the time. He had the new complex that I did not like France. You know how Jean sees only the black side. He now has a young pretty actress called Marie Mauban, he takes her out every night and thinks I am with my "Generals." He treated me so terribly, accusing me of sleeping with everybody I talked to, that I knew I could never live with him.

Then, in Berlin, with all the emotional up-set, I ran into the so suddenly open arms of "Abelard" like into a haven. And I did not sleep with him. Which does not make me any purer. Then he wrote me wonderful letters and wanted it to be the "great thing or nothing" and when it happened with Mutti he brought me there and was kind and did not push himself into the picture. He calls every night from Reims where the camp is and he will come here on the 18th and leaves for New York on the 21st. He will call you. Although he is very shy he promised to do it. Just say that you know of my admiration and devotion for him. So as to make it easier for him. He will get a divorce not because of me—his daughter is twelve. They live in Washington. He does not know what he will be assigned to. For your information he is the pioneer of the paratroopers, started with a handful of men in '41 against all odds. Went through the Sicily, Anzio Campaign, Normandy, Holland. Only Division which has four Combat Jumps. The red things on his shoulders are the Belgian and Dutch Fourageres. Maybe they will have the French by the time they get home. But for that they would need one more shoulder. He was born 1907, I am nine months older than he, see?

Actually she was six years older than her Abelard at the time, but then arithmetic always confused my mother.

I just made myself some tea, made a little sack of an old piece of panty, tastes awful, like soap. The food you sent was wonderful. Find out when one can send clothes officially, because civilians can't wear uniform things and no shop is allowed to dye them.

Got all the books. How do you like Remarque's new book [*The Arch of Triumph*]? Didn't you laugh that "Jean" kills me in the end? I wondered how Boni would solve the problem because he couldn't wait until I first played it out for him. It is badly translated and the love scenes are too "literattur" and boring, but it is a good film story with action once it gets started. He paints me worse than I am in order to make himself more interesting and he succeeds. But everything from Fouquet's to Scheherazade to Antibes, Chateau Madrid, Cherbourg, Lancaster Hotel, even "Jo" on the boat. Of course, he couldn't make it a woman and the actor he really makes ridiculous is in it. I am much more interesting than Joan Madou.

Jean has a wonderful story he is making for Gaumont. He wants me to play it, now that the other film is off. Two in a row together would not have been good. If I make that picture, I will stay here. First to be here as long as Kater is here, and then for that kind of a part it is worth it. Should it not work out and Gaumont wants a French woman, which might be an argument, then I will come back. No reason to sit alone in a hotel in Paris. I will cable and write. Don't worry—my stars are wrong, that's all. Can't last forever. Carroll Righter has been right again. I told Jean to have the contract signed before September 12 and he did not. Righter said it was important because after that date there would be trouble. He was right. They have paid me only my expenses since Oct. 15. I hope I get the rest. I will let you know. Don't worry. I am tired, inside, not physically, emotionally.

All my love as forever,

Mutti

December 7 '45

Papilein,

I am going to Biarritz for a week. First to get away from here—am really too lonely, every evening, reading old Kaestner books and Rilke. That's fine if you are quiet inside. But I am too nervous after all the misery. I'll give lectures on films for the GIs at the University there and sing in the evening. Abelard called from London last night. They are moving there but he will come here on the 18th and leave on the 21st.

Was with Chevalier for a few hours yesterday. He stars at the ABC and then goes on to New York to sing for the Shuberts. He said that I was the climax of his life. He is so very much like Jean when he talks. He also said that he could understand Jean's jealousy. Must be typically French.

All love for now. Mutti

For my twenty-first birthday, my mother wrote me a letter using one of her precious sheets of crested stationery. Whether the Dietrichs' or von Losches', I never did find out, and she never commented on it—just used it with aristocratic flourish when a "grand" occasion warranted it. As far as I know, it was the only memento she took for herself from her mother's house.

Still in Paris, being Jean's *"Ma grande"* while waiting for her Abelard, my mother went to a play, saw Gérard Philipe and swooned, told everyone how beautiful he was, what a brilliant actor he was, every night sat through his play—hugging her knees, on the edge of her seat—entranced. Went backstage, glowed, draped herself against his sinuous frame, looked up into his handsome face and—melted. He, very young, was flattered, enchanted, and returned the compliments.

ON A COLD WINTER NIGHT, we did our play in a deserted schoolhouse in Bad Hamburg. Icy rain beat against the fogged window panes. There was something ominous about all those regimented desks, still in place, where only a short time ago tow-headed youths had been indoctrinated. Their spirits hovered. I ran my hand along a scarred desk and felt the sharp outline of a swastika. Christmas Eve is not a time for such feelings.

In January, General Gavin wrote from Fort Bragg that he had called my father and had a visit with him in New York, adding: "A good man and I can understand your deep and understanding friendship."

Having done our six months, our show was sent home on a huge Victory ship jam-packed with jubilant GIs. My father was at the New York pier to greet me—without Teddy at his side, somehow incomplete.

A letter from my mother awaited me:

Paris, February 10, '46

Angel,

I am so blue it isn't even funny. I have lost all my last straggling ends of sense of humor. With you gone, nothing seems to matter. This Europe I loved so much has dwindled down to some vague form of memory. I still long for it, forget that I am here, and then realizing that it too has probably gone forever.

Only when I walk up the Champs-Elysées and see the Arc is it still the same place and just as beautiful. I am always looking for the Beautiful. That is probably what is wrong with me. During the war there was Beauty in the people but now all that seems to have gone. Everything is ugly. Everybody thinks of how he can outdo the other and schemes to get around the law and thinks nothing of it. Maybe all this is natural. I don't like it. And that's why there is no joy. Nobody is gay. They are too busy scheming to make money and keep it. Maybe that is natural too.

When you read this letter you will be in your "Holy Land" and probably you are hating the civilians just as I did.

Don't forget me. Here life with Jean is very difficult.

I love you more than life.

Mutti

Back in my father's penitentiary, Tami was my first concern. Her condition was deplorable. The many forced abortions endured over the years to ensure no scandal sullied the purity of my mother's marriage had finally taken their catastrophic toll. While my mother and father still believed that these "shocking" consequences of Tami's love for my father were entirely her fault, and scolded her for her irresponsible behavior, Tami, the conditioned victim, accepted the guilt and proceeded to punish herself for it. False pregnancies had begun to appear and disappear, first accompanied by euphoric joy, then black despair. As her emotional pendulum swung out of control, her desperate need for drugs had become imperative to escape from her worst nightmare, her own reality. To acquire them became the goal of her daily existence. When she ran along the streets of New York, from one drug-store to another, buying amphetamines, stuffing her handbag as she ran, her frenzy making her oblivious to her surroundings, as she searched for yet another and another source, I would fol-low, catch her, coax her into coming home with me, hoping we would make it back before my father returned and punished her for once again disobeying his strict order not to leave his apart-ment without his permission.

When she pummeled her bloated belly, trying to kill the child she believed was inside her, I grabbed her frail wrists, held her as she shivered from shock at her own bestiality. When she tried to ram a bread knife up inside her, I tore it from her hand, held her as she screamed—reentering reality, cradled her frail body as she wept her sorrows against my heart.

I tried to discuss her "treatment" with my father. I was highly critical of the doctors my mother had hired with instructions to "do some-thing to make my friend, Miss Matul, behave—normally." But my father refused to discuss her, adding that if I insisted on questioning the ex-pertise of respected medical authorities that my mother, out of "the goodness of her great heart," had found and was paying for, I could find myself another place to live. If I left, Tami would be utterly alone, completely at his mercy. I kept my mouth shut, cleaned her, fed her, guarded her, loved her, and stayed.

My mother's letters continued to arrive. Gabin, knowing how my mother loved Remarque's Cézanne watercolors, had given her two, throwing in a Degas for good measure.

> . . . at first I did not want to accept them and then sometimes I think that I am very stupid always feeling like that. Jean has so much property here—is really a rich man.

A scrawny street urchin in a little black dress became the sensation of postwar Paris. With a big guttural sound, she sang of suffering, lost love, and impossible dreams. Hands on hips, legs braced against the onslaught of life, she epitomized the indomitable spirit of the French masses, and they adored her. Of course, my mother fell under Piaf's spell, and as always when enamored, mothered her, showered her with presents, advice, and whatever drugs her new love required. Gabin, always appreciative of raw talent, agreed that my mother had good reasons for her crush on Piaf the performer, but reserved the right to his opinion of Piaf the woman.

The script they had been working on finally became a reality, and they began shooting *Martin Roumagnac*. A film so full of self-conscious embarrassment, it is amazing they didn't stop after the first rushes and walk away from it. Gabin, his wonderful unself-conscious acting stilted even in his own language, hobbled by tricks and contrived characterization. Dietrich is just plain awful. Trying ever so hard to be "provincial, small-town French," she achieved a look and acting style that made you want to take scissors and, like a paper doll, cut her out around the edges. Jean must have seen it, for he tried, worked with her on the dialogue: "Don't speak so perfectly. Pull the syllables together, you are not playing a baroness." When she had a scene without him, he sat beneath the camera, coaching her. But even "Gabin and Dietrich" together could not lift this film out of its mire of mediocrity. They had been lovers too long for any vibrant sensuality to register on the screen and perhaps save the film.

When her old pal director from *The Lady Is Willing* called and offered her one hundred thousand dollars to play a gypsy, *and* at Paramount, she accepted without a moment's hesitation. Phoned Nellie to prepare a black wig "with long bangs to give the look of mystery, and lots of shine to give the look of hair *greasy*. Gypsies always smear their hair with goat grease—that's why they stink so. If the hair shines, it will look 'real' gypsy!"

Of course, Gabin didn't want her to leave. They quarreled:

Martin Roumagnac was filmed in France in 1946. Its stars, Gabin and Dietrich, tried, but to no avail. They had planned to marry after the film but, by the time it was finished, my mother was in love with another Jimmie and blamed Gabin.

One of my mother's prides: the day she marched, wearing her medals, in the military parade commemorating the liberation of Paris.

"But I need *money*! American money! *Real Money!*" Having made up her mind to leave him, yet always with an eye on "history" and to make certain that Gabin would be the one blamed, she wrote out all her reasons in one of her trusty notebooks:

> Paris, July 25, '46
> This is a story which I write down so I don't forget the facts of this strange end to my life with Jean.
> I also write it down so that I can prove to myself later that I did not dream it up or elaborate on it as time went by. . . .

Jean only sent a final letter, as always in French, delivered to her hotel. For "an uneducated peasant," as my mother so often referred to Gabin, rather beautifully expressed. My father thought so too—that's why he kept it safe after my mother sent it to him. A long true letter from a man who loved her—that ended with:

> . . . Ma Grande, listen, there is a commonplace remark that has been said thousands of times, "You have been, you are, and will remain my one and only true love." I know, this has already been said to you but, believe me, it is said by a man who has a lot of experience. . . . I hope you will appreciate its real value. As I once told you: I would rather lose you alive than lose you dead and unfortunately, I feel I have lost you, al-

though we did have such a good time together. I don't care about what will happen
next, I don't mind what the future holds in
store for me, I just remain with an immense
sorrow, a deep pain within me and an infinite grief. There it is, that's all I wanted you
to know.

J.

The only thing wrong with Gabin was his
character and his love. Both were strong and
unmalleable. Impossible attributes when in love
with Dietrich, whose entire emotional structure
was built on quicksand that she shifted to suit
herself—then blaming her victim for what she
herself had manipulated.

Jean Gabin walked away from his damna-
tion and I was proud of him.

SHOWTIME

A NEVADA divorce became possible, and I left my wounded Tami for my own selfish needs. As my mother was paying the legal costs and required a trained handmaiden, I was told to report to her in Hollywood after being granted my "freedom." We moved into a little house in Beverly Hills. All "bungalowy," a happy nest fit for contented mother and child. As the one bedroom contained an enormous bed, she absolutely refused to let me sleep on the equally huge couch in the white and petal-green living room, insisting we share the bed. I knew I wouldn't be there for long, a new romance was sure to come along soon and I'd get the couch.

"Good morning, Miss Dietrich. Good morning, Miss Hei— Oh! Excuse me, Miss Maria!"

We drove through the Paramount gate. The dawn pink, the air crisp. We had been assigned our old dressing room. Nellie, now the head of the Hair-Dressing Department, stood waiting, wig block with greasy wig under her arm; Crosby crooned, saws hummed, the perfume of sawdust, that charged hush before a studio woke . . . I was home!

If ever *Golden Earrings* is remembered, it

is for the look of Dietrich in that black wig and matching face. She out-gypsied every gypsy that ever was or ever will be. That hair dripped grease. The heavily black-rimmed eyes, with their inner line of stark white in a modeled nut-brown face so mysterious, could see into any future in any crystal ball. Barefoot, beragged, beshawled, bejeweled, bracelets, earrings, gold coins jangling, she smeared grime and dirt on herself, plucked fish heads from suspended black iron pots around smoky campfires, stank to high heaven, and had a wonderful time. She even had a costar to make fun of again.

"Now, really! *That* they pay! *That* is considered a star? Can't be! Probably Mitch has a crush on him and that's why he wants him in the picture!"

Through the whole film, Ray Milland very carefully kept out of Dietrich's way, appearing at her side only when a scene called for it, and then you could see the clammy sweat begin to form on his gypsy makeup. It drove his makeup man crazy, he kept having to run into shots to "blot." This moisture was not due to passionate desire held in agonizing check for his gypsy woman, but from trying desperately not to throw up in her face. The day of the campfire scene— that did it! My mother plunged her hand into the pot, stirred it around, extricated a big juicy fish head and sucked out its bulging eyes. Under his dark makeup, Milland turned dead white— and ran. I think she rather enjoyed turning her costar's stomach—it became a game to see what she could come up with to make him sprint to the bathroom.

In the evenings, going home in the car, she would be deep in thought, then murmur:

"You know, tomorrow, in the wagon scene—I could itch my crotch. All gypsies have lice. The petticoats pulled up, against the brown naked leg will look very good, then move the hand down the leg, pull off a hunk of bread, put it in his mouth . . . very gypsy! Shows she loves him that she gives him her food. I told Mitch when we do the disguising scene, I'm going to use my goose grease to smear him with . . . so it looks *real*!"

In later years, she always referred to Ray Milland as "That awful Englishman with the delicate stomach, who was finally taught to act by Billy Wilder and then never did anything again after that 'drunk' picture."

The hottest new find on the Paramount lot, an athletic young man fresh from his triumphant debut in a gangster film—*he* interested her in an entirely different way. Soon our weekends revolved around making him happy. As he was married at the time, he would arrive around ten in the morning and have to leave by five in the afternoon, so I never got to sleep on the couch.

After seeing to it that his favorite foods were in the refrigerator, helping my mother put her special Irish linen sheets on "our" big bed, I made myself scarce, reappearing when I knew our young actor had gone. As handmaiden to the queen, my role had not changed, except that now I was considered old enough to listen to sexual tidbits of her romances, as well as changing the sheets.

She rhapsodized about her latest's physique. His amply muscled torso held special appeal. Between filming, I ordered gifts for him that my mother decided this "future star" required. The gold watch, the Cartier cuff links, the cigarette case, Hemingway to lift his mind from his "sideshow mentality," as she put it, up to her superior level, the cashmeres, the silk shirts, and opulent dressing gowns. One day, I was sorting the bills in the dressing room, when she turned away from painting on her gypsy eyes and said:

"Sweetheart. He wants a gramophone— No! What are they called now? Record players?— Yes, that's it. He is dying for one with all the 'very latest inventions built in.' That's what he told me. Can you get it for him? . . . The best they make and have it all ready on Saturday so that he can take it home with him in the car when he leaves. He can tell his wife the Studio gave it to him, so when you find it, buy it under the name of Mitchell Leisen—they can charge it to him—I already talked to Mitch about it."

Soon after the latest hi-fi presentation, our weekend visitor lost interest and faded out of our life. Over the years, my mother often referred to this "interlude" in her life as, "the time we made that terrible film with that English bore— What was his name? And that son of a bitch went to bed with me for a record player!"

He became one of the few lovers she never saw again, who did not remain a lifelong supplicant.

During the filming of *Golden Earrings*, we had a strike.

"A strike—for what? Who is allowed to strike in Hollywood? We make pictures—not cars," said our 1930s Movie Star and meant it. As a matter of fact, it had confused her for years that she now paid union dues and had something called an SAG card. "What is SAG?" she asked me, very puzzled.

"The Screen Actors' Guild, Mutti."

"Oh—I thought it was a union?"

"Well—it is."

"No, it is *not*! Says 'guild'—that's when actors get together, like that place in New York, where they all are so proud they belong to— You know— What's it called? Something . . . monk . . . something . . ."

"You mean the Friars Club?"

"Yes! That's the one! In Hollywood they call it 'guild.' In New York they call it 'club,' but it's the same thing. They get together to have drinks, sit in leather armchairs, and talk about themselves!" So, when her union, which was supposed to be only a 'social club,' informed all the actors working on the Paramount lot that they risked breaking a strike if they came to work, my mother was outraged and refused.

"Mutti, please listen. The strikers are lining the gates. There are rumors they are threatening to throw acid in the actors' faces if they insist on crossing the picket line." *That* got her attention.

"I am going to see Mitch about this stupidity," and she marched out of the dressing room.

The Studio was battened down for a siege. The companies of all pictures in production were ordered to stay on the lot, remain inside the Studio until the strike was settled. The Property Department heeded the call to arms—trucks hauled mattresses and cots out of their storage lofts and distributed them, pillows, blankets, and sheets were issued, canteens were set up for dinners and breakfasts and an entire Hollywood studio went camping.

In the Writers' Building, cots, pretty typists, and booze mingled in erudite abandon. The Make-Up and Hair-Dressing Departments merged, set up their cots in one, then threw a party in the other. Dressing rooms became a fiercely contested possession; the stars having their own private ones reigned supreme. Everyone who had ever thought of sleeping with someone on the lot got their wish. They were "locked in—by order of the Studio," the excuse of all time—to live one night within one's fantasies *and* get away with it!

My mother's dressing-room door stayed securely locked, but Nellie didn't stand guard—she was busy somewhere else. I had my studio bicycle and rode around, listening to the radios blaring "Zip-a-dee-doo-dah," taking in the gay sights and squeals of delight!

The next morning, disheveled, bleary-eyed, and dazed, the Studio went back to cranking out its product, not quite sure they could take another night like the last one. My mother really did not blossom from one-night stands, especially when a very bad, very untalented actor had shared it, and so was in a lousy mood. She was drawing the white line down her nose when I came back from dawn breakfast.

"Well—did Milland get you?" my mother asked, her gypsy eyes fixing me through the mirror. She had been making these innuendos through the whole film, irked that I wasn't having an affair with someone. Anyone would have done. Just as long as my behavior was worse than hers, it would make her feel more the "lady." I hated to disappoint her; besides, anyone who had spent a whole night with Murvyn Vye deserved something, so I gave her a present:

"Oh, he wasn't good at all," and seeing her satisfied smile, left to pick up her gypsy skirts from Wardrobe.

We had just come home from the Studio when the telephone rang. I answered it; that French growl I knew well, I passed her the phone. She said "Oui," her face quite calm.

Jean told her he was getting married. Her face whitened, she clutched the receiver, she began pleading with him. He was making a terrible mistake, no woman he had suddenly found "like that" could be good enough, could ever make him happy enough to warrant marrying her.

"*Mon amour*, sleep with her if you have to but MARRY? WHY? Is it all just to have a child, that you feel you have to be so bourgeois?"

But no matter what she said, how much she begged him, reminding him how he had loved her, how she still loved him completely, unconditionally, she couldn't sway him. Finally, he hung up on her. She put down the receiver. She looked drawn and completely lost.

"It's a mood," she whispered, "another one of Jean's moods. A trick, to make me come back to him. It wasn't necessary. All he had to do was call, tell me he loved me, and I would have rushed back to him—*after* we finished the film."

That evening we were scheduled to go to a

big party at somebody's Bel Air mansion. I don't remember whose. Travis, now a disenchanted man running his own dress business, designing clothes for poolside cocktail parties and bored executive wives, had designed a special evening dress for the occasion, of palest blue chiffon, its trailing oversize stole bordered in blue fox. I, too, had a special dress, a spectacular black silk jersey made for me by Irene, so it must have been a very important affair. All I remember of that night are illuminated gardens that stretched for miles, playing marble fountains, the who's who of Hollywood dripping jewels and charm, and my mother floating about in a pale blue daze, getting blind drunk. It is my first memory of what was to become the tragic reality of the years ahead, of picking my mother up off the ground, hustling her quickly into a limousine, having her pass out in my arms, getting her safely inside her place of residence, to undress her limp form as she snarled invectives at me. Back then, in the fall of '46, I had been cold sober for twelve whole months and was determined to remain that way forever. In my so-new self-pride and crusader innocence, I believed that I could now help my mother to conquer her demons, but although I tried for more than forty years, I never managed to extricate her from the final dismal pit she dug for herself.

· · ·

MY FATHER WROTE, saying that he had an offer of a job with a French film company and that he was eager to return to Europe. If, after a few months, he found that it worked out, he would give up his apartment in New York to live permanently in Paris. He planned to leave Tami in New York, send for her and their belongings if things went well.

"Good. Finally Papi has something to take him away from Tami's craziness"; and assuring him of her financial support, my mother involved herself in the arrangements.

She did wonderful gypsy portrait-sittings; we packed up the dressing room. The stench of goat grease clung to everything. I felt sorry for whatever star would be occupying it next! Apparently, Jean had not rushed into marriage after all, and so deep, intense astrological discussions began, until my mother was assured the stars were in the right position to return, persuade "the love of her life" that he truly was that and more, do away with all his foolishness, and be his—forever! Poor Jean, I wished him well.

As Carroll Righter advised against flying for all Sagittarians and Capricorns, we took the train to New York.

"Endless! This country never stops, and we used to do this all the time? Why? It takes forever—but then, we used to do a lot of crazy things in the early days—remember that heat, before this air-conditioning? Which is just as bad. Cook or freeze—always American exaggeration."

We still washed at the Blackstone, that hadn't changed.

My mother continued on to France by ship. I remained in New York to look for work in the theater and take care of Tami during my father's absence. A convenient solution for a tricky problem that gave everyone what they wanted: My father got his bachelor trip to Europe, my mother the safety of having someone take on the duties of nurse within the family, thereby eliminating the risk that was always present of possible exposure to the press of Tami's true position in the Dietrich household.

Alone, Tami and I were actually happy at times. Being together, without the powerful presence of our usual taskmasters, was a relief. I searched for the hidden pills, followed her on her daily foraging of unscrupulous pharmacies, fed her, washed her, helped her dress in my mother's cast-off finery, and tried to shield her from harm. I didn't succeed—I just tried.

My mother wrote from the new pride of the Cunard Line, the SS *Queen Elizabeth*:

> Angel,
> These are notes as I think of things I need, not a letter.
> 1. Ask Dr. Peck if the depilatory he spoke about, the one that does not smell, is ready to send.

2. Also need Vitamin C, ascorbic acid, against my red hands.

3. Cream for Papi's hemorrhoids.

I have the same stewardess from the *Bremen* who asked me about "Little Heidede."

Saw *Darling Clementine* yesterday. How terrible—Ford, our greatest director, to make such a bad film! The title is so misleading, too. Gloomy tombstone in slow motion. Today we have *M. Beaucaire*, with that awful Bob Hope.

Unbelievable passengers. Unbelievable boat. I have made a motion to give sunglasses with every passage ticket. The lights are hospital lights and so are the walls. The vibration up at the grill is so strong, your teeth chatter—and you are supposed to dance on a carpet! For that at the grill you pay extra.

Wally Simpson's husband, I mean Mr. Simpson, runs after me and I hide which is difficult with all these bright lights. People stare at me so openly, it is almost insulting. There are mostly rabbit coats and old fox coats worn over evening dresses and I leave my new coat in the cabin. Today we are going to the Cabin class dining room instead of the "Vibration" room.

Six days of complete boredom. "Next time, take the plane." Should you come over, ask Carroll and fly if possible. Although you might love the boat as you can sleep for days and days.

I think we have a good time when we live together. I love you.

Mutti

One of the string of quacks that my mother collected had convinced her that electric shock would certainly cure her friend and so, before leaving, she had issued orders for Tami to be taken for weekly treatments, signed a blank check, and hired a very strange-looking woman to make sure she went. When I promised that I would follow all orders laid down if only I might be permitted to take Tami myself, my mother fired the "Auschwitz warden" and said: "You'd better! I paid!" and stepped into the waiting limousine.

The doctor was near, I walked Tami to his office, then helped her as we slowly retraced our steps. Each time we went, she whispered: "Don't leave me." Each time we returned, I had ceased to exist.

In 1946, there were no tranquilizers as we know them today—three years yet before the first, Miltown, long before the mighty pacifier Valium. If any anxiety-reducing drugs did exist, the "doctor" hired to electrically unscramble Tami's brain did not believe in them. Two burly men, in white coats, lifted the trembling creature that I loved so, slammed her onto a metal slab, strapped her to its icy surface. The restraining cuffs around her ankles and wrists were thick leather, the straps securing her body of heavy canvas. A wired leather band was tightened around her head, electrodes placed against each temple, a wooden wedge jammed between her teeth, and the switch pushed forward. I remember noticing that the ceiling lights dimmed, just as they did in movies at an electrocution. As Tami's limbs jerked, a low scream escaped through her wedged mouth, like the howl of an animal at bay, a faint smell of singed flesh—then silence.

Some days it took hours before Tami emerged from that long black tunnel she had been slammed into, knew who she was. Other times only a few minutes, but with each "treatment," she lost a little of herself, her memory, her quick intelligence, her lovely humor, her giving tenderness. The essence of the woman that was Tamara Matul became diffused, bringing fear, confusion, and utter desolation into sharp focus. She had trusted me and I had stood by and let them torture her. Deep down in the depths of her madness, she never forgave me— neither did I.

Fordham University in New York was justly famous for its unique triple stage and innovative productions. Its theater department was headed by Albert McCleery, the one-time aide-de-camp of General Gavin who had been so diplomatic and protective of his general the night I arrived in Berlin. He called and asked if I would be free to assist him in directing his production of *Peer Gynt.* I agreed to come to a rehearsal and see what I could do.

When I walked into the darkened theater, I saw a lithe figure of a man focusing lights onto the huge barren stage. I turned to McCleery as he joined me, and said:

"Are those going to be the lights for the first scene? If so, aren't they too bright?"

The man on the stage turned, peering into the darkened auditorium.

"Who said that? Al? Is someone out there with you criticizing my lights?" He sounded very annoyed.

McCleery escorted me down to the apron of the stage and introduced me to William Riva, the university's teacher of scenic design. I, who had grown up in a profession that had practically invented "love at first sight," I, who had always ridiculed such unrealistic "Valentine's Day" behavior, who cringed when my mother swooned, fell madly in love, never regretted it, and never looked back. Although I came to realize almost immediately that the object of my sudden passion was a superb artist, a consummate teacher, and brilliant craftsman, it took him a while to get over his antagonism against "movie stars' daughters who thought they knew the theater and, worse, believed they had the talent to teach its craft." Besides knowing that I was hopelessly in love, I came to respect his judgment in things of true value. After forty-five years of loving him, I still do. I worked hard to gain his approval, but it wasn't easy. He watched me direct a scene and that seemed to impress him. I volunteered to work all night to finish building one of the intricate sets; that he liked. I joined the paint crew, found an old pair of pants, put them on, needed something to hold them up, couldn't find a belt, so tied an old curtain chain around my midriff—that got him!

I got a job touring as understudy in the Theatre Guild's first production of Eugene O'Neill's *A Moon for the Misbegotten*. Bill came to visit me whenever he could get away, and soon O'Neill, the great stage designer Robert Edmond Jones, James Dunn, everyone smiled their approval of the romance traveling with our company through Columbus, Cleveland, Boston, and points west. When, in Kansas City, the police closed O'Neill's beautiful play because its language offended the decency laws of that fair city, I returned to New York, caught Bill on the eve of a dress rehearsal for another one of those complex, extravagant, exciting productions that the dear Jesuits of Fordham loved so. Three days without sleep, Bill was dead on his feet; I saw my chance, and asked him to marry me. He nodded his head—he was too tired to say no. Best thing I have ever done, as well as the most courageous.

I kept my mother carefully uninformed. This was never hard to do. Such mundane questions as "How are you?" "What are you doing?" "Tell me about yourself" were never part of her speech pattern, but I called Brian:

"Oh, Kater—my dearest girl. What wonderful news! God bless!" and went to visit Remarque, just to tell him of my love for Bill—not to stay long. We talked the night through, never noticing the time, until the electric lights became too bright with the morning light streaming in through the tall windows. Good friends can do that for each other—open old wounds, let accumulated poison flow, cleanse each other's spirit. He was so happy for me having found a home to set my love in. For him, the need for my mother remained unaltered.

The morning of my wedding day, I settled Tami in her favorite chair by the window, put a roll of tangled twine in her lap—she liked to pluck at the knots, a preoccupation that calmed her—kissed her and wished she were well enough to see me marry. On the 4th of July, 1947, I walked up the aisle of a beautiful church, feeling right in a very white dress, and married the man I loved—who loved me. No fuss, no extravaganza, no press, no photographers, no "world movie-star mother." But Albert Mc-Cleery, ever her fan, did manage to send our wedding picture via Reuters news service to her in Paris, and so, she managed to find someone in New York to break into our apartment and strew masses of fresh rose petals all over our white bed sheets. It was reported to me that she was furious, but made sure that everyone had the impression that she was only concerned about getting champagne and flowers to her wonderful daughter who was getting married—*without* her loving mother by her side.

She never got over my choosing to marry a man who had served overseas longer even than Eisenhower, sported seven hash marks on his uniform against her not too "official" three. In Dietrich's world, *she* was the designated hero soldier—certainly not some Italian-American with dark eyes and black hair. When later all my sons were born with their father's eyes, she shook her head in Aryan disapproval and was heard to mutter: "I knew it! The moment Maria married him, I knew her beautiful blue eyes would be lost forever! Those dark men—their genes always win!" For years, she waited for the moment she knew would certainly come, when I would return, my marriage another dismal failure, and gnashed her teeth as the years passed and I did not appear to whisper "Mutti—can I stay here with you tonight?"

JEAN MARRIED, and, completely distraught, my mother returned to New York and fell in love with the only man I ever thought the perfect husband for her. Elegant, handsome, intelligent, cosmopolitan, trilingual, and rich. Bill and I liked him enormously. The only thing that worried me was his gentleness, that and his genuine "niceness" might be a real handicap. This cavalier had so little armor to enter into an emotional siege with Dietrich.

Between being swept off her feet by her storybook Cavalier, she met my husband. He was polite, she was reserved but determined to make the best of what she considered was yet another emotional mistake of mine. She visited our third floor walk-up, commenting with girlish giggles how the linoleum on the stairs reminded her of the servants' quarters in her mother's house in Berlin, tasted my tuna casserole without comment, and shuddered at the roar of the Third Avenue El as it clattered past our bedroom window. Finally, a long sleek limousine drove her away—only to return an hour later, laden with boxes of expensive gifts: smoked salmon from the coldest rivers of Scotland, tins of perfect caviar, cheeses, breads, squabs, exotic fruits, bundles of white asparagus, cakes, and filigree cookies, and the inevitable bottles of Dom Pérignon.

My husband, who could not afford to lavish such gifts on me, was stunned. I was frightened, tried to laugh it off:

"Bill, love. Don't let my mother get to you. She is world famous for her overdone generosity and no one ever questions, nor understands her motives behind it. But I do. You know why she sent all this luxury? Because what she really wants to say to me is: 'You see, with him you have to eat tuna fish, with me, you would have caviar!' Let's have a party and get rid of all this junk!" A brave speech that I hoped would convince him that he was not letting me down by having only his love and canned tuna to offer the "daughter of a famous movie star." I knew he so wanted to give me the moon. He had yet to learn that what he had to give was much more precious to me, but the warning bell had sounded inside me. She knew this time someone might finally take me away from her, and desperate to repossess what she had always believed was hers alone, to keep forever, she would not stop at gifts of food.

Billy Wilder came to my rescue. He offered her the role of a nightclub singer trying to survive amidst the ruins of Berlin. She hated the character, the whole idea, but trusted Wilder and needed the money. She left for Hollywood in '47, quite sure that once she had designed the clothes, sung the Hollander songs, and made sure that "Billy won't insist that the woman was really a Nazi during the war," *A Foreign Affair* would become a Dietrich film. She duplicated the old sequin dress that she had worn during her GI time and looked fantastic. With an old German buddy as director, she had a wonderful time making the film. She phoned me constantly, sometimes didn't get me—which angered her—because, as I was teaching graduate classes at Fordham, I was not instantly available. Her leading man did not interest her. She referred to him as "that piece of petrified wood," and to her costar Jean Arthur as "that ugly, ugly woman with that terrible American twang." An attractive athlete she had met at one of Warner's many parties was paying her court. "Just like your Bill, '*ever* so Italian,' but not romantic-looking like yours, a little more low-class—like down more towards Naples. In the summer he hits a ball and then runs 'home' in that childish game the Americans are so crazy about—you know the one I mean. He is a little dumb—but sweet!"

So I knew my mother was well taken care of and hoped her Cavalier's corporate position would keep him safely in New York and out of the way until DiMaggio struck out.

With the recommendations of her admiring

generals, the War Department announced that Marlene Dietrich had been selected to receive the highest honor the nation could bestow on a civilian, the Medal of Freedom.

She called me, sobbing, full of pride and elation:

"Sweetheart—I am having it framed for you. Nellie is going crazy sewing the little red-and-white ribbon I can now wear in the lapel of my suits. And I have a small medal to wear for state occasions—besides the official big one. Most children get medals from their father. You will inherit yours from your mother!"

I became pregnant, and my mother, ever the soldier's daughter who faces defeat with stoic resignation, returned to New York to oversee her daughter's "glorious" pregnancy, but not before asking me if I didn't really want to get rid of it.

"Once you have a child, you won't be able to get out of this marriage so easily. I know you keep harping on wanting children, but a child brings you nothing but trouble."

The look on my face must have frightened her, for she never dared to mention this subject again, allowing herself only to observe, in a tone laced with acid disapproval whenever I announced over the years that I was once more expecting yet another child:

"Again? Another one? Haven't you enough

trouble already? What's wrong with Bill—won't he let you douche?"

In the spring of 1948, at the urging of her Cavalier, who knew the proper background his lady deserved, my mother rented the Lady Mendl suite in the Plaza Hotel. A four-room concoction of Vertès hand-painted murals of smirking nymphs scampering through watercolor woods of palest greens.

Bill was building a nursery out of a little storeroom we had, and as only oil paint was available in those days, we escaped the danger-ous fumes engulfing our apartment by staying for a few days at the Plaza in my mother's suite. With her charming Cavalier in residence, every-thing was serene. Whenever he was not at his office or with his wife, he resided with us, show-ering his lady with superb gifts of impeccable taste. She lived up to his visual concept of her, wore beautifully simple suits, Valentino dresses, cut slim, unadorned, their line as elegant as a Ming vase. A figure-eight knot, first used in *For-eign Affair*, sculpted her hair against her neck; understated pearl earrings completed the look— Aunt Valli had come to stay, was living at the Plaza!

Russian broadtail and silver-tipped Russian sables were a must to complete this picture of ladyhood. Stoles were very fashionable in the late forties; my mother hated them. In her opinion, they had been invented by "fat old ladies who wanted to show that they were rich enough to own furs but couldn't afford the whole coat." It became a family problem what to have made in sable. My father, back in his apartment on the upper East Side, unencumbered by Tami, whom he had locked away in a sanitarium, preferred the full-cut Chesterfield-style coat. Remarque, still at the Sherry Netherland, a belted model with a flared skirt. I, horizontally worked skins. In Paris, Chevalier, when asked his advice over the phone, wanted cuffed sleeves. Noël's comment was a pertinent: "Whatever you do, Marlenah, make certain that you have yards and yards of the delightful stuff." Hemingway's laugh boomed over the Cuban phone lines—said it had to button. Piaf didn't like the whole idea:

"Why do you want to spend so much of your own money? Keep it. If he wants to buy you a sable coat, that's different—that's business!"

My husband was included in this summit meeting of pelts, by being asked to sketch the many suggestions. My mother smoked, paced the imitation Aubusson, and said:

"Have you seen that sable coat Tallulah wears? I don't know where she got it—but she looks like someone kept by a rich gangster!"

The Cavalier smiled his cosmopolitan smile, remarked:

"Whatever, you decide—Dietrich should be

wrapped in Russian sable," and the idea for my mother's famous fur blanket was born.

She finally made a ten-foot runner of horizontally placed skins and, like a tall tube of Christmas paper, wrapped her body in sable instead of cellophane. She referred to it as her "Indian blanket." Years later, it became known as "the Thing" or "the Animal," and starred in one of Dietrich's renowned self-parodies:

"Do you see this 'Thing'?," pointing to the yards of sable taking up its own chair. "I looked wonderful wrapped in it when I arrived, right? No money—but covered in Russian sable! The story of my life! You know Rudi had it insured years ago for a fortune. I still have to pay every year for the insurance—waiting for it to get stolen, but you know, no one steals it! Everything else they steal—but not my Animal. So I think, why not lose it? One night, I just happened to leave it lying under my seat in the theater. No one noticed. So I call Rudi in the middle of the night to tell him the good news. The next morning, the manager of the theater appears at my door, beaming, and hands me my Indian blanket! Of course, I had to appear overjoyed and gaga grateful. He wouldn't accept a check, so I said, 'Tell me *how* I can thank you,' which, of course, was a dangerous thing to say—but all he wanted was autographed pictures for his whole family. I finally got rid of him. . . . I leave it in taxis—it comes back and costs me a fortune in tips. I let it sort of slide off as I walk through Bendel's or Bloomingdale's . . . and they find me wherever I am in the store and are *ever* so happy to bring it back to me. One time, I was on some ship crossing either to or from Europe, and we hit a storm. It was terrible. Everyone was sick—the ropes were up, wind blowing so hard no one was allowed on the upper decks. So, I put on my 'Animal' and took the elevator to the promenade deck, as though I wasn't feeling well and needed to walk, then I crept up the stairs to the top deck. The wind nearly blew me overboard—that would have been funn-eee!" She always laughed at the sudden thought of her going over the side together with her sable.

"So there I am, struggling to hold on to the rail—I loosen the 'Thing' so the wind can just take it and blow it away! In case some sailor might happen to see me, I couldn't just throw it into the sea—it had to look like a real accident. I was freezing, my hair, my evening dress completely ruined from the salt spray. It took me an hour to lose that thing! I got back to my cabin and immediately placed a call to Rudi to tell him the good news! Two hours later, the captain bows and hands me my Indian blanket! It had flown off the top deck and landed on a man's head in third class, four decks below! . . . I am jinxed with this thing. But the day I cancel the insurance—*that*'s the day someone will *finally* steal it!"

I had always dreamed of having one of those royal bassinets, all lace and ribbons and ruffled canopy for my firstborn. I looked all over New York City for one to live up to my exaggerated MGM-type concept, but as this was 1948, before Grace Kelly's Monaco princesses, there were none to be found.

"You want a Victorian bassinet, my darling? Easy. We'll make one," said my scenic designer husband and went in search of white organdy, eyelet for ruffles, and as I was determined to have a boy, wide blue satin ribbon. Ever the executive, the Cavalier had his secretary buy a sewing machine and ordered card tables to be installed in the Plaza suite.

My mother caught the bassinet fever, decided that Austrian field flowers were the only motif to complement the ruffles and ribbons, had the chauffeur drive her to the garment district in search of silk cornflowers and poppies. Santa's gnomes had nothing on us. Bill measured, cut, and pinned while the Cavalier sewed perfect ruffles as though born to the trade, my mother kibitzed, ordered coffee and sandwiches to keep us nourished and working. I, by now the size of a house, was allowed to sew the finished splendor to the wicker basket. I had to do so standing up, bending had become impossible. It was a happy time that I have remembered, because despite the rather theatrical circumstances, it felt so normal—like a real family.

In June, John Michael Riva was born and made Marlene Dietrich a grandmother. *Life* magazine ran a cover, proclaimed her "The Most Glamorous Grandmother," Walter Winchell called her "Gorgeous Grandmarlene," and *A Foreign Affair* opened to raves. The press kept pouring it on, until universally, she became known as "the World's Most Glamorous Grandmother," a title she secretly despised but officially embraced with seemingly passionate devotion; but never stopped blaming my husband for making me pregnant, thereby "complicating" her life. I, of course, was sublimely happy—my guard was completely down. A dangerous thing to let happen when Dietrich was near.

I even allowed her to play grandmother, or so I thought. Actually, she took on the role she preferred, the one of mother. Bill and I were young, in love, we wanted a few days together, and as I was not nursing, gave our baby to her to look after. It was late summer, friends had left the city, so she took over their house, draped off the downstairs in sterile sheets, scrubbed everything down with Lysol and Ajax, taped the windows against possible drafts, ordered nurse's uniforms, dressed in one, and moved our child from his sweet new nursery into Dietrich's Surgical Ward—and took over. Boiled bottles, made, remade, and remade again formula until she was certain no germs could possibly have survived, touched the baby only when absolutely necessary or to check if he was still alive. Fortunately, he was too young to be harmed by this exaggerated sterility. By the time we returned she had convinced herself that my son had sprung from her womb instead of mine. At the age of ninety she still accused me of taking him away from her:

"You left him with me and went off with Bill. He was mine! I got that house, moved all the furniture out, washed and sterilized everything, made that formula over and over—all that steam in that terrible New York heat. Never slept, listened every second to hear if it was still breathing and, when you came back, you *tore* him out of my arms and took him from me to your apartment!"

For years, I was confronted by outraged ladies, with: "Is it true you tore a baby out of your mother's arms and just marched out of the house after she nursed him for a whole year for you?" Sometimes, I actually caught myself explaining that I had only been gone five days, that I had actually borne him. Really, I could prove it!

Later, she loved to tell my son how I had

deserted him, beat him when he was little, how she had been his only hope, tell him her "hidden secrets."

He was a young man, nearly grown, when he asked me:

"Mom. Is it true that you used to beat me when I was a baby?" He saw my face and quickly put his arms around me, held me close. "I'm so sorry, Mom. I knew it couldn't be true, but she used to tell me you did . . . all the time. I just had to ask you."

Charles Feldman called, offered her a film to be made in London for Alfred Hitchcock. She would have complete control over her choice of clothes and be allowed to pick any Paris designer she liked to execute them. She agreed to do the film. I called Charlie and thanked him. "You're welcome," he laughed. He was a good friend.

Before leaving America, the life insurance that von Sternberg had bought for her in 1931 matured, and my father and mother had one of their most vehement quarrels. It was my father's contention that as I had been the sole beneficiary of this policy, the matured amount was rightfully mine.

"But, I am still *alive*!" she screamed at him. "Anyway what would she do with sixty thousand dollars?" After a few weeks of this, my father found a lovely brownstone house on the upper

East Side, convinced my mother to buy it with the proviso that she allow me and my family to live there until it could be legally gifted over to me.

"A house! Maria *has* to have a house? For what? All that work, rooms and stairs? The garden is good for the child, but who needs a whole house? You two are so alike—always talking about a 'home'! When she is with *me, then* she is home, and not in some house in New York with a strange man!"

My father persisted. Finally, she bought the house and lots of lovely rubies for herself with what was left over. My father knew that we had no means to furnish a house on our teachers' salaries. His plan had been to use the rest of the monies to make the house habitable and put a nest egg by for our son. But although he seethed inside, he knew when it was time to back off and be satisfied with what he had achieved. Years later, before he finally died, I was able to tell him of the house he found and fought for me to have, that became the Riva house, full of joy and love, children and grandchildren, youth and age—a real home, full of memories, and I thanked him for it. Over the years, my mother got so much good publicity out of this fabulously generous gift to her beloved daughter, I had no guilt about the house at all as far as she was concerned.

Clutching a dirty bib as a talisman of "her baby," my mother left for Paris and began making clothes at Dior. Remarque was in Paris and they saw each other constantly. He understood her longing for Gabin and the seething anger at his recent marriage. She encouraged Remarque's love and allowed him to share her suffering over Jean. Her Cavalier, still the innocent, followed her to Europe.

Paris, June 6 49

My Angel,

The pain of having to leave you was all over me running like a fine toothache into my hand with the bib. Arrival at Orly, photographers, press. I played gay and almost felt like it. Had a date with Remarque at Fouquet's, we went to dinner at the Méditerranée and as we sat at our old table, I had the first funny dull thought in my head. The thought made no sense but it was there: Why isn't Jean here? The baby is expected in October. We joked that in France they now make babies in a much shorter time than it usually takes and said that it must have happened the first night he knew her.

Anyway, that was the first evening. Remarque probably had a good time, knowing that Jean's expecting a child would close the door to any future between him and me, enjoying the dramatics of it all—and planning to use it somewhere in his next book. He was sweet though, full of fatherly pity and advice.

The next morning, after a night I passed somehow, I went to work. I spent all day at Dior's while the sketches were made and materials picked to be sent to London. Then I got sick like I cannot remember ever having been, except when I was a child and had eaten unripe cherries. I had eaten almost nothing since I arrived, but my stomach kept turning upside down all night. I was so weak that I could not walk on the street. Chlorodine helped but the weakness stayed for a week.

Like blood and rubber and snake venom, another one of those "great discoveries": Chlorodine, came in tiny, very thin, cobalt blue glass bottles with a tight cork stopper. Wrapped like Worcestershire sauce, its parchment proclaimed this elixir could cure stomach cramps, diarrhea, malaria, dysentery, influenza, typhus, cholera, and the bubonic plague. Black, thick, and sticky, it looked like boiled-down opium—which it probably was. My mother loved it, couldn't be without it, gave it to anyone who had the slightest upset stomach, for years smuggled her little blue bottles everywhere she went.

It's a holiday here, PenteCote, auf Deutsch Pfingsten. In Germany and Austria they put young Birch trees or branches in front of their houses and anyone can come in and drink young white wine. Here they go to Deauville instead.

Dresses, shoes, stockings, gloves, handbags, coats, negligees, suits, jewelry, foundations, scarves, hats—nearly all was ready, and so she finally left Paris for London to make the wigs.

Her Cavalier awaited her with open arms at Claridge's. *Stage Fright* began shooting in England on July first.

Michael Wilding had all the prerequisites to attract. He was handsome, a storybook British gentleman, tender and shy, with a medical affliction that marshaled all of her protective powers. They became lovers quickly and remained so for quite a long time. In many ways, Michael reminded me of Brian. Although he had a more pixie humor, he also had that capacity to step back into the shadows whenever she became involved with someone else, ready to emerge again with love whenever she finished with his rival. Both men had the compassion of a saint and the patience of Job.

During the Wilding time, my mother kept up her devotion to the Cavalier, became involved with a famous American actress known not only for her talent, pined for Gabin, received her baseball player whenever he needed cosseting, loved Remarque, her charming general, Piaf, a gorgeous Teutonic blonde who became her German pal, and worked full out at being indispensable to her immediate entourage.

Golden Earrings (1947), the gypsiest gypsy that ever was.

With Hemingway. They met so often, talked about each other in such glowing terms, the world believed they must have been lovers.

In June 1948, Dietrich became a grandmother. She thought the headlines proclaiming this momentous change in her status ridiculous hysteria. (Photograph by Arnold Newman)

Photographers pounced when they caught Dietrich out with her daughter and son-in-law.

The fine talents that made *Foreign Affair* a success. My mother disliked everyone in this picture except the man in the hat, Billy Wilder. He was her German-speaking chum, and she trusted him and his talent. In such things, my mother was never stupid.

Stage Fright, filmed in England, was another matter. Alfred Hitchcock was not to my mother's liking. They stayed as far away from each other as possible, and the film suffered. My mother didn't—she fell in love instead.

I liked Michael Wilding.
He reminded me of another
one of my mother's loves,
Brian Aherne.

An opening night somewhere. On seeing this
picture, my mother said, "*I*, who can't stand
jealousy in a man, went out with two of the
most jealous men I ever knew in my whole
life? Von Sternberg *and* Remarque *together*?
Why would I do such a stupid thing? Must
have been *quite* an evening!"

After a romantic week with Wilding in the south of France, she returned to Paris in October, called, complained that it had rained the "whole time" in St. Tropez and that the fuss everyone made about the Côte d'Azur was ridiculous. "Before the war, *then* it was luxurious. Now *concierges* take their whole families there for vacations!"

Stage Fright finished, she booked passage for New York, called her astrologer, and then flew instead. Arrived back on November 5th, furious that American Customs had charged her one hundred and eighty dollars for the Dior clothes, worth thousands, that she had brought back with her. That night, she and her Cavalier had dinner at our house and she told her stories:

"You know how I worship penicillin, how it saved my life during the war, so I told Spoliansky, I saw them all the time while I was in London, I said: 'All I want while I am in England is to meet Alexander Fleming, the god who discovered penicillin. I want to tell him how he saved my life during the war!' The next day, the papers said I had gone over to Alec Guinness at a restaurant and said, 'You are the second most important man I want to meet,' to which he was supposed to have replied, 'Who is the first?' to which I answered: 'Sir Alexander Fleming!' Can you imagine my doing that? I was furious, but the Spolianskys swore they didn't tell anyone.

But one evening, I go to dinner at their apartment and—who is there? Fleming! He just stood there and said: 'Hello.' I sank to my knees in front of him and kissed his hands. I must have been very boring at dinner. All I did was stare at him in awe—like a schoolgirl with a crush. Then we went dancing and the most terrible thing happened: When he held me, I felt him trembling! I couldn't believe it, so I said, 'Sir, are you all right?'—and you know what he said? 'Oh, Miss Dietrich, it is such an honor to meet you!' Can you believe it? A great man like that—the god who brought the world penicillin —turns out to be just another fan, like everyone else. Isn't that sad? I asked him for an autographed picture, and you know what he did? He sent me the very first penicillin culture under glass. I am going to frame it with his picture. Sweet man, but like all geniuses, only intelligent in the one thing they are interested in." She helped herself to more of the Camembert she had brought and cut a huge hunk of bread. As usual, she was starving.

"Let me tell you about Hitchcock! A strange little man. I don't like him. Why they all think he is *so* great, I don't know. The film is bad— maybe in the cutting he does all his famous 'suspense,' but he certainly didn't do it in the shooting. Richard Todd is nice but nothing there. You know the kind of Englishman who has those thick white ankles? Also the hands? Todd's fingers are like little uncooked sausages and he's *engaged*! Jane Wyman, she is very sweet. Michael Wilding? Oh, a British version of Stewart. He mumbles, is ever so shy, and being English, gets through the film on charm. The best thing in the film is me doing 'la Vie en rose.' I called Piaf for permission. I didn't want her to think that I thought anyone but she had the right to sing it. Of course, she said yes and was flattered that I called her—and the *very* best is 'Laziest Gal in Town.' I did it with marabou feathers on a chaise longue, making fun of it. Cole will adore it—if he ever sees the film. The hair is very bad—the whole picture—too 'old lady little curls.' I always have said that the British can't make women's films—I should have listened to myself."

As she was between pictures, my mother now launched herself into the role of "fairy godmother" for the benefit of "her son." She had seen him looking at the pretty pictures in a book of fairy tales, and when next she appeared to take him to the park, she arrived in costume. Gone were the hospital-matron brogues, the surgical uniform, the antiseptic look of purity and dependability. She didn't walk into the house, she skipped—layers of starched petticoats awhirl about her beautiful legs. She hadn't been able to find glass slippers, but those she wore were see-through plastic and did the job. Golden curls bobbed on her shoulders, satin bows adorned her wrists, a blushing rose nestled in her cleavage.

My one-and-a-half-year-old was enchanted. "Puetty wady," he lisped, and they became inseparable—until he cried, then she quickly handed him over to me, worried that he might be dying and that she would not know what to do to save him: "With you, I was always frightened. Always! Never a day went by that I wasn't frightened about something happening to you. I drove Papi crazy in the early days with you in Berlin, then in America with the kidnapping—it only got worse." When she saw that my son was truly still alive, not threatened by some ominous unknown disease, she plucked him out of my arms, and they went back to happily cooing at each other.

My mother's new maid addressed her as "Missy Dietrich," and for some reason, my son liked the sound of "Missy," giving it his own pronunciation of "Massy," and that became the name my mother was referred to from then on by all of those within her intimate circle. A great relief to have found a name at a time when I was desperately looking for an acceptable substitute for "Granny."

Tauber died, and my mother went into her mourning routine, came out of it to voice her fury when the Kinsey report was published:

"Sex, sex, sex! What is it with people? Put it in, pull it out—*this* they have to *study*? And the money it costs! All that research—for what?"

Oh, how my mother objected to my second pregnancy.

"You have a perfect child. You need more?" she asked, genuinely confused by my obvious joy. When I answered that I hoped I would have many more children, she marched out of my front door in her best Nazi officer manner. All through that Christmas of '49, she suffered my obvious bulge with ill-disguised censure, throwing particularly juicy barbs when a dinner guest in my home:

"Look at her," she would point me out to my friends. "All her life she has hated being so fat— Now— Suddenly— She is as big as this house I bought for her and now she doesn't mind! She will find out someday the terrible trouble children are, then it will be too late!"

Convinced as she was that I could not give birth without her magical presence, she was once again in attendance in May 1950, when Peter was born. Although Bill was right there, it was again to Dietrich that the doctor came to announce that it was a boy. She played the role of husband so well, it was an automatic reflex for the doctor.

Hemingway sent her the galleys of *Across the River and into the Trees*. She brought them over to the house, plunked the long, thick stack onto my kitchen table.

"What has happened to him? Read this and tell me. Something is wrong, but I can't tell Papa until I know what it is!" She unpacked her schlepper, took out a tall jar of beef tea, put it in my refrigerator. "What have you got in here —Jell-O? You don't give *that* to the child? I'll make him fresh applesauce," and proceeded to do so.

"Pat took me to see a play, called *Death of a Salesman*. How depressing! And SO American. Little people with little problems, all done up like Big Drama! And you must see a thing called *South Pacific*. Not-to-Be-Believed! During a war— They SING! And big to-do because Mary Martin washes her hair on the stage with shampoo and real water? Now really!" The apples were boiling merrily. "She even does a cutesie-poo song, all about 'washing her man right out of her hair.' No! A bad Technicolor musical maybe, but not in the theater! And you can't even imagine the way the *man* looks— Old—Big—and Fat, like an opera singer. Which, of course, he is, but couldn't they at least have put him in a corset and dyed his hair?"

She was awarded the French Legion of Honor for her service to France. To be selected to become a member of such an exalted body was the high point of my mother's aristocratic life, topped only by being promoted from the rank of Chevalier to Officier a few years later by the then president of the French Republic, Pompidou, and finally, to the ultimate glory of Commander by Mitterrand. I certainly did not begrudge her this high honor, only wondered what she had done for France as a nation that was *that* important. Loving Gabin? Worshiping de Gaulle? Knowing the lyrics of the "Marseillaise"? And living in Paris just didn't seem enough, somehow.

"Jean should have been with me. He would have been proud. Why they never gave him one I'll never know. After all, he is still the greatest French actor they have. He even fought in the war. Strange, a German they honor, but a man of the people they don't. But then, I have always loved de Gaulle, a wonderful man and I always tell him so when we see each other."

The first rumors of war began in Korea. Proclaiming that if I insisted on having babies all the time, she had to earn more money for me, my mother signed to star in *No Highway in the Sky*, to be filmed in London. She had a tearful farewell with "her child," clasped him to her bosom, whispered, "Don't forget me, my angel," while my son tried to come up for air. My new baby didn't warrant a look. He didn't interest her. He had dark hair, like his father, was chubby, healthy, and unromantic-looking. And she left for Paris.

Dior was again given the singular honor of

designing her costumes for the film. The clothes they conceived were so perfect, so utterly Dietrich, that throughout the film she looks as though she is doing a portrait sitting for *Vogue*. Although her costar was once again her old heartthrob from *Destry*, and even Elizabeth Allan had a part in this film, she never mentioned either of them. In her daily phone calls to me, she complained about the "lackluster script," the "half-asleep director," then spent the rest of the hour telling me how sweet Glynis Johns was on and off the set.

In December, she returned aboard the *Queen Elizabeth*, complained that the cabins creaked, that she really had enough of the British four-o'clock tea mania, but conceded that Elizabeth Firestone and Sharman Douglas had made the crossing bearable. She launched herself and her newly acquired salary into a frenzy of Christmas shopping. Her Cavalier was grateful to have her back. She had a new film, to be directed by an old lover, scheduled for the New Year in Hollywood, where Michael Wilding was waiting for her, and her favorite general was expected to pass through. My father was sorting and recording her European expenses, Tami was stashed safely away in a new asylum, my two-and-a-half-year-old had recognized her immediately when she walked into his nursery, and I, for once, was not pregnant—all was right in my mother's world.

. . .

LIVE TELEVISION, originating in New York City, had become the new marvel, the wonder that kept families at home together, clustered around their precious eight-inch screens. My mother had nothing but disdain for its amateurish growing pains and predicted television's rapid demise. Having handed down her obviously correct judgment, she ignored its existence until I called her in Hollywood and announced that I had auditioned and been given a starring role in an hour-long play on CBS Television. She was happily ensconced in Mitchell Leisen's apartment complex in the hills above the Sunset Strip. Michael Wilding, in better health than he had been when they were together last, was functioning as a most inventive lover, so her diary states at that time. Although she writes that she is "staining," she adds that hopefully it is Wilding's "steeple chasing" that is causing it and not something else. She goes on to say that she inserted a "firecracker," Dietrich's name for Tampax.

For the next fifteen years, not a day went by without her recording, in one way or another, her evaluation of her menstrual cycles, its erratic signals, its sudden absence or appearance, swelling, pressures; no symptom from that part of her anatomy was too minute to record. Her comments always underlaid with that silent panic that was to continue until 1965, when I finally forced her to face the possibility of cancer, and then hid the truth from her while she was being treated for it in Geneva.

So, when I called her that day in '51, she was happy with Wilding, worried about what "staining" might mean, in preproduction for the worst film she ever made, and knew it, and was in no mood to have me "prostitute myself for a few dollars, trying to act on that tiny, little stupid screen for little people."

Thanks to my husband's urging and encouragement, I summoned up the courage to try and was very successful. I loved television. I always have, working in it, or simply being a viewer. I always felt I belonged to it, that it was my friend.

A very special relationship emerges when an actor must wait to be invited into his audience's home. The welcome mat may be out the first time, but the performer must earn the privilege of being invited back. Once your host approves of you, you become a friend, a bonding not to be taken lightly. The live television camera has an uncanny perception. Its range of intimacy leaves no room for falsehoods. If by some clever maneuver they do get by, the viewer will eventually catch the insincerities and resent anyone trying to make a fool of him in his own home. As friends are supposed to be honest with each other, TV demands it.

My mother was afraid of this intimacy between a medium and its audience, and, therefore, hated it, had to discredit it whenever possible. For her very few TV appearances in later years, she drank herself into an anesthetized stupor. Her only TV special became a parody on herself, a personal tragedy.

EXCEPT FOR GIVING HER THE IDEA for a costume she was to embellish and perfect years later for *Around the World in 80 Days*, *Rancho Notorious*, the film she made in March of '51, had nothing to recommend it.

Since the day when Fritz Lang had "betrayed" her to Jean, he had ceased to exist as her one-time lover and friend. Now she erased him as a director as well. She showed her antagonism openly to anyone she chose, calling him "a Nazi."

"No wonder he did all those frightening pictures. A man who can do a film like *M* has got to be a sadist."

In April, her diary records the end of shooting with:

> End of film—Another tough one—
> No more Germans!!
> Resolution!!

During this period, a "Jimmy" figures prominently in her diary as taking up her evenings "steeple chasing." Trying to decipher my mother's somewhat crowded sexual calendar could be confusing. There were so many Jimmys, Joes, Michaels, and Jeans, both the Anglo-Saxon and French versions, that one welcomed those lovers who sported such exotic names as Yul— it made them easier to identify.

Hitchcock was quoted as saying that Dietrich was "A professional cameraman, a professional makeup man . . ." and so on. My mother never noticed that he omitted "actress" from his long list, nor did it ever occur to her that he might, just might, have meant to be slightly sarcastic, enumerating her many accomplishments in every category but her own. But those of us who lived within her immediate control, we understood and sympathized. We knew that Dietrich thought of herself as an indisputable expert in anything that she decided was important enough to warrant her interest.

Medicine was one of her most dedicated specialties. She told doctors what diagnosis they should come up with, changed, replaced, and manipulated them without the slightest hesitation, bullied nurses, reorganized hospital routines, ignoring completely the wishes of the patient in her zeal to save his life as "only she could." All of us tried, whenever possible, to become ill only when she was safely out of town.

My father had major abdominal surgery

while she was away working in Hollywood. She constantly phoned everyone, waking my husband in the middle of the night, screaming that the hospital would not put her call through to "her own husband" at two a.m., so that she could make sure he was still alive! When Bill told her, for the hundredth time, that I was in attendance twenty-four hours a day, she calmed down a bit, hung up, and turned her energies to instructing her lovers and friends to send telegrams to "Poor Papi—who is suffering without me in that terrible American hospital in New York, with only Maria there to make sure that they don't kill him. While I am stuck here making a film to get the money to pay all the doctor bills!"

"Poor Papi" was recovering rapidly when the telegrams started arriving. I was with him the day he opened his daily stack, while muttering angrily: "More! They only send them because she tells them to! Does she think that I am really so stupid that I believe they care what happens to me? She tells everybody, 'Send poor Papi a cable!' and so they do it for her! Not me! Never me!" With every word, his voice grew hoarser. I watched him. I knew that inner rage that burned inside him at his own weakness, his dependency both emotionally and financially on the woman it had become his habit to love. This impotent fury had already damaged his kidneys, destroyed three-quarters of his stomach, and I wondered what part of his body he would sacrifice to it next!

"Papi, please! Stop! Why don't you try to have a life of your own? Try just once to get away? Do something *you* want to do that she has nothing to do with, over which she will have no control. Take Tami and just go!" I pleaded. At least, if my father decided to escape, it would get Tami away from the dubious psychiatrists reorganized for her by my mother.

It took him quite a while, but finally, with borrowed money from his only true friend, my father bought a little ramshackle house in San Fernando Valley, California. With two rows of meshed cages and a few dozen scrawny chickens, he proclaimed his independence by going into the egg business. He was "his own man" once more; he was happy, he had hope, and Tami blossomed. My mother was furious. Immediately on hearing who had made his independence possible, my father's friend became her mortal enemy. Then she launched her campaign to make sure that her husband would return to his rightful place of pliant "family retainer," the position he had filled so well for nearly thirty years. From then on, my father's acre plot of dirt and dust, the rickety rows of lopsided cages and clucking hens became "My Husband's Ranch," giving it the intonation one might use when referring to L.B.J.'s four-hundred-acre spread in Texas.

Later, when she had finally maneuvered the takeover of my father's debt, it became "Papi's ranch—that I bought for him." But by that time, my father knew he was beaten, was working on his second massive coronary, and just didn't care anymore. He had lost for the last time, and he knew it.

In the spring of '51, she returned to New York into the waiting arms of her Cavalier and, within days, was madly, insanely in love with someone else. As her love for Gabin had consumed her, so now did her infatuation for Yul Brynner. For four years, their secret affair blazed, flickered, smoldered, simmered, then flamed anew—only to repeat its erratic, agonizing pattern all over again. They kept up this emotional upheaval, giving it the name of "love" until, finally, her possessive romanticism began to choke him, and he walked away from what had been an impossible situation from the beginning. He always remembered her with tenderness and joy. She came to hate him with as much passion as she had once adored him. Thirty-four years after their blazing affair, she sent me a newspaper clipping of Yul in a wheelchair, looking pitiable, returning from yet another unsuccessful cancer treatment. Across his haggard face, she had written in her big silver marker: "Goody—goody—he has cancer! Serves him right!"

But in 1951, she thought Yul a "god," was wildly jealous of his wife, although relieved that she was supposed to have "mental problems," and spent her days sitting by her phone hoping he would call. He did. Every moment he could capture the privacy needed to dial Dietrich's number. He was the toast of Broadway, the catalyst force in a most demanding musical, ever perfecting his brilliant performance of the king in *The King and I*, which was to be his lifelong triumph. He would call the moment he arrived in his dressing room, during the overture, intermission, the second the curtain came down; escaped from friends, admirers, and dignitaries who expected him to join them for their after-theater celebrations, to rush into the trembling arms of his divine goddess. My mother rented a hideaway on Park Avenue, furnished it in Siam silk and gold to complement her lover's Broadway persona, stocked her kitchen with Russian caviar, superb champagne, and five-inch filet mignons, had my husband install strip lights under the base of her king-size bed, and—Dietrich was in business.

It was my mother who insisted on all the fanatical secrecy. She, who had slept with married men all her life as nonchalantly as lighting her cigarettes, now became the nun who sinned behind cloister walls—all to "protect" her lover's reputation. Soon her "King" appeared for breakfast, stayed through lunch, rushed to play his matinee, and, still in his dark body makeup, returned to take his passion to bed between performances. She, who adored romance, but usually complained bitterly about having to include the necessary sex in order to "keep the man happy," now gloried in Yul's seemingly inexhaustible virility. On matinee days, after he had left for the evening performance, she would call me to come over to see "the bed." As this was usually around six o'clock in the evening, when I was busy putting my three-year-old and my baby to bed, my husband would volunteer to go over to her apartment and play the appreciative audience. She so loved to show off her disheveled bed, particularly proud of her once-white sheets now smeared with Yul Brynner's body paint that he had been "too aroused" to take the time to wash off. Bill found all this very funny. It was easier for him, he was not related to her, he didn't need to feel the shame that I did at this tasteless vulgarity.

She enjoyed being raunchy with my husband. She constantly sought opportunities to be ever so "naughty" when in his company. Whenever she greeted him in public, she executed her specialty—a type of standing body-press. Arms around neck, feet firmly planted, her pelvis would slide into its forward motion until it connected with the recipient's pelvic region, then glue itself into position while the rest of her body followed into line. It was something to watch! It was a famous "Dietrich" maneuver. Later, she even used it on my grown sons, those she preferred, of course. Their embarrassment she never noticed, she was too busy pressing.

Yul, who had been a respected TV director before becoming Broadway's idol, counseled my mother not to ignore television's potential nor the role that he believed I would play in its development. As my mother never had any cause to be professionally threatened by me, she had always been renowned for her supportive attitude toward her daughter's acting career. Now, between waiting for Yul to telephone, appear, and love her, she embraced her new role of "mother to budding TV star" with her customary dedication. She crept into studios during dress rehearsals, so broadly intent on not attracting attention that all action stopped to pay homage to the important movie star who had kindly descended from her Hollywood Olympian heights to grace a lowly television studio with her presence. Quite naturally, the young pioneers of this fledgling profession were awed by her and the industry she represented and completely charmed by her whispered comments: "No, no. Don't let me disturb you. I am only here to see my wonderful daughter, Maria. . . . I don't want to be in the way." Out of the darkness of the control booth, the famous voice would ask: "Does that light really have to be so low on her face? It makes her nose too long. If you lift it just a little . . ." They listened, flattered by her interest.

Of the director, intent on his three cameras, viewing his shots on different monitors, making hurried notes for changes, giving commands, sponsors hovering, the incredible pressure of live television bearing down on him, she would ask: "Do you really want her to wear her hair like that in this scene?" or "Have you noticed that her hat is throwing a shadow?"

She drove them crazy, but after all, she just wanted to help her daughter, and who could fault a mother for that, especially such a famous one? I spent most of my first year in television being embarrassed by the undeserved spotlight my mother's presence gave me, apologizing for her interference and trying to convince my employers that I did not expect to be handed instant stardom just because of my relationship to it.

She asked my husband to find her a secluded beach house on Long Island, then rented it for the summer. Announcing she had made it possible "for the children to have a nice summer," she let us live there during the week, then ex-

pected us to vacate the place by Friday afternoon, so that she could arrive and prepare the
house for Yul's late arrival Saturday night after
the show. Sometimes Yul even managed to escape during the week; then we made ourselves
as scarce as possible, hoping the children
wouldn't make noise and disturb the young lovers. My mother was happy that August, and
without telling Yul, tried to get pregnant. When
she told me of her "secret plan," I listened, but
refrained from reminding her that at the age of
four months short of fifty, this might be a little
difficult to accomplish. One, I knew she would
never believe that she was older than thirty, and
two, I had learned long ago that it was much
easier to follow her delusions than try to oppose
them. I also had learned that nothing seemed
impossible for Dietrich to achieve once she had
made her mind up. This time, though, I hoped
the laws of nature would defeat her. Yul's little
boy, Rocky, had enough trouble to face in his
uncertain future, and my children certainly did
not need a sudden "uncle" younger than they.
Her diary reads:

> August 21, 1951
> Here till 3 AM
> Two thirty— Tried again
>
> August 22
> Northport

August 23
Heaven
Leave at 3:15 for New York
He bringing Rocky
I behaved well, but suffer

August 28
Terrible night
Knew that all my courage would be going
once he left.
2 Dexadrine
Misery. Nothing helps.
He came at 4:30— Better

On and on it went! Misery when Yul missed
an hour, a day, when his sick wife needed him,
when he tried to save his marriage or his child,
or his work and all those responsibilities that
went with being a star took up his energy. Eu-
phoria, when he managed to stick to the strict
schedule her life had become dependent upon.
As she had done since 1941, she consulted her
astrologer, driving him crazy with constant questions whenever she was uncertain, then ignoring
his advice completely when she felt back in control. As with all her previous lovers, Carroll
Righter had been sent Yul's date of birth the
moment after she had met him, but not the actual
hour that he was born, nor the place, which
Righter, being the skilled astrologer that he was,
usually insisted upon. As Yul was then still claiming to be a Russian gypsy by birth, and as gypsy

wagons are supposed to roll through moonlit nights going nowhere, his place of birth needed to remain as vague and mysterious as the intriguing background that he had manufactured for himself. His looks and manner so suited this romantic fairy tale, no one wanted to spoil it by the truth. Mystery, after all, doesn't go with being born a Swiss.

> September 12
> Called at 5:30
> Said would call tomorrow at 12:30
> Fight with DiMaggio/Stork Club
> Saw *him* there

> September 23
> 12:30 called
> Pictures of DiMaggio and I. God, I hoped *he* might worry.
> Call Righter. Seven o'clock called. Called 11:45

> September 14
> Lunch, he ordered lamb chops. Small talk, I finally told him I could not worry anymore about what he thought or felt. He then said that he loved me. Left at four. I on cloud. Called at seven. Sent him love letter. Will come after show.

Yul's dresser, Don, became their loyal confidant and go-between. As neither could use their distinctive first names in messages, to escape detection Yul invented monikers for them:

He, of the shaved head, became Curly, my mother he christened Crowd, in my opinion, the most wonderfully appropriate name my mother was ever given by anyone.

As her evenings were structured by the running time and acts of *The King and I*, she was free between the hours of eight-thirty and eleven, so continued to see her Cavalier for dinners. Often her diary states that she waited for a call at one, spoke to Yul at four, and, as he had no time between shows, she went to her Cavalier's home, then rushed to be back at her apartment for Yul's eight-fifteen call. Later, Yul worked out a calling schedule that even included those moments during the play when he was not on stage. When Gertrude Lawrence was doing her big number, "Getting to Know You," the King, offstage in all his bespangled splendor, was probably once again dialing Dietrich's number.

Between yearning and glorying in Yul's appearances and calls, she managed to fit in Michael Wilding as he passed through New York. She so hated to disappoint lovers of days gone by and considered it only natural to allow them to partake of what, after all, had once been wholly theirs. I tried once to question the basic ethics of such generosity. She replied:

"But they are so sweet when they ask, and then, they are so happy afterwards. So . . . you do it!" adding coyly, "Don't you?"

All year, her diary continues to record the hours when Yul came, called, stayed, canceled, didn't call, or was with his wife, whom Dietrich always referred to as Her or She.

> September 15
> Left at 6 AM. Heaven. Called at 6:30
> The world stood still. Called at 12:00.
> Came here for breakfast.
> Happiness!!!
> Called afternoon.
> Don called at midnight—message:
>   "Don't forget I love my Crowd."
> To Hell with "Her."
>
> September 25
> No word all day.
> Misery
> Flowers from him at 6:00
> Call at 6:30. All is well.

My mother poured her heart out to those who "knew," which meant my home became her daily forum. She either appeared between Yul's visits or phoned me constantly: He called; he didn't call; had I heard anything? What did I think? I was his friend—I should know. Had his wife really left him? Was he lying? Was he perhaps still sleeping with his wife? Was I sure that he loved only her? What did Bill, as a man, think? Et cetera, et cetera, et cetera. When I was busy with my children or in rehearsals, she either badgered my husband at work or left repeated messages on the switchboard of CBS for "Maria Riva to call her mother *immediately*."

Bob Hope left to bring Christmas cheer to the fighting men in Korea. My mother was so in love, I don't think she even knew there was a war going on. Certainly Dietrich never volunteered to entertain "the boys" in this one. But then, this time her "only love" was safe on Broadway.

We were never allowed to celebrate my mother's birthday. The world, yes. The famous of that world naturally, but those she considered her family, never! That was punishable by her deep-freeze method of ostracizing the offender from her hemisphere. A banishment to be wished, but as it never lasted forever, the reentry was made so unpleasant it didn't warrant the primary mistake. No cards, no flowers, no gifts, no cake, no party. This did not mean that one was allowed to forget the date of her birthday. She would call and say:

"You know who called me . . ." Usually there followed a list of several presidents, political leaders, famous writers, musicians, physicians, and a sprinkling of privileged actors and directors—then came the flowers line:

". . . and you should see the flowers! The baskets are so huge they won't go through the door! The roses are too tall for all the vases! No one can move! The apartment is like a green-house! I can't breathe and I don't know where to put all the cases of champagne!" She paused for breath.

This was our cue to complain "pitifully":

"But, Massy, you told us not to send you anything—you don't want us to—you gave strict orders not to do anything for your birthday!" so that my mother could reply:

"Of course I don't want *you* to do anything—but I just wanted you to know how everyone else makes such a fuss for my birthday!"

It was a game we played for fifty years, until I heard from a trusted source that my mother had called, thanked an unknown fan for remembering her birthday, adding that his flowers and card had been especially welcome as "her daughter never remembered to send her anything." From then on, I cabled my mother or phoned her on the morning of her birthday, always beginning with the words: "I know it is against the rules, that you have forbidden it, but . . ." She still told everyone I had forgotten. But at least, now I knew she lied. My children were confused by all this game playing, and, when they were older, resented it terribly, as indeed they should. My husband simply refused to play. It did not endear him to her, but then, he had the strength not to care.

The fifties were full of fascinating men—Yul Brynner (ABOVE), the King; Edward R. Murrow (BELOW), the Crusader—to name two who loved and were loved in return.

After only one year on live television, I made the cover of *Life*, with a "little" help from my famous parent.

At the age of fifty-two,
the Las Vegas years
with their "naked"
dresses begin.

Louis Armstrong, for
the first time upstaged
by a pair of gorgeous
gams.

ABOVE: Each year she played Vegas we had to come up with new ideas for her big finale. This chorus line, à la Rockettes, caused a sensation. She used it later in her world tours. BELOW: There was a reason her necklaces were placed so close to the neck—they hid the secret that was underneath.

THE HOTEL THAT MADE LAS VEGAS ... THE ENTERTAINMENT CAPITAL OF THE WORLD
HOTEL SAHARA

On December 27, 1951, Marlene Dietrich turned fifty. She had altered her birth year so often that very few people knew the truth, my mother least of all. She always had that amazing ability to believe unconditionally whatever lies she invented, so, as far as she was concerned, she was—maybe forty? And who was to say no? She looked no more than thirty and behaved, at least in her romantic life, like sixteen.

Noël sent champagne and an offering of Coward rhyme for the occasion:

To celebrate your birthday most adorable Marlene
I have been to an immense amount of trouble to get you this expensive little bottle of champagne.
Please remember that my love's in every bubble.
From Mr. Noël Coward
with compliments to Miss Dietrich
and a smacking great kiss

She thought it extremely inferior. Not the champagne, that she drank, the rhyme she gave me to throw away. Yul gave her what she wanted. She wrote in her diary on that day:

12:00— Evening
Yes and Heaven!
Wish my birthday was every day!!

As everyone had known, *Rancho Notorious* was a lackluster film. In the hopes of stirring up some interest, RKO announced it would present two of its stars, Dietrich and Mel Ferrer, "in person" the day the film opened in Chicago, in March of 1952. I never did know how anyone managed to get my mother to agree to do such a thing. Starlets were made to prance suddenly onto lit-up movie-house stages, to do their saccharine speeches into hastily placed microphones in front of ogling movie fans, but Dietrich?

I was scheduled to appear with Charlton Heston in a scene from *Jane Eyre* at a Westinghouse convention and promised to fly from there to Chicago in time to help my mother through the trauma this personal appearance was certain to be. I arrived on the 4th of March to utter bedlam. Once again, completely out of character, my mother had gone to Elizabeth Arden to find an evening dress to wear for the occasion. The style had to be exaggerated and flamboyant enough so that she could be seen down on the stage of that vast movie palace. Years later, she fully agreed with me that she must have been slightly deranged at the time to have gone to Arden in the first place, let alone choose a huge concoction of layers upon layers of ruffled, stiffened tulle in graded shades of hot pink! Dietrich, who had invented evening dresses with sleeves, now stood in this exaggerated lamp shade, the bodice of which left her shoulders and arms bare, her breasts flattened shapeless under pleated net.

She looked like a huge boiled lobster in drag.
As always in Dietrich's life, this ridiculous personal appearance, the awful dress, her desperate
embarrassment and fury at finding herself in such
a situation, having to show herself in the flesh
for nothing more important than to promote a
very bad film, caused her to come up with a
solution that later contributed to her glorious
success in Las Vegas. Still in her fit of madness,
she had also agreed to warble the atrocious song
from the film, plus a second one for good measure. I was stunned and decided her agent must
have caught her between "heaven" visits from
Yul, otherwise she would never have agreed to
any of it.

She had designed a revealing dance-hall costume for the film that showed off her legs to perfection. After seeing herself in the lobster tulle,
she knew that she had to get out of it as fast as
possible, show the people how she really could
look, and so, her later to be world-famous "fast
change" was born. Fast changes, most under a
minute, were a standard necessity in live television, and one of my specialties. I used to get
jobs because I could do a sixty-second change
from elegant evening dress to fleeing downtrod-
den refugee. It was "Iron Curtain" time, and I
was escaping from the KGB constantly. I now
taught my mother the trick and timing of un-
derdressing. When she walked out onto the vast

stage, under the voluminous skirts of her dress she already wore the black tights and high-laced shoes of her film costume. As she exited into the wings after her introduction, I ripped the dress off, she stepped into her foundation on which the entire costume, sleeves, swag, bustle, bolero, and jewels were sewn, zipped her up, and back onto the stage the "real" Dietrich stepped— from fat lobster to luscious dance-hall queen in sixty seconds! The crowd went wild, just like her GIs during the war. She had them, knew it, and basked in the feeling of power such moments always achieve. We did this magic act for the twelve, three, six, and nine-forty-five shows, and each time, it got the identical reaction of stunned surprise, followed by adulation that we had planned for.

When she returned to New York, she signed for her own weekly radio show, a concoction of espionage and mystery called *Café Istanbul*. Between agonizing, rhapsodizing over Yul, she rewrote radio scripts, recorded songs with Mitch Miller, kept up her close relationship with the Cavalier, took her favorite midnight planes that in 1952 still offered berths to Los Angeles, spent a secret weekend with her King in Palm Springs, and when he returned to New York, remained in Hollywood to guest-star on Bing Crosby's radio show, had dinners with Tyrone Power, indulged in a romantic interlude with a very handsome star who accompanied her openly to the homes of the James Masons and Van Johnsons. Her diary states that it was all "fun." A very unusual word for my mother to use in relationship to herself. I congratulate "Kirk" for accomplishing it.

Still in the "happy glow" of her new California romance, she returned to New York:

May 12, 1952
Arrived late 1 PM
Y here
Till 6 (He does love me)
Called at 6:45
Will come at 12:00
Am astonished but don't get too hopeful so not to be disappointed if it means nothing.
Y at 12:00 Midnight till 12:45
It means nothing

May 15
Decided I love him too much. Such longing is ridiculous after a whole year.
Lunch

May 17
Breakfast

Sunday May 18
All alone.
Remarque—dinner

May 20
All for nothing.
Make up my mind there is no love no nothing.

May 21
Y here breakfast tell him of decision.
Telephoned— All is well. Wilder dinner
Stork.
Yul here

My mother always had the ability to create
her own amnesia. She chose those realities that
she feared or considered expendable and simply
erased them from her conscious world. As she
had done throughout her thirties, she recorded
the first day of her menses in her diary with an
X, not to be confused with the sign of the double
X, which stood for sexual intercourse. My
mother was in her fifty-first year, when she wrote
on May 22, 1952:

X— Big Jump— Almost two months!

Stricken, she came over to my house and showed
me her panties.

"You see? All this time you and I thought
I was pregnant and now we know—nothing! But
why did it stop for so long? Do you have that
too? That it stops for no reason?"

I took her to my gynecologist, who put her
on hormones and tried to explain what meno-
pause was, but gave up when she turned to him
and said:

"But, if you say these hormones are so
great, why don't you give them to my daughter?
I am sure she needs these shots too!"

One morning, she rushed into the house, the picture of outrage tinged with fury: "He says he cannot live without me and then—goes and fucks Taylor!"

For a second, the "he" confused me: "Who?"

"Michael Wilding! He married that English tart, Elizabeth Taylor!! Why? Can you tell me why? It must be those huge breasts of hers—he likes them to dangle in his face." And, a few months later:

"She got pregnant rather fast, don't you think?" and that finished poor Michael—that is, until they were divorced, when he returned, was chastised for his "insanity," and forgiven.

CBS Television had signed me to an exclusive contract and, as my face had become known to American audiences, *Life* magazine decided to do a "famous mother and daughter" layout. My mother and I had posed together once before for *Vogue*, but then I had only been "the daughter." Now I had a name of my own, an identity, so it meant something special to me. We reported to Milton Greene's studio in June; my mother always stated that it was her idea to have me pose looking down at her in the famous photograph, but it was Milton Greene who decided to print the composite photograph in reverse, so that I was the image and Dietrich the reflection. It was his version the editors decided was important enough to use for a *Life* cover. The article inside was mostly about Dietrich, but lo and behold, when it spoke of Maria Riva and there was no "daughter of" appendage, I knew I had made it—I finally had a name of my very own. My mother took to carrying *Life* around to people's homes along with her latest records.

"Isn't it beautiful? Of course, I told them — No, No. ME on the bottom—Maria must be on top. She is 'the star' and my hair looks better spread down. Of course, the article is on me, but they were nice. Good people at *Life*, they wrote about her big success too."

In August Yul was scheduled to go on a two-week vacation, after Gertrude Lawrence was due back after her two-week hiatus. Although my mother always maintained that "Gertie" was one of her best friends, never once do her diaries of this time refer to Miss Lawrence's failing health.

We packed training pants, spades, sandals, and teddy bears, bundled summer necessities into our Ford, and we were off to our little rented house on Long Island. My mother stayed, waiting for the phone to ring.

> August 2nd
> Breakfast 10:00 here till 1:00
> Pretty vague laboring conversation about show. But then, why does he come here? Cannot be for that cup of coffee? Never saw

anyone so preoccupied with himself. Flowers came while he was here and it suddenly occurred to me that he never sends me flowers or brings me something or makes the slightest effort to return all the things I do for him which should embarrass a man. Maybe he thinks he repays with the afternoons. What a horrible thought.

He is coming tonight. I asked him what he was doing tonight and he said—I could come to see you. I said you do love me if I have to ask.

He probably thought he was here yesterday and that takes care of his obligations. What horrible thoughts I have today.

I write all this to explain to myself why I swing back and forth and don't keep the resolutions I make—not to doubt his love.

Sunday, August 3rd
Sunday all alone. Time to think about my Sucker-ism.

August 6th
It is terrible now, he has not called or come. How inconsiderate, if he could not get out of appointments, he could call to say so.

This weekend with the maid on duty he could have even spent a good part of Sunday with me, including the evening. I'm his little whore, let's face it!

On the 6th of September, Gertrude Lawrence died of liver cancer, having suffered the agonies of this disease while continuing to perform in *The King and I*. She gets top billing in my mother's diary:

> Sept. 7, 1952
> Gertie died
> Here for breakfast.

And, on the 9th, the day of her funeral:

> Funeral, with Maria
> Here 4–7:00
> Y drunk
> Ferrer dinner

Sometime during this period, my mother's Cavalier divorced his wife in the belief that she would marry him and attain the worry-free male-cosseted life my mother always claimed she so desired. During the years of emotional upheaval of her passionate affair with Yul Brynner, those years when she suffered, mooned over her "gypsy king," still managing to "keep happy," as she put it, Michael Wilding, Michael Rennie, Harry Cohn, Edward R. Murrow, Piaf, Adlai Stevenson, Sam Spiegel, Frank Sinatra, Harold Arlen, Kirk Douglas, and an impressive array of those ladies and gentlemen who must remain nameless for various reasons, yet never relinquishing her passion for Gabin, she often referred to the Cavalier's proposal of marriage with:

"Thank God I didn't marry him. Can you see me, the grande dame in Palm Beach, with nothing better to do than play canasta all day?"

JUDY BROUGHT BACK "two shows a day" at the Palace. We went to her opening *en famille* —well, not quite: My father was plucking chickens in California, so one of my mother's "pals" was her escort. That sweet voice, with its inner heartbreak, soared, filled that famous shrine of vaudeville, then left a bitter taste in my heart as it faded. The audience, on the edge of hysteria, screamed their adulation. My mother—who pretended to admire Garland but secretly couldn't stand her and never was able to understand her magical talent as it stemmed from inner creativity, not contrived, manufactured art, as it did in Dietrich's case—clapped as enthusiastically as the rest of the audience. Judy had become a homosexual fetish, and my mother, being another, knew she was being watched.

We went backstage to congratulate the star of the evening. I took her in my arms, it seemed the natural thing to do. I held her carefully, like those blown-glass souvenirs one buys at fairs— she seemed highly breakable. Our reunion was soundless and suspended. As the hordes of gushing admirers pushed into the dressing room, we let go of each other and the moment.

That evening, my mother insisted on holding court at the El Morocco, in her favorite, its exclusive inner sanctum, the Champagne Room. My mind was on other things than Dietrich being Dietrich, so much so that I did not hear Piaf say to my husband, in French, which he spoke very well:

"Well—how does it feel, living off your mother-in-law's money?" It shocked him so, he asked her to repeat it, to make sure she had actually said such a thing. She did. That's when I heard it, at the same moment as my mother.

"Oh, Mon Amour!"—both Gabin and Piaf rated "*amour*"—"but he makes Maria so happy!"

As other tables were as usual watching the goddess and her entourage, I rose without saying a word. My husband looked at my eyes and stood. We made our polite good nights and left before I could explode. The absolute coarseness of that French guttersnipe did not surprise me; unfortunately, neither did the basic nastiness of my mother. Neither did their love affair—the Lady and the Tramp.

My mother was very proud of being Piaf's "best friend," as she publicly put it. When Piaf married, it was Marlene who had her dress made for her, a copy of her own chiffon Dior, dressed her, hung a delicate Cartier cross around her little throat, and like the cavalier lover she was to most of her women, sent her into the arms of another. Later, when Piaf's pugilist lover was killed, it was Dietrich who calmed her grief-stricken Sparrow with comforting *"amour."*

Remarque announced he was thinking of getting married to—of all people—Paulette Goddard! My mother was appalled; I have to admit, so was I.

"What insanity! He is not really going to marry that Goddard woman, is he? Doesn't he know she only wants him for his paintings? I am going to talk to him," and she did. Boni asked my mother to marry him; if she refused, he was marrying Paulette, which he finally did. My mother's only comment:

"Now, just watch. Now—she'll try to kill him. He was a great writer, but about women—always so stupid!" and sweet Boni was no more.

When Remarque died in 1970, Dietrich declared, "Well! It took that terrible woman a few years, but she finally did it. Now she's as rich as Croesus and can rot in her luxury," and went into her room to mourn him as the rightful widow she believed herself to be.

Hemingway's masterpiece *The Old Man and the Sea* was published and my mother, who had fallen madly in love with it when he had sent her the first galleys, went about like a proud wife who had always known her husband had even deeper greatness than was realized by those not privileged to know the real inner man.

Thanks to Yul, I became involved in raising funds for the wonderful work done by the United Cerebral Palsy Organization. In the spring of 1953, when John Ringling North gave this charity the opening of the circus at Madison Square Garden, stars volunteered their services in everything from sweeping up after the elephants to flying through the air. Without jockeying for position, everyone joined in the common goal of raising money for the children afflicted with this devastating brain injury. My mother did not involve herself in charitable causes. I never knew her to make a donation to any charitable organization, and yet she was renowned for her limitless charity—another Dietrich myth that no one ever challenged. It is true that she was extremely generous, but only if it benefited her in some way: fur coats to maids, who then felt too overcome with gratitude to quit, no matter how she treated them; doctor and hospital bills paid for the children, wives, and husbands in her employ, acquaintances, and friends, who, then consumed by gratitude, could be counted on to keep their mouths shut about the intimate secret things they knew about their benefactress and be on call, day or night, to give service. Dietrich was ready to help anyone.

She used her money, her energies, her time,

her fame, but never for the benefit of an organized charity. My mother demanded that her generosity be known by the individual recipients—in that way she could control them through their gratitude. All my life I heard my mother complain about those she helped, when they did not repay her generosity in ways she expected. It went something like this:

"Sweetheart. Can you believe it? The maid, just now, she can't come on Sunday! Because 'it's Easter' and she has to be with her child! Remember two years ago, when she told me all about that child of hers? How he limped and how I called all the doctors—remember when they said he had to have a special shoe? How I ordered it for her right away and how she thanked me, kissed my hands and cried? And, after all that, *now* she can't come because of some stupid holiday with that child! Ridiculous! You see how people are? You do everything for them and then they still do what *they* want!"

This extended all the way to ethnic levels:

"I gave up my country—my language—for them, and now, what do I get? The stores are closed for Yom Kippur!"

This time, knowing that cerebral palsy was Yul's favorite cause, I hoped to be able to persuade my mother to participate, particularly if she was offered a role in the circus that was unique, one that she would not have to share with any other celebrity. When we offered her the position of ringmaster, she immediately agreed and began designing her costume. Long before the era of "hot pants," Dietrich wore tiny velvet shorts above black silk tights, high-heeled boots, white tie, scarlet tailcoat, shiny top hat, and, cracking her whip, was a sensation. *Vogue* ran a full-page color photograph of her in her circus splendor, every newspaper proclaimed her the "star of the evening," and United Cerebral Palsy gained a lot of additional publicity. Ask Miss Dietrich what cerebral palsy is, and she would reply: "Oh, that's when I designed that beautiful ringmaster costume."

Eisenhower ran for president, and my mother's rage knew no bounds. When he was elected, she threatened to return her passport, but not her Medal of Freedom.

"That coward! *He* is going to lead a nation? The whole country has gone insane!" and went to call Hemingway.

I signed to star in what was to be the first TV adventure series in color to be filmed overseas. My husband would be the production designer, and our children would accompany us. My mother was furious. But, as Israel was to be our base of operations, she couldn't publicly show her disapproval; privately was another matter:

"All the Jews that didn't make it in Holly-wood are there. What do you think you are going to be able to get done there? An American television show in the desert? It will be worse than what we went through in *The Garden of Allah*! And why must you schlep the children with you? They can stay here with me . . . and who will do your hair?"

Yul thought it a wonderful adventure and wished us well. So, on the 24th of May, 1953, we stepped into Pan Am's trusty Clipper and left for Gander, our first refueling stop on the long journey to Tel Aviv. My mother continued to fly to California for weekend meetings in Palm Springs with "him." As I was away, I am not sure who this "him" is that her diary refers to. Knowing her, it could be anybody. Between lovers, she visited my father.

As our daily language was now English, even her letters to me acquired an American rhythm.

> Angel,
> I saw Papi. He is working terribly hard, much too hard I thought after the operation but he is stubborn, you know. Tami is nuttier than ever and I was crying into my beer driving home from the ranch because it still affects me to see the crazy be stronger than the sane. He had promised her that she did not have to cook in the beginning and they went with me where they always go for dinner, a lousy little joint with a loud jukebox.

The food was so greasy that I had some cottage cheese instead and did not touch it. He ate all this terribly heavy greasy stuff and I asked him (I ask, you know, well trained as I am) if I should not cook Pot-au-Feu and bring it out, they could heat it for three days at least and he would have something good to eat and no work. I was told yes, I cooked a whole day, vegetables ready to eat, etc. When I arrived, Tami yelled she could not keep it all, she would still have to wash dishes even if she would only heat it, and I calmly packed everything together, washed the dishes after dinner and left too sad to say a gay good-bye. I never went out after that because I don't want to cause any trouble for him.

I could see my mother arriving at that little house, her limousine laden with enough expensive groceries to feed a family of twelve for a month. The chauffeur lugging the hotel-size kettles containing her famous pot-au-feu into Tami's tiny kitchen, throwing out whatever was in her refrigerator in order to make room for all the things the wife had brought, while Tami stood helplessly by. In one grandiose gesture that others would once again interpret as Dietrich's "wonderfully selfless generosity," she had invaded another woman's home, claiming her domain, belittling her ability to care for the man she loved, made her feel useless, poor, uncaring, and ungrateful, and to top it all off, my mother's pot-au-feu was so good, one even felt like a lousy cook. I knew exactly how Tami felt—I had been there myself. At least, I had a husband who made me feel wanted, even disliked my mother's cooking, whereas my father had probably given Tami hell for making trouble again and causing wonderful, generous Mutti to feel that her "great effort" was not appreciated.

We set up our house in the Sharon Hotel, between Tel Aviv and Haifa. What a country! Wild and serene, young and ancient, a land of contrasts—its life force guided in anticipation of a great dream yet to be fully realized. All pioneer countries have this sense of grabbing the future. Here, antiquity added its own dimension. Timelessness and newly born, the fire-brand cactus children and the sage survivors.

We ate kosher, learned the rules, customs of the ages. We didn't have to—we chose to. We wanted our young children to respect all religions by becoming involved, understanding their laws before making up their minds which one suited them, gave them the haven in which best to grow their own spirit.

The gentle young woman placed a dish before Michael, who, in his five-year-old treble, asked, intrigued:

"Sarah, why is your telephone number written on your arm?"

She looked at me, hesitant to give such a young child an explanation. I loved her for not being shocked or angry at his innocence.

"Tell him, Sarah. It is important for him to know."

And she did—simply, without rancor or personal anguish.

We looked for pebbles on the beach that day, a very serious, highly dedicated activity.

"Mommy, look—look! A pretty one, all shiny white with silver spots! I'm going to give it to Sarah, for her poor hurted arm!"

In New York, my mother wrote to me:

> I am writing an article for *Ladies' Home Journal* on: "How to Be Loved," for which I get 20,000. Yes! You read right, $20,000. Remarque was furious at the price. It did not help me that I pointed out that crap is better paid than good stuff, he was burning up.
>
> . . . I can see the men who claim to have been so miserable with me say: Why didn't she act like that with me? I give the women sugar too so that everybody is happy.
>
> Then I have signed to write a book on beauty for Doubleday. There Remarque was not so furious because it is about beauty. About love he felt the competition. Only I can write about love and the workings of it.

She worked on "How to Be Loved" during the hours she waited for Yul to call or appear at her door. She wrote of those emotions she wanted him to be aware of, then showed him her work in the hope that he would recognize all the feelings she was trying to communicate to him. Actually, most of the article was written to enchant Yul, and when he offered to help her, they spent some of the best times they had together collaborating.

For many sad reasons, our series collapsed without a single segment having been filmed. I cabled my mother that we were returning to New York.

August 13, '53

My love,

This is going to be one hell of a fast letter so that it gets there in case you leave.

The Las Vegas thing: I signed with the Sahara the biggest joint there. Not the Sands, the chicest joint there, where I stayed and went on with Tallu. She introduced me and I went out to see if I could get them to whistle. The Sands is a plush real night club that everybody prefers because it is small. They whistled all right, I sang three songs and then finished with Tallu with "May the Good Lord Bless and Keep You." But it proved to me that I was not nervous even without rehearsal, naturally discounting that it is easier to give a benefit always than performing for money.

The Sahara offered me $30,000 a week for 3 weeks against the highest price ever paid, $20,000 which Tallu got at the Sands. Also for the next year again. So I took it. December fifteenth I open, till Jan. 5 '54. Isn't it funny that I should have a year with big earnings and all outside of films? I am trying to contact Orson because I want to do the mind-reading act which I have completely forgotten. Danny Thomas is frantically searching his material to remember what he did with me. I thought after my songs it would be a good thing to get the audience to participate in the mind-reading. Then the chorus is going to do a Circus number with a clown act from Paris in it and Mitch is having a Circus song written. I will come into the dancers with a whip and finish my act with the Circus number so I can wear the costume from the Madison Square Garden evening. I only have to do 25 minutes, they beg you to be short so that the people go out and gamble. I could not say no to this fabulous offer. I am not scared either. I was so at home on the stage there that I am sure even when it is for real I won't shake like Van Johnson and Tallu did.

So I won't be home for Christmas.

The wandering Riva family headed home. Each of us a little wiser in a lot of things.

My mother's diary makes no mention of the

Las Vegas deal. She recorded only those vital moments that were really important to her:

September 30
Here for lunch.

October 1
Here for same.

October 2
Here for same 12
After show to stay

October 3
Left 12:45

The next day, she records that Yul came back for "the same," which I do not necessarily think was lunch, and that she went out with Otto Preminger to the Stork Club that evening, and that Yul called her there at two a.m., came over to the apartment, and stayed the night. How that man managed to be the pivotal force of that exhausting musical astounds me still.

She told me that Yul was against her idea of doing Orson's mind-reading act, that he thought it would cheapen her to involve the audience in such a way. I agreed and counseled her to either play against the Vegas image or top it, but never to join it. She turned to Yul, saying:

"What is it that you two always agree? Just like that so important charity thing of yours. But, you know, Maria is right, Dietrich must be a *sensation* and that we can only do with what I wear."

She left for Hollywood to begin her first meetings with Jean Louis at Columbia Pictures. She knew that only a Wardrobe Department of a major studio was equipped to execute a costume worthy of Marlene Dietrich's first appearance on a Vegas stage. Hollywood had cornered the market in skilled beaders way back in the twenties, when Theda Bara slithered across silent screens. Her first choice had been the wonderful Irene, but as that was impossible, she had decided on Jean Louis, whose work she admired. As he was Columbia Pictures' top designer, my mother had to get permission from his boss to use him and the Studio's workshop. It was sheer chance that at this time Harry Cohn, one of the most feared and disliked of the movie moguls, was interested in hiring her to star in the film version of *Pal Joey* that he was just beginning to develop, or she might never have been allowed to make her famous dresses on his lot. Years later, when Harry Cohn finally banned Dietrich from the Columbia lot for disrupting the Studio's entire Wardrobe Department, she loved to tell her many stories about him. How she had first approached him in 1953, begging to be allowed to make her costumes and how he had agreed only after demanding her sexual favors: "Right there, in his office, he wanted it! In the daytime!

In return for the services of his seamstresses!"
As Harry Cohn was despised by nearly everyone
and a renowned lech, she could get as raunchy
as she wanted when telling her stories about him.
Yet her diaries make no reference to his demands, nor to her "shocked" refusal. They do
say that they discussed *Pal Joey* and that she
dated him frequently over the next two years,
until he dared to throw her off the lot. At which
time, she told me that she asked Yul to get his
gangster friends to intercede for her, or, if that
didn't work, to beat him up in a dark alley. Dietrich loved this imagery of planned mayhem to
one she considered her enemy. All who wrote
books on her were wished this bloodied fate in
shadowed alleys. I am extremely careful whenever I have to pass one!

Who finally did persuade Harry Cohn to
change his mind and reopen the Columbia Studio
facilities to Dietrich has always been an intriguing mystery. One version has Frank Costello the
avenging angel, another had the Mafia threatening to set fire to the Studio, another that Rita
Hayworth had been sent by Dietrich's supporters
to Harry Cohn's office with orders to "soften him
up"! Another that Hedda Hopper, with all the
power of her position as the queen of the Hollywood gossip columnists, was willing and ready
to divulge "all" she knew . . . if Harry insisted
on being so mean to "Marlene."

During this time of upheaval, my mother notes in her diary:

Cohn here Talked left at 2:00 AM

and shortly after:

Resumed fittings Columbia.

Dietrich didn't need gangsters to do her dirty work. But she so loved the idea of the underworld going to bat for her that she perpetuated many scenarios that showed her as being unjustly treated, only to be saved by "Dorothy di Frasso's boyfriend Bugsy Siegel's friends" and embellished such stories with her own inventiveness whenever she chose.

The basic design of that gold sequined dress that had served her so well during her "army days," that had called forth those wolf whistles from adoring GIs, was now pressed back into service. This time, the object was to entrance a civilian audience who had paid a huge fee for the privilege.

First, she and Jean Louis took Birannccini's "souffle," dyed it the color of Dietrich's skin, and constructed her foundation. Next, they covered her from neck to toe in the same diaphanous material, molding it to the foundation that formed her body. Only then could the work of "gilding the lily" begin.

My mother's stage career boasted many

such works of art. Each dress cost thousands of
dollars and, more important, thousands of hours
of work. Hundreds of people labored to achieve
their perfection. Each bead was placed by hand
into its strategic position to form the intricate
patterns, then sewn individually into place, only
to be removed with trembling hands from the
fragile material, to be repositioned for what was
often the fiftieth time. Thousands upon thousands of beads were treated with this fanatic per-
fectionism, until Dietrich saw in her reflected
image what she wanted the audience to see—the
sublime woman, the perfect body, technically
completely clothed, appearing naked to the human eye, yet remaining the untainted goddess.

Each year that Dietrich played Vegas, she
strove for a new effect, hoping to recapture that
stunned moment when the audience first saw her
and gasped. And each time she achieved it. Over
the years, she shimmered in gold, white, black
bugle beads, sequins, mirrors, rhinestones, crystal tassels, balls, and fringes, trailed rivers of
feathers behind her, enfolded herself in giant fox
shawls, installed wind machines to blow masses
of chiffon away from her body—so that she appeared as exposed, as magnificent as her favorite
sculpture, the *Winged Victory of Samothrace*.

The wind effect she had used in *The Garden
of Allah*, the chiffon shawl bordered in yards of
fox had enveloped her in *Desire*, even the collar

and sleeves of her justly famous swan coat were amazingly familiar in design to that swansdown jacket she wore in the boudoir scene in *The Scarlet Empress*. I am sure that my mother never realized that she was reinventing perfection from the past. Besides, it was all so perfect even the second time around, there was no reason to draw her attention to it.

By the time she designed her two masterpieces, her iridescent bugle-bead dress that we christened "the eel," because she looked like one swimming through clear water when she moved in it, and her swansdown coat, with its eight-foot circular train for which two thousand swans were said to have given the down off their breasts—willingly—she had outgrown Las Vegas, was performing her concerts in legitimate theaters.

In 1954, her second year in Las Vegas, when she achieved a one-minute change from her elaborate dress into her tails, it was not only to bask in the appreciation of such a metamorphosis, it also afforded her the opportunity to sing those songs whose lyrics she felt demanded a man's attitude. Though most songs written for men can be sung by substituting *she* for *he*, my mother was convinced that only male lyrics were truly worth singing. She believed that as men had their priorities right, only they could sing about love and its disenchantment with the proper authority. Women, being so unpredictable, were prone to emotional exaggeration and, therefore, could get boring singing about their loves. Dietrich, the woman who sat by the telephone all day mooning over her married lover while pining for her Frenchman, actually believed herself exempt from her critical judgment of all women.

I began choosing her material, structuring the emotional progression of her performances, giving her a dramatic format that she could handle and feel comfortable with. The opening segment of her show was easy, "glamour and sex," both visually and vocally, combined with her Dietrich standards from her films and records: "See What the Boys in the Back Room Will Have," "Johnny," "Laziest Gal in Town," and all the others. The applause would carry her to the wings. She would exit to shed her extravagant coat, in later years using this moment to also wash down her painkillers with champagne or scotch, and reappear, uncovered—divine fragility—to perform those songs that had a tragic impact, the Weltschmerz Dietrich knew how to communicate so very well. This was the hardest category for her to perform, but when she managed to sustain its dramatic impact without allowing herself to get maudlin with self-pity, she could be truly outstanding. "Go Away from My Window," "When the World Was Young," "Lili Marlene," and of course, "Where Have All the Flowers Gone?" She fought me often on my choices, especially with "Flowers." She absolutely refused to sing it, saying:

"All that toodle, toodle, toodle about where flowers have gone—it never ends! It's only good when the girls pick them!" When I explained to her that she should sing it with condemnation, that she should bring to it a hatred of war, she mumbled that, again, I was "asking a lot of her 'feeble' acting talent," but as I had been right about the other songs, she was willing to give "Flowers" a try. Occasionally, she found and fell in love with some awful songs, insisted on singing them—no matter what I said. As there were always more than enough idolizing fans in the audience who could be counted on to scream "bravo" if she did nothing but stand before them, she used their enthusiasm as proof positive that, despite my opinion, such songs as "Boomerang Baby" were after all just "perfect."

Once she was in her tails, I gave her material that she could relax with, could enjoy. She had fun with "Whoopee," indulged her favorite fantasy of the lonely lover in "One for My Baby," and explained love as she perceived it with "I've Grown Accustomed to Her Face"—Dietrich could always sing real love to a woman better than to a man. Sentimental love, *that* she did better as a woman. But these polished performances evolved over the years, when she performed her one-woman shows on concert stages and not in nightclubs.

Her first opening in Las Vegas in December of 1953 was a triumph, the "naked dress"—a sensation. Her diary is blank for the rest of that year. She was riding a new wave of success—no time, nor necessity, to record it.

Dietrich loved Las Vegas. She basked in the nightly adoration of her audiences and was proud that the elite group of Vegas entertainers accepted her as one of their own. Gone were the hours of waiting by the phone for Yul's calls, she had a job to do. As always, her entire energies were now marshaled toward her work. Only when her duty was done, her show over, did she allow herself to "play." During the years that she appeared there, Vegas was the entertainment capital of the world. In one night, one could see Dietrich's first show, run next door, catch Peggy Lee's, dash down the main drag to Tony Bennett's second show, Betty Hutton, Jimmy Durante, Lena Horne, Nat King Cole, Sophie Tucker, Louis Armstrong, Luis Prima, Noël Coward, Frankie Laine, Frank Sinatra, Rosemary Clooney, etc., etc. The celebrities at ringside often outshone the stars on the stage! My mother, who never wanted to be a part of the Hollywood community, who refused to fraternize with her fellow contract stars at Paramount, now experienced and welcomed, for the first time in her life, the warm feeling of belonging to this exclusive family of her peers. From all over the world, people flew into Vegas to catch Dietrich's act at the Sahara.

The night Harold Arlen came to see my mother's show, he fell madly in love with her and remained so till the day he died. In her nightly telephone calls to me, she described her first reaction on meeting this famous composer.

"I just stood there, in awe, in front of him. But you know he looks white! How can the man who wrote 'Stormy Weather' be white? He also wrote that Bluebird thing that Judy Garland insists on singing with all her blubbering, but— you know his hair is very kinky! I am going to ask Nat King Cole if Harold Arlen is black or white. He is also very ugly . . . but sweet." Arlen became my mother's first Vegas lover, and later, her ever devoted victim.

Always self-conscious of her lack of vocal range, she heard that a thing called cortisone was supposed to open the vocal cords and began swallowing this drug as though it were candy. This was long before cortisone was suspected to trigger certain forms of cancer. But even if she had known about these dangerous side effects, my mother would have continued taking it. She always believed that she was immune to all afflictions that mere humans are heir to.

Before the end of her Vegas engagement, Noël Coward called to tell her that when a Major Neville Willing announced himself, not to ignore his presence but to receive him, for he had had a most wonderful idea and could be trusted.

The major, a dapper little man, as elegant and spiffy as the nightclub he represented, offered to spread London at Dietrich's feet. A four-week engagement at the famous Café de Paris, throwing in the Oliver Messel suite at the Dorchester Hotel, and all the Rolls-Royces, complete with liveried chauffeurs, that she might desire. My mother, unimpressed, wondered why Noël had wasted her time. Then the major played his inspired trump card: He suggested that each night England's leading male actors would introduce the divine "Marlenaaa," that they might even be persuaded to write their own euphoric introductions of her. That did it! She accepted, but only after making quite sure that when the major said "leading actors," he had meant such luminaries as Laurence Olivier, Ralph Richardson, Michael Redgrave, Alec Guinness, Paul Scofield, and anyone else brilliant enough to warrant calling upon, reminding him that Noël had assured her that he was supposed to be "trustworthy."

My mother closed in Vegas, flew to Hollywood to repair and rebead the dresses she would need for London, then returned to New York.

. . .

We had gone to visit someone, maybe it was still Remarque at the Sherry Netherland, and as my mother had a fitting, we decided to walk the few blocks down Fifth Avenue to her tailor. Dietrich never strolled or window-shopped. Like most visibly famous people, she moved through a crowd rapidly, intent on reaching her destination before being recognized. Suddenly, her gloved fingers gripped my arm, and she jerked me into Tiffany. As my mother, besides never making such erratic gestures, loathed what she called "the most boring jewelry store in the world," I knew that something must be very wrong. Urgently, she whispered to me in German:

"My legs. I have pain in my legs. Pretend you want something, then we can lean on the counter as though we are looking," and pushed me against the glass showcase. One of those cool, polished Tiffany salesladies, her inner excitement veiled as she recognized her famous customer, brought forth her diamond wares for Dietrich's inspection. Taking her time, my mother examined each piece, murmuring such phrases as:

"Not bad stones, but the setting—really! Do men really buy this sort of thing for their women?" As she twisted a magnificent diamond solitaire, "Haven't you anything purer? Only the quality of a stone can excuse the vulgarity of such a size." Finally, my mother signaled me that the pain had subsided and we exited back onto Fifth Avenue, leaving a very disappointed Tiffany lady behind us. I hailed a taxi to take us to Knize, where my mother stood for the next two hours, ramrod still, while tailors worked on perfecting her tails. On the way back to her apartment and Yul's hoped-for call, I suggested that we pursue the cause of our morning's emergency by going to a doctor for a thorough check-up.

"No! Most doctors don't know what they are doing and the really great ones, you can't go to until you know what you have—because they are all 'specialists.' You see, my legs are fine now. You saw how I stood all that time at the fitting. But that was funny today . . . I mean 'ha-ha' funny, at Tiffany's. I wanted to tell that woman the story of Paulette Goddard on the train . . . remember? I told Boni but he wouldn't listen."

It was one of Dietrich's favorites, and as with all of her routines, needed to be heard in her unique cadence to do it justice.

"It was one of those terrible trips on the train, on the way to Hollywood, before we took airplanes. Paulette Goddard was on the train— I think it was when she was still married to Chaplin, or maybe after. She came to my drawing room and we talked. Now, you know me, I must have been *very* lonely to want to talk to Paulette

Goddard! I think it was something that Papi had done or Chevalier or Jaray, or maybe it was later with Aherne or Jean. I can't remember, but it was someone, and I told her how he had treated me badly and she stood up, left, then came back schlepping a large jewelry case—a trunk! Like those that jewelers use when they come to your hotel to show you their whole store— They are made of ugly Moroccan leather and have drawers? Well, Goddard had one of those in *alligator*, and it was full! Nothing but diamonds! Like rocks! And she says to me, very serious, like a professor: 'Marlene, you have to get diamonds. Colored stones are worth nothing. Only pure white stones have lasting value. A man wants you? It's easy! You say no, right away. The next day, he sends you long-stemmed roses, you send them back. The next day, when his orchids arrive, you send them back. His little gifts, expensive perfume, handbags from Hermès, mink coats—things like that, you send everything back. Rubies and diamond clips—back, even emerald and diamond pins. When the first diamond bracelet arrives, it's usually small, so you send *it* back, but you call him and say thank you—sweetly. The next day, when the larger diamond bracelet arrives, you send that back, but now, you let him take you out to lunch— nothing else! The first diamond *ring* never is big—give it back, but say yes to dinner . . . go dancing. The only thing you have to always remember: *Never, ever* sleep with a man until he gives you a pure white stone of at least ten carats!' "

My mother always intoned this credo in a stage whisper, full of breathless admiration, then paused, adding:

"It's true! She really said all that to me. It must work! She has all those enormous diamonds. Terrible woman! But isn't it amazing how those women do it? Get away with it like that?"

The disabling pain, that was like a sudden cramp, came and went. Some days she could walk three whole blocks before having to stop. Some days, two. Other times, after only a few steps, she had to find some excuse to rest and wait out the seizure. She searched for a pattern that might give her a clue as to its origin. Were the legs bad when it was humid? About to storm? Too hot, too cold? Were they better in high heels, medium or low? She discovered that when she had had three glasses of champagne, her legs felt less constricted, and so, tried a couple of glasses at breakfast, and when that seemed to help, took to carrying champagne in a plastic bottle in her handbag. When the legs got better, she forgot for a while that they had ever bothered her, but still refilled her glass as well as her plastic bottle, just in case. She did not stop smoking.

Those in her immediate circle were sworn to secrecy. She spoke of her pains to only those she trusted not to gossip and alert the press to what she perceived as a sudden flaw in the perfection of the Dietrich image. Goddesses who beget physical infirmities descend to the rank of lowly humans, and lose their right to deity.

She subscribed to medical journals, health-food publications, listened attentively to anyone who spoke of anything to do with pains of the lower regions of the body, asking what pills they had found that cured them—then ordered them from her trusted pharmacies around the world who supplied anything without prescription, just for the honor of serving Dietrich.

Over the years she swallowed enormous amounts of her favorite cortisone as well as Butazolidin, phenobarbital, codeine, belladonna, Nembutal, Seconal, Librium, and Darvon. Although my mother would swallow any pill she was given, she actually trusted medication by injection more. She now searched for a doctor who could be "trusted to say nothing," not insist on tests or examinations—just be willing to shoot magic potions into her behind that would do away with all her fears and woes. Reminding her of Tami's tragic history would have done no good; for my mother the thought of being like anyone else was beyond her comprehension. There was only one Dietrich.

"Sweetheart! Sweetheart!" she ran into my house, laughing: "I found him! He gave me one shot and, see—I ran in! He is wonderful! He just looked at me and said, 'All you need is vitamin B shots!'—and he is right! I feel wonderful. I told Yul he has to go there right away for energy."

Even my husband was persuaded to have a "magic" vitamin shot. It took three days to get him down off the wall! Yul was twirling his costar through that famous polka—like a whirling dervish—but my mother believed that she was cured, that all her troubles were over, at least, the physical ones.

Years later, this doctor was arrested for trafficking in amphetamines, but by that time, Dietrich had gone to so many doctors just like him that he no longer remained in her memory. When she boarded her plane on the 15th of June, she carried in her hand luggage the precious vials her "miracle" doctor had prepared for her to see her through the London engagement.

On the plane, she wrote to me, discussing her eventual departure from my life. Still distrusting planes, she was always very superstitious and full of last-minute thoughts whenever she flew, setting everything down on paper before the "final end" she was certain was about to happen. Once she landed safely, she sent the letter off anyway. No use wasting momentous thoughts that proved her eternal devotion just because she found herself still alive.

Angel,
  I never knew fear of death before I had you. But I used to lie awake all night at the hospital already fearing the possibility of your being left without me. I am replaceable everywhere. In all categories. Except in one. And maybe that is what they say is Hell. Should one still know and be removed without power to protect?
  Don't get too tired. You always needed sleep. You and Papi. Let the house go. The joy of a clean house is short. Here I sit with my nails broken, skin cracked on my fingers—I had joy cleaning your house—but I never took a minute away from the children because of the house. There I am again, "knowing the true values."

Massy

Ah! Those famous broken nails and roughened hands—they got a lot of mileage! Her stories of cleaning her daughter's house were famous and appeared in the press the world over. Ridicule by innuendo was her favorite game, and we all drew her fire. Some more than others. It was a lethal execution, devoutly to be escaped —whenever possible. The routine went something like this:

Scene

Manhattan
Elegant dinner party
Elegant people assembled in Elegant Town
House
Living room
Famous World Star rushes in—stops—hes-
itates for an instant, until assembled guests
notice her and respond to her magic aura
All heads turn upstage—toward her

"Marlene!"—the Russian-born hostess ex-
claims as she moves toward her in greeting.
     Furs, white kid gloves are handed to
hovering oriental servant as Marlene
speaks: "Sweetheart! I rushed—I thought I
would never finish and had to miss your
wonderful Stroganoff! Maria called at four,
the baby-sitter *again*—she always has such
trouble with her baby-sitters—of course, I
had to go and help her. So I run over to the
house and my Michael is still asleep! He
must have been fed a very late lunch—I was
worried he was sick—sleeping *so* long in the
afternoon? But Maria rushes out— No matter how big and pregnant she is, Bill *makes
her work*. Don't ask me where she *has* to
go—you know me, too well brought up to
ask questions. Remember last week when I
cleaned the nursery? All the walls and inside
the drawers? The things I found! Well
today—all afternoon—I washed all the
floors! The entire house! That girl she has,

that I found for her and pay, she uses a mop—one of those rag things Americans use! Ridiculous! They think that is cleaning? All they do is smear dirt around! So I did it correctly—on my knees with a scrub brush. You can't imagine the dirt! I'm sure they never clean—and I had to listen for the child, then the telephone rang and I have to answer it. Someone from CBS. I told them that Maria was out and I am washing the floor, so they hang up quickly. Finally, Maria comes back. She was at the supermarket—all this time? I don't know what she cooks for them—from a supermarket! Can't be any good— So I ordered six filet mignons and steak ground for steak tartare and a dozen lamb chops from my butcher the moment I got back to my apartment. Just had time to dress—but I couldn't fix my hands! Look at them! (She stretches her rough and reddened hands out toward the audience.) All my nails are broken! I had to use three new pairs of stockings— they tore every time I touched them with these hands . . . and you should see my knees!

My mother's repertoire included many such monologues. She performed them brilliantly, making every point. Her audiences sympathized, and condemned her verbal victims in absentia. She was a master at character assassination.

On her arrival in London, my mother called

to tell me that Major Baby, her nickname for her new majordomo, had been true to his word, that the Messel suite was like a stage set too beautiful to live in, that all the great actors had agreed to introduce her, were writing their own elaborate introductions, that her feet were swollen, especially the left one but was sure that it was only because of the flying.

She had heard of a young man who was touted to be the best theater critic in England. Having read some of Kenneth Tynan's articles, she had asked to meet this young "genius," as she called him. She described their first meeting:

"I walked into that enormous Oliver Messel suite at the Dorchester and, suddenly, from behind the couch, pops up a white worm—like the ones you find in flour. And this white little thing turns out to be this 'brilliant' writer everyone respects! Well . . . I couldn't just throw him out, after saying to everybody how much I wanted to meet him, so I had to offer him a drink before asking him to leave . . . just to be polite. He was all nervous and shaking and I thought how sad —just another fan! Then we started to talk and he was wonderful! Brilliant! The things he said about Olivier . . . to die! It's so wonderful to finally find someone intelligent to talk to."

During her London engagement, she and Tynan became inseparable. When old lovers arrived, he delicately stepped back into the shadows, reappearing when the coast was clear. Kenneth Tynan wrote many things about my mother, always brilliant, always correct, always to the point, but nothing as true as my favorite: "She has sex without gender"—in my opinion, the best analysis of Dietrich's professional enigma.

FROM ITS OVAL SHAPE to its red velvet trappings, to its gold-leaf rococo plaster columns, the Café de Paris was the perfect cabaret for Dietrich. The place resembled one of those exaggerated sets that stars used to be photographed in front of for fan pictures in the old Studio days. Now, it suited the movie-queen image in the flesh that people had come to see. At midnight, on June the 21st, 1954, Noël Coward, with his famous haughty glance, surveyed the splendid audience before him, real royalty as well as those nearly royal due to fame and fortune, then spoke his party piece:

We know God made trees, and the birds and the
    bees,
and the sea for the fishes to swim in.
We are also aware that He has quite a flair
for creating exceptional women.

When Eve said to Adam, "Stop calling me Ma-
    dame"

the world became far more exciting
which turns to confusion, the modern delusion
that sex is a question of lighting.

For female allure, whether pure or impure
has seldom reported a failure,
as I know and you know, from Venus to Juno
right down to La Dame aux Camélias.

This clamor it seems, is a substance of dreams
for the most imperceptive perceiver,
the Serpent of Nile could achieve with a smile
far quicker results than Geneva.

Now we all might enjoy, seeing Helen of Troy
as a gay cabaret entertainer,
but I doubt she could, be one quarter as good
as our legend'ry, lovely Marlenah.

At the top of the curved staircase, she
moved into her spotlight, onto her mark. Stood
very still, allowing the adulation to wash over
her. Slowly, she began to descend the stairs that
led down onto the small stage. Like the famous
show girls of the Folies-Bergère, she moved,
measured, regal; eyes front, never lowered to
check the distance of a step. Her tight beaded
dress caught the light, molding each leg from
long thigh to satin shoe, all fluid movement. Suddenly she paused and, ever so slowly, leaned
back against the white pillar, snuggled her body
deeper into the fur of her voluminous coat, and
surveyed her ecstatic audience through those

amazing hooded eyes. The flicker of a teasing smile played momentarily around her mouth, then she continued her descent, while the orchestra struck the first notes of her opening number.

Everyone came to London that June to hear and applaud the "legendary, lovely Marlenah." Harold Arlen flew in; her diary records that he left after five days, was jealous of Tynan, but "at least" got something out of the trip by Oliver Messel agreeing to design the musical that Arlen was in the process of writing with Truman Capote, *The House of Flowers.*

The difference in time, her performance schedule, and Yul being only reachable in his dressing room made phoning practically impossible. So, they had worked out a letter system: He wrote on Tuesdays, Thursdays, and between shows on Saturdays, she on all the others.

> My only love—
> This is my day for a letter, I guess I'd better type so that you can read. (I know that you can read it *quietly* and then tear it up.)
> They played the score of the *King* and the polka tore into my heart. I have never had the desire to openly belong to someone and rather laughed at the people who wished so much for it. But now I wish I could be yours, bright in the spotlight of every-

body's eyes, and dance with you to that melody which will forever mean you. And I look at photographs of Sinatra and Ava and I feel really jealous because they made it after all. To think, that I ever would bother to look at photographs of those two, seems frightening. But there it is. Michael was there last night with Liz, sitting rather stiffly in a corner and looking at me quite steadily and sadly, and I thought that that could happen to me, seeing you with another woman and I felt quite sick.

She told me she had to send her dresses and coats to the Queen's dressmaker, Norman Hartnell, to shorten the front by a quarter of an inch as she was having trouble maneuvering down that staircase. When I suggested that she should rest one hand on the curved banister for balance, she got angry and refused, saying that then the audience would immediately think she needed to steady herself like an "old lady." I knew the image of age was so repugnant to her that I did not insist, but on those nights when she called to tell me that her legs felt funny, "heavy, like sacks of flour," I had visions of her falling down those stairs.

On the 4th of July, 1954, she records that for her day off she flew to Paris at ten a.m., had lunch at Fouquet's in the rain, then dined with Noël and their special friends, Ginette and Paul-

Emil Seidman, Vivien Leigh and her husband, and Peter Brook, the director. She stayed in Paris overnight, and the next day Gabin's niece took her to Le Bourget Airport in time to make her show in London and Tynan stayed with her that night until six a.m.

Those amphetamine-laced injections, plus my mother's astounding stamina, were obviously in full swing. On July 15th, she hit her right foot against the leg of the fruitwood piano, breaking two toes. That night she called, said she had to cut into one of her precious handmade shoes to relieve the painful pressure, a heralding of what would become routine in a few years.

When the Cavalier arrived in London, all of her English admirers were asked to withdraw until she could call them forth once more. So, for the three days he was there, he was happy, innocently believing that she was still his alone. The moment he left, Arlen returned, Christopher Fry came to lunch, Tynan for tea, a sexy new Swedish blonde to supper. After closing in London, she installed herself in the Hotel Palais-Royal in Paris, where Sam Spiegel and Chevalier awaited her. She made records, ordered clothes from the new collections, spent a weekend at Dior's country house with someone whose initials were G.P., and, hiding behind dark glasses, crept into a movie house to feast her soul watching Gabin's face in his latest film.

She accepted to sing at a gala in Monte Carlo and, having learned the value of being introduced by one as famous as, or, preferably, more famous than she, asked her "pal" Jean Cocteau to do the honors. She showed him what Noël had written about her and suggested that Cocteau might like to come up with something similar, or, if he felt like it, better? She didn't get Cocteau himself—he sent another pal of theirs, the pretty French actor Jean Marais, to speak his tribute for him. It was one of Cocteau's better efforts, and Dietrich was so impressed that she got Fry to translate it into English, later reprinting it often in her theater programs. Of course, brilliance written by an unknown would not have been acceptable. Dietrich was a real "celebrity" snob—funny, in one so famous.

On the 21st of August, looking very military and serious, she was photographed marching down the Champs-Elysées in the front rank of the American Legion in the Paris Liberation anniversary parade, wearing all her medals.

By September, she was in Hollywood to fit her new dresses for her Vegas engagement and to meet Yul. As usual, when she wasn't at the Beverly Hills Hotel or hadn't rented a secret house, she stayed with Billy Wilder and his wife, Audrey. They were good friends, listened to her endless yearnings, kept her secrets, could be trusted. This did not stop her from voicing her private opinion on their characters, habits, and life-style:

"All they do, those two, is sit in front of the television set! Billy even eats in front of it. They both sit there like Mister and Missus Glutz from the Bronx, little mennubles—eating their frozen dinners! Unbelievable! That's what happens to brilliant men when they marry low-class women! Sad!"

Yul was now on a grueling schedule of touring his play, juggling his performances to fit in hurried trips to Hollywood to confer with Cecil B. De Mille for his role of Ramses in *The Ten Commandments*. Reading his schedule and comparing it with the dates and notations in my mother's diary for this period of August to October 1954, I don't know how this man managed to be in six places at the same time and still give the glorious performances he did. Probably his supply of doctored "vitamins" had something to do with it!

MY ELDEST STARTED SCHOOL—real school, with teachers, friends, show-and-tell. He even had a real lunch box, with a picture of Howdy Doody. I loved it so, the homework, the school trips, the PTA, class projects, even gym! Couldn't wait to get up every morning, wanted to share it all—going to school through my child.

Over the years, I drove my poor sons crazy, but they were kind and let me play—not minding the reputation of having a completely crazy mother who packed red lunch boxes on Valentine's Day, made green sandwiches in the shape of clovers for St. Patrick's, and miniature galleons for Columbus Day. Well, that's not entirely true, they minded—but not enough to spoil my fun. I even joined them in measles, chicken pox, and mumps—well, Japanese gardeners, servants, bodyguards, and Studio personnel don't give you those kinds of things, and I wanted a real childhood in all its aspects. By the time I was thirty-six, I too could boast, "I've had all my childhood diseases!"

In Hollywood my mother had her fittings, waited for that one phone call that would make her life worth living. Believing that Yul had heard rumors of "other" men and was angry, she wrote him:

> My love, I talked to you a couple of hours ago and feel sick with misery. What have I done to deserve this? I made my letter of last week funny because I thought it was better than to write you a weeping letter. But, funny or not, I made it clear that I had done nothing wrong. I am certain you believe me: That you are my only love and my only wish, that I don't look at any other man, let alone be interested in another man.

Please don't throw me away—if you change your mind about us and end the love that you called "infinite," you must know that it will end my life. It cannot be that you want to do this without a reason, to me who loves you so much since so long.

She sent me a copy for my comments and suggestions of what she should do next.

On October 12th, she had an early morning rehearsal in Las Vegas, had a bad cold, then recorded her opening night as though it was nothing special. The next day, instead of the usual notation of wild success, she simply wrote: "Feel awful." The entire Las Vegas engagement was a repeat of this feeling of her being half alive while being the toast of the town. This shimmering, glorious image that stood so regally before her jubilant audiences each night wrote: "All days alike—dull."

Noël kept in touch. She sent his letters on to me. I had now graduated to the dubious position of being sent all the mail she received— my father got the carbons.

1/11/54
Noël Coward
17 Gerald Road
S.W.1

Darling.
    The photograph is absolutely wonderful and the dress looks like a dream and Oh,

how I wish I could see you whirling on in that tiny hurricane.

I am having a lovely rich success at the *Café de Paris* and I got a beautiful laugh on the opening night by whispering "Hello" huskily through the mike and kicking an invisible cloak! I also leant against the piano with that imperious look and they cheered like anything.

I shall be in New York in the 1st week of December.

Kindly keep a lamp burning in the window and oblige.

Love, Love, Love, Love

Noël

I was doing a Cerebral Palsy Telethon, in Cleveland or Columbus I think. In those days, before Jerry Lewis mega-telethons, state organizations had to do their own to benefit local chapters. My mother was also in town, accompanying Harold Arlen on pre-Broadway tryouts of his new musical *House of Flowers*. After eighteen hours of continuous pleading on live television, I was groggy, but I stopped off at their hotel to say a fast hello before returning to New York.

I walked into Arlen's suite as Truman Capote, his Kewpie-doll face distraught, squeaked:

"Dear—Dear Marlene! Sweetie!— One simply cannot rhyme MOON and SOON—and EVER show one's face in public again!"

"Why not? Berlin would go crazy if he lost double *o*'s!" Pearl Bailey always cut to the bone. Everything that came her way was stripped of folderol, put into its proper place.

My mother, hand in trouser pocket, other holding her cigarette as in *Morocco*, very Tin Pan Alley Tunesmith, acknowledged my presence without breaking her stride or concentration:

"But Harold, sweetheart!" she crooned. "You don't want *that* kind of schmaltz—do you?"

"My love, his kind of schmaltz I have nothing but admiration for!" said Arlen with his usual humility.

"Me, too! Me, too!" Capote had a way of speaking that reminded one of an excited little girl clapping her hands at her own birthday party.

My mother gave him one of her "looks." Arlen's worker's hands skipped across the keyboard; it sounded like "Got the World on a String" played backwards.

I didn't want to interrupt all these creative geniuses, but I had a plane to catch, gave "Pearlie" a hug—I liked that big woman, big in stature, big in heart—kissed the sharp southern belle in man's disguise, my mother, the gentle man so full of magic, and left this odd quartet to their work in progress.

I don't care what the Broadway critics finally

said—*House of Flowers* had true beauty. Like a perfect butterfly whose time was just too short to be fully appreciated.

CHRISTMAS WAS NEAR—my father wrote one of his rare letters:

9th December: 6 AM

Dearest Mutti,

I am so grateful to you for many things and I have been wanting to thank you for so long ago but you know how much I work! And in the evenings I am always so tired that I always mean to do it tomorrow. Now I am trying to write in the early morning hours, before starting work.

Well, your records are wonderful—out of this world, the introduction from Noël Coward. The Las Vegas photos great.

And now I would like to thank you for the money which helps me so, you just can't imagine how much! Every dollar counts now for me. And I could earn a lot of money— of course not like you as a star—but I have a sound business, i.e., a good clientele. I never have enough eggs to satisfy them, and therefore I have to buy eggs because I do not have the money to extend the layer-hen installation in order to have more hens. But I must say I now have 4000 hens—I had only 3000 when I took the farm over, with a pro- duction of 2100 eggs a day. The couple who

is working with us has to go in January because I cannot afford to keep them—so that
means even more work. Thank God I am
healthy and can work. Tami works as I never
would have expected, from dawn to sunset
—we eat at home every day except one day
when "the cook" gets "a free night" and
then she goes out with me. Wednesday is
the night out but we did not go out yesterday
because of "bankruptcy."

I am not discouraged—I love my work,
my life here, the animals—I realize I have
achieved a lot, quite a lot and that I cannot
be down now. It must go better. Things will
go better.

Mutti, please get something for the boys
for Christmas, a small gift from Papi! I am
so sad that I cannot give any present to
Maria and Bill—what can I do—one cannot
pee against the wind!

I have to work now. I thank you again,
dearest, for everything—I take you in my
arms.

Papi

My father had become a pitiable man, possibly had always been, I, just too young and full
of anger to recognize it. I never forgave him for
what he did, allowed to be done, to Tami, but
I learned to pity him for what he had allowed to
be done to himself. Living with love makes nour-
ishing ground for compassion. I even hoped I
might, one day, think of my mother within the
context of human frailty.

My mother called, read me my father's letter, adding this epitaph:

"How can Papi be 'happy'? Working like that—for what? What is he trying to accomplish? He doesn't *have* to work—and Tami? Works? Nebbish! I work enough for all of you. Like your Bill, working all the time—why? Even you, now the Big TV Star—why? I do Vegas for you, just for you, all of you, and still everybody wants to work? You're all nuts!" and hung up.

Hemingway was awarded the Nobel Prize in literature, and every parent in the world built a private shrine in their heart to Dr. Jonas Salk. I looked down at my sleeping children and cried, thanked God for him who had lifted the specter of polio from their lives.

NINETEEN FIFTY-FIVE WAS A BUSY YEAR for my mother. She prepared and played a second engagement at the Café de Paris in London, triumphed again in Las Vegas, mourned Alexander Fleming, appeared in Michael Todd's *Around the World in 80 Days*, rented a secret California hideaway, where she kept house for Yul while he prepared for his role in De Mille's *Ten Commandments*. Repeatedly returned to New York, where she continued her old romance with the Cavalier, and indulged in numerous new ones, although her passionate involvement with Yul continued unabated.

Adlai Stevenson was only an interlude, as she explained it to me: "Such a brilliant man! How can a man who can write such beautiful speeches be so uninteresting? Remarque was difficult, but at least he could carry on a conversation! I had to say yes to Stevenson when he asked for 'it'—he was so shy and sweet, like a little boy!"

The physicist Oppenheimer apparently didn't ask for "it," and so was allowed to stay immersed in his brilliance and nuclear secrets, and escaped, although she often commented:

"Wonderful face . . . all those bones! Like me. Is his hair that short because he is radiated or because he likes it that way?"

The playwright William Saroyan did ask for "It" and was, of course, rewarded. One of the few civilian one-night stands in my mother's long history of bestowing herself for the enjoyment of others. Edward R. Murrow and Frank Sinatra lasted longer.

She met "E.M.," as she referred to Murrow in her diaries, on the 14th of January at a cocktail party she attended with Stevenson. By the 18th of February, they were lovers.

All her life, my mother was convinced that I would automatically agree with everything she did. After all, as she had been responsible for giving me her "superior intelligence," it was only natural that I would recognize and approve her judgment, opinion, and subsequent actions.

Since first hearing that deep, melancholy growl vividly recount the agonies of the London Blitz, Edward R. Murrow had been an idol of mine. His professional courage, his personal dedication to the principles he believed in, his deep love for his country, his hatred of McCarthy, and his crusade to expose this dangerous man's fanaticism made Murrow a very special man—a real live American hero.

When he became my mother's lover, I was shocked, but that reaction lasted only a second. Brilliant men infatuated with Dietrich were, after all, nothing new. The paradox of such beauty also being endowed with such polished intellect was, after all, an irresistible combination. Still, I was saddened that such a man as Murrow should be in need of casual companionship, no matter how seductive. But then Dietrich made bumbling adolescents out of many worldly, respected men—why not this one? So, Murrow began to appear, between meetings, conferences, rehearsals of his acclaimed television shows, to love my mother in the bed recently vacated by his friend Adlai Stevenson.

At first, she dedicated her energies to being wholly his, and in her usual style of possessive lover, wrote him longing letters, this time tinged with more Americanisms than those she wrote to Yul. The letters were secretly delivered to

Murrow's headquarters at CBS by a trusted lackey of my mother's, hastily recruited as go-between, when I, for once, refused to play the role of courier. This did not exempt me from receiving a carbon copy and a Dietrich snarl:

"Oh! Suddenly you are so 'holier than thou'? Really—such 'goody-good' affectation."

My mother's need to continually prove to herself and others that she was more than just a movie star was so all-consuming, men of intellectual as well as international stature were vitally important to capture and hold. This did not stop her from making fun of him.

"Sweetheart! You should see Murrow. He walks around the apartment with nothing on except those underpants that flap—like the kind that old men wear, and with his cigarette, of course. He smokes even *during*—you know what I mean. But he is *so* brilliant—you just have to listen to what he is saying and try not to look down at those thin legs of his sticking out of those funny bloomers—otherwise, you have to laugh —and you know me, then I pee!"

Murrow was chastised for more than just his boxer shorts. She complained constantly of his penny-pinching. The day he gave her a pair of earrings, she strode through our front door, carrying the small jeweler's box.

"Now, you have to see these! Not to be believed! Little-itsy-bitsy-pearly-whirlies, all strung in a little row like five-and-ten-cent store! I said: 'You must be joking! I need a beautiful desk for this apartment—and you buy me dangling earrings?' "

The day he bought her that gorgeous antique desk she had picked out, they had dinner at our house. She was especially soft and beguiling that evening, while keeping a weather eye on the clock not to be late getting back to her apartment for Yul's call.

My mother considered my home a "safe house," a logical place to bring secret lovers. After all, as she had bought it, it was hers. During those hours that Yul was on stage and Murrow free from his many projects, they spent many evenings with us. It was difficult, at those times, to keep the Cavalier away, pretend that I didn't know where she was when Arlen or the others phoned, but lying to my mother's victims in order to spare them additional hurt was such second nature, I no longer questioned its justification.

Dietrich used her affair with Frank Sinatra as her private placebo against the loneliness of yearning for Yul, and later, out of superstition. She thought him romantic, gentle, and sweet. She explained to me that what she found most attractive about "Frankie" was his infinite tenderness. "He is the only really tender man I have ever known. He lets you sleep, he is so grateful—in a nice way, all cozy." In later years, she also loved him for his less gentle qualities. Whenever Dietrich saw another headline proclaiming that Sinatra had smashed some reporter's camera or face, she cheered: "Oh! How I love him! He hates them all—like I do! He wants to kill them too! What a wonderful man! You know, I only spent one night with him. . . ." Then there would follow the verbatim recitation of one of her lasting fantasies of the "only" night she had convinced herself she had spent in the arms of Frank Sinatra, and how to avoid detection, she left his house at the break of dawn to wander alone down amongst the honeysuckle in stocking feet searching for a cruising taxi that would carry her back to the Beverly Hills Hotel and safety. Actually, their first romantic encounter was way back in the early forties, and in her later diaries, "Frankie" reappears often.

In the autumn of '55, she was back in Hollywood, a guest of the Wilders in the throes of her usual suffering over Yul.

Sept 2
109 degrees
Nervous Stomach. Have too much to bear. Put on radio but music makes me cry. Feel have lost "Him" forever. No use living. But have to get money Vegas first. Would be foolish anyway to kill myself in Wilder's house. Have to find out better way. Wish I

could drink—but too hot and cannot breathe easily anyway. I ask nothing. He called at 4:30 said Wilder and Hayward told him I had taken Harold [Arlen] with me to London and how wonderful it was for Harold to have me. I did not cry. Did not behave badly, said how terrible London had been, how desperate I was and asked "You know how much I love you." He said no, so I told him and that if he was worried that he had made me suffer in these four years they were nothing compared to this summer. That I was sure he had had another woman, and that I nearly died those last days. He said he was going to San Francisco till Monday night "family business" and he would call when he came back. I said when will you call I want to be here. He said either Monday or Tuesday morning.

Betty Furness party.

Sat next to Frank, he talked of 1942. I was stunned.

That Sunday, she went to brunch at the Stewart Grangers', then:

Frank, Italian restaurant—here— Nice

September 5
Never moved waiting for phone
"He" called from airport
Called again 11:45 drunk—
Called again 12:30— Talked hours. Angry

because of Arlen. Could not argue.
He was too drunk. Don't know what to do.

September 6
Start dresses for Vegas
F. called 9 PM
Sweet and tender
Called again 12 AM

Billy Wilder and his wife must have been the perfect hosts—multiple lovers underfoot, phone calls at all hours, and—they kept having her back for more!

September 7
Frank called at 4 from rehearsal
Plans for Vegas

September 8
Left for Vegas 7:30 Together with Frank
To bed at 7 AM

September 9
Las Vegas
Sahara after noon while Frank rehearsed
F drunk but nice. To bed at 9 AM

The next day, she woke Sinatra at four as he had a five o'clock appointment and commented, as usual, that he was "sweet and tender"; then she went to the Sahara to try out the microphones for her next engagement there. Instead of staying at the Sahara, which would have been the normal thing for her to do, she was staying with Sinatra at his hotel. Yul called her that day and asked her to come back to L.A., using the word "home." She refused. She remained with "F."

> September 11th
> F To bed asleep in chair at 9:30 AM
> Got up without kiss
> Bad day did not behave as usual. I went to Sahara. F staying in sun with usual gang
> Came home, talked to Harold. Asked him [F] in car to Dunes what was wrong. He said plans. TV show, picture—but he was different. Talked about Harold Arlen twice but I did not attach any importance. Up till 9 AM went to his room. He said "Go to bed"—I was thunderstruck. Left. Harold told me to leave and not wait till private plane with F at 4 PM. Left too miserable to think clearly. No word from him [F]. Fitting— Fainted.

"Miss Riva, I am so sorry but there is an urgent phone call for you downstairs."

I apologized, being the star of a show makes it a little easier to leave a full rehearsal, ran downstairs to the office, worried something had happened to the children:

"Sweetheart! I fainted! Today—at the Studio! Do you think I am pregnant?"

"Well, Massy—I don't really think that is possible—"

She interrupted me: "Why not? You know how I have always yearned for Yul's child—it has to be his, no one else in my life. What do you think? Should I call Carroll Righter?"

"Yes, good idea—you do that! He'll know!" I said and hung up on my fifty-four-year-old incorrigible.

On the 17th of September, she went to a party at Sidney Guilleroff's, got drunk, and flirted openly with Harold Arlen.

September 18th
Better day because if Harold the reason for "F" behavior there is hope that "He" also could have thought the same.

The days were long. No calls from Yul, no calls from Sinatra. She called me daily to ask for advice, forgetting it as soon as we hung up.

September 24th
Garland party. F came alone. Formal "Hello." Later I said, "How are you?" Drunk! And he was more than I have ever seen. I took cigarette, he pulled out lighter and said: "Like the lemon peel." All I could do was to put both my hands around his and light the cigarette—"Lemon Peel" having been our romantic word because I like his hands twisting it into my drink. It was stunning again, coming again at this moment when he was so drunk and like a stranger otherwise. He said formal good-bye after

saying he was going to Palm Springs. Horrible Sunday again because "lemon peel" stirred everything up again. Why did he say it? And why did I not say something?

M. Rennie who took me to the party here afterwards scene jealous about F. Wanted to stay—but no— Lonely day— Lonely day.

September 26th
God. I have to get down to work. Help from somewhere. Please! "He" called—came. Is everything all right? Heard about Frankie. Said I could do what I wanted to but don't "Bull shit me." I can do what *I* want?

She must have convinced Yul that she was his—and only his, for, on September 27th through the first of October, her diary pages are blank except for: "He came."

She opened in Las Vegas and was an even greater sensation than she had been the year before. How she found the time, not to mention the energy, to fit in the next few weeks is beyond me.

October 19th
Came to L.A. two hours Beverly Hills Hotel.

Sometimes my mother could get very confusing. Did she dash so gallantly from Las Vegas to a clandestine rendezvous in Beverly Hills with

Frankie? Michael? Arlen? Murrow? Yul? I suspect it was good old Yul, for on November first, she notes once again:

> To L.A. Beverly Hills bungalow
> "He" came.

Two days later, she worked for Michael Todd. Her costars in that famous scene were David Niven, Cantinflas, George Raft, Red Skelton, and lo and behold, "tender" Frankie. She had been flirting outrageously with Michael Todd ever since they met, telling me he was the "sweetest," most "brilliant" man, and giggled when whispering in my ear the great secret she had discovered: that his real name was Goldenberg . . . "but he doesn't *look* Jewish. More like a Greek, and you know, he is much too passionate for just a 'Goldenberg'!" and was livid when Todd fell in love with Elizabeth Taylor. "That terrible woman again—who ruined Michael Wilding's whole life," but kept right on trying to get him for her own, switching to "bestest pal a man could ever have" when Taylor won out.

She looked absolutely stunning in her segment of *Around the World in 80 Days* and basked in the deserved admiration accorded her on the set. She molded herself into her "Goldenberg," reminisced with her old pal George Raft, ignored Cantinflas, rhapsodized over Danny Thomas to

Red Skelton, rekindled tender Frankie's still smoldering embers, and tried to heat up David Niven.

In Alabama, a brave woman defied the racist law of that state by refusing to give up her bus seat to a white man and Dietrich flew to Vegas for Chevalier's opening night—then recorded clandestine meetings at various bungalows on the grounds of the Beverly Hills Hotel.

I signed to star in a touring company of *Tea and Sympathy*, a craziness only made possible by a husband who invented the term "supportive." Not to worry, he would look after our two children, see them to school, help with homework, be there for them—all would be well, I *had* to play this wonderful part that I would surely be brilliant in, and sent me on my way to Buffalo.

True, it was a part worth leaving your loved ones for—*if* acting was your world, in the marrow of your bones. After two months on the road, with four still to go, I knew what my marrow was full of: "Get me out of this—and Home!" But my run-of-the-play contract held me to our schedule.

THE SCRIPT OF *The Monte Carlo Story* was awful, but as Vittorio De Sica, the genius who had made *The Bicycle Thief*, was to be her costar and director, with Sam Taylor, a victim of the Mc-Carthy witch hunt, as the official one, my mother agreed to do the film.

Once again, Harry Cohn was wined and dined, and Columbia Studios embarked on executing Dietrich's glamorous wardrobe for a film to be shot not on their lot, not even in the States, but in Monte Carlo and Rome! She had more than ten costumes to design with Jean Louis, then send the sketches with swatches of the various materials and colors to Italy for the producers' approval. She was so busy that the entries in her diary are preoccupied with preparations for the film. The usual "He came," "He called," "Here," are vague and unidentified—although on March 31, she records:

Left Vegas 5:45 AM. Home 7 AM. "He"

This could mean that it was Sinatra who came from Vegas or that she, who had been in Vegas with Sinatra, had flown to L.A. to be "home" when Yul appeared. Whoever it was stayed around for a week until the 9th of April, when my father was hospitalized with his first heart attack.

In Delaware, after much discussion, the producer allowed his wife, who was up on the part, to take over the lead so that I could fly to the bedside of my dying father. At least I thought he was dying after listening to my mother's frantic announcement over the telephone. As the final curtain came down on the third act, I walked off the stage, grabbed my coat and bag, was on my way to the airport and made the last plane with connections in New York to L.A. I remember thinking, Thank God it's a modern play—I would really look crazy doing this mad dash as Mary Queen of Scots!

Knowing that I had an hour's wait between planes in New York, Bill managed to bring the boys down to La Guardia despite the late hour for a fast kiss and a hug from their disappearing mother. The missing of each other was getting too hard. He didn't know it yet, but I was ready to give up the foolishness of so-called "fame" for something I should have known was far more valuable and rewarding.

Hours later, still dressed in the costume I had walked off the stage in, I entered my father's hospital room as he said: "Mutti, when you bring me my martini tomorrow, tell the hotel that the one today needed a little more vermouth, and don't forget, tomorrow *fresh* lemons and the correct melba toast for the caviar."

My mother whirled on hearing my laugh and shrieked: "Papilein— She is here! Look at her! Still in her makeup—straight from the stage!" and flung herself against me, sobbing—the "nearly-was widow"! Over her bowed head, my father and I looked at each other. With his index finger, he tapped his forehead, a gesture he often made when silently commenting on Tami's irrational behavior. I wondered where she had been hidden away during this time, when the world press was monitoring Dietrich in her role of "distraught wife at dying husband's bedside."

I told my father how happy I was to see him so far from death's door, then listened to my mother's grievances against the various private nurses assigned to her husband's case:

"Sweetheart! They are so rude. They behave as though they are doctors! And they are all black! Can you believe it! How can they allow those people to be nurses?"

While my mother was busy instructing the doctor in the latest techniques of coronary care, I went in search of Tami. I knew nothing and no one would pry her too far from my father's side. I finally found her in a waiting room on another floor—all alone, bony knees pressed tightly together, her gnarled hands fidgeting with the metal clasp of her worn handbag, her big eyes desperate, her frail body in its cheap summer housecoat, trembling in fear. She had accompanied the ambulance, come straight to the hospital as she was, stopping only to snatch her purse on the way. No one had bothered to tell her what had happened to my father. She believed him dead and was waiting for my mother to tell her so. She had been in that room, forgotten, since his arrival at the hospital ten hours earlier. She reminded me so of a wounded animal. I approached her cautiously:

"Tamilein—it's me, Kater. Papi is not dead. Do you hear me? Papi is not dead—Papi is alive."

"Oh, Kater! The truth? That's the truth? Kater, really," she pleaded.

I nodded my head, put my arms around her, and held her close—until the tears came and she allowed herself to believe me.

The next day, I rejoined my company. I arrived at the theater just in time to change my clothes and be discovered, serene, "terribly controlled" in a chintz-covered armchair, knitting, as the curtain rose on the first act.

Everybody lauded my mother's courage and superhuman stamina during her husband's illness. She fitted day and night, in between dashing to the hospital with her husband's lunch and dinner, supplied by the foremost restaurants of Beverly Hills—loaded with cholesterol. Tami was not allowed to visit. She was given strict orders to become invisible, remain at the "ranch," stay inside, and speak to no one. When my father left the hospital, my mother gave him back to Tami to take care of and flew to Paris to make hats and shoes. She arrived in Monte

Carlo in time for the start of principal photography.

During the making of this film, she wrote me some wonderful letters, Dietrich at her best:

Hotel de Paris
Monte Carlo

June 10 '56

WELL, MY ANGEL—this is the first Sunday and no work. Have a cold and antibiotics keep me in shape to work. Voice doesn't matter which still seems funny. Entire film will be dubbed. Still, they fell into each other's arms when I played the first scene words and all. They are not used to that. They more or less mouth their lines like we do when we shoot a song and the soundtrack is playing. They do a silent picture and concentrate on the expression and the eyes and say the words rather tonelessly. I had a hard time playing to De Sica because there was no meaning to the lines. This all happened after they had just gotten over the shock that I was there in time, or there at all. The politeness is killing me. After the day's work, which was two lines at a time at the most and over my shoulder (I had to remind them gently that this was Cinemascope and I would be on the screen in full shots e.t.c.) I was kissed and hugged for performing molto bene bellissimo and: "How do you do it with all the expression

ABOVE: Harold Arlen, the composer, and her pal Noël Coward. Everyone who adored her came to witness her triumphs. BELOW: In her glitter dress, she sang to men; in her tails, to women.

In Michael Todd's *Around the World in 80 Days*, she appeared with a number of her pals and one who was far more than just a pal.

Dietrich thought Edith Piaf was a lonely sparrow with a busted wing. My opinion of that corroded steel in "a little black dress" is unprintable.

This evening, my husband and I must have found a baby-sitter and played "Dietrich's happy family."

Italy has a way of inspiring romance.

But Vittorio De Sica, her costar in *The Monte Carlo Story*, filmed in Monaco and Rome in the summer of 1956, was not a candidate.

My sons, Peter and Michael, thought going out with their grandmother (Massy) meant "money is no object." Yelling for taxis was part of the fun.

in your eyes and in the voice." I should have been a silent Film Star or Italian to start with. They sure have an easy life. Also found out that Lollobrigida and Sophia Loren, Mangano, e.t.c. don't even dub themselves. They have other actresses dub for them. Their accents are too low-class for Rome consumption, also their acting talent when they speak.

The young girl in the film is called Trundy. Never made a film and looks not only 12 years old, but also has my color hair and complexion plus a few freckles. I thought they were kidding because in the script there is a lot of talk of her being 22, but to choose the same color hair for the other woman in the same film seems ridiculous. Everybody says it wasn't his fault and that's how it was until at midnight we saw the rushes in the local cinema and I saw her on the screen I finally said to Sam Taylor who takes director's credit on the screen, "I don't think it's funny anymore." He then asked *me* to put my foot down and ask the producer to change the girl. He said he couldn't do it. Well, you know that my hands are tied, because I can see the stories in print when the girl returns home: I was jealous, she looked too young, e.t.c.

DE SICA gambles all night at the Casino and I see him only during the day when we work. He is charming, but a little stiff, very conscious of his profile, this being the first part of an elegant man and lover. His make-up is thick and pasty and I told them last night: that in America people will laugh at a man who looks made-up, men don't make-up with grease in Hollywood. For color they have a water-soluble makeup which does not show, just for color sake. Sam Taylor said: "I know nothing about all these things." The little, very good cameraman was very sad and DE SICA was still gambling and had not seen anything. I suggested they get another makeup man and make tests with DE SICA before we get into the indoor scenes, which, by the way, will almost all be made here in the actual Hotel lobbies, restaurants, gambling rooms. There is very little left for studio work in Rome, which is very disturbing, because I looked forward to a dressing room and calm studio work instead of this location business where you have to change behind your retinue spreading their skirts. No mirror, no light, no place to stretch out or take your clothes off in this heat.

My wardrobe girl only speaks Italian and I understand everything she says but I still cannot speak it. Some words which don't make sense at all I have to ask for, like who can know that Left is sinistro, although Right is diritto, which makes sense. Pronto is the most important word on the set. And I run like the circus horse when I hear it.

The Hairdresser is very good and speaks

French so we can communicate. Guilaroff will leave soon which I don't regret, but if I hadn't brought him I would have had more sleepless nights before I got here than I had.

My test was all right, they again fell into each other's arms about it, although they must have *known* that there was film in the camera when we made it! The eyes were not blue but some sort of mush and I told Peppino about the eye light we have and when I see my first rushes I will know more.

The Make-Up man is a little short fellow who speaks an Italian I can hardly understand and has hot, fat hands and they are *heavy*. He has already lost onto the floor, or they must have glued to his pants, 6 pairs of my precious eyelashes, but I always say: Non importa, non importa. (They say everything twice here) and he takes out another pair. Then he squooshes the liquid adhesive onto the band with a big squoosh which makes it get all over the lashes and sticks it onto my eyes, much too far into the corner, and I signal to put it further out. He then pulls on the band which by now is stuck to my lid and my lashes, presses it down on the outside and says: Va bene. I have slits for eyes and as I can still see the clock ticking away I say: Va bene too. When he is gone, I pull them off and get out another pair, because these being full of guck and he had them too long in his hot fat moist hands and the lashes are going every which way. I now get up an hour earlier and make-up myself. But he still insists on starting on the eyebrows and put his fist into my cheeks, twisting it while he sketches the eyebrows while I twist inside. He also loves to pat my face from the jaws up to the eyes using the same moist fingers from the darker color over the lighter highlights. I have stopped that with: Stop! which they *all* understand.

Yesterday the crew took me to St. Paul de Vence in a very fast Italian racing car for dinner. There I finally met Coxinelle, the young man who is a dead ringer for Marilyn Monroe, except he has a better voice. He sings in Juan-les-Pins and I must go one night, when I don't work in the morning. I naturally couldn't help looking at the beautiful décolleté of "her" evening dress and it was quite something. "Hitler should have had them for tonsils!" You should have seen the reaction of the Americans, Taylor and his society wife and Guilaroff (for more reasons than one)! We took a picture together, I will send it. Although I wish I could do one with me in tails that would be much more fun.

Grace has returned to the Castle we hear and Guilaroff claims he telephoned her, but I don't know if he just says that to impress me. He is like all MGM people devoted to her which is rather nice. I have a suite of rooms, if you could only get the kids into the air, even if it is not this air, which is not very bracing anyway.

I love you
Massy

Live television gave up, as it had to. America's different time zones were impossible to handle for sponsors and scripts alike. So, the drama shows and many other categories moved to Hollywood and on to film, and the studios that had so feared television, cried doom—predicted the death of Hollywood—suddenly had a brand-new industry where all their brilliant know-how could flourish anew.

I began having to commute from coast to coast. I never unpacked, I was like a visitor in my own home. No question of moving our family out to swimming-pool heaven, no matter how enticing. My husband's work was in New York, and I alone knew the hazards that such a move could create within a marriage. I had chosen to use my married name professionally for that reason—no "Mr. Manton" would stigmatize Bill, as had "Mr. Dietrich," my father. I was lucky that Riva went so very well with Maria. If your talent is such that it drives you beyond yourself, is a consuming need outside of your control, then all is fair in love and war. You really can't help yourself. But, my acting talent was not of the "glorious monster" type and therefore could be laid to rest quite easily without regret at something precious forfeited. I flew out to L.A., did one more big show—and quit. At the age of thirty-one, I had come to my senses. Thanks to Bill, our sons had weathered the motherless time extremely well, greeted my sudden reappearance with undramatic appreciation. My husband wasn't dramatic either, but appreciation? Wow! Was he appreciative!

My mother moved to Rome to shoot interiors. The film nearly finished, her letters were full of self-anger and depression:

> September 10 '56
> WELL? I'm on the homestretch—four more days and I am through. I hate myself for having succumbed to fatigue and rundown nerves and spoiled so many days for myself and work. But I just couldn't fight it alone. I felt too lost and it shows. And this time it wasn't my perfectionism that made me over-critical. I hardly bothered about the clothes. I just put them on and forgot about them. That shows too. But that isn't bad. I wanted to play this film lightly and fast and without a care. I thought it was the only way possible to do this uninteresting part. I never thought that I would have to fight for realism with Italian film-makers. But I had to fight every inch of the way and was hampered enormously by the most old-fashioned camera direction. But I am afraid

I didn't fight hard enough. I got tired or because it was hopeless to keep good humor around me and fight at the same time. Not that they were not all charming. They just didn't know what I can do if I don't feel harnessed. Besides this I had De Sica on one side who saw me and the part one way and Taylor who saw me another way. De Sica says I have the face of Duse and that he loves the melancholy which hangs over me and Taylor wants the cynical "Femme du Monde." Both did not want "love." Well, I hope I gave them both what they wanted. It is difficult for me to forget completely what is being said to me just before the camera starts to roll. And Taylor would always talk to me quickly just then.

One never has a chance to see all the rushes put together again and again when one records directly. This way I see myself on the loops again and again and every fault sticks out, every timing that is off, I have to follow with my dubbing. It is like being put through torture to have to do the same mistake over again, just because the lips move and you have to go with it.

I am as thin as a herring and the cameraman instead of getting better photographed me rather badly ever since we came into the studio. The makeshift lighting in Monte Carlo became me much better. Also London Technicolor found that our little cameraman is inexperienced and in order to save money asked him for more and more light, and he complied without telling me. I could not open my eyes anymore and he swore up and down that I had the same amount as before. Only when I had to interrupt every take because of tears rolling down my cheeks did he take some lights off. I know enough about light not to confuse it with heat. If you saw the rushes it looks like Nazi torture, a desperate face trying to keep the eyes open and be funny and interrupting all the time saying I'm sorry I cannot or "Excusate" or "je ne peux pas." I sit there with my hands over my face and the camera keeps rolling and I try again and again and every time the scene is over I hide my face in pain. It wasn't the pain that upset me so. It was the knowledge that something was wrong, that it could not be good on the screen. And I hated myself to be so well brought up that I could not walk off the set and say: If you want me to act fix your lights so that I can. The American cutter I forced onto them through Michael Todd's help from United Artists is not first-class and not bright enough for the people here. He does not quite know what we are saying and he is cutting by the script I guess. I had so hoped he would give them a list of retakes to be able to speed up the picture which is very slow. But as we have no protection shots the best cutter cannot speed it. But I asked for a cutter with authority because my main reason for getting the cutter was to have someone other than me saying we needed added shots to be able to cut the picture for tempo. Even if De Sica dubs well, which I doubt, and could read some lines faster, we have no head of mine to insert to pull his lines over. This way he has to dub in the same slow tempo to match his lips. I have a terrible cold and could not dub today that's why I have time for this long letter. I am all packed; again I have put the unworn dresses back in the suitcases, again I have folded everything carefully to carry it back home. I never went out in Rome and in Monte Carlo I worked every night. Mostly I wore Blue Jeans. The fountains gush outside, it is still hot. I have seen Rome at night three times. I wished so much I could have left here not feeling like a "gutted chicken."

I salute you Americans.

Massy

Except for her middle-European sentimentality, Dietrich would have made a good director, perhaps even a better-than-good. What a shame she never took the time from "being in love" to concentrate on becoming one.

Somewhere, after this film, she got involved with an Italian actor, a cheap, very cheap version of Gabin. She always claimed their love was "pure," that he was impotent—then wondered out loud how his wife had managed to have so many children. Ensconced with her new heart-throb at the Hotel Raphael in Paris, at fifty-five she was in love again, and of course was convinced I would want to hear all about it.

Tuesday night
Sweet love,
It is 12:30 a.m. We came home from a dinner at his producer's house. He was beautiful, separated from me, opposite me and he dominated the conversation—brilliant and articulate.
. . . I could now come to him and he to me without hiding and only imagine to "Faire l'Amour" with me. I told him then that it wasn't only that that I had wanted—per se. I wanted him to attach me to him. Something physical, like you spit a dog in the mouth—so he stays—or sleeps in the same bed.

Her Hemingway-acquired truisms were always so fascinating!

That is what I had wanted. He said how terrible morning is, after a night of love and how wonderful his mornings are when he finds that I have put out the light and signs of love—like his clothes hung up and his socks gone—taken by me to wash. And I sat there and knew he was right but I knew also that I would forget his eyes which now seemed to be the only happiness I wanted to look into.

Page after page after page of subliminal love—until:

> I will go to bed now. It is 2 a.m. No use sitting optimistically on the red couch in my gold dress. Should he wake up, he will not call. Such is not our relationship. He tells me often he woke up and read. I also wake up all the time since I am here. I don't read, though. His room is cozy. Mine isn't. I have no talent for that—I just have the longing.
> I kiss you.

For the first time, she had quite forgotten she was in Paris—and that this had always meant, Jean was near.

My mother returned to New York, found that I had decided to give up my successful career, and, to prove the point, was pregnant. She was not pleased.

As she had signed for another Vegas stint, she flew to Hollywood in November for the third and final fittings.

Michael Wilding, now free from his marriage to Elizabeth Taylor, came back into the fold. She planned to take him to the privacy of my father's "ranch," then noted in her diary that as Papi had friends visiting him, this was now out of the question. It made her angry. If she paid my father's bills, she felt it only just that she should be able to use his home to bring lovers to whenever she chose.

Yul was also in Hollywood, and so she began waiting for "Him" to call. When he didn't, she called me:

"Why doesn't he call me? I know he knows I am here! You think it is all because of that Swedish horse? How can an internationally known whore be allowed to star in films?" She was wildly jealous, certain that Yul was having an affair with his costar from *Anastasia*. Dietrich's hatred of Ingrid Bergman was born that winter. Years later, she would tell outrageous stories about anything connected with Bergman: How Rossellini had confided in her, told everyone how he would knock on her door, begging her to let him in so he could seek comfort in Dietrich's arms, there to unburden his soul by recounting Ingrid's many, many infidelities.

My father's friends finally left, and my mother was able to rendezvous with Michael Wilding at her husband's house in the Valley. She called me from there:

"Sweetheart. Tami cooked a wonderful dinner for all of us. She is so much better since they let her out of that place I found, but she is so tired all the time, I gave her all the Dexedrine I had. You should have seen how Michael ate!

He is a new man, now that that awful woman that made his life so miserable is gone! Now, we have to get his children away from her! Here, he wants to tell you himself how happy he is," and she put Wilding on the phone, so that he could tell the daughter in his own words of his refound joy with the mother. Poor Michael, like Brian, he had manners and these calls embarrassed him so.

Quickly I whispered:

"Just say it, Michael, make her happy, keep the peace, but for God's sake, don't ever let her near your boys!"

She took the receiver back to inform me that Carroll Righter had said that, according to her stars, nothing would be resolved with Yul until the 2nd of December.

For eight hours a day, she fitted the new dresses for Las Vegas. Her diary is full of her usual astute observations of what is wrong with the cut, beading, placement of every stone and bauble and what must be done to correct it. Then, suddenly, all work is forgotten:

> November 28th, 1956
> "He" possible divorce. Am quite sick.

Sobbing uncontrollably, she called me. She was convinced that Yul was having an affair with Bergman, and now was getting a divorce for that "whore." I calmed her, reminding her that Yul and his wife, Virginia, had been on the verge of divorce many times. I knew my mother always hoped that when Yul actually decided to divorce, it would be because of his great love for her. She asked to talk to Bill. Perhaps, being a man, he could explain why after all these years that she had loved Yul, been faithful to him, "only him," he could now treat her so cruelly! Bill listened to these fantasies, mumbled something appropriate and noncommittal, and shaking his head in disbelief, handed me the receiver.

"Sweetheart! I told Bill. I will call the moment when I know more!"

She hung up, called one of her string of ever-obliging doctors, asked him to telephone her Beverly Hills drugstore to instruct them to deliver yet another hundred refill of Miss Dietrich's favorite amphetamines to her bungalow, then called Remarque to ask his opinion of Yul's strange behavior. When her blond movie-star lover of days gone by suddenly phoned that evening, she was still so miserable about Yul that she accepted Kirk's invitation for a cozy dinner at his beach house.

The next day, December 1st:

Ordered *fur* sample for Vegas.
Sick
Called Doctor. Lie down. He comes at five.
Says heart OK.
Party for Hornblow.

Tony Martin
Home with Frank
Finally, some love

December 2nd
Home at 3:30 PM
F called at 9:30 PM
Finally some sweetness
Slept well and long

She had known when she moved to the Beverly Hills Hotel that Anatole Litvak, the director of Yul's film, and his wife, Sophie, lived in a bungalow across the walk from hers. She had even accepted Sophie's invitation to tea, a thing my mother never did, in the hope of seeing Yul or hearing news of him. My mother's private stake-out of the Litvak bungalow finally paid off:

December 6th
His car parked here. Caught him coming out of the Litvak bungalow, but he was with agent—so walked by, saying "Hello."
Nothing all day. Home. Miserable.

December 7th
Decided accept 125,000 this year. Work Tropicana Vegas February
Studio 2 PM First time black dress together
No good. Looks like evening dress. Too even.
Put extra fringe from samples on blouse to give accent.

Home at 6, over to Litvak's. Stayed for dinner.
Nothing.

December 8th
One o'clock. His car parked in front of my bungalow. Missed him going to Litvak. He came out with Litvak into car to lunch. Litvak came back on foot alone at three.
Separation notice in columns. What more can I suffer. Seeing him breaks me.

She went to see *Baby Doll* with the writer Charles Brackett. When she got home, recorded:

He stood in front of theater.
Saw me get out of car.

December 10
Did not send letter as planned. How can he believe that I am in despair if he sees me with Strange man, looking O.K.? called at 1:30 AM

December 12th
Feldman to screening *Anastasia*. "He" was there. Alone with De Mille.
De Mille came to me at end. Kissed me, took me over to him, said I was the most wonderful woman, what he would not do for one kiss, etc. I shook hands and said:
    "You are wonderful in the film."
Then left, direct for home. Was so miserable that I could not whisper to him to call me.

. . .

She returned to New York to complicate our Christmas and tell us of all her despair at the cruelty of those she loved. It was time for United Cerebral Palsy's yearly telethon. That year I believed I had something very special to contribute—the image of a woman expecting a child, surrounded by children born impaired. I spoke of my belief that a whole and healthy child was the true miracle of birth, not the norm—but the glorious exception. I implored the parents who had been granted this gift to help us help those who strove against such terrible odds to achieve their own wondrous miracles.

My mother was furious: "How can you show yourself on television, with all those sick children? You are pregnant! All that sickness can mark the child! It's ridiculous, this obsession you have about those ugly, twisted children!" and she left for California, checking her handbag to make sure she had her favorite knockout drug for the plane.

She had found a sleeping pill in France. Actually, not a pill but a potent hypnotic in the form of a suppository. Dietrich preferred medication to enter her body through her rectum. It worked faster. She also mistrusted the ability of the stomach to know what was food and what was medicine, then have the intelligence to know where to send it.

Another advantage of suppositories was her

belief that, due to the lack of space, one could not commit suicide inadvertently by shoving too many things "up there." Because this French medication worked so well, put her to sleep so quickly, she christened her suppositories with the name of the actor she considered the most boring man in Hollywood, Fernando Lamas.

The moment my mother arrived in Los Angeles, she called to tell me of the terrible thing that had happened to her on the plane, what Yul had done to her "in the air," then sat down to write Noël Coward the whole story from the beginning:

> Last week in New York, I stood at the door when he came. I was not going to do one wrong thing. He came in smiling, bottle under his coat. He came into the bedroom and told me about Paris, the fog around the Eiffel Tower, the streets, the bridges and how he thought about me. I stood there thinking this is not a dream. He is really back and he loves me. Then the hurricane broke over me for three hours and I fell asleep, for the first time in two months to the day without torture and sleeping pills.
>
> He woke at eleven, said he had an appointment at twelve. I made coffee as usual, gave him emperin as usual after a drinking night. He left as usual a little bit vague and at the door I said AS USUAL: When will I hear from you? and he said: "Later."

He did not call. Sinatra opened that night at the Copacabana. I went at midnight. He was there. I went home. He did not call. All day Friday I waited. As I had made plans to leave for California on Saturday (I open at the Sands on Feb. 13), I called him at 6 p.m. I said my name and he answered. I said I was leaving Saturday and he said he was on the same plane. He said I'll see you then. My heart stopped again. There was something wrong. I thought, maybe he hated himself for having come back and there would be scenes again and I said: Won't I see you before? and he said: "No, I have no time." I said I want you to know there will be no complications again, no scenes, no trouble ever, no questions. He said, "Thank you, ma'am." He said, "How did you like Sinatra?" (he saw me there and smiled to me very sweetly and intimately). I said: I thought it was terrible, Sinatra was drunk, had no voice, very unprofessional. He said, "I sat with him till 8 in the morning." Again I said: "Can't you phone me later tonight?" He said "No." I said: What is wrong? He said, "I want nothing anymore. I have no confidence in anyone or anything anymore. Not in you either. You asked for it."

I said: No confidence in me? He said, "Yes." I said: Don't you love me anymore? and he said, "You said you would not ask any more questions. I have to stop, someone is coming. See you tomorrow on the plane."

Horrible night. Wanted to cancel trip, but then thought I better go because if I don't go I will reproach myself and I went.

I was taken to the plane first. He came later. Walked by me and took a seat on the other side furthest away from me in the seat section in the back of the already made-up berths. The empty plane took off. He had three drinks and went to his berth without ever looking at me. Thank God I am German. Otherwise I would have jumped out of the plane.

I went to my berth. I took a Fernando Lamas but could not fall asleep. Dozed off and on. Then suddenly I FELT HIS HANDS ON ME AND HIS BODY FALL-ING HEAVILY ONTO ME. I did not know where I was only that he was there. I took his hand, heard the noise of the motors, knew he was in my berth on a plane and wanted to hide him and pull him in. He pulled himself up and half out and said something. I said: Come here! still half dazed. He started to crawl back to me, then he pulled back again and said, "No, there are too many people around." I let go of his hand. I opened my shade and saw it was light. I said I dreamt this. I looked through my curtains and saw his foot in the shoes I brought from Italy on the floor of the opposite berth. He sat again on his seat of the night before.

I went over to him and said: Good morning. He said, "Good morning. How did you sleep?" I took *Match* with his story in it so I could bend down, gave it to him.

If you are still with me after reading so far let me thank you.

Please write to me. I will be here at the Beverly Hills Hotel till February 8. I have to work which is the worst part of it all. Work usually helps unhappy people. But my kind of work cannot be done with unhappiness. A film would be different because one is being pushed and does not have to create everything alone.

I don't know how to do it yet. I have no "Lebensmut." And, without that it is difficult to exist, let alone go and dazzle the people in Vegas with a performance which is a fake anyway and took always work to put it over.

Now it becomes a mountain of silly, superficial exploits, which only my sense of humor of myself could surmount.

But where do I find that?

As long as I don't know what he feels I will have no rest.

If the jealousy angle is true then he must love me still. If not then why did he come back at all? Why did he call you? Why did he tell me he'd "missed me"? Why did he want me so badly?

How can one forget the one one loves when one has no pride at all and no way out like nervous breakdowns or trips around the world or jumping out of a window?

I love you and I wish I could behave in the proper fashion.

Noël replied immediately:

> Firefly Hill
> Port Maria
> Jamaica B.W.I.

Oh, darling,

Your letter filled me with such a lot of emotions the predominant one being rage that you should allow yourself to be so humiliated and made so unhappy by a situation that really isn't worthy of you. I loathe to think of you apologizing and begging forgiveness and humbling yourself. I don't care if you did behave badly for a brief moment, considering all the devotion and loving you have given out during the last five years, you had a perfect right to. The only mistake was not to have behaved a great deal worse a long time ago. The aeroplane journey sounds a nightmare to me.

It is difficult for me to wag my finger at you from so very far away particularly as my heart aches for you but really darling you must pack up this nonsensical situation once and for all. It is really beneath your dignity, not your dignity as a famous artist and a glamorous star, but your dignity as a human, only too human, being. Curly is attractive, beguiling, tender and fascinating, but he is not the only man in the world who merits those delightful adjectives. . . . Do please try to work out for yourself a little personal philosophy and DO NOT, repeat DO NOT be so bloody vulnerable. To hell with God damned "L'Amour." It always causes far more trouble than it is worth. Don't run after it. Don't court it. Keep it waiting off stage until you're good and ready for it and even then treat it with the suspicious disdain that it deserves. . . . I am sick to death of you waiting about in empty houses and apartments with your ears strained for the telephone to ring. Snap out of it, girl! A very brilliant writer once said (Could it have been me?) "Life is for the living." Well that is all it is for, and living DOES NOT consist of staring in at other people's windows and waiting for crumbs to be thrown to you. You've carried on this hole in corner, over-charged, romantic, unrealistic nonsense long enough.

Stop it Stop it Stop it. Other people need you. . . . Stop wasting yourself on someone who only really says tender things to you when he's drunk. . . .

Unpack your sense of humor, and get on with living and ENJOY IT.

Incidentally, there is one fairly strong-minded type who will never let you down and who loves you very much indeed. Just try to guess who it is. X X X X. These are

not romantic kisses. They are un-romantic.
Loving "Goose-Es."
Your devoted "Fernando de Lamas"

She read me Noël's letter over the phone, then
got angry when I said that I agreed with him
wholeheartedly.

"Oh, you two Sagittarians! You two always
agree! Neither of you can understand how one
man can be a woman's whole life! Noël does it
to boys in the ass—and you? You play house!"
and she hung up on me.

On her arrival, Yul left Hollywood. "Frankie" was more than willing to lick her wounds.
Two days later, she notes in her diary:

> F.S. called at 1:30. Had just come from New
> York. I went there till Monday 5 A.M. Sweet
> and tender—hope it helps.

She hired a new accompanist. She was enchanted by his boyish charm and talent. He was
handsome, vital, virile, and gifted. Strangely
enough, they were never lovers, undoubtedly
Burt Bacharach's sense of good taste. He did not
believe in mixing work with pleasure.

Secretly, she did resent Burt's capacity to
elude her famous charms and camouflaged this
resentment by telling outrageous stories about
his sexual escapades with others, always sounding like his private madam. Until Burt became
famous in his own right and finally left her, those

of her immediate entourage were told, innumerable times, of how she would case the Vegas chorines for likely candidates to share Burt's bed.

Dietrich's most tasteless story involving Bacharach was one of her lies she enjoyed telling the most. Of how she had first diagnosed his gonorrhea, then found ways to cure it for him. Her clutch of avid listeners at these times would gasp and gush:

"Marlenah! That's just too, too hilarious for words! Absolutely divine!" tears of derisive laughter running down their cheeks. By this time, Bill and I had usually left the scene, my mother's voice following us out:

"You see what I told you? About Maria? The manners? She was brought up with only the best manners! And now . . . where have they all gone?"

On the 13th of February, 1957, with Burt Bacharach at the piano, she opened in Vegas. Looking superb in her perfect diamond-fringe dress, she accepted her usual tumultuous accolade.

After closing in Vegas, she returned to Hollywood, flirted Paramount into copying her black wig from *Golden Earrings*, rummaged through the gypsy section of the Wardrobe Department, and appeared as the madam of a Mexican brothel for Orson Welles in his film *Touch of Evil*. She had agreed to play the part as a favor to Orson, and when he told her that he had no money as usual, she did it for nothing. They shot her two short scenes in one night. The glowing reviews she received for her work in that film, the cult that regards that as probably her best acting since *The Blue Angel*, always amused her. I once asked Orson what had given him the idea of Dietrich for the madam of his brothel. He smiled that naughty "little boy" smile of his: "Never heard of type-casting?"

She returned to New York in the spring of '57, comforted Murrow, and made sure I could give birth. My third son was born physically handicapped. My mother was the first to be told that something was wrong. She took charge, ordered the doctors to say nothing to me, then in her best "Prussian officer" manner, announced to my anxious husband:

"Bill! We have a terrible tragedy! Maria's child is not perfect like the others! Is there something wrong in *your* family? No! No! You cannot see her now! They had to do a cesarean to get it out! *I* will tell you when you are allowed to see her!"

My loving husband never told me of this terrible moment. My outraged doctor and the shocked nurses did. My mother began sending cables, telephoning, alerting her private friends of the "tragedy" that had befallen her. Later she would embellish this by adding, "You know, Maria took that terrible pill when she was pregnant—that one . . . what is it called?—'tha'–something . . . the one that makes babies with no arms and no legs . . .'' Branding my child with a horrendous lie.

Billy Wilder and his superb timing—again came to my rescue. Three days later, my mother was forced to leave my bedside to prepare for her dual role in his film *Witness for the Prosecution*. Her parting words:

"You should have stopped after Michael. *He* is perfect. All this having children to-do is nothing but vanity. I told you—but you wouldn't listen. You had to do that 'cripple' telethon!", gave me a "sorrowing" embrace, pulled on her white kid gloves, and left.

Softly, Bill opened the door of my room, hesitant, face drawn, eyes haunted, so afraid it was he who had brought me this hurt —somehow. I reached out for him, we held each other, hard and close, more in apprehension than sorrow. Would we be able to help our child? Were we up to the task, were we good enough to do it right, was love enough to teach us the way? Then we squared our emotional shoulders and went to work, to be the very best parents we could be for our Paul.

This child was never given into Dietrich's care. What a cripple she would have made of that courageous little boy. By the time he did visit her alone, he was all of five, had conquered handicaps that doctors had deemed unconquerable, and even a Dietrich could not daunt him. She cooed, hovered, clucked, sighed, played the sacrificial nurse to the "afflicted," liked the connotation of complete dependence that she assumed he would be forced to exist under. As he said, when returning home that day:

"Massy was really silly, Mommy. She put on my shoes, cut all my food in little bits and got real mad because I didn't want her to feed me. I can do that now all by myself! I can, I learned it! Why was she so *mad*?"

I hugged him close. My lovely child, whose valiant battling spirit had conquered his physical destiny.

"Don't let her bother you, honey. Massy is not very bright about *really* important things."

He nodded his head—his "professor" nod he often used when contemplating anything he considered profound.

"Yes, Massy's *dumb*!" and went off to play with his favorite thing in all the big, big world —his little brother David.

Why did we keep it up? Why indeed. I think I so wanted to believe that a normal life was possible, I was blinded by my need to make it so. Bill inadvertently abetted my delusion—for him, "mothers" were people who belonged within a family unit. His world knew nothing of what my world knew too well and was afraid of. So I thought I could make it all "nice" by hiding all the ugliness from them, letting it corrode my spirit instead of theirs. I was conditioned to being ashamed of the "parent" Dietrich, they were not and should not be until they were old enough to judge for themselves. But they had to live with the backlash of my efforts and that was wrong. Being innocent spectators to fame and the adulation it begets, regardless of character content, being raised within the traditional boundaries of correct behavior, yet witnessing my mother's lack of any—and worse, seeing me condone such actions with what must have seemed to them as children, a suspect moral ease—harmed them. I should have cut—and cut deep—but did not. In subtle ways, it marked my children, for I notice the scars it left—even small, they should not have been inflicted at all. It is a crime I allowed, for which I am punished still and will be forever, and there is absolutely nothing I can do to make it right.

One of the tragedies of loving is the moment when "Kiss it and make it better" no longer works.

My mother was so busy making herself ugly for the cockney woman for *Witness for the Prosecution*, she didn't notice that I had ceased to call her, and when she called me, was too "busy" to talk. In July, when I notified her by telegram that we were moving to our little house on Long Island, she became so overly effusive, she must have been apprehensive. Her *professional* intelligence remained intact:

Saturday, July 13 '57

Oh my love,

What Joy your telegram is and what joy it gave my heart.

I have moved to a bungalow. This is my first morning at home and it is all too beautiful for me alone to have. But knowing you are at the seashore makes it less difficult to bear.

Everything is happening here. By now Laughton is co-directing me with Billy. He is a sly fox and Billy who is "in love" with him does not notice what he is doing. Through his advice I was made to yell in the first Courtroom scene which I think disastrous as I have no place to go.

But it was a beautiful foil for Laughton's long interrogation because he played it cynically sweet and led up to the end of his scene just yelling suddenly the word "Liar" after all the soft spoken proof of my lies. My yelling my answers made his sweet cynical attitude much more effective than if I had done it as I had thought of doing it. My: "No, I never loved him . . ." I wanted to say coldly which is emotional, and the spectators' reactions would have been the emotional impact against me, as they are supposed to be against me. And I always feel that people are more antagonistic toward cold and bitchy people than against anyone showing emotion.

But there were long conferences after every one of my takes, between Laughton and Billy and I just stood there and took it. I know that I have this terrible legend to overcome: that I am only interested in looks and have never acted before, and everything I would say would sound either that I did not want to distort the immobility of my face or that I knew I could not act emotional outbursts.

In the meantime Ty Power sits in the prisoner's box. He wears a beautiful tweed jacket, light in color, therefore more elegant than if the jacket were brown. His shirt is *immaculate*, cuffs freshly pressed. He wears *extra large* square *Hollywood* cuff links shining bright gold. He wears a beautiful wrist watch and a large signet ring on his little finger which has to be constantly rubbed with wax because the reflection hits the camera. His hair is brilliantined and *combed* before every take. He looks like Tyrone Power, American! When he has to bury his head in his hands out of despair about my bitchery he is very careful not to touch his hair. Like Claudette Colbert used to do because of the false bangs.

He looks as guilty as hell. None of the

innocence and bewilderment the man should have so that you believe he is not guilty. None of the poor English appearance of the wrinkled cuffs and sleeves of a man who is in prison on top of that. They spray him with perspiration to make him look worried. When he makes a worried expression he looks quite guilty. But no one dares to say anything. I had gotten tiny pearl earrings from the dime store, and I was told they made me look too rich. I am photographed harshly so that nothing reminds anyone of my usual beauty, and there sits a Hollywood LEADINGMAN so out of character and his beautifully manicured hands with ring and cuff links and watch lie on the edge of the prisoner's box. I have not seen him in the witness box where he will stand in all his glory and say that he is out of a job since he lost his job, that although he is hard up he never got a chance from the old lady he is accused of having murdered. Well? One should laugh, I guess.

Now Laughton told me that he thought as I was so military in court as Mrs. Vole, I should go to the opposite and be fuzzy feminine as the Cockney woman. With a bee-stung mouth and flirtatious fiddling constantly with my hands on my clothes. When he showed it to me blinking with his little eyes and fiddling with his shirt I had to think of the joke about the analyst who tries to get the butterflies off himself that the patient says he feels on his own body.

We have also tested numerous scars. All of them too shocking to Hornblow. Until in the general discussion how wrong everything was, my makeup man said: "But I read in the script that the scar is the reason for this woman's hate and also that she shows the scar only for a flash. If it isn't horrible, why does she wear her hair hanging over it? She could put some pancake over it and cover it easily if it were just a red streak." "Ah," they said, "yes, that is true," and okayed the scar.

Billy has great trouble with the set as I anticipated. The Old Bailey is reproduced in solid wood to the specific measurements. As you know, photographically measurements mean nothing, with light you can give depth and space that is nonexistent, and can also crowd if you want to. But there they are, proud that they have the *real* thing. Except that it is new. That they have forgotten. The side ceiling, where the wood paneling stops is painted fresh and almost white, looking like a Hollywood set. The expert British Barrister we have on the set agreed with me that it is dirty up there from the years and even if they painted there each year it would never look like that. The leather on the benches is brand-new too.

On those benches sit the Hollywood extras. In their own clothes. Up-to-date hairdos, hats, jewelry à la Hollywood. Pretty faces. The men have white shirts that glare distractingly behind the actors' big printed ties. No narrow knots like the British are wearing, no middle-class English faces, all American, so wrong you cannot believe that nobody sees or objects to it. All that in the "true-to-life" Old Bailey set. No characters who go to murder trials but nice California good-looking ladies.

It is none of my business but these are the same people that judge me!

Una O'Connor played her scene exactly as she played it on the stage except she had trouble with the changed lines. She wore her same clothes and her long earrings dangled alongside of her face giving her sharp head turns a lot of life. She plays the old housekeeper of the murdered woman. There they had respect and let her do.

What else can I tell you? I have played whores all my life. And this one they don't even think I can contribute anything to.

Not that I feel they can spoil my performance altogether. I still will get Mrs. Vole on the screen, maybe not as perfect as I could have played her, but good enough.

As I have no other picture coming I find myself in that awful spot with interviewers: "What are you going to do afterwards?" All I can say is: "I go home."

I kiss you with my heart,
Massy

She kept her diary up to date:

Wednesday July 24th
Learning lines. Big end scene.
　　He called. I thought I was dreaming—
Slightly drunk but not much. Enough to call
me though.
　　Working hard and back still bad. One
hour talk first time since January.

This reference to Yul's back pain may be the first
indication of the virulent cancer that would de-
stroy this talented man. On the 19th of August,
she wrote:

Without brace first time. He said I came to
tell you that I love you. He had three drinks
when he said it. He was lying in bed when
he said it.
　　After saying good-bye at the door and
decided to stay.

August 20th
Finished *Witness*.

August 22
Home all day waiting. Billy called, said I
was wonderful in film. I Academy Award
performance.
　　Means nothing as *He* did not call.

September 4th
He came at 1:30 left at 4:30. Sweet, tender,
looks wonderful (taking Ginseng). In bed
an hour and a half. I should be happy.
　　Difficult because it's love that matters,

not the bed. Although that was always his sign of love.

Dubbing Thursday Cockney woman.

September 13
Miserable. No call. Why?
To studio to see Billy. 3 PM
Chevalier
Ty Power

September 14
Dark bloodstain backache
No blood on Tampax at 9 PM put in at 12 noon
But still backache. Worried.

She had continued to record erratic staining in her yearly diaries and would continue to do so until 1964. She refused to go to a doctor.

Tami took more and more refuge in the voices only she could hear. When they told her not to sleep, she sat for days, unmoving, eyes fixed, her frail body rigid in its suspended state. When her voices urged her to open her veins and she obeyed them, my father had her committed. It was the end of her long tortuous journey. I should have rushed to save her from that final anguish, but I was too engrossed with my own sorrow and fears to muster the strength to do battle for that sweet woman I loved. By the time my child had triumphed over his handicaps, it was much too late.

Witness for the Prosecution, with Charles Laughton and Tyrone Power, directed by Billy Wilder (BELOW). This is the only film I can remember my mother ever actually wanting to make. In it, she had a chance to play a dual role. I never thought she got away with the disguise, but she believed she did—one of the few times her sharp intelligence concerning film deserted her.

My mother wrote me enumerating all the faults of this
famous court scene in *Witness for the Prosecution*.

One must read her letter to appreciate her talent for criticism.

LEFT: Another Vegas, another see-through vision, another huge success, while yearning to be with her sexy "King of Siam" (BELOW).

My mother summed it all up:

"Finally she is really crazy and put away! Now Papi can get some peace!"

His reaction was to continue his affair with Linda Darnell, begun before Tami's final collapse.

My mother returned to New York, and as her backache persisted, she resumed her daily doses of her favorite, cortisone. The moment it entered her bloodstream she felt really well. So well, in fact, that she recorded it in her diary. She also mentions that when she stopped it a week later, the numbness in her feet returned as well as the backache and so decided to continue taking cortisone on a regular basis.

When Michael Todd's plane crashed and he was killed, she went into her widow's mourning, ridiculing his real wife for doing so.

We campaigned for John Fitzgerald Kennedy, and I thought how this had been Big Joe's supposed destiny, not being shot down in a war, was glad that Jack had picked up the fallen torch, and wondered if he had really wanted to. Funny feeling to have a president who once made your knees woozy. I wished him well and wore my Kennedy button with "family" pride.

Gable died, and when I told my mother so had Henny Porten, the movie-star idol of her youth, she said, "Who? Never heard of her!"

Yul slowly began to fade from the pages of her diary. She had once said that if she could hate him, she could then stand the pain of losing him. With her Teutonic discipline, she was now true to her word. By the end of that year, the obsessive love that had so dominated her life for so many years, she had turned into an equally consuming hatred.

Unknown to my mother, Yul and I remained friends. I admired him for many reasons and always had a soft spot in my heart for Dietrich's victims.

THE WORLD

AS VON STERNBERG HAD ILLUMINATED, glorified what only his gifted eye had seen, so now after a year of working with her, Burt Bacharach began to mold, then hone Dietrich's talent to mesmerize a live audience vocally. He rewrote all her orchestrations, trimmed her excessive use of violins, allowing them only when their lilt would be most effective, injected American rhythm into her old standards, then taught her how to sing "swing." He coached her, directed her, treated her as a knowledgeable musician whose ability needed only polishing to be recognized as laudable talent. As her confidence grew, so did her ability to take command of a stage as a performer, not simply a Hollywood glamour queen come to warble her ditties. From time to time, as I found songs I knew were particularly suited to her philosophy of life and loving, I discussed them with her, then sent the music to Burt to write his orchestration, that is, if he agreed and approved of my choice. No one ever was a better arranger for Dietrich's vocal capacity than Bacharach. By the time she embarked on her first international tour in her one-woman show, the Dietrich nightclub image had been replaced by a powerful performer, in full command of her talent and, under the constant watchful eye of her musical mentor, her material. All that was left over from her Las Vegas days were the shimmering dresses and the extravaganza of the swansdown coat. At sixty, she had found at last the lover she had been seeking since her adolescence: one who worshiped without complaint, demanded nothing in return, was grateful for all she might give, constant, welcomed the sweet agonies of loving she offered, accepted her sorrows as his own, enjoyed her with an exaltation devoid of all physical contact. This new lover was completely hers to control, he was even punctual. As she had so meticulously noted the minutes, the hours with Yul, she now recorded the exact time her new and perfect love affair with her audience could begin with "Curtain—8:30."

With Burt's talent protecting her, she began to tour the world. She triumphed on the concert stages of South America, Canada, Spain, Great Britain, the United States, Israel, France, Portugal, Italy, Australia, Mexico, Poland, Sweden, Germany, Holland, Russia, Belgium, Denmark, South Africa, and Japan. Knowing the people of Israel, I persuaded her not to cut her German songs from her repertoire as she had planned, but to sing them, and in the original language. She was hesitant about it. I said, "Believe me, do it," and she did, was loved and respected for her honesty.

She called me from Tel Aviv: "They loved me. They cried, kissed my hands. The theater was full—full! So many that did not get killed by the Nazis. Amazing!" and had a fast affair with one of Israel's more flamboyant politicians.

Brazil, too, offered more than just popular adulation:

Hotel Jaragua
São Paulo—Brazil

It's autumn here— Beautiful!

My love—quickly just so that you know. Great opening here. And Ricardo Fasanelli (the same FASAN—*Gold*fasan my sister used to call me "Golden Pheasant": the bird). Thirty years old. Basque and Italian ancestors intermarried . . . so out comes that delicately boned narrow body and face. . . . Giant black eyes very short-sighted, sometimes with horn-rimmed glasses. Baby-hair dark brown. Brilliant—and rubs his eyes with the fist like babies do. See what I mean? To die, no?

I said at one point: "This is ridiculous— I promise you I will pull my net in." (We had just been talking about the ocean and fishermen and boats.) He said: "You do not make sense. You said you were in love with me and now you say: I promise to pull in my net. You couldn't do that if you are in love." Can you see how I greet all this with passionate delight? After all these years of emotional idiots? Maybe we should keep this the way it is, just loving each other's souls. Anyway I do no seducing or even suggesting anything else. But God, how he looks at me. It makes your teeth rattle.

Kisses.

Massy

When an egg was thrown at her during a performance in Germany, the audience nearly lynched the offender, then gave Dietrich a standing ovation for refusing to be driven off the stage by a "mere Nazi." One night, during her triumphal German tour, she fell off the stage into the darkened orchestra pit. My phone rang:

"Sweetheart— I fell!" Her frightened voice was barely audible.

"Where are you now?"

"In bed, in my hotel."

"Where did you hit when you fell?"

"Not my legs. Don't worry; only my left shoulder. It hurts but I tied my arm against my body with one of the men's ties and I finished the show. Thank god, I was already in the tails, so the dress didn't get torn when I fell."

"Now listen to me carefully. There is an American hospital near you in Wiesbaden. First thing in the morning, you go there and have them x-ray you—"

She interrupted:

"Oh! Nothing is broken! Just the stage was so dark, I didn't see the edge and suddenly disappeared from view. . . . Must have looked very funny to the audience."

"Don't try to get out of it. You go to Wiesbaden tomorrow for X rays. That's an order!"

On her return from the hospital, she called:

"I said to them, 'You see how my daughter is always right? She told me I had to come here and be x-rayed. She sits all the way back in New York and is the only one who knows that there is an American hospital in Wiesbaden.' You were right, as usual—they say my collarbone is broken, whatever that is, but I am just going to tie my arm to my side, like I did yesterday, and so, I can go on with the tour."

She did just that, and the added pathos of this indomitable soldier, gallantly performing despite her busted wing, endeared her even further to her German audience. I had a suspicion that too much champagne, and not just the darkened stage, had contributed to her fall. Her drinking had accelerated, not only before and after a performance, but during it as well. I knew the constant ache in her legs and back had become the perfect excuse to increase the intake of narcotics and alcohol she had been taking for years. Somehow, I had to get her to be examined by a reputable physician.

. . .

Again I was waiting for a baby. Again I spoke on television, again my mother accused me of putting my unborn child at risk. In the summer of '61, she was in Hollywood filming *Judgment at Nuremberg* but managed to fly back to New York in time to announce to my husband that I had given birth to another boy. She was genuinely surprised that this one was "unmarked by that telethon thing!"

By this time, my mother had decided which of my children were special enough, in her opinion, to be awarded her undying devotion. She informed me Michael had inherited her "elegant, thin bones," and as his hair was also blond, she considered him her own. The fact that I had borne him was a mere happenstance, not worth a thought. Peter she tolerated—just. At the innocent age of two, he had looked at her one day and piped:

"Massy—you look old today," which put him out of the running for her favors for the rest of his life! He never rated porcelain bells, delicate silver sleighs, not even scampering Bambis. His Christmas "package codes" were always the least pretty, usually in shades of blah brown. Paul she had immediately adopted as her "serious cause," played "St. Bernadette to the afflicted," and would have wrapped him in emotional cotton had I let her. My new baby did not interest her in the least. He looked like my husband and screamed whenever she came near him. From birth, David was very intelligent.

She came to the hospital, cautioned me against having any *more* children, and returned to Hollywood, where she gave an amazing performance as the righteous wife of a condemned Nazi general. She never realized and would have been outraged if anyone had suggested such a thing, but the woman she portrayed so skillfully in *Judgment at Nuremberg* was a meticulous, brilliant recreation of her mother—masquerading as Tante Valli. How sad that her most vivid subconscious memory of her mother should be one of stoic self-aggrandizing loyalty to duty—in a black velvet suit.

That summer, Hemingway committed suicide. My mother, in flowing black, took his letters out of their special strongbox, locked herself in her room, and played widow. Read his words over and over again, searching for a phrase, a thought, that might give her a clue as to—why. She never really came to terms with her friend's death nor ever forgave him for deserting her. Secretly, she blamed his wife:

"If *I* had been there with him, he would never have done it!"

Gary Cooper's death did not stir her to widowhood. She just went to his funeral and was photographed looking "stricken."

A wall went up—dividing Berlin and Germany; the *Tropic of Cancer* was finally allowed to be legally published in the United States, and Dietrich allowed herself to be examined by a competent physician.

The first X rays showed massive occlusions of the lower aorta. Because of this blockage of her main arterial branch, her legs were being literally starved of their normal blood supply. This accounted for the practically nonexistent pulse in both of her legs. Naturally, she refused to believe the diagnosis. In her view, only "old" people got advanced arteriosclerosis.

"That's what they told me my mother died of. You see how stupid they are? Of course, she had it because she was *old*!"

I persuaded her to consult the leading cardiologist of the day for a second opinion, and when he not only confirmed the original diagnosis but added the warning that if she did not have immediate attention, she faced the possibility of amputation of both limbs in the future, she refused to have anything more to do with any of them:

"Surgeons! All they want to do is cut. That's why they are surgeons. Ridiculous!"

For the next thirteen years, my mother played her own deadly version of Russian roulette with her body's circulatory system and nearly got away with it. Whenever she read or heard of anything that was touted to increase the flow of blood, she got it and took it, regardless of what it was or where it came from; found a weird little Frenchman who called himself a doctor by wearing a white smock, let him inject a secret potion into her groin with a horse syringe, for he had assured her that only his magic mixture could flush all the blockage from her arteries.

Her legs worsened, particularly the left one, which had the least pulse. The foot and ankle swelled, an ugliness she found abhorrent. So, once again, what she had done by chance for quite different reasons years before, now worked to her advantage and offered her the camouflage she needed. She resumed wearing her famous trousers. They hid the elastic stockings she was now forced to wear, and later, the bandages. For her tours, she invented tall boots, wore them with her new short-skirted Chanel suits, and set a fashion trend. For those times when she was forced to wear more elaborate clothes, she designed shoes that were elegant but did not attract the eye, then had them made in the same color as her stockings to further emphasize and enhance the illusion of the perfect unbroken leg and foot line.

When the first support tights came on the market, they were a real boon to her. She redesigned her foundation to include them. First, she eliminated the garter belt construction, substituted a row of eyes on which the tiny hooks sewn along the top band of the tights could be fastened around the waist, making them an integral part of the foundation design.

As the swellings were erratic and completely unpredictable, the left foot being sometimes two sizes larger than the right, boots and shoes had to be made in varying sizes. It was not unusual for Dietrich to pack eight pairs of identical boots in various graded sizes, repeated in twenty different designs and materials, before departing on one of her international tours.

Why the mystery? Why the desperate need to conceal the truth? Simple. She believed that no human flaw must ever be permitted to mar the perfection of the legend that was Marlene Dietrich and—history proved her right. But this game of hoodwinking the public produced a dangerous side effect—as long as she looked an unblemished Dietrich, she believed it herself.

In 1962, she narrated the *Black Fox*, gave this documentary on Hitler the prestige and impact it deserved, winning for it the Academy Award the following year. She again played Vegas, replaced her customary champagne with scotch when she learned that it opened veins, rekindled her affair with Michael Wilding so energetically that they broke the double bed in the guest room of the home of my friends. When she heard that Elizabeth Taylor was in need of a better bra to wear under her costumes in *Cleopatra*, she took Wilding with her for advice as to the correct size, scoured Hollywood for the perfect brassiere, found it, and sent three dozen off to Rome. Had a fling with Eddie Fisher and observed, *now* she understood why Taylor had left him, was so "gaga" over Richard Burton.

By July she was back in New York to help us move to Europe. As our two eldest were scheduled to enter boarding school in Switzerland for their junior and senior high school years, and as Bill now had his own design business, we were "movable" and decided to set up camp near them with the two youngest.

While we drove through Switzerland looking for a town we could afford to settle in, my mother rented a little house near Geneva and took care of our year-old baby. I knew he was safe. He didn't cry anymore when she came near him—just gave a look of "don't you *dare* lay a finger on me." She wore her nurse's uniforms, starched and pristine, sterilized everything in sight, then received carefully screened friends to witness how superbly she was taking care of Maria's "neglected child." After many visits, Noël Coward had enough material to do a wonderfully amusing routine entitled "Visiting Marlenah's Nursery in Jussy."

I did love Noël. For some reason, I felt very

maternal toward him. Always got the urge to reach out, put my arms around him whenever we met. I don't know why—just felt he was hurting inside that polished frame and needed comforting. For Dietrich, it was his style, brilliant success, and the "Noël Coward," as he lived his own creation of himself, that was her "chum." The sensitive, vulnerable, serious man, so easily lonely, hidden so well beneath the throwaway charm—him, she never took the time to find. And if she had? It would have confused her.

We returned to "Marlenah's nursery" to find my mother's sister in residence, utterly bewildered by all the rules of hygiene she was expected to adhere to and scared stiff that her adored Pussy Cat would once again be annoyed by her usual clumsiness. My Aunt Liesel welcomed my return with sighs of relief, her little wren eyes brimming with tears of joy. I should have known from past experience that once my mother had been given authority over anyone, she assumed they were hers in perpetuity. She greeted me with:

"David—walks! *I* taught him to walk!" as though God, nature, and his age of thirteen months had absolutely nothing to do with it. From then on, whenever she saw David, the first words out of her mouth were: "*Who* taught you to walk?" said in a tone of military challenge, *daring* him to give her a wrong answer. This can

In her "lady" suit for *Judgment at Nuremberg*, looking like her mother.

She liked Spencer Tracy because Katharine Hepburn loved him, and was terribly jealous of the protection from scandal MGM accorded these two stars.

ABOVE: In *Touch of Evil* she played the bit part for nothing as a favor to her friend Orson Welles and was probably better than she had been since *The Blue Angel*. BELOW: When we ran out of ideas for finales, we sometimes switched from black to white. In Rio de Janeiro, it looked great.

be a little embarrassing in the crowded lobby of a Broadway opening night when you are twenty-five.

With my mother and her latest girlfriend, very smart in Chanel suits and inherited wealth in residence, our first Christmas in our new home near Geneva was a disaster. It was Europe—my mother's domain—and French-speaking to boot! She ran everything. Me, my home, my children, the village. When she tried to extend her field-marshal tactics to my husband, he balked—"No way! New Year's Eve with those two females is out!"—and I put in an SOS to Noël, fifty-some miles down the road at Les Avants:

"Dear child! Simply send the German lady and her latest on to me!" which we did and for which I thanked him with all my heart.

It was around this time that my mother invented her story of why she suddenly stopped smoking. We all knew that the doctors had been horrified at her continuing to smoke despite their warnings and that finally she was frightened enough by the increasing leg cramps to stop. But the gestures of smoking, the cigarette held so elegantly, the cupped hands shielding an offered flame, the emphasis of cheekbones as she pulled the smoke into her lungs with obvious pleasure, the pucker of her lips as she exhaled, were so much a visual part of the Dietrich image, she knew the press would notice their absence and want to know why. She told her cover story so often, she finally believed it herself:

"Sweetheart! You know the year I stopped smoking—the legs, always the legs! But you can't tell people that's why. So I said to Noël, 'You should stop smoking too. You don't walk so well either and we will tell them that we made a bet—whoever smokes loses. That's fun, not something medical. We can play that very bon vivant, à la man-of-the-world—you know, like: "Of course! I would *adore* a cigarette! But I simply *can't*, I have a bet on with Marlenah!" ' "

Years later, when Noël resumed smoking, she was furious and called him:

"What about our bet?"

"What bet?"

"I have dreamt of a cigarette ever since you made that bet with me. Not a day goes by that I don't *yearn* for a cigarette. I haven't slept one night since I gave up smoking!"

I could hear Noël chuckling all the way from Jamaica:

"My dearest Marlenah—it's been six years! You must be exhausted!"

My mother never appreciated sarcasm. Anyone daring to make fun of her was such an outrageous thought, that she never contemplated its possibility. But she had the last word:

"You see! Even without sleep, I have more

discipline than you have. You lost our bet!" and slammed down the phone.

Near Montreux, just below where Noël had his Swiss home, a doctor, a pioneer in live-cell theory, ran his famous clinic. Although he boasted many cures for legitimate ills, the international fame of his treatment was perpetuated by those who spend their lives and fortunes searching for the fountain of youth. Patients checked into his elegant château on a Tuesday. The patient guest list was secret, and meticulously guarded. Wednesday they were tested and questioned:

> Memory flagging?
> Skin going to flab?
> Bones creaking?
> Perhaps a bored libido?

After these briefings, the patient returned to his lovely room to gaze out of French windows at fluffy pregnant sheep grazing contentedly on emerald green meadows. Thursday was slaughter day. The woolly sheep were cut open and their fetuses removed for their abundant supply of unused cells. A few very fresh brain cells for the memory. A half a teaspoon of bone cells for those creaking joints. A pinch of newborn liver cells to refresh that toxic one. A bit of this, a bit of that—put them all in a blender, mix until it looks like a rusty-colored malted, fill into enormous syringes, then shoot all those "miraculous" goodies into the willing and waiting behinds of the rich and desperate.

I always pooh-poohed the entire concept, but my mother took this cell treatment four different times, and knowing what she went through, what she was able to endure over the rest of her lifetime, I often wondered if that ghoulish intramuscular cocktail didn't have something to do with her amazing endurance. That incredible fortitude of hers just couldn't have been due to Prussian genes alone!

THE REST OF 1963, she toured the United States, performing in Washington, D.C., where she visited the charming son of her old boyfriend, Ambassador Kennedy.

September 6, 1963
Open Washington
Sold out

September 9
Women's Press Club. Walton drinks.
Visit Harriman.

September 10
With Walton Lunch White House.
Senator Pell
White House
Saw Jack 20 minutes
Show sold out.

September 11
Lunch Bobby at Bill Walton's
Schlesinger, Buckley (*Newsweek* and Mrs.
B. Kennedy)
Wrote letter Papa Kennedy
White House drinks Jack
Jewish congregation to give me plaque. Had
to cut White House visit short.
Not the first time the Jews interfered with
my life.
Show at 10:30–250 sent away.

As we had rented our house in New York, my husband, when in America on business, stayed at my mother's apartment. He was there the day she returned from Washington. She came through the door, saw him, opened her large black crocodile handbag, extracted a pair of pink panties, and held them under his nose, saying:

"Smell! It is him! The President of the United States! He—was—wonderful!"

My husband moved to a hotel.

WE SETTLED IN LONDON for the young children's schooling, and, in order to be near us, my mother moved to Paris, where she rented an apartment opposite the Plaza Athénée.

Two of my mother's French "friends" died in October. To one, she had been a lover, to the other, a lifelong "pal." From both, Dietrich learned valuable lessons that enriched her stage career. Edith Piaf gave my mother her song "la Vie en rose" and taught her the art of economy of stage gestures. Jean Cocteau, the art of exaggeration to achieve the maximum theatrical effect on a large stage. My mother mourned Piaf like a husband his child bride, and took great comfort from the fact that her "little Sparrow" was buried wearing the gold cross she had given her on her wedding day. Cocteau's lyrical tribute to Dietrich she framed along with his picture and hung it next to Hemingway's.

She came over to London for the anniversary gala of the Battle of El Alamein. The Royal Albert Hall was jammed; many famous stars had agreed to appear to commemorate this great British victory against the "desert fox," the mighty Rommel. I dressed my mother in her golden sheath, walked her through the catacombs of that bastion of Victorian culture, sent her out onto its vast platform stage.

She stood in a single shaft of light, like a sword reflecting the rays of the sun, Excalibur made woman! Took a beat and began "Lili Marlene," and that giant domed concert hall took on a silence of such awe and respect, it vibrated like a living thing in that hushed air. The hall was filled with the veterans of that terrible desert war, and they accepted her as one of their own. She was quite magnificent that night and she knew it, but was angry we hadn't remembered her medals.

"Tonight, finally, I could have worn them —all of them!"

In November, my mother returned to appear at a royal command performance. As handmaiden conveniently in place, I took her through the rehearsals and dressed her. There were many famous stars who were scheduled to appear that night. We stood together backstage, waiting for our individual rehearsals to begin.

"Sweetheart—look. Look over there," she whispered. "What *are* those? They look like monkeys with all that hair! What are *they* doing backstage? All this big 'security' and *they* got in? Just look at them—how terrible!" and pointed to the Beatles.

"Massy, I think it would be a wonderful idea if Dietrich were photographed with them—"

"What? With those *monkeys*?"

"Yes—they are the new rage, kids adore them. It would create a big stir if Dietrich were seen accepting them! Trust me!"

She gave me one of her "the things I do for you" looks, and I walked over to John Lennon and said that Miss Dietrich had expressed the desire to meet the Beatles. When the photograph of The Legend and the soon-to-be ones hit every newspaper in the world, my mother was heard to exclaim:

"The Beatles? *You* don't know who the Beatles are? How is that possible? They are geniuses—they don't look it, but they are geniuses and so young! I asked them if I could have their autographs for Maria's children, and they said all they wanted was a picture taken with me—so of course I had to say yes!"

I WAS WORRYING where in London I was going to find real cranberry sauce for Thanksgiving dinner and Crisco for pies . . . and pumpkin? The TV was on. Suddenly—that pink suit . . . all I remember is that *pink* . . . scrambling out onto the back of the speeding car, reaching, a blur of bright color . . . over and over again, in slow motion, in speed, again and again, that pink haunted, became a part of our life—and I, so far from home, sat stunned, disbelieving, praying it was not true, knowing that it was, and . . . I saw him, tanned and lean, diving off the highest cliff, bowing in his white tuxedo jacket asking for a dance, laughing over tea, walking away so sure of himself toward that sexy convertible, so handsome, so wonderfully alive! He would be mourned by many, the great and small of many lands; I mourned him for the youth he wore so well.

My mother donned simple widow's black, her face a white mask of personal sorrow, sat erect, her voice hushed and reverent as she repeatedly told of their last romantic encounter.

By Christmas, a writer of children's books asked for "it," and helped ease her sorrow. They enjoyed each other so, this lady appeared often at our door during the holidays. My small children were oblivious. My older ones, home on vacation, asked a few pertinent questions and were given straight answers. They had observed enough of my mother's romantic entanglements, spent summer days with Yul, teas with Murrow, Christmas Eves with her real husband while the acting husband carved, to have no illusions about their grandmother's life-style.

Unfortunately, her lady author was killed in a plane crash soon after the New Year, and so, my mother went back into "widowhood" before she was completely through with the last one.

IN HER CRYSTAL DRESS, she stood before the velvet curtain, an incandescent diamond against the ruby-red curtain of the Queen's Theatre. She had made it. She had performed, been acclaimed on the same stage that had witnessed the brilliance of Olivier, Richardson, Gielgud, Ashcroft, and most of the great actors of England. It was her opening night in London and she had given the best performance of her life and knew it. We all did. The exuberant audience response merely confirmed this fact. The entire first London stage engagement was magical. She basked in being the toast of the town. London was at the feet of a Hollywood movie star who had stepped off her turf onto their hallowed boards and been accepted. She worked hard, played hard, slept little, was thin as a rail, at sixty-three—she had never looked better.

Only two things marred this successful time: the new pain in the region of her rectum, and the need to wear her trusty Tampax continuously to staunch the persistent pink staining. When she heard that an ailment called colitis could cause sharp pains similar to the ones she was experiencing and that a concoction known as slippery elm would cure it, we went shopping at London's health-food emporium and bought out the store. If slippery elm could cure "pains down there," why not find something to cure everything else that was bothering her? We returned to her Dorchester suite and set up "Dietrich's health clinic" in the spare bedroom. She particularly liked the idea that apple-cider vinegar, mixed with honey, was supposed to be the true elixir of life. She proceeded to mix half-gallon jugs immediately, and had them delivered to Burt's dressing room, along with his freshly laundered tuxedo shirts.

"Not that Burt needs any *more* energy, but you never know what he might pick up from those girls of his!"

Bill refused to partake, after he heard my mother exclaim in wonder how amazed she was that what she had been douching with all these years, she was now drinking!

She continued losing weight. We had to unpack the foundations marked "very tight." The thinner she got, the better she liked it, and in those incredible dresses, she did look divine.

The day after she closed in London, I took her to the great gynecologist Prof. de Watteville in Geneva. She was frightened and therefore full of fury. She called Noël:

"My private Gestapo, Maria, is dragging me to Geneva just so that her precious doctor can examine me. That's all she does—have me examined by strange men!"

After her initial consultation, she returned to Paris; I continued on to Gstaad to meet Bill and visit our boys' school in the Swiss mountains. I was so certain that my mother had cancer that I had arranged with the professor to secretly call me there the moment the results of the tests were in. He did, told me that she had cancer of the cervix.

My mother thought of cancer as a slow process of inner decay. I knew that she would never accept this process going on inside Dietrich. She, who was so proud to proclaim herself a soldier's daughter, always lacked the courage to face up to stark reality. If my mother had been told that she had cancer and that a hysterectomy was mandatory, she would have jumped out of the nearest window, German or no German discipline. So, the professor and I discussed alternatives. He was a wonderful man. He had many famous world beauties as patients and understood how vulnerable, how immature some of these women could be about their bodies. He suggested that it might be possible to do a series of radium implants; if, by some slim miracle, these radioactive packings resulted in checking the cancer, surgery might be avoided, for a while at least. We agreed to buy time. I suggested he tell my mother that the treatment he proposed was for a precancerous condition only and not in order to treat an already developed cancer. This script would be the only one she might accept. She was furious, balked, finally consented to being treated, but only if I accompanied her, stayed with her the full time.

In March, I flew from London to Geneva and met my mother as she arrived from Paris. She was so drunk, I had to help her into the waiting car. At the hospital, she gave orders that a cot be placed immediately in her room for me to sleep on. The nurses were alarmed and attempted to explain that if I were to stay in the room with her, I too would be exposed to radiation and any future children I might want could conceivably be at risk. My mother was not impressed.

"My daughter doesn't need any more children! And risk? She does that to them all by herself! She will stay here in this room with me!"

March 6, 1965
Curettage and first implant.

March 7
Taken out 3 P.M.

Before taking her back to Paris, I made her give me her solemn oath that she would return with me for her second treatment, scheduled for March 27th. I had to force her, but she went.

March 27
Second implant.

March 29
5:30 A.M. OUT.

As my mother was not allowed to have a telephone in her room, a nurse came, conducted me to a glass-enclosed booth in the Victorian lobby of the infirmary, to take my father's call from overseas. So I was alone when I heard his voice telling me that Tami was dead. I remember the pretty colors the sun made as it hit the cut-glass panels of the little booth; how glad I was to be in a private place where I could cry. Sweet Tami—forgive me. You should not have been left to die alone amongst mad strangers.

I returned to my mother's room. She was annoyed that I had been so long on the phone. I gave her the news of Tami's death. She paused, sighed, and said:

"Poor Papi! Anyway, it's good that he has that pretty Darnell woman—so he's not alone," and that was Tami's epitaph from the lady who had destroyed her life.

On the 24th of April, three and a half weeks after her last radium implant, Marlene Dietrich opened her one-woman show in Johannesburg, South Africa, to jubilant acclaim. While I glowed a little in the dark, my mother, at sixty-four, had beaten cancer and didn't even know it!

By August, she was appearing in Edinburgh and became involved with a gentleman she referred to as "P.D.," and, years later, as "that sentimental old Jew I had in Edinburgh." Next, she toured Australia, where she fell madly in love with a reporter, of all people, who looked like a pugilist or a very, very, very poor man's version of Gabin—depending on how much he had had to drink. As he had a wife and children, their affair, which lasted for nearly two years, took on the intrigues of a French bedroom farce.

She couldn't remain in Australia forever, so in the guise of helping Dietrich write her memoirs, her new love persuaded his paper to give him a leave of absence and followed his lady love to Paris. Although his official address was the home of my mother's loyal friends, he secretly lived with her in her apartment. To justify his remaining for longer and longer periods, my mother devised a scheme of introducing him to other famous people for the purpose of writing a series of profiles.

For the first time, Dietrich was willing to use her rather awesome connections. She called everyone, telling them about this wonderful young Australian writer she had found, who would be *so* grateful if they granted him a moment of their precious time to write a piece about them. While my mother was busy lining up the world's celebrities for her lover to interview, our happy-go-lucky reporter lived the life of Riley.

Of course, she kept me informed. I was constantly amazed by my mother's absolute conviction that I would be intensely interested in everything concerning her. I was expected to listen to every detail of her life with him: his habits, his likes, his dislikes, his abilities both in and out of bed, his problems with his wife.

"You know, he is like a child! Excited to be in Paris. I don't think he has ever eaten such food," her voice dropped to a confidential whisper. "I don't think he comes from a very good family, so I am teaching him how one behaves in first-class restaurants."

All that restaurant-hopping must have caused her to gain some weight, for she complained: "You and your doctor fetish—I was so *wonderfully* thin in London! But *you* had to force me to go to that hospital in Geneva, and *now*—all my waistbands are too tight!"

She flew to London, with her Australian, and arrived at my house with him in tow. For some reason, this lover made my flesh crawl, an instantaneous reaction that interested me as much as it confused me. I had long ago stopped being affected one way or another by the array of flotsam my mother brought to my door—still, with this one, I balked. Somehow, I didn't want my children exposed to him—there was an aura of contagion about him.

On July 22nd, her brash Australian had the guts to write his own entry into my mother's "sacred" diary:

> *His*: Tonight she told me that men like I, know "Only about getting into bed and going 'Bam'—'Bam'—and that's it." She added that we lack the imagination of men like another she mentioned. This, as someone said before, was the unkindest cut of all. I always thought going to bed with her

a joy. Especially when it was not a fight night and, instead, we made love, sometimes—it seemed—forever. Those ruddy medicos tell us that women always get more out of that than we do. It appears that she is an exception. Or, does she want me to *think* that she is? I hope so. I love her.

Finally, he just had to return to his wife and job, but they made plans to meet secretly in Hollywood and, later, in Australia.

She returned to London for another triumph and arranged for her sister to fly in to witness it. In between sitting her down, making her listen to her "Pussy Cat's" many LPs for hours on end, Liesel was taken for slow walks, while being reminded to "take it easy" because of her varicose veins, her weight, her arthritis, her failing eyesight. "Oh, Lieselchen—be careful!" "Lieselchen, are you cold?" "Are you hungry?" "Are you tired?" "Are you all right?"—bounced about in such tones of speaking to the mentally afflicted. I cringed for my aunt, who didn't. She had been a victim so long, one couldn't victimize her.

While my aunt was in residence, I remember a bizarre family dinner in my mother's Dorchester suite. My clever husband had, once again, found something "urgent" to keep him from joining us. Bill had a way of doing that successfully that I envied. Over the lobster bisque, Michael and Peter, now seventeen and fifteen, asked Liesel what it had *really* been like to live in Germany during the Second World War. While my mother served our resplendent room-service banquet, hovering as usual over the table, anticipating her guests' slightest wish, completely oblivious to whatever was being said, we listened in growing amazement to her sister expound on the moral integrity of the German Reich. Assuredly, there had been some bad Nazis, but one could not deny that during their reign, Germany had regained its lost glory. We finished dinner, my sons took flight, slightly critical that I stayed. I couldn't blame them, yet I was sorry for this strange little woman, now so complex in her loyalties, who once had been so far-seeing, so politically astute. Somewhere she had lost her way or, more likely, the way had never been hers to lose.

A few years after that dinner, in yet another London hotel suite, my mother received a phone call informing her that Liesel had died. She turned to stone. I pried the receiver from her rigid hand, poured her a double scotch. She did not cry. From then on, whenever my mother referred to her sister, it was "Remember that day in London, when they called me and told me that Liesel was dead? I performed that night—I forget where I was playing, but I know I went on. I did my job! 'Do your duty,' my mother always told us. Poor Liesel, that terrible husband of hers, she wouldn't listen. She stayed because of her child. When I searched and found her in the concentration camp the day the British liberated Belsen, she wouldn't leave. All because of that son of hers! He was, of course, in the German army and she was frightened that if she moved he wouldn't know where to find her! So, I got Gavin and the British to find her a better apartment and got permission so that she could stay in Belsen and wait for her son."

Dietrich said these words to many people and never once did anyone challenge her, ask for explanations of the so obvious discrepancies. It is this nonchallenging, this automatic acceptance, without corroboration of utterances made by "living legends," and even nonliving ones, that angers me. People, and this includes those famous for their intellect, seem to have an inbuilt aversion to pick at surface gold, get down to those possible feet of clay. The fear of tumbling man-made gods is a really powerful phobia.

TWO HUNDRED THOUSAND U.S. TROOPS, under the guise of a nonaggression force, were now fighting in the jungles of Vietnam. The napalm bombing runs had begun.

My mother returned to California, secretly met up with her Aussie, took him onto the set of *Who's Afraid of Virginia Woolf?*, was ever so friendly with one of her pet hates, Elizabeth Taylor, and basked in the "looks" Richard Burton threw her way.

"Sweetheart! Oh, he is so beautiful! Those eyes! That voice! So Welsh! He *is* Welsh, right? I felt his eyes on me the whole time and had to pretend I didn't feel them, because everyone was watching. That Bitch—is even going to *act* in this picture because he is carrying her in the palm of his hands through the whole film with *his* talent. But, you should have seen them both—ever so jealous because Burton couldn't keep his eyes off me. I wore my rain jacket, the shiny black one with the red lining, low heels—very simple, no big 'glamour.' I knew Taylor would do the 'star' bit enough. Maybe that's what Burton liked? Wasn't he once a coal miner?"

IN 1967, DIETRICH CONQUERED BROAD-WAY. Although her producer had asked me to come to New York to fill my usual role of peacemaker between outrageously difficult star and the suffering minions, I couldn't. My husband was gravely ill. So I wasn't there for the nightly traffic jams, New York's finest on nervous horses trying to control the surging crowds blocking all of Forty-sixth Street, she—Chanel skirts hiked to her crotch—balanced on the top of cars, throwing autographed pictures like confetti to the screaming multitudes down below; nor when Dietrich accepted her special Tony Award for her one-woman show, broadcast live on national television. As she made her entrance, she stumbled, nearly fell, then slurred her thanks. Her words overlaid with that thick comic German accent that appeared in her speech whenever Dietrich was thoroughly soused. Those who called me in London to report my mother's shocking condition that night assured me that as she looked so absolutely fabulous, probably no one had even noticed. The next season, when Dietrich returned to Broadway, I was able to heed her producer's SOS and went to baby-sit his star. I arrived in New York, went straight to the theater, and was greeted with, "The witch is on her broomstick," and walked into a hornet's nest. The place was buzzing with fury and borderline mayhem.

"Well! Finally! The plane landed two hours ago! *Look* at this dressing room!" She stood aside for me to get a better view. In her honor, it had been painted, decorated, furnished—all new, all clean, and very un-Broadway. It is one of those affectations of the legitimate theater that dressing rooms have to be stark, ugly, with overtones of small-town morgue. This one was actually quite pretty.

"See? Garden furniture! Bent sticks and orange cushions? Not to be believed! And *dangerous* for the dresses!" Knowing she had a point about the rattan possibly catching the fine soufflé, I didn't even try to cajole her into accepting the decor.

"Okay, Mass. Don't worry. This is easy to fix. You concentrate on the really important things, do your scheduled orchestra rehearsal—I'll do the dressing room."

A fast change in furniture is a bit harder to do, but we did it.

With the help of a courageous salesman, we collected floor models, stripped the French furniture department of Bloomingdale's, roped it to the roof of the gleaming limousine, stuffed the rest in the back, and two hours later, Dietrich had a gold-and-powder-blue "French château," instead of "Adirondacks porch." Her poor producer, when he got that bill, he flinched—but paid. One thing about Alexander Cohen, he always tried to make her happy, no matter what fortunes it cost him.

Next came the Flower Rooms. Just like the old days, when the trunks had their own allotted rooms in hotels, now our traveling florist shop and its special personnel had their own "dressing room." Having heard that the "cavalry" had arrived from London, they now descended on me like butterflies in heat.

"Mrs. Riva! Mrs. Riva! We haven't got our

flower rooms yet! Where *shall* we put our boxes? And the pink ribbon they got for us—it won't *do*! It's all *wrong*! It's *synthetic*—not satin! And the pink is too *deep*! . . . Oh! It's all so disorganized—and tables? Where are our *tables*?" The Flower Boys always got very rattled as an opening night approached. One calmed them down with lots of soothing appreciation of their *tremendous* responsibilities, gave them the importance they craved, a strong cup of herbal tea, and then they were as good as new.

It was one of our best gimmicks; the organized running-down aisles of handsome young men, waving their lovely bouquets to present to their Queen. They were well rehearsed, their floral tributes in shades of complementary pinks, their attitude: "This is the first time I have *ever* done such a thing!" They did this act twice, once before "Honeysuckle Rose," so that Dietrich would just "happen" to have received a perfect nosegay trailing pink ribbons to swing in tempo to its jazzy rhythm, and at the end, in staggered runs, to lift, frame, prolong the homage to the vision so beautiful gathering up the many floral tributes offered by her young admirers. This also gave the audience the courage to join in the homage with their own posies. A lot of young men met on those euphoric sprints and remained friends forever.

I stood in back of the theater and watched

my mother—star—on a Broadway stage. I who had seen her be superb, so many times, now saw her do a mediocre imitation of herself. The shimmering look, the incredible body, the pearl-pink skin, the golden hair, the military carriage, the hypnotic gaze from beneath those famous hooded lids—all was there, perfect and sublime, but the spirit was not. Vibrant energy had become diffused by spirits from a bottle, and her art lay heavy in the throes of mediocrity.

The audience went wild, gave her a standing ovation, the Flower Boys sprinted with their nosegays—still, her second Broadway triumph was more in memory of the first than its own.

I was never an audience fan of Dietrich's. Having been part of constructing the platform for her performances, I knew each transition, the split second of each gesture, every look, every pause and intonation. Being the innate, trainable soldier that she was, the structure of her performances never varied. Even when she was drunk, one could set one's stopwatch by when an arm would lift, a special pause would occur, a look punctuate a meaning of a lyric, a measured silence, a lowering of the head. With her amazing discipline, she Xeroxed her performance, night after night, year after year. It was this ironclad, unwavering construction that so depended on an inner vitality, a sudden burst of magical adrenaline, to bring it into glorious existence, make her come to life.

All great performers who go on forever live with this danger of becoming their own carbon copies. It is just that my mother started out as one, and so, to infuse it with ever new life became harder and harder as time passed. Finally, the drugs dulled even the spark of its ignition. As Dietrich believed her audience was there to only listen and worship, she didn't consider them having a life force of their own to contribute to her performance and, so, never called on it to help her when she needed it most. In this unawareness of her audience as possible energizing participants, she was forever the real Movie Star—remote, removed, up there looking down from above at those who had come to pay her homage. It made her later years as a performer terribly hard, and very lonely.

While I was still with her, she decided to fly my father, now infirm from long-term heart disease, in from L.A. to witness her Broadway triumph. The cuffs of his heavy silk shirts were frayed, the Knize suits hung on his old-man frame, his vicuña overcoat had thinned. His swollen legs made walking difficult; he used a cane to find his way, the splendid one my mother had bought for herself to wear with the broken ankle. He hadn't completely lost his air of elegance, only its polish of authority. He was a proud man—without pride.

Strange to have them together again. I tried to keep them both on their feet long enough to appear as a happy, healthy couple whenever they were seen in public by strangers. When the show closed, my father fled back to his ragged dogs and leftover chickens, I to my family in London; my mother continued on to San Francisco to be her own ageless, glamorous, living legend.

IN APRIL, Martin Luther King, Jr., was killed. In Europe, his murder hardly caused a ripple— it was an American, home-brewed tragedy. Two months later—"Oh, no! Not again!" our hearts cried as Bobby lay bleeding, life leaving him so quickly. That sharp mind, that daredevil spirit behind that organized intelligence, my octopus authority was no more.

My mother was back in Australia, performing in one town when her Australian was killed in a freak accident in another. She called me in despair. As he had a legitimate widow, Dietrich could not expose her sorrow publicly, nor her personal interest in his death, and gave me a list of telephone numbers to call for her in Australia in order to find out the details of the tragic accident, send the proper flowers to his funeral, and went into her room to mourn.

She closed in Australia and returned to Paris to be with her favorite Michael. My son was studying at the American College in Paris, and my mother threw off her widow's weeds and blossomed. Found, furnished, and fixed him a sump-

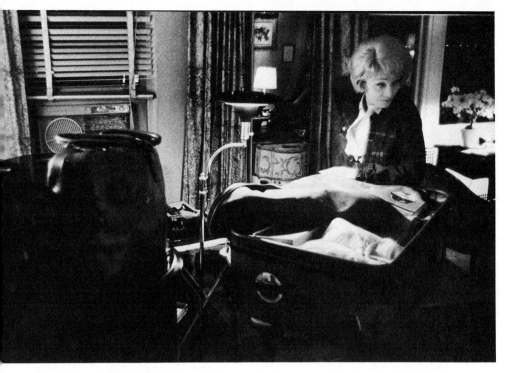

Packing—always packing.

The golden years of success, acclaim, adulation, and wild applause. She stood alone upon the stages of the world and let it wash over her.

LEFT: She loved to lead Burt Bacharach out before the cheering audience to acknowledge his genius as her arranger and conductor. His being young *and* handsome was certainly a plus. RIGHT: During one of her Paris triumphs, Jean-Pierre Aumont and Jean Cocteau, old nonlover pals, vied to light her cigarettes.

On stage, Maurice Chevalier was allowed to show his long, undying devotion.

Every night after the performances, the London bobbies lost their battles with the surging crowd at the stage door.

Christmas together in London. David was a little shy of the lady by the tree, and she was miffed that Paul thanked his father for his present before opening hers.

The bugle-bead dress we christened "the eel" because my mother looked like one swimming through clear water wearing it. She loved being at her thinnest that winter of 1964. I worried about it.

LEFT: Her name in lights on the Queen's Theater where England's greatest actors had performed. She was justly proud to have made it.

Her Broadway triumph
and its marquee, New
York, 1967.

My mother hid her pain.
My father could no longer
hide anything.

Every night cheering crowds blocked the streets.

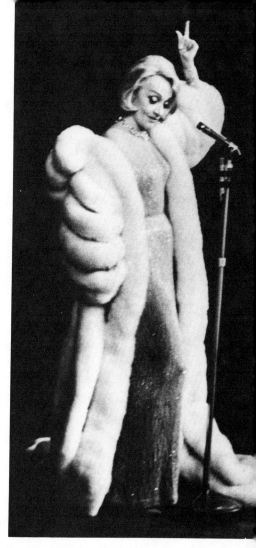

ABOVE AND LEFT: The fabulous dress, the superbly tailored trousers hid what she needed to hide, and kept her secrets.

ABOVE, LEFT: Noël smiled when the cameras clicked but worried about her pill consumption.

Wheelchairs at airports now often became a traumatic necessity.

In Moscow with Bacharach, one of the last carefree tours before his own fame took him away from her and her accidents ended it all.

To
my
Love
my
Love
Mass

The enraptured audiences never knew
what was happening to this icon glittering
before them.

tuous bachelor pad, then never left him in peace long enough to enjoy it. She had her own key and entered whenever she felt like it, to clean, stock his refrigerator, and check his bed. On weekends, she took him to expensive restaurants, entered clinging to his handsome, tall frame, seated him next to her most aggressively homosexual friends and—waited. He came home to London for the Christmas holidays and asked my advice on how to make her stop.

So she was trying with her grandson what she hadn't accomplished with her daughter? I thought: She never gives up. I had suspected long ago that my mother had subconsciously wanted me to be initiated into a lesbian life-style, even maneuvered my sexual abuse in this manner, in the hope I would follow this path into maturity. No man could then have taken me from her. Certainly in later years, this would have served her well. Her daughter, unencumbered by husband and children, would have been available, by her side, ever the happy, willing companion, her lover, an added handmaiden to fetch and carry. A truly contented *ménage à trois*. As Dietrich always proclaimed "all homosexuals *worship* their mothers," I figured, as she thought of Michael as hers, she was now, once again, investing in her future cosseting. As an added little love token she had given my son a "few," about a hundred, amphetamines—just to help him with his "so difficult" studies. It was one of the too few times I told her off. Shocked, outraged, stunned silence descended, and our Christmas was minus one legend, and, bliss!

JUDY LAY on a bathroom floor; she, who had died so long ago, was finally, officially, dead. I mourned my friend as one does a child who had a life to live and was not able to.

That summer, man invaded the moon.

My mother called: "Sweetheart, Papa Joe has died."

"I know."

"Remember Antibes? When he was Ambassador? You used to swim with his children. He was old then already, but sweet. Used to follow me around. Boni was jealous—Jo, too. I never hear from *her* anymore. Strange. Probably still on that island of hers with all her black people?"

In December, von Sternberg died in Hollywood. For the man who had given her professional immortality and loved her so, Dietrich did not play widow nor attend his funeral. The story most often told in reverent admiration is that Marlene Dietrich denied herself this last poignant farewell in order not to upstage her Svengali in his last moment of supreme importance. That after the ceremony, she appeared at his home wrapped in chinchilla, weeping, to console, give her loving support to his grieving widow.

Those of us who really knew Dietrich knew how frightened she was of all funerals, how she hated the press and the obvious, intimate questions they would certainly have focused on at this time, and knew, once again, she had instinctively chosen a path that the world would later interpret, laud, and recount as yet another example of Marlene's sublime thoughtfulness— while simply serving her own needs. Through the years, she continued to court Jo's widow as well as his son. Keeping the shine on the image never hurt—"You never know, said the widow . . ."

In the spring of 1970, Burt Bacharach received his first two Academy Awards. That definitely rated a phone call:

"Sweetheart. Now *you* know I love Burt, but 'Raindrops Keep Falling . . .'? Where has he got them falling? On his head? Why? And it is such toodle-toodle—for *that*, he deserted me? For raindrops?"—and hung up.

In Paris, my mother had to have her shoes and boots enlarged, received daily injections into her groin by her quack, and prepared her first Japanese tour.

Remarque died—warranted two whole days of my mother's murmuring routine, plus a letter to friends of mine.

. . . I was alone when Remarque died. But I had known of his illness and, by chance, I tried to telephone him and he answered. I talked to him, sent him flowers every day and wires, all to arrive in the mornings because that bitch Goddard only came in the afternoon after her beauty sleep. Maria wrote to him and I also talked to Rudi on the phone and he sent a cable to him which he got during the few days when he was lucid, before he died.

He had many strokes, but recovered and even wrote a letter to Maria, showing her how he had learned to write again. But then, life for him without his favorite, wine, was not good anymore. He loved to drink a lot—not for the effect but for the taste. Now the bitch has all the riches: van Goghs, Cézannes, Modiglianis, etc., etc. And the most beautiful carpets—all priceless. Maybe this is why she never allowed him to see me. Maybe she thought he would give me some of his treasures. It could not have been jealousy, because she never loved him. I could not go to the funeral last Sunday. If I survive Gabin, it will be the same thing. I could have had it all, the name and the money. But I said: "No." I couldn't do it to Rudi.

She emerged from her widowhood just long enough, to go right back in when De Gaulle died.

. . .

MY MOTHER WAS BACK in Paris the year the Duke of Windsor died. She called, laughing:

" 'David' is dead! Remember Clifton Webb always called him David? I once went to dinner at their château. What an evening! She sat there, 'ever so elegant skeleton,' and after dinner, clapped her hands—like calling a servant—and said in that affected American: 'David, go! Put on your kilts and do your dance for our guests!' and this man, who once was a king—goes! Comes back in full Scottish costume like some chorus boy from *Brigadoon* and does his little dance—on toes, skirts whirling—frightful! And those dogs! Did you ever see those ugly dogs they have? They wheeze! Long things drip out of their pushed-in noses and their pop eyes water. . . . What a way to live! Terrible people! They deserved each other!"

Although my mother was in London when our son Peter was married, she did not attend the wedding. Practically impossible to explain to the bride's parents, as was our family's relief at having this beautiful day unmarred by the famous grandmother's presence. My mother's diary makes no reference to this marriage. Actually, as far as Dietrich's diaries are concerned, she has no grandchildren, she recorded none of their births, or later her great-grandchildren's.

· · ·

For years, I had been trying to negotiate a television deal for Dietrich's one-woman show, but her demands, the special conditions she set down, were so outrageous, so unrealistic, that neither a network nor an independent producer could be persuaded to risk it. For an American TV special, my mother insisted that it be filmed in Europe, during an actual performance, and in a legitimate theater of her choice. She wanted Orson Welles to direct, Bacharach to conduct, her stage-lighting genius, Joe Davis, to light her, and for Dietrich to have full and unlimited artistic control over everything but the color of the toilet paper in the washrooms. My mother's prime objective for considering "a special" in the first place, besides the obvious money, was to record for posterity the tumultuous response to her performance. Believing that foreign audiences were much more prone to exuberant adulation, she absolutely refused to listen to our arguments that if she filmed in America, she would have the superb quality control of the entire television industry at her disposal. What my mother really wanted was to record her show in Soviet Russia. She believed that as artists in that country were so revered, applause from a Russian audience was the ultimate accolade. Copenhagen was her second choice, possibly Paris, Edinburgh, even Rio de Janeiro.

When I first discussed such a project with Orson in 1961, he fixed me with his shoe-button eyes, squeezed his soggy cigar; that wonderful voice rumbled up from its subterranean cave and said:

"Maria, if this should ever come to pass, I shall be out of town, conveniently very unavailable. You don't have to tell Marlene that now. You know how she is—this idea of hers may never get off the ground, but if it ever does, I want *you* to know that I shall be very, very far away."

Ten years later, the ever-courageous and willing Alexander Cohen took on the challenge and lived to regret it. After months of negotiations, trying to explain to my mother the astronomical complexities of shipping skilled American crews and their sophisticated equipment to foreign lands in order to film a television show best suited to a controlled soundstage in Burbank, California, Alex finally found an available theater in London that my mother was willing to approve, and the preparatory work could finally begin. Like an army preparing for battle, we marshaled our forces, each of us responsible for our own specialties—everyone geared toward one goal: to keep our star functioning and happy in order to capture her magnificent performance on film. While Alex negotiated with sponsors, unions, and the BBC, my job was to keep Dietrich cooperative, content, and, secretly, as sober as possible.

The Savoy Hotel was to be my mother's

billet. This elegant establishment, with its beautiful river suites, the fast, silent, meticulous service of its staff, was my mother's favorite London hotel.

A Cinderella dream of a suite, its chandeliers ashimmer, awaited her. Everything ready, just waiting for our queen to grace its splendor with her presence, and I had two days before my mother's arrival to transform its beauty into Dietrich's "working headquarters." I was the best majordomo Dietrich ever had. Not only because I knew her better than anyone else, but because I believed that making enemies was not the way to achieve the cooperation and support of the people one needed. I knew my mother would be able to generate her own anger and dislike without any help from me.

I thought it was only fair that the Savoy Hotel should be warned, given basic instructions on how to face this imminent upheaval that would interfere not only with the smooth running of the entire hotel but intrude into the private lives of its staff as well. Being treated as slaves usually generates acute stress in normal human beings. I tried to set myself up as someone they could come to, commiserate with, relieve their stress. This time I was lucky. An eager, young assistant manager had been assigned to see to the special needs of Miss Dietrich. He was, even then, one of those rare people who know instinc-

tively how to handle VIPs, solve their problems
with the minimum of pompous fuss. Today, this
likable man holds an exaulted position within the
great Ciga hotel chain and often has the charm
to claim that what I taught him about handling
Dietrich was a valuable lesson for a young man
making his way up the management ladder.

"Mrs. Riva? May I introduce myself? I am
Mr. Butavaba. May I be of service?"

"Mr. Butavaba and how! Have you about
three hours to give me?"

Rather taken aback by my American exu-
berance, the small, rotund gentleman blushed:

"Certainly, madam."

"Wonderful! Come on. Let's go and inspect
Miss Dietrich's suite and I will try to explain what
we have to do to it," and I strode toward the
discreet elevator of that Edwardian emporium.
Mr. Butavaba, the tails of his staid morning coat
flapping, rushed after me. We entered the suite
and stood for a moment, appreciating its beauty.
The dazzle of pinks, yellows, peach, lavender—
flowers everywhere; the sparkle of everything,
the brocade and lace framing the great views of
the Thames embankment.

"How lovely you have made it all! Thank
you. But, my mother is not a movie star in the
style of Miss Elizabeth Taylor. I am going to be
very honest with you, Mr. Butavaba. If we are
going to work together, I have to trust you—I

have a feeling I can. Now, let's start with the largest bathroom."

We opened a paneled door, two steps led up to a pink-tiled ballroom!

"Mr. Butavaba, please listen to me carefully. No one must know this. No one. You must give me your word. If ever Miss Dietrich should find out that I told you, she would kill me. My mother suffers from a circulatory problem of her legs. She must never injure them in any way. Anything that might cause her to trip, fall, stumble, even knock against her legs, is extremely dangerous. If she should ever receive even the slightest wound on any part of her feet or legs, her lack of circulation would make it impossible for the wound to heal. Gangrene would follow and, possibly, eventual amputation. Therefore, this suite must be made safe for her. Steps leading into a bathroom are out. She might forget they're there and trip. We will have to use this one only for 'hair washing' and the 'storage of supplies.' Show me what the other bathroom is like." Not a ballroom, and with a window that let in daylight, but as it had no steps, it would have to do.

"Okay. We will need a curtain of heavy cloth to black out the window. Miss Dietrich always puts on her stage makeup in her hotel, never in her dressing room at the theater. I need an electrician to install a row of lights above the mirror, with mesh-covered bulbs to protect her face should one explode for any reason. This door has to be removed, so that she can exit and enter without difficulty. I need two tables along this wall for her makeup, a board over the top of the bathtub to make a counter for the wig stands, and a special outlet for her professional curling irons. Please have the chambermaid remove all the towels and, especially, all and any bathmats and throw rugs. Make sure that the housekeeper instructs the staff that this bathroom is not to be touched, or supplied with daily linen. Miss Dietrich uses her own makeup towels and will clean this area herself. In the other bathroom, we will always need at least twelve extra-large bath towels for when she washes her hair, but again, remember to caution the maids that no bathmats or scatter rugs are to be furnished to this suite. The special rubber mat for the inside of the bath, I have here in my bag. Make sure that the maids replace it securely each time they clean the tub. We don't need this chair in here —Miss Dietrich never sits when making up.

"Now, let's do the bedroom. . . . The hotel must have some blackout drapes that were used during the war. Please have them brought up and hung over Miss Dietrich's bedroom windows. As she prefers artificial light in her bedroom, we will be able to tape the edges of the curtains. Even the faintest crack of daylight wakes her instantly. I will also tape the edges of the carpets in the entire suite, to avoid her tripping anywhere where the joins may not be completely flush. Also, luminous cloth tape will be put down across every doorway. This is a precaution, so that if she gets up during the night, she can immediately see where to put her feet in the dark. You must impress on the entire staff that under no circumstance must these tapes be removed—ever."

The Savoy had a wonderful room-service system, a fully-fitted serving kitchen on each floor, presided over by its own room-service captain. He was my next target.

"Madam, this is Charles—he is in charge of this floor."

"Charles, let me be the first to offer you my condolences. These weeks are going to be murder. But, maybe I can give you a few tips that will make it a little easier for you and keep Miss Dietrich from being too irritated. First and foremost, when Miss Dietrich rings, grab your menu and run. Always react as though it were an emergency. By the way, Mr. Butavaba, you better tell that to the telephone girls—anytime they see any one of the phones from this suite light up on their switchboard, they must react as though it is a matter of life and death. I'll see them all individually myself later, but that is a cardinal rule for everyone. The faster one obeys Miss

Dietrich, the easier it will be on everyone's nerves in the long run. Now, Charles—never expect to *serve* Miss Dietrich a meal. When admitted, simply roll the table into the room, arrange the order, do not wait for her to be seated, and never, ever expect her to sign a room-service check—simply bow and exit. Miss Dietrich is not an American and, therefore, dislikes glasses filled with ice water. Neither does she appreciate butter curls swimming in ice. Always see to it that there is an ample supply of seeded rye bread and pumpernickel in the bread basket. Never try to convince Miss Dietrich that the coffee is freshly brewed when it has been sitting for fifteen minutes waiting for her summons. Never, ever try to convince her of *anything*. Remember, she is always right—no matter how unjust it might seem to you and your staff. If she orders broccoli, and, for some inexplicable reason, they send up spinach and she commands you to explain this crime, you can only resort to one course of action that will get you out of the suite with your job intact: Bow, apologize profusely, and suggest that it must have been one of those very young apprentices who are being trained to be cooks by the great chefs of the Savoy kitchens and that you will report their negligent behavior immediately. This is the only scenario that Miss Dietrich would find engaging enough to forgive a mix-up from room service."

Next came the housekeeper, the doormen, bell boys, flower girls, and chauffeur. During the weeks that followed, I supported my little army with lavish tips and, much more important, gratitude.

Our star arrived weeks before rehearsals were to begin. New wigs had to be made, old ones redyed and shaped, and her private falls cleaned and set. I think it was Vivien Leigh who first introduced my mother to a genius wig-maker by the name of Stanley Hall. She had dinner with the Oliviers one night, and, knowing Vivien was going bald, was amazed by the beauty of her thick hair and asked her what pill she was taking. My mother told me later that Vivien laughed, gripped the bandeau encircling her head, removed it from her head with most of her "hair" attached to it. Wig-making has always been a special craft in England, where most actors wear wigs not only in period plays but in modern ones as well. Stanley Hall and his staff were so skilled, used such superb quality human hair, dyed and curled it with such expertise, that they made wigs and hairpieces that could be worn in life for daily wear. The design that my mother had seen close-up on Vivien Leigh and had been so impressed with, a short, bouncy, gleaming half-fall attached to a bandeau, became Dietrich's official hairdo from then on. She wore it for the rest of her life. My mother had dozens of them, dyed perfectly to match her own hair color in front. She covered the bandeaux in velvet to keep them from slipping, in colors to match her wardrobe, but mostly she preferred her favorite, the beige velvet ones; their color blended with the hair and camouflaged the line between her own hair and the false one.

How that TV special was ever completed was a miracle. Cohen did everything to please his star, gave in to her every whim, sometimes even to the detriment of his own investment. As she began to realize that something was not working for her, that perhaps she had been wrong to insist on filming in a real theater and in Europe, she panicked and, as usual, blamed everyone but herself, refused to listen to advice, and turned to her trusty bottle to escape having to face the truth. I searched for her scotch, hidden in the most outlandish places. Watered what I found, called for time-out when I thought she might pass out, and prayed that the visiting sponsor would not notice her condition.

As Dietrich's alcoholism was such a well-kept secret, the psychological adjustment that the entertainment industry usually makes unconsciously, before and during work involving a known alcoholic, was not in force for her. So her seemingly undisciplined, sloppy, and abusive behavior was observed and judged without the usual cushioning benefit of previous knowledge of her problem. After this fiasco, my mother gave out interviews, implying that her TV Special had been less than perfect due solely to the producer not living up to his promises, for which Alexander Cohen sued her for slander. In my opinion, he had ample justification to do so. Professional loyalty, although always associated with the Dietrich myth, was not one of my mother's strong suits. Whoever got to her first with an offer and worked her ego correctly could make a deal. She made out legal documents for sole representation as though they were postcards.

In later years, no one with any professional integrity would touch her with a ten-foot pole. You just couldn't trust her. Powers unto themselves are often treacherous.

To advertise her TV special, she returned to New York for a portrait sitting with Milton Greene. The famous pose of Dietrich enveloped in swan, just one leg showing as though completely naked underneath, was taken at this time. In glorious color and golden wig, one would never guess she is seventy-one, yet there is something terribly wrong. When I first saw it, I thought of my old San Francisco friend, she looks so much like a drag queen "doing a Dietrich," while doing one of her own. After she retouched the hell out of this picture, it looked even more unreal, except for that slightly swollen foot, *that* she couldn't completely erase.

Watergate. Nixon was reelected in a landslide. Only twenty-four thousand troops remained in Vietnam—the other forty-seven thousand had come home in shiny new boxes, while three hundred thousand more were strewn about in military hospitals, trying to mend more than just their physical wounds.

When my mother had flown back to Paris as Chevalier was dying, it was naturally assumed she was rushing to his bedside to bid him a last farewell, but her plane reservations had been made long before that date—it just worked out to her legend's advantage. Years later she made up a moving story to cover up Chevalier's adamant refusal to see her when she had arrived wan and beautiful at the hospital:

"When Chevalier was dying I flew all the way to Paris just to be with him. When I got to the hospital where he was—they told me that he had given strict orders that I was not to be admitted into his room! You know why? He didn't want me to see him like that. He loved me so— he gave up seeing me one last time—just so I wouldn't have to suffer. Wonderful man!"

She returned to tour the States, then the British Isles. Wheelchairs became a sometime necessity for arrival and departures at airports; trying to avoid press photographers catching her in one, a constant nightmare. Noël died at his home in Jamaica. His famous friend blamed his smoking and lack of discipline.

"You see? After our bet I never smoked and I am still alive, but poor Noël couldn't stop. He was my friend. Now those two chorus boys of his will get those beautiful houses—everything! How awful! Now they will live like kings on Noël's money. Well, they stayed all those years with him, so maybe they earned it."

On the 17th of May, 1973, my mother and father celebrated their golden wedding anniversary—he wringing chicken necks in the San Fernando Valley, she lunching with her "latest" in Paris, very annoyed that a reporter had ferreted out the date, insisting that as I was only twenty-five, he got it all wrong anyway and planned to sue him.

On the 7th of November, at the Shady Grove Theater in Maryland, on the outskirts of Washington, D.C., my mother finished singing her third encore to jubilant applause. Being a theater in the round, the audience seated in a circle all around her, she had shifted her position at the microphone often to encompass every section of the full house. Now she turned her shimmering body, walked the few steps to the edge of the stage to salute the orchestra and her ever-attentive conductor below. She went into her famous bow, legs ramrod straight, her upper body bent down from the waist—so low that the top of her wig nearly touched the floor, her right arm stretched out in gallant tribute toward her conductor, Stan Freeman. Suddenly, she wavered and pitched from the stage into the orchestra pit. Freeman, seeing her begin to fall, jumped onto his piano stool, trying desperately to help her, but could not reach her in time. She lay amongst the music stands, ominously still. As anxious hands reached out for her, she snarled:

"Don't touch me! Clear the theater! Clear the theater!"

The sharp ring of the phone woke me. I grabbed the receiver to hear the alarmed voice of my mother's dresser:

"Maria—we are calling you from the dressing room. Something has happened. Here is your mother . . ."

I am instantly awake.

"Mass?"

I hear her breathing, trying to get out the words. I look at my clock, four-thirty a.m., London time. Must be eleven-thirty her time in Maryland, right after the performance.

"Okay. Mass? Take a deep breath—speak slowly—tell me what happened." I say it like a military command. It is the only way to make her function, come to attention.

"I fell," she whispers.

The fear and shock are alive in the room with me. I bark out my interrogation.

"Anything broken?"

"No."

Although I knew the wig would cushion her head in a fall, I still have to ask:

"Did you hit your head?"

"No."

"All right. Now . . . tell me, *did you hit your legs*?"

"Yes."

Oh, my god! I take a deep breath and continue: "Which leg?"

"The left one."

Jesus, the one with the least pulse.

"Tell me, slowly, exactly what happened."

The shock has softened her tone, she sounds like a little girl recounting an accident at school:

"You know—how I always bow at the end and present my conductor, how I reach out my hand toward him so that the audience understands?— Well, tonight, for some ridiculous reason, Stan Freeman thought I wanted to shake his hand and so he jumped up on the piano stool, grabs my hand, lost his balance and fell, pulling me down off the stage with him. The moment I hit the floor, I knew it wasn't bad—the dress was all right and the wig was still on. But you know the dress is too tight for me to get up, and I didn't want the audience to see me . . . so I lay still and yelled at the shocked musicians to leave me alone and to clear the theater. Then I felt a funny wetness on my leg and saw there was blood, and so I knew I would have to be carried back to the dressing room and *that* I couldn't let the audience see, so I stayed on the floor until everyone left and they got me out— All I kept saying was, 'Call my daughter— Call Maria.' "

"I'm here. Now listen to me—carefully. Do *not* remove the tights—do *not* remove the elastic stocking underneath. Wrap a clean towel around the leg, leave it as it is and get to the Walter Reed Hospital. Do not let them touch your leg there before they know you have only peripheral circulation—"

She stops me: "We pulled off the tights already. We had to, they were full of blood and the stocking too."

Now I knew my mother was in bad trouble. By pulling the elastic stocking off the leg instead of cutting it off, precious skin had undoubtedly been removed. More in command of herself, she begins to argue:

"I can't go to a hospital. The photographers, the reporters . . ."

I'm already looking up the number for Pan Am. "Mass, I'm coming. If you won't go to a hospital, you must at least call a doctor. You must not get an infection. Do you hear me? You have to get the wound cleaned, bandaged, and get yourself medicated. Also you need a tetanus shot—the theater floor is dirty. Call Teddy Kennedy. He will know the best man in Washington."

"You're coming? When?"

"The earliest flight out of London is at ten this morning. I'll try to get on that one. I'll be there . . ." I looked at my clock—it is five a.m. "I'll be there about six tonight, your time. Now I want you to take two cubes of sugar and dissolve them under your tongue. Have them wrap you in a blanket, keep warm, go to the hotel, and don't put your leg up high."

"*Not* up high?" The way she said it, I knew that was exactly what she had done.

I got a reservation on the first plane out. As Bill was in New York on business, I called my married son who was living in London:

"Pete, forgive my calling so early—I need your help."

"Yes, Mom. Shoot!"

"She fell in Washington and opened the leg."

"Jesus!"

"I have to go . . . can you and Sandy take care of Paul and David?"

"Sure! We can come over right away, give them breakfast, and take them to school. Mom, everything will be taken care of at this end—just go!"

I arrived in Washington, D.C., late that afternoon, rushed into my mother's hotel suite, and found her bandaging her oozing leg, preparing to go to the theater for that night's performance. The wound was deep, the size of a man's fist. Because of the lack of blood supply, it had stopped bleeding almost immediately after the accident; for the same reason she felt no pain. At this point, the greatest danger was infection.

For me, Senator Kennedy has never changed from the little boy I knew as Teddy in those long gone summer days of 1938. Being helpful and conscientious was a very serious matter to him. One only had to say, "Oh, Teddy, I forgot my book," and his chubby little legs would go into action, all the way up to the hotel from the sea. My mother had reached him—he had arranged for her immediate admittance to the great hospital in Bethesda. When she refused, gave her the name of a doctor in Washington who she could trust instead. He did not mention the personal tragedy that had struck his family. Within days, his son would lose his leg to bone cancer.

Of course I had to force my mother to see the doctor. As he didn't issue her orders nor prescribe "magic potions," she didn't like him. He was a good man and knew that without the proper blood supply the leg could not, would not, heal. As she refused to listen or even discuss the possibility of surgery, all he could do was try and protect her against the dangers of infection, giving her injections and antibiotics and routine dressings, in the hope of keeping the wound sterile until she came to her senses. None of this satisfied her, so she called Geneva, asked Prof. de Watteville what to do. He, knowing her *very* well, prescribed as many injections of new "miraculous" medications that he could think of. Most of them vitamins, concentrated proteins, and harmless hormones, and, as none of them would be available in America, a courier service was arranged. When he reminded her that she had too little circulation, she hung up on him. I insisted on canceling the rest of the Washington engagement.

Any inactivity drove my mother crazy. If I wouldn't "allow" her to go to work, she could at least be permitted to organize the suite to function as a first-aid station. Setting up a field hospital was right up her alley. As the suite boasted a pantry kitchen, she commandeered it, disinfected the walls and counters, then stocked it with every medical supply available in the District of Columbia. When she was through, we could have performed brain surgery in that kitchen. While my mother was busy and happy preparing her MASH unit, I took care of business. Although I had grave doubts that she would be able to continue her tour, open in Montreal by the 26th, I asked her personal musicians, those who traveled with her, to remain on standby and wait for my call. I phoned Bill in New York, Michael in Los Angeles, and my other children in London, bringing them all up to date. Typically, my mother had not asked about them.

The next day, a gaunt Stan Freeman accosted me in the hotel lobby. His bloodshot eyes searched my face, his voice pleaded:

"Maria! I didn't pull your mother off the stage! I swear it! She says I did—but I didn't! I would never hurt her. You must believe me!"

I tried to comfort him: "Stan, of course you didn't. You and I both know the real reason why my mother fell. I know it must be terrible for you—but Dietrich can tell any lie she wants to believe is the truth and the world will accept it as gospel. We're canceling the rest of the performances here in Washington. But keep yourself free. Knowing her, she just might make Montreal. Remember, when Dietrich has marked you the culprit, there is nothing we lesser mortals can do about it. Now you must get some sleep. Try to forget it. The people who love you will know what's the truth—that's all that really matters."

Brave speech, excellent advice, one I tried constantly to follow and often failed to do.

The wound remained open, slightly oozing precious protein. We became experts at changing the sterile dressings. The "medications" arrived from Switzerland, a nurse was hired to give daily injections. My mother felt well. Besides my constant presence, the actual rest was doing her good. We even celebrated Thanksgiving with room-service turkey:

"Well, because if *you* don't have your *precious* Thanksgiving, you will be impossible to live with—besides this American hotel probably has nothing else but that stupidity on the menu!"

Refusing to admit that her wound was not healing, she insisted on fulfilling her contract and continuing on to Montreal. I felt I had to accompany her at least as far as the next stop of her tour. I wanted to be there in case the injured leg gave her more trouble than she could handle. I was not sure that it would support her through the strain of an entire performance. During our hiatus in Washington, I had been watering her scotch and controlling the daily intake. Each time she put her half-filled glass down, the nearest flowers would receive another generous dose of J&B. She kept saying, "Why is my glass always empty?" but never caught on. I must say, the flowers did remarkably well on this diet of booze.

For the first time in years sober, she strode on stage, her swan's coat a huge marshmallow wave rolling behind her, and like the phoenix, the symbol of resurrection she so adored, she rose triumphant and gave a performance that, in my opinion, she never had nor could equal. No one who was privileged to witness her triumph that night in Montreal would have believed that under that lithe incandescent form oozed an open wound, swathed in wet gauze and thick bandages. For a full hour, she stood unwavering, immobile, sang encore after encore, bowed her famous low bow, finally begged her audience to stop, left the stage, and walked firmly to her dressing room. We had to strip her dress off in order to change the bandages. She had a second show to do. The next day, this review said it all. I don't believe in reprinting reviews, but this one Dietrich deserves to have recorded:

The Gazette, Montreal, Monday 26, 1973
—Dave Billington

When she was a teen-aged girl, the gassed and shell-shocked troops of Ypres and Vimy crouched in their slimy trenches. . . .

Twenty-five years later she was touring military bases crammed with the sons of many of those "war to end all wars" veterans. . . .

Twenty-five years later, on a concert stage in Montreal, Marlene Dietrich, Hemingway's Kraut, sings "Lili Marlene" for the umpteenth time in her life and a century of turmoil, hatred and hope clings to the changeless edges of a torn calendar caught on a blossoming thorn bush. . . .

She sings as the merciless white spotlight fails to find a flaw in the slightly sunken cheeks of the face which refuses to age. . . .

It's as if one were seeing this century personified. Past its prime and supposedly in its decline, but still proud with the hope in which any century (or person) begins life, she is still there, still alive and still refusing to yield. . . .

Perhaps it is stretching credulity too far to see Dietrich this way. After all she is only a human being, possessed of all the frailties implicit in that word; she is only a singer and actress of honestly average talents and skill. So why should she, above all others, be seen in other than this light? . . .

The lady herself provides the answer when she sings a simple children's "round" song first popularized by Pete Seeger— "Where Have All the Flowers Gone?" She provides it, not because she includes this antiwar plea in her repertoire, or even because of the passionate way she sings the song, but rather for one fleeting second of the splendid last verse. . . .

For more than an hour without break, without artificiality and without milking the audience for false sentimental appeal, Marlene Dietrich entertains—swinging from message, to love song, to vamp, to humor, in a perfect mixture which left the audience grinning like cats sated on Jersey cream. . . .

When it was over, the senseless calls for encores, echoing cheers and a mild (but fervid) attempt to rush the stage as if Dietrich were a talisman of immortality which must be touched.

The curtain closes and the lady disappears again into mythology, like a brief messenger from Olympus. . . .

And when it does this, the dimension which has made Dietrich more than just another phenomenon in a milieu which abounds in them, stands revealed. She ceases to be Marlene Dietrich, woman singer, actress and worshipped idol of an audience which would have given Freud a nightmare. . . .

She assumes the dimension of time given shape and substance. She seems to embody the whole century of Western man's worst and finest hours. For she was born when the century was born, and lived through and seen that century retreat from the greatest promise any century ever began with and yet still be unable to fully deny that promise. . . .

And she and the century are still there —perhaps tired, perhaps jaded and perhaps fading from hope but still there . . . and still able to ask with honest anger, "When will they ever learn?" . . .

Put aside symbolism, forget the phenomenon and just accept the fact that this was a consummate performance. The timing, the mixture of songs, the hand gestures, the lighting, the makeup—all of it a distillation of the elements which make audiences love great entertainers.

She had my admiration as well. Before returning to London, I tried to impress on her, once again, that although she had triumphed this time, it was madness to continue touring with an open wound. Only surgical intervention could effect a healing process, and I begged her to see the eminent heart surgeon Michael De Bakey, in Houston. Still heady after her triumphal resurrection, she hardly listened and complained about my continual prophecies of doom. I agreed with her—I was beginning to bore myself. I returned to London, my mother continued on to San Francisco, the next stop of her tour that was scheduled into the next year.

On January 10, 1974, my mother opened in Dallas. She was booked into the Fairmont Hotel for three weeks. She phoned and, on being questioned, admitted the wound was still open, its edges turning black. In London, I took matters into my own hands and dialed Dr. De Bakey's office in Houston. It was late afternoon, Texas time, and the great man answered the phone himself. For a moment, I was speechless, and rather scared by what I was about to attempt. I introduced myself as "the daughter of" and, as precise and to the point as possible, I launched into "the secret saga of Marlene Dietrich's famous legs." The eminent surgeon listened without comment.

"Please, Dr. De Bakey, if I can get my mother to fly from Dallas to Houston on Sunday, her day off, will you see her?"

"Of course, Mrs. Riva. Tell me the time and I shall arrange to be in my office here at the hospital."

"Oh, thank you, Doctor. Please, may I take one more minute of your time? If, when you see my mother, you decide she must have surgery, please—just look at her and say that if she doesn't, her leg will have to be amputated. This is the only way she will ever consent to an operation. You have to frighten her into it. Forgive me for assuming to tell you what to say—but I know my mother, she won't listen otherwise."

I gave him my London number, he promised to call me after he had seen her . . . now all I had to do was to get her to Houston to see him. She complained, argued, snarled, bitched—but she went. The moment she walked out of De Bakey's office, he called me:

"Maria, I didn't have to pretend at all. I told your mother that if she did not have immediate surgery, she could lose the leg. Because that's the truth. But she insisted she had a contract to fulfill first."

"Doctor, she will never do it unless I am there with her. She closes in Dallas in three days, on the 25th. Is it possible for you to schedule the operation around that time? Somehow, I'll get her to you."

On the 26th of January, 1974, Marlene Dietrich, known as Mrs. Rudolf Sieber, secretly checked into the Methodist Medical Center in Houston, Texas. I arrived from London the day after. Dr. De Bakey's staff was used to incognito VIPs. Their handling of my mother was a lesson in diplomacy. The doctor's personal assistant, complete with limousine, had greeted her plane and whisked the patient to a special suite in his famous hospital.

To determine the exact position and extent of the arterial blockage, first she had to go through a rather drastic procedure of an arteriogram done under full anesthesia. The moment she was wheeled out of the room, I began the search of her luggage for the pills and booze I knew she had stashed there. My mother was not beyond medicating herself in secret, swigging down a few shots of scotch the morning of surgery, the doctors none the wiser until their patient suddenly went into convulsions and cardiac arrest on the operating table. Despite her reputation of being a medical authority, her actual knowledge was appalling.

I dumped everything I found onto the bed. By the time I called the head nurse to verify what I had found and impound it, the bed was full. Although this type of raid was not unusual in order to protect a patient from themselves, I had not done one since my days when I looked after Tami. I was stunned by the quantity of my mother's stash, her true addict's inventiveness and duplicity. She always loved those tiny bottles of booze handed out on airlines and usually had a few dozen tucked away in her hand luggage. For this trip to the hospital, she had emptied their vodka and scotch contents into bottles marked "cleaning fluid," refilling the liquor bottles with the cleaning fluid. I shuddered at the thought of someone by chance drinking one of those. Skin lotions had done the same switch of identity, so had hair-setting lotion, mouth wash, and perfume. The most lethal hypnotics had become "European vitamins—special," her Fernando Lamases now were suppositories "for constipation." Those drugs impossible to camouflage because of their identifiable shapes and colors she had stuffed into sewing kits, dressing gown pockets, handbags, into the cardboard tubes of Tampax.

She was in an extremely agitated state when they brought her back to the room. By the evening, when the anesthesia had worn off, the first thing she asked for was her traveling bag. When I suggested that anything she wanted from that rather large and heavy satchel she could tell me and I would give it to her, she became furious, ordering me to do what I was told! Frantically, she searched the bag until, suddenly, it dawned on her that what she was seeking had been removed, surreptitiously, without her consent. From then on, I, the nurses, the state of Texas, were the Gestapo, and open war was declared on those who "keep me locked up in this concentration camp."

Dr. De Bakey is enormously proud of his personal battle against infection. His rules of hygiene, governing every aspect of his operating theater as well as his entire hospital, are strict, immovable, and border on the possessed. His victories over infections justify his fanaticism. His surgical patients were required, without exception, to take a shower, wash themselves with a special disinfectant solution in the early hours before surgery. I reinforced my identity of Gestapo agent when I woke my mother at five a.m. and informed her that she had to take a shower. Fear made her even more abusive than usual.

"I'm not dirty! Now you all think you have the right to tell me I have to *wash*? You're all Hitlers! You— *You* made me come here . . . You and your sick love of hospitals and doctors! I am not going to wash! Such ridiculous stupidity!"

It must have been a terrible time for her.

Worse than any outsider could possibly comprehend. This woman, who reconstructed her aging
body to suit an illusion of youth, who concealed
the crepe-flesh of her hanging thighs in a thousand ways, who hid her thinning, wispy hair beneath golden wigs, who folded sagging breasts
into gossamer harnesses, ever re-recreating the
Venus the world wanted and expected Dietrich
to be . . . was about to be laid bare. The legend
exposed to the clinical gaze of many strangers.
From that day on, there would exist in the world
a group of people who had seen the real Dietrich,
the seventy-three-year-old woman whose body
bespoke her age even if her face lied. The major
surgery she was facing did not frighten her as
much as being discovered did.

Somehow, I got her into the shower. Knowing that she would be sedated before being taken
down to surgery, I was still worried that they
might not heed my advice—to do so as quickly
as possible. I knew she could still change her
mind and walk out of the hospital. It was five-
thirty a.m., I was toweling her down, when she
said:

"We are leaving! The leg will heal without
all this to-do! You can make up a story, tell your
precious De Bakey I'll come back after I finish
the tour," and marched out of the bathroom in
search of her clothes. I edged myself toward the
bed and the nurse's call button. I needed help.

Being forcibly deprived of her drug-alcohol fix, my mother was in the throes of acute withdrawal. She would have to be sedated quickly before she became too agitated, even violent. I pressed the bell without her seeing, then approached her cautiously—she was stark naked, trembling, her hands in spasm, hugging her waist.

"Easy, Mass. Easy—let me help you. We'll leave. I'll get your bra and panties but before you get dressed, remember? We have to put a dressing on the wound? Lie down on the bed for just a second, so I can bandage the leg."

Ten minutes later, my mother was being wheeled toward the elevators, a gentle smile curling her lips. She gazed benignly up at me beside her bed, sighed contentedly. A body that craved scotch was quite willing to accept a good hefty dose of Valium instead! I prayed she wouldn't remember how lovely she felt and get hooked on all the other narcotics her veins were about to sop up. I squeezed her hand, the elevator door closed. After all those years of worry and pain, finally a real doctor's skill could focus on saving Dietrich's famous legs. That morning, Dr. De Bakey successfully performed an arto right femoral, left iliac bypass, and a bilateral lumbar sympathectomy.

It is always so cold in intensive care. The machine breathed for her. My mother lay silent—for the first time since I had known her, utterly helpless—and I had the strangest sensation of feeling suddenly safe, unhurtable. I hadn't realized until that moment how much I still feared her. For one terrible moment . . . Then I turned and left her to the machines that would resurrect her.

During the early hours of January 30, the ring of the phone woke me. The agitated voice of the head nurse in intensive care:

"Mrs. Riva, I know it's three o'clock in the morning, and I am sorry to have to wake you, but it is your mother. No, no. Nothing to worry about. It's just that we are having trouble handling her. She's breathing on her own now and she keeps insisting we get you. She says she wants to see her daughter *right away*! We tried to reason with her but she is extremely agitated. We have put her in a section by herself."

"I'll be right there."

I entered the darkened unit. Still forms in long rows, monitors whined, singing their high tunes of hearts in transit, the monotone hiss of respirators, the soft squeak of rubber-soled shoes hurrying—machines and dedicated angels working to hold death at bay.

I entered my mother's secluded cubicle. She was yelling:

"You call yourself a nurse? I told you to *get my daughter. She* will tell De Bakey what you are doing to me. . . ." She was completely lucid, wide awake.

If her body hadn't been hooked up to the

miracle machinery of modern medicine, no one would have believed that this woman had undergone major bypass surgery less than twenty-four hours before.

"Oh! You are *finally* here! I told them, 'Get my daughter.' They told me you were *sleeping* and I said to them, 'My daughter *sleeping*? She wouldn't sleep when her mother is in here! *Get her!*' I had to fight them—can you believe it? I lie here, I am the patient, and they *argue* with me? What a terrible place . . . they even dared to tell me to lower my voice, that they have other patients out there who are dying. The *great* De Bakey has patients who *die*? Since when?"

Intensive care nurses are always so happy when they can remove a patient's breathing tube. It is a moment when life again takes over from apparatus, and they wait for it with anxiety, dedication, and hope. With my mother, they now probably regretted having done so and felt guilty for wishing to put it back.

She gestured me to come closer, whispered: "They won't even give me an injection to sleep. Tell De Bakey, and tell him some young student is allowed to come in here to take my blood every two minutes. I call him 'Dracula.' He doesn't know what he's doing. Look at the blue marks he made on my arms. . . ." Suddenly, she froze, stared up at the soundproof ceiling: "Look—look," she hissed. "There they are! See? See them? They have cameras! They have cameras! See the reflection off their lenses? There are little men up there—with *cameras*. . . . Tell De Bakey!"

It is quite normal for patients to hallucinate after surgery, but they never remember those times—when the brain recovering from anesthesia emits disjointed thoughts. But my mother referred to this visit of mine often in the years to come, repeating the exact words she said to me. It was eerie. It gave my memory of that sparsely lit scene quite another dimension.

Three days after the operation, my mother was brought back to her room. Her usually icy legs were warm, their bluish whiteness replaced by a rosy hue. For the first time in fifteen years, both limbs registered a steady pulse. We celebrated—that is, everyone but Dietrich. Oh, it wasn't that she was displeased with the results, just enraged that no one would give her a proper drink. If it had not been for the anesthesia and the many drugs her system had been forced to absorb, my mother would have been pretty well dried out by this time. As it was, she was still irritable and unpredictable, going through the latter stages of withdrawal. To see her through this period, she was put on Thorazine, and heavenly bliss descended on our floor, the building, and the state of Texas. She was even heard to say "thank you" and "please." We looked at television together and laughed. My mother had turned into a human being, actually nice to be with. Until the day she received her new pharmaceutical encyclopedia, looked up Thorazine, and discovered that it was a medication used to calm patients in insane asylums. That finished Thorazine! She refused to take her medication from then on and the real Dietrich returned.

It was time to return to my family. I hugged Dr. De Bakey, thanked him for his kindness, infinite patience, and consummate skill. Kissed my mother and, in secret, the valiant nurses, wished them luck, strong nerves, and put my mother into their capable hands. We would be in constant touch by telephone. I was sure that the next operation, the skin-grafting, would be equally successful now that the leg had its sufficient blood supply. My mother had only to follow her doctor's advice, convalesce, hold on to her hard-gained sobriety, and all would be well.

On the 7th of February, with shaved skin from her thigh, the graft was performed and took on the first try. Once again, Dietrich was victorious—she would keep her leg.

Six weeks after the operations, my mother walked into her New York apartment, opened a bottle of scotch, and without a moment's hesitation, started down that familiar road that would lead, eventually, to her own destruction. By April first, after a traumatic fall, three consecutive full anesthesias, vascular surgery, and skin-graft surgery, Marlene Dietrich, at seventy-three, was back on tour.

M. DIETRICH 1974 Tour

New Orleans 4 3–13	Fairmont Hotel
Los Angeles 4 15–16–17–18	Chandler Pavilion
Washington 4 22–23–24–25	Kennedy Center Opera House
Honolulu 4 29–30 5 1	Waikiki Sheraton Hotel
Phoenix, Ariz. 5 16–17–18	Phoenix Symphony Hall
Toledo, Ohio 5 21–22–23–24	Masonic Temple
St. Paul, Minn. 5 25–26	O'Shaughnessy Auditorium
Chicago, Ill. 5 28–29–30	Chicago Auditorium
Sacramento, Calif. 6 2–3–4–5–6–7–8–9	Music Circus
Mexico City 6 11–23	Fiesta Palace
Danbury, Conn. 7 10–24	

She called me daily. Her legs, unaccustomed to the sudden rush of blood supply, were swollen, pulsed painfully. She drew pictures of what she called her "barrel leg," sending them to De Bakey. She was frightened that the "stitches" would rip and the Dacron "tubing" that he had spliced onto her arteries would tear loose. So, in a small drawstring bag, she carried a spare, an exact duplicate of what De Bakey had used —in case of such an emergency. Repair jobs had always been suspect; Dietrich hated them on her dresses, her costumes—it was only natural she would not trust them inside her body! Another worry plagued her: Since the time the catheter had been removed after the last operation, my mother at times could not control the flow of urine. With her amazing Spartan attitude, she decided to devise a way to overcome the possibility of leaving puddles in her wake. Sanitary napkins were the only logical protection that she could hide effectively under her stage dresses. They had another advantage; if anyone, like hotel maids, found them, they would automatically assume Dietrich still menstruated, not that she might have become incontinent. She suffered terribly under this new affliction; by its very connotation of old age it marred her own criteria of elegance and beauty. The fact that the more she drank the more she "dribbled," she refused to acknowledge. It was easier to blame De Bakey and wear two pads instead of one.

· · ·

AFTER TWELVE YEARS in Europe, the Riva family was finally coming home. Paul pulled my arm: "Look! Mom! Look! Your Statue of Liberty!" and there she was, constant and true. This would be our first summer back in America. Oh, it was going to be wonderful! We rented a little house near good friends on Long Island, told the kids stories of when their big brothers had summered in the same place, fished for snappers, clammed, cooked real American steaks on a backyard barbecue, witnessed the workings of a true democracy—the impeachment proceedings of a president on national television.

On the 9th of August, a Capricorn president finally got the message and resigned, and the other Capricorn flew from Paris to Geneva for her annual checkup with Prof. de Watteville. As usual, my mother's Dutch courage routine was in effect. Back in Paris that night, she made a half-turn as she approached her bed and collapsed. The phone rang. I recognized the voice of one of the many young men my mother allowed to wait on her for the honor of serving their Queen.

"Maria, your mother fell. Something is very wrong. Here she is . . ."

Accidents sobered her fast: "Sweetheart, this whole thing is ridiculous. I just made a funny turn and fell—right here, in the bedroom—on the soft carpet. But when I tried to get up, I suddenly couldn't. Now you *know* that's stupid. The graft is okay, De Bakey's Dacron is okay, so *now* what?"

"Mass, listen to me carefully. Call Dr. Seidman, he's still in Paris. You must be x-rayed. Call him right now—I'll wait here. Have him call me."

While I waited, I called Prof. de Watteville at his home in Geneva, asked what had happened while she was with him that day. He informed me that he was extremely pleased, that he had found no sign of recurring cancer, that she had shown him the graft, and that in his opinion, it was a beautiful piece of work.

"Your mother is a truly amazing woman and an extremely lucky one, but I am very concerned about her drinking. I hesitated to mention it to her but felt that today it was necessary. Her reaction was most astounding. She insisted that as she hated the taste of all alcohol, she never drank anything more than an 'occasional' glass of champagne. But I must tell you, she was exceedingly drunk."

As its elevator was too elegantly small, my mother was taken by emergency stretcher down the back stairs of her Paris apartment. With her screaming directives, frightened to be discovered by lurking photographers, they took her through the subterranean garage to the American Hospital in Paris. After being x-rayed, she refused

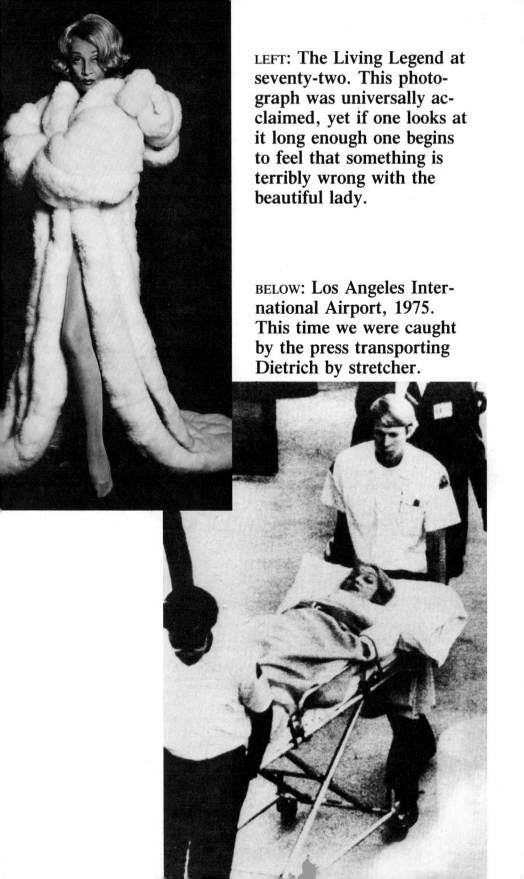

LEFT: The Living Legend at seventy-two. This photograph was universally acclaimed, yet if one looks at it long enough one begins to feel that something is terribly wrong with the beautiful lady.

BELOW: Los Angeles International Airport, 1975. This time we were caught by the press transporting Dietrich by stretcher.

My mother during one of the last visits to my father's "ranch."

Just a Gigolo, the last film that she should not have had to make —the last costume that she should not have had to wear.

to remain there, insisted on being returned to her apartment. She had broken her hip.

She called to give me the news. By now, she was cold sober:

"Sweetheart—I can't stay in France. They kill people in France. London is out—the British press is vicious and since the Nazis killed all the Jews, there are no more good doctors in Germany. So maybe Sweden? Or America—again? Call De Bakey and ask," and hung up.

I called Dr. De Bakey and asked him for the best hip man in the world; without hesitation he said: "Frank Stinchfield," and gave me his New York number. I tracked him down at his home, introduced myself, and gave him my mother's full medical history. He was wonderfully kind, assuring me that there was a highly respected and skilled orthopedic surgeon in Paris that he could recommend. When I explained that under no circumstances would my mother consent to being treated in France, he said that if I could manage to have her flown to New York, he would make the necessary arrangements to have her admitted to Columbia-Presbyterian Hospital for hip surgery. I thanked him and promised to have her in New York within twenty-four hours.

First, I had to call my mother and convince her to be flown to New York. Second, I had to find someone trustworthy to accompany her

stretcher from Paris. Third, I had to find an airline that would accommodate a stretcher and
keep the entire procedure confidential. Fourth,
hire an ambulance to meet the plane at Kennedy
Airport. Fifth, organize my home so that I could
leave for New York City. As the young man
attending my mother held a British passport,
which required him to have a visa before entering
the United States, it would take too long for him
to accompany her. Time was of the essence, not
only because of the medical emergency, but because of the world press. The longer it took to
get Dietrich from one country to another, the
more time the press had to find out about this
latest accident.

As I had to organize the New York end, I
called an old flame of my mother's who held an
American passport and was living in London,
told her what had happened, asked for her help.
She refused. Desperate, I called a friend I could
trust, asked her if she would fly from her home
in Canada to Paris, pick up my mother, and deliver her to me in New York. Her instantaneous
"Of course," I shall be eternally grateful for.

I and the ambulance were waiting on the
tarmac as my mother's plane landed at Kennedy
Airport. The passengers disembarked, then we
lifted our precious cargo off the plane. That the
press of two countries did not get wind of all this
was a real feat. A year later, we weren't so lucky,

but this first time, as I climbed into the ambulance next to my mother's stretcher, I was jubilant.

"How is that for superb cloak-and-dagger? We made it! No reporters! The security system at the hospital is briefed, everything has been arranged. Stinchfield is the best in his field. We'll get through this too. New York is not Houston, but I think we'll get away with it. I have arranged to sleep in your room, as it takes two hours to get to our place out on Long Island. . . ." I kept up the chatter, trying to distract her. To be in an ambulance is a frightening experience for anyone. For one who was as petrified of cars as my mother, a really harrowing one. For her stretcher trip across the Atlantic, Dietrich had chosen to wear a candy-pink caftan; around her pale face she had draped a Chanel chiffon shawl of the same color. She looked vulnerable and absolutely gorgeous. Only the fear in her eyes marred the pretty picture she made. I held her hand and calmed her as best I could each time we hit another New York pothole. She was sure that every jar dislodged her broken hip even farther.

The next day, my mother was wheeled into yet another operating theater to undergo major surgery. Just five and a half months after the last one. When she regained consciousness, Dietrich's hip boasted a brand-new, man-made ball joint. She christened it "George." Much more intriguing to say, "You know, George feels funny inside me today," than "My prosthesis is bothering me." She had completely forgotten that this had also been one of Yul's code names—or had she?

While my husband kept the home fires burning and the kids teased him about his cooking, I concentrated on getting my mother back on her feet and walking. It was normal for her to feel fragile, breakable, petrified of testing the safety of that stainless steel inside her body. She refused all attempts to make her stand, canceling therapists right and left. Even when Dr. Stinchfield finally forced her out of bed, the moment he left the room she hoisted herself back into it. I mentioned that she was scheduled to open at the Grosvenor House in London on the 11th of September and casually asked if she wanted me to now cancel her contract. She lay there, just looking at me. I knew now she would get up and went to dial the therapist's extension.

Once again, my mother was being forced to undergo the stages of alcohol withdrawal and hated the whole world for its cruelty, especially the Columbia-Presbyterian Hospital staff. The one that received the most abuse was her young therapist. I remember that young girl's incredulous expression when my mother announced to her that it was a complete waste of her time to be forced to practice climbing stairs, informing her that Dietrich absolutely had no reason nor further need to do so—ever again. The mere idea that anyone had the power to eliminate stairs from their life was beyond the girl's comprehension. Privately, she asked me:

"Is your mother serious? Does she mean that? She is never, ever going to have to use stairs again?"

"Exactly. If my mother decides stairs are 'out,' they will cease to exist for her. You and I might have to maneuver such mundane obstacles, but Dietrich? She can change the world to suit herself!"

The steps leading up to the stage at the Grosvenor House were eliminated. Twenty-nine days after hip surgery, Richard Burton introduced Marlene Dietrich to her glittering audience. She strode onto the stage, steady as a rock, without the slightest limp, bowed low into her famous bow, and triumphed once again.

She called me the moment she got back to her dressing room: "Sweetheart! The dribble wasn't too bad and the sound wasn't right for 'Where Have All the Flowers Gone?' because you weren't here to fix it. But De Bakey's Dacron held, the graft looks okay, the legs didn't swell too much after the flight from New York, and 'George' didn't snap out when I did the bow, and you'll be proud of me—I didn't limp."

I was, but I would have been even prouder if she hadn't slurred her *r*'s.

An hour later, she called back: "You know

who insisted on seeing me? That little gnome—Princess Margaret. You know how I never let anyone come backstage and see me in the dress? Well, all this to-do with 'royal protocol,' I wasn't allowed to let a 'princess' wait! Big Deal! So I had to see her right away. Don't they have anyone who can tell them how to dress? You should have seen her. I hear she drinks—she looks puffy. Remember when Noël took me to dinner at her house? What is that palace where they live called? And how we were all taken on a 'grand' tour to see her new bathroom? All ruffles and ugly marble and solid gold rococo fittings and how I laughed that with all that to-do, in typical British fashion, the cold and hot water were *still* coming out of separate taps? I am going to take my Fernando Lamas now and go to sleep. Call Stinchfield and tell him I will send him the reviews in the morning."

By December she was touring Japan.

EARLY IN '75, she played a week's engagement at the Royal York in Toronto, and I flew up to see the show. She had asked me to check and fix the sound. I balanced the microphones, repositioned the speakers, stayed to dress her and see the show to double-check the system.

During the day, my mother had been particularly irritable and irritating. Using the imagined pain of her hip as an excuse, she had swallowed six of her new love, Darvon, with a fifth of scotch. By the time she stood waiting in the wings for her cue that night, she was a mess. Her eyes glazed, her wig off-center, her makeup sloppy, her lipstick smeared. She slumped, holding onto the weighted curtain for support. When her entrance music cued her onto the stage, she ambled, disinterested, and took up her position at the microphone. Her dulled glaze tried to focus on her audience. Despite the bright lights shining into her eyes, she could distinguish the faces of those seated at their tables at the very perimeter of the stage. I, standing at the back of the room, watched her anxiously, expecting her to pass out any moment.

She missed a beat, hesitated over a lyric, and stopped cold. Her body froze—a sudden stillness descended, and before my eyes, my mother metamorphosed into vital, magnificent perfection. She sparkled! Teased! Commanded! Enslaved! Became the "golden Venus" her audience had come to worship. I had been witness to this startling transformation and still couldn't believe my eyes. What had provoked it? I searched for a possible clue among the faces at the ringside tables, and there he was—Yul Brynner. It was the sight of his face that had galvanized my mother into becoming "Dietrich."

Yul called her repeatedly that night. He was

staying in the same hotel and wanted to see her. At first, she made me tell him no, then decided to tell him herself. She was not depressed. She obviously enjoyed reawakening Yul's burning ardor, only to extinguish it. She felt on top of the world.

She continued on to Dallas, Miami, Los Angeles, Cleveland, Philadelphia, Columbus, and Boston. Whenever I could, I flew to where she was, listened to her suffering entourage, smoothed over irate hotel and theater managers, checked the speakers, microphones, and consumption of scotch. She always greeted me with heroic expectations—now everyone would fall back into line, do as they were told, behave— Maria had come to slay all her dragons.

As her drinking increased, her performances lost the crystal sharpness of brilliance, dulled into "good" instead of "great," bookings into concert halls waned. Anyway, she had played them all when truly magnificent, so return engagements for a lesser impact became hard to find, and so luxury hotel chains often took the place of legitimate theaters. These were the hardest for her. She had outgrown those audiences that sit at tables drinking, expecting a floor show. No matter how much it cost them to see a legend in the flesh, these were not parishioners come into an awesome temple, but merrymakers out for a good time expecting their money's worth. I knew how difficult this "downscaling" was for her and chose those times to appear, take up my old post of handmaiden, and dress her.

As she lived in the hotel she worked for, she could prepare for the performance in her suite. First the makeup—god, she was good at that! When she was really drunk, she messed it up, but when even half sober, one marveled at her skill and lightning speed. Now the wig. This one's side wave was not correct, try another. No. 12A, marked "L.A. Chandler Pavilion opening night" was finally chosen. Now the all-important tray for the table that was always positioned stage right at the edge of the curtain—her safety net to exit to. Flashlight, hand mirror, comb, brush, lipstick, lip brush, Kleenex, pressed powder, Allenberry lozenges, glass of champagne, glass of scotch, four Darvon—individual capsules laid out ready to grab—three Dexedrine tablets in a row, one cortisone. All the essentials to get through yet another working night.

The foundation marked "No. 3 tight Denmark," then the golden dress. I took its heavy beaded coat down in the service elevator to the Cotillion Room, the Empire Room, or whatever name this particular hotel had chosen to impress its clientele with, then returned to take—her. The revealing dress hidden beneath a silk kimono, she stood waiting, breathing slow, body erect in gossamer harness of glowing armor. I was always so sorry for her when this moment came—the gladiator, ready to go into the arena, all alone. The tight dress, the distances, the alcohol-induced unsteadiness, the excuse of the hip, now made a wheelchair an acceptable convenience as long as no "strangers" saw her use one. I positioned it, she lowered herself carefully into it. The dress, always that worry for her dress. She adjusted the kimono, making sure that her revealing front was completely covered, reached out for her tray, positioned it securely on her lap, I made sure there was no one in the corridor, and we began our journey. Usually service elevators empty adjacent to hotel kitchens, and that is where we exited.

It was definitely Shrimps Casino tonight, with a faint overlay of broiled lamb chops. The cooks smiled at their nightly visitor, they all had received photographs especially dedicated to them and were her fans. Harried waiters, scurrying bus boys, acknowledged her glamorous presence as they weaved, avoiding her chariot. She was not disturbed at being seen by them, somehow she knew they wouldn't talk; besides, she always felt comfortable in kitchens. I pushed her wheelchair amidst the bustle, the pungent smells, and wondered if she too was remembering all those kitchens we had run through— laughing—young—so very long ago.

. . .

Her latest tour done, my mother returned to her Paris apartment. Paul graduated from high school and fell in love—with a Chevrolet; David was looking forward to getting back to our summer house and his special fishing cove. I had positioned a few loyal people in Paris who knew when to water my mother's scotch and keep an eye on her pill consumption. Darvon was now her daily favorite, she acquired hundreds of the red-and-gray capsules, ate them like candy, washing them down with her J&B. This, combined with her various sleeping pills, made up a really lethal combination. Everyone on my Paris surveillance team had their instructions and my telephone numbers in case of an emergency. I left for Long Island, convinced that this summer of '75 I would get to spend with my family.

On the 10th of August, my father suffered a massive stroke, was resuscitated by paramedics, then taken to Holy Cross Hospital in San Fernando Valley near his home. He was not expected to live. I called my mother, broke the news to her as gently as possible, said I was on my way to California. She cried—said she would remain in Paris until she heard from me.

My son Michael was waiting at the airport and drove me out to the Valley. My father was still alive. His right side paralyzed, speechless, but alive. I called my mother, gave her as much hope as I possibly could, minimizing my father's critical condition, trying to make it easier for her. Her only question: Were there reporters at the hospital already? When I said no, she was not convinced, saying that I should watch out for them, protect Papi from any publicity, to call her every half hour, that she would remain in Paris, sitting by the phone until I told her he was out of danger.

I was relieved. I had been worried how I was going to manage to keep her from rushing to her dying husband's bedside. Long ago, during one of those rare times when my father and I spoke to each other as friends, he had said to me:

"Kater, when I die, see to it that your mother does not stand looking down at my grave."

It was the least I was prepared to do for him.

Michael got me dimes for the pay phone, reminded me that there was a nine-hour difference between California and Paris, and left for a few hours' work.

As potential mourners, those who wait outside intensive care units develop a special kinship. They may never see each other again or know each other's names, but while they share their sad vigil, they bond.

We whispered hopeful platitudes to each

other, needing to believe them, shared our prayers, coffee, and Kleenex. The long wait for life or death to flee had begun.

Every hour I was permitted five minutes to stand by my father's bed and witness his struggle. I held his good hand, repeated words I knew he couldn't comprehend, yet said them anyway:

"Papilein, I am here. It's Kater. I am here. You are safe—you are safe, I promise," and imagined it calmed him. After each viewing, I called Paris. As the hours dragged on, she became less emotional, more resigned to my father's critical condition, and began issuing orders. Her primary concern was his diaries. She was terrified they might fall into the wrong hands, be read, and all her secrets revealed. She ordered me to leave the hospital, go to my father's house, and remove the diaries to a safe place. I thought it a bit macabre to pick over the corpse before it actually was one, but assured her that I would see to it that the precious diaries were removed immediately, as ordered. I did nothing of the kind. I had more important things to worry about than my mother's reputation, her fear of being finally discovered the less-than-perfect "wife."

Nurses are always so concerned of possible bedside thefts; I was given my father's personal possessions for safekeeping, his wallet, his gold Patek Philippe wristwatch, and his teeth. I noticed that his large signet ring was missing. It and my father's hand had been inseparable. I remember how the square-cut emerald caught the light whenever he clenched his hand in anger. He would have liked to have been buried wearing it. Now the ring was gone and I wouldn't be able to, I thought, as though it mattered—as though he would ever know. Waiting for someone to die, one thinks such silly thoughts.

On my next call to my mother, I had nothing new to tell her, but she did. I was to see to it that my father's dogs were taken to the pound and gotten rid of. With true Germanic thoroughness, she was cleaning out her husband's home. I suppose, being so far away, having no actual control over events, she had to involve herself in something. Again, I assured her I would execute her orders immediately, but I had no intention of destroying what my father loved.

The doctors agreed and approved my request that my father be allowed to die in peace, not be subjected to further "heroic" methods of resuscitation. He was given extreme unction. We waited. The hours dragged on. My father continued his struggle, refused to die.

The Holy Cross is a wonderful hospital. Its staff skilled and dedicated angels, but for a seventy-eight-year-old stroke victim determined to remain alive against all odds, a more sophisticated, technically equipped institution was necessary. His doctors and I discussed the advisability of transferring him to the UCLA Medical Center in Westwood. We agreed that as he was fighting so hard to survive, he deserved to be given every chance to succeed. I began to make the complicated arrangements of transferring a critical patient from one hospital to another. Seven days after suffering a massive stroke, my father, hooked up to his life-support systems, was lifted into a private ambulance. No one really believed he would survive the long journey to UCLA. I rode with him. If he died on the way, Tami would want me there with him.

My father was still alive as our ambulance came to a screeching halt at the emergency entrance of UCLA. Expert hands lifted his stretcher and rushed him inside. While I handled the necessary paperwork, my father was being hooked up to IVs, monitoring devices in the intensive cardiac care unit on the fourth floor of one of the greatest medical centers in the world.

On the 22nd of August, twelve days after his stroke, my father resurrected himself, became aware that something was terribly wrong with Rudi Sieber. Now his real torture would begin—yet he must have wanted it, to fight so hard to reach this moment.

I called my mother with the incredible news. She refused to believe me. She had never fully comprehended the reason for my father's serious incapacities nor what had caused them. She was convinced that he had had "just" another heart attack, and could not understand how that could have paralyzed him, robbed him of speech and comprehension. As she was scheduled to begin rehearsals in Melbourne on the 26th, I suggested that she stop off in L.A. on her way to Australia, see her husband for herself, confer with his doctors. I felt it was time for her to take up some of a wife's responsibilities, besides paying for them.

I sat outside on the hospital steps, waiting for my mother's limousine. It was a cool, clear evening, the sky full of early stars, the air heavy with mock orange. The car swung into the driveway. Dietrich, looking every inch the breathtakingly beautiful, distraught wife, swept into her husband's special enclosure—and ICCU Four was never the same again. Although my father could not recognize her, she insisted that he did. The doctors were patient, drew her pictures indicating where the blood clots had lodged in his brain, where they had wrought their havoc. They tried to explain why her insistence that they operate "immediately" was impossible in her husband's case.

Lips tight, she waited for the doctors to leave, then fixed me with one of her looks: "*These* are the 'great' doctors you are so in love with? They are idiots! They say they can't operate on Papi because they don't know *how*. I talked to all the greatest doctors in Europe. They all tried to tell me that the Americans are the best brain specialists in the world! But nobody really knows anything. I should have taken Papi to Niehans to get fresh cells years ago."

She took a suite at the Beverly Wilshire for the night and was furious when I insisted on returning to my room near the hospital. The next day she got busy organizing her husband's future. First, she discovered that I had not killed off the dogs as ordered and was livid, then when I insisted that they be removed to a kennel instead of the pound, granted me their reprieve. With her beautiful eyes luminous with unshed tears, she informed the doctors that after she finished her Australian tour, she planned to return to California, rent a small house in Beverly Hills, and devote the rest of her life to pushing her husband's wheelchair in the sunshine. Her voice a soft caress of utter sincerity, she meant every word of it.

The listening male physicians melted, charmed by this so-beautiful woman's wifely devotion. There were many who, over the years, heard my mother pronounce those words, heard the plans she had for her crippled husband. Neither the doctors then, nor those who heard it later, ever challenged her idyllic script. No one ever said, "To devote your life to caring for your infirm husband is commendable—truly wonderful—but wouldn't it be better to dedicate yourself to his recovery? Help him to walk again? Help him to regain his pride, rather than pushing his wheelchair in the sun?" She left for Australia, I remained.

On the day my father was strong enough to be transferred to the neurological wing, I came to say good-bye. Hoping somehow my father would understand the meaning of my words, I tried to tell him how proud, how full of admiration I was that he wanted life, was willing to fight so hard for it, squeezed his good hand, touched his good cheek, and wished I could do more for him.

Back in New York, I kept a close check on his progress, calling my mother twice a day in Australia to give her the latest news. She was so convinced he would have to be institutionalized, she persisted in her obsession with the dogs. As she would pay for having them killed, "even buried," why did I continue to refuse to execute her orders? As for my father's house, it was to be stripped of his belongings, then sold.

Fortunately, my mother was so tied up with her tour, I was able to stall her. It was essential for my father's possible recovery, no matter how impractical it might seem, that his home, his possessions, his animals, all he treasured in his life, were kept safe for him to return to. It was the lodestone he needed to survive—he had no other.

Rumors of trouble began to filter back to me in New York. The Australian tour was going badly. I received a call from one of the irate producers—Miss Dietrich was complaining constantly about the sound, the lights, the orchestra, the audiences, the management. She was abusive, she was drunk, both on and off the stage. Her concerts were not sold out, the management was considering canceling the rest of the tour, I was asked if I would take on the task of preparing my mother for such an eventuality. I, and her faithful agent, negotiated a compromise. We would do our very best to persuade Miss Dietrich to consider terminating the tour, attempt to straighten out some of the more unpleasant disagreements if they, in turn, agreed to pay her contractual salary without any deductions. Fortunately, by now all they wanted was to get rid of her, cut their losses.

It was left to me to get Dietrich out of Australia as gracefully and as fast as possible.

"Mass? Listen. They say the ticket sales are not good at all. Oh! I agree with you. It is *their* fault entirely for not spending enough money for publicity. Yes, the ads are *much* too small but . . . they are willing to pay your full salary, even if you don't perform. So, why not take it easy. Take the money and get the hell out! Who needs all this hassle? With all these worries you have about Papi, you can just take the money, go back to California, and be with him!"

"What? He is in a hospital and I have a contract! I can't leave in the middle of a tour! They only say to *you* they will pay me, but you watch, the moment I left—Nothing!"

"I would insist that you were given a banker's draft before boarding the plane. That's the least of our worries."

"No! I have a *contract*! I go next to Canberra and then I open in Sydney. They are not going to get rid of me! How dare they! Don't you have anything more to do with gangsters like that!" and she slammed down the phone.

Filled with her usual Darvon, Dexamil, and scotch, Dietrich opened in Sydney on the 24th of September, 1975. Mike Gibson, of the *Daily Telegraph*, reviewed her performance that night correctly. Unfortunately, this one too she deserved:

> . . . A little old lady, bravely trying to play the part of a former movie queen called Marlene Dietrich, is tottering around the stage of Her Majesty's Theatre. When I say bravely I mean it. Without a doubt her show is the bravest, saddest, most bittersweet concert I have ever seen. . . .

. . . With the aid of the best in lighting, cosmetics and modern-day underwear engineering, for more than an hour she defiantly stands there trying to recapture the magic of a woman who gave soldiers goose pimples in a war over 30 years ago.

Her fans adore her.

Like a wind-up doll, a camp impersonation of a German legend, she brazens her way through songs like "My Blue Heaven" and "You're the Cream in My Coffee." . . .

She sways unsteadily as she shuffles her way offstage to take off her fur. . . .

When it is over the applause from her fans is tremendous. The compulsory roses conveniently placed in front of the footlights fly through the air onto the stage.

Now you can see why the little old lady sings on. It can't just be money. She wouldn't try as hard as this. . . .

Hanging onto the red curtains for support, she takes bow after bow. She is still bowing, and waving, still breathing it all in as we leave.

When we get home the baby-sitter is watching the late-night movies on Channel 9.

It is called "Shanghai Express," it was made in 1932, and it starred Marlene Dietrich.

"Wasn't she marvelous," said the baby-sitter.

"Yes, she was," I replied.

Five days after this scathing review, my mother arrived at the theater for that evening's performance. My friend, that rescuing angel who had flown from Canada the year before, was in Sydney, had offered to "watch-dog" her for me, and help dress her. My mother was so drunk that she, together with the girlfriend of one of the musicians, tried desperately to sober her up in the dressing room with black coffee. Finally, they managed to zip her into the foundation and into the dress. Supporting their precious burden between them, they exited the dressing room as the first strains of Dietrich's overture came over the loudspeaker. They made their way to the wings and placed her by the curtain. She slumped and collapsed.

Her conductor, seeing Dietrich had missed her entrance cue, signaled the orchestra to repeat the overture while Dietrich was being carried away from the stage back to her dressing room. The shock of falling had sobered her sufficiently to realize that something was wrong with her left leg. It would not support her.

The performance had to be canceled, a crippled Dietrich had to be gotten out of the theater as fast as possible. But she absolutely refused to have fans waiting for her at the stage door see her close up in the stage dress and insisted on changing first. As she had to be held upright in order to remove the dress without tearing it, my mother locked her arms around the neck of the distraught producer, and just hung there, while the two women peeled off her costume and re-dressed her into her Chanel suit.

Back at her hotel, not knowing I had already been informed of this new accident and was in touch with Dr. Stinchfield, who was contacting doctors in Sydney, my mother forbade anyone to call me. With her usual luck, the international convention of orthopedic surgeons was taking place in Sydney that week. Within the hour, two leading physicians, resplendent in their tuxedos, came to my mother's suite. Though she believed that Dr. Stinchfield's hip joint was the culprit, it was obvious to the doctors that she had probably broken her thigh bone. They did not tell her this, preferring to wait for the X rays to corroborate their diagnosis. She refused to be taken to the hospital.

All that night, my mother lay in her bed, hardly daring to breathe. Early the next morn-ing, she finally allowed herself to be smuggled out of the hotel into St. Vincent's Hospital. The X rays confirmed the doctors' suspicions. She had a broken femur of the left leg.

Alcoholics are always at risk, especially in the field of orthopedics. In order to protect them from the added danger of bone infection, tremors during traction, and other complications indigenous to their specific problem, it is essential that any surgeon be given the whole truth about a patient's alcoholism. I arranged for Dr. Stinchfield to confer with the Sydney doctors. But my mother absolutely refused to remain in Australia—where to take her?

Finally it was decided to place her into a protective body cast and fly her to the nearest medical center in California, into the care of the chief of orthopedics at UCLA, whom Dr. Stinchfield had recommended. After making the arrangements for her to be flown by stretcher from Australia, I flew to L.A. to prepare for her arrival, booked the ambulance to meet her flight, selected a room in UCLA's VIP Wilson Pavilion. Suddenly I realized that my mother and my father were about to sleep under the same roof! The thought of these two damaged people finally coming together this way saddened me.

I met my mother's plane on the tarmac and transferred her stretcher to the waiting ambulance. This time, the press caught us and snapped the only picture ever taken of Dietrich on a stretcher. Again I rode in the ambulance with her, holding her hand, trying to calm her fears. She was furious. I asked for her forgiveness, for I knew she held me responsible for the break in our usual tight security. Once installed in her new domain, across from the suite where John Wayne would die a few years later, my mother sent me out on all sorts of concocted errands so that she could unpack her little bottles and secrete them away in her night table, behind a stack of Kleenex.

More X rays, conferences, and discussions. In between, I visited my father. He was so proud of his latest feat: When the therapist placed a soft rubber ball into the palm of his once useless right hand, he had not only progressed to recognizing the touch of an object, but was able to actually curl three fingers around it! The day was not too far off when he might manage to give that little yellow ball a squeeze and know he was really alive!

The renowned surgeon, very handsome and "movie starish," flanked by his brilliant young assistants, leaned against the wall facing my mother's bed. Patiently, he tried to explain a relatively new, yet highly successful surgical procedure—the cementing of broken bones, as opposed to placing them in traction to wait for time and nature to heal the break. My mother was not impressed. She dismissed the three men as though they were bell boys, then ordered dinner for both of us.

"Did you see how young that doctor is? And those two on either side of him? Like little boys! Children like that can't know what they are doing . . . they are much too young! It's all too elegant here to be any good. Only in Hollywood would they have a hospital that looks like a movie set!

You better take all my X rays back to New York, show them to Stinchfield. Explain to him what they want to do to me here and ask him what he thinks."

I kissed my father good-bye, told him to keep up the hard work, that he was terrific, and thought I saw a flicker of pleasure in his good eye. Before leaving them both, I asked my mother if she wanted to see him, and when her answer was a sharp "No," I wasn't surprised.

Dr. Stinchfield feared that further surgery might expose her to dangerous infection, and as she objected to remaining at UCLA, distrusted the doctors there, but he was still acceptable, it seemed the safest solution to fly her back to New York, install her in her old room at Columbia Presbyterian, and now that she had normal circulation, put her leg in traction.

On the 7th of October, I met my mother's plane at Kennedy Airport and helped transfer her stretcher to yet another waiting ambulance. She had been confined in a body cast since the 13th of September, flown from Australia to California and from there to New York, she was exhausted, scared, and, understandably, extremely cranky. She might have been worse, except that a very attractive blond, ex-army nurse had accompanied her—whose hand my mother held and patted until the doors of the ambulance shut behind us. I took her vacated hand; the potholes seemed to have increased since our last trip along this same route. As we rolled her stretcher into Columbia Presbyterian, I thought I felt the floor staff shudder.

It had been hours since her last drink on the plane. She was getting frantic and unmanageable. She slapped the first nurse who tried to sedate her, then tore the hypodermic out of the second one's hand and hurled it across the room. Finally we managed to put her under. The cast could be cut off, and the complicated procedure of placing and aligning her broken leg into traction could commence.

Normally, the time for such a break to heal in one of my mother's advanced age is from two to three months. It took my mother's alcoholic body four months to heal—until February of 1976. How she endured all those weeks, those screws through her flesh, her leg stretched, strung out, weighted, completely immobile, amazed me. It must have been torture. Granted, she was a terrible patient.

No one was allowed to enter her room without permission. She refused to allow any black or Puerto Rican maids to clean. The nurses were frantic, so were the poor maids, who feared for their jobs should any doctor report the deplorable condition of Miss Dietrich's room. I scrubbed the floor quickly whenever I could, and tried to coax my mother into more receptive and democratic attitudes, and continually apologized for her awful behavior. I had a refrigerator installed, where she stashed the hospital meals she ordered, then refused to eat.

"The food in this terrible, filthy hospital is not fit for human beings to eat! I had them put it all in the icebox for you to take home for dinner."

Sometimes I was able to get her to watch that "low-class form of entertainment," television. The night she saw a Robert Redford film for the first time, she fell madly in love with him. That helped. Now we had orders to bring her fan magazines, anything that mentioned him. I found a pillowcase with Redford's picture, she loved it—she could sleep with him and dream.

My friend, who, like St. Christopher, had brought my mother's stretcher safely over the seas, first from Paris, then from Sydney, who had valiantly struggled to sober her up, supported her, caught her as she collapsed, arranged X rays, doctors, packed up the dressing room, costumes, hotel suite, hid her as best she could from the Australian press, then accompanied her stretcher to L.A., was exhausted. Before flying home, she came to the hospital to say good-bye. As she entered my mother's room, she heard her say:

"You know why I fell? Why I have a broken leg? Just as I was going on the stage in Sydney, that friend of Maria's—tripped me!"

The enormity of my mother's lie stunned her so, she turned, left the room without uttering a sound, and never saw Dietrich again. She did write her a very detailed letter, in which she chronicled exactly the events leading up to the fatal Sydney fall, but my mother never recanted, nor ever modified her blatant lie, repeating it to everyone. Over the years, my friend's continued absence puzzled and irked her greatly. After all, she felt that as she had actually never blamed "that woman" for tripping her, causing her all that "agony and expense," why then did Maria's friend feel she had the right to be *so* offended? As usual, my mother simply refused to accept the truth—even when it was laid bare before her eyes.

Through Thanksgiving, Christmas, and New Year's, she gnashed her teeth: "Vacations! Everyone is on vacation! You ring the bell and nobody comes. You call the doctor's office and nobody answers. The whole world stops! What is this—this obsession with holidays? In every country, people find excuses to not work. *But* they want to get paid! If I see one more Santa Claus! . . . What has he got to do with somebody being born in a stable? That's what Christmas is, isn't it? Because someone was born in some stable?"

My mother was never too sure about the

Bible. The Lutheran dogma of her childhood got mixed up with her agnostic sentiments, which, in turn, were confused by her superstitions. Actually, she was never too sure if she was an agnostic or an atheist. All she was really certain of was that God couldn't exist—for if He did, He would show Himself and do as He was told!

Angry that I wasn't with her constantly, that I was trimming a tree, cooking that awful thing known as turkey, spending time with my family, she took Polaroid pictures of her stretched leg with the pins through it and sent them to my sons as a Christmas greeting, inscribed: "No money —*this* Christmas!"

She phoned me incessantly, any hour of the day or night. The entries in her diary during this time have one recurring theme: "Haven't talked to Maria," "No one came," "No food," "All alone," and her perennial favorite: "No one called."

As my mother never recorded that she had called me ten times that day, any outsider reading her diary would be filled with justifiable outrage at her daughter's cruel neglect.

Finally, the traction could be removed and she was put back into a partial body cast. Because of her fragility, she remained in the cast even after I brought her home to her New York apartment. Her bed had been built up, the mattress reinforced, the bathroom transformed into her favorite first-aid station. The rented wheelchair, parked at the foot of her bed, she never used. She preferred staying in bed.

Although still partially paralyzed and speech-impaired, my father was declared strong enough to be brought back to his home. As he was being lifted from the car, his dogs swarmed around him, barking their joyous greeting. I was told that he cried when he saw them, knew he was home.

My mother decided that before returning to Paris, she would fly to California, make sure that her husband was being taken care of properly by all the people she was paying.

The day came when I took her to the hospital to have the cast cut off, then brought her home with a brand-new walker. Strangely enough, my mother did not shun this stark reminder of infirmity. She loved it. Suddenly, she had something to hold onto that moved with her, she could drink and still be mobile. She had no fear of being seen pushing her metal frame about. As she never went out on the street, had no need to enter a car to be taken to a theater to perform, her basic reasons for leaving her apartment were now nonexistent. Drunk, she shuffled, pushing her walker before her. Without its support, she couldn't walk, didn't even attempt to. We knew that she had to be weaned from this latest dependency.

As she refused to go outside for the pre-scribed therapy, Dr. Stinchfield arranged for therapists to come to her. These she either didn't like, objected to their touch, their manners, their looks, their age, certainly resented the truths they tried to make her understand. Instead of lengthening her shortened left leg through dis-ciplined, conscientious therapy, she just built up her left shoe and fired the therapists for their obvious "stupidity."

For one so stoic, so enamored of military discipline, Dietrich's pathological refusal to fol-low the rules of systematic therapy astounded me each time anew.

Slowly I got her to let go of the walker, but only after she insisted one was sent ahead to my father's house and another to her Paris apart-ment. I phoned my father's doctor to warn him of my mother's impending arrival and the havoc she would accomplish. I was so sure she would maneuver my father's ultimate defeat by yet again belittling his accomplishments, destroying his hard-earned pride in himself. She had given me a very good idea of what she was capable of toward this struggling soul:

"Sweetheart. You won't believe this. I talked to Papi's two nurses today, and you know what they are doing? They are trying to teach Papi to speak! A waste of time! Why does he have to talk? I'm paying all those people just to take care of him so they should *know* what he wants! I said, 'All my husband needs to learn is "shit" and "fuck"—that's all that's important!' What other words does he need the way he lives now? And all that to-do . . . the Big excitement—that he can stand and 'diddle' in the *toilet*? Why? The moment I get out there, I will get him one of those wheelchairs that he can pee in while he sits. Then he can stay there, nice and comfortable all day, and pee without having to move. Why do they have to torture him? And why does he have to learn to walk? I *pay* people to *wheel* him! All idiots!"

My poor father, who for the first time in his ineffectual life had accepted the challenge to save himself, who had grasped a little pride by once again urinating as a man, not as a helpless infant, was about to be cut down by his loving, caring wife; I feared—this time for good.

On the 7th of April, having escaped the press from seeing her at the airport in a wheelchair, I put her on the plane for California. By the middle of May, after reorganizing my father's home, his therapy, his life, she was back in her Paris apartment. By the end of June, my father was dead.

I flew to California to bury him. My mother used the threat of the reporters she was convinced would gather around Dietrich's only husband's grave, as excuse to remain in Paris.

· · ·

Amidst mahogany, walnut, satin, and brass, Michael helped me find the plain pine coffin I knew my father would have wanted. In one of his white silk monogrammed shirts, Hermès tie, Knize suit my mother and he had treasured so, my father was buried in the cemetery where Tami lay. I could let them rest together in the same place, but side by side?—*that* my heart refused to allow. I placed my cross on top of my father's coffin to help him on his long journey and turned away into the arms of my son to cry. The few friends present thought I was crying for the loss of a father. I was not. I was mourning the terrible waste of a man's life, for Tami's suffering, for his, for all the wasted years.

I received many suggestions for the wording on Rudolf Sieber's tombstone. Some were outrageous, some insulting to the man my father could have been, some simply banal. So I did what I thought he would have wanted. The husband of one of the world's great legendary women lies buried under a shady tree, his grave marked by a simple slab of Florentine marble in his favorite shade of green:

RUDI
1897–1976

It was time for me to leave. I went down the path to say good-bye to Tami. Looking down at that little piece of grass—it seemed impossible it could cover all the thousands of things that made up a human being. I spoke to her, asked her forgiveness, hoped she approved of what I had tried to do for Papi, because she loved him so.

Soon the telephone calls began: "Maria, how could you? Your poor mother called me. She told me how you did not let her come to Rudi's funeral. She was weeping. How could you do that to your mother? She said she was all packed, just sitting by the phone night and day, waiting for you to call! But you never did!"

I knew my mother had not wanted to be a witness to the actualities of her husband's death and was now simply assuaging her guilt, polishing her widow's image by laying the blame for her absence at her husband's grave on me. Besides, I had welcomed this need of hers to once again hide from reality. It had given me the chance to keep the promise I had made my father.

Dietrich lost two husbands that year. Soon after my father's death, Jean Gabin died. She was shattered, mourned him for years. It was not only his actual death that destroyed her so, it was also the realization that her long, secret dream of someday having Jean return to her was now at an end. Within weeks of each other, my mother lost the two men she loved the most—had betrayed the most.

They became her "ghosts." She looked for them—listened for their voices—complained when they didn't materialize, refused to give her signs of their comforting presence.

When Fritz Lang died, she celebrated; whenever someone else disappeared, she called me: "Did you hear Luchino Visconti died? Remember when he did that film where that bad actor he liked so, his boyfriend, played me in drag—in the *Blue Angel* costume? . . . And now with Howard Hughes dead, who is going to get all *those* millions? He used to chase me around Las Vegas, before he got that thing about living locked away with Kleenex boxes—and what is all this to-do suddenly in America, about a book about Negroes? I read something about it in *Newsweek* . . ."

"You mean *Roots*?"

"Yes—that's it! Who wants to read about them? It'll never sell," and hung up.

For the third time, she sold her unwritten autobiography to yet another American publisher. Refusing all help, advice, and counsel, she recounted her life as she believed she had lived it—pure, dedicated, a hymn to duty, honor, virtue, and motherhood.

In 1978, her agent brought me a deal for her to appear in a film being shot in Germany for world-wide distribution, to be called *Just a Gigolo*. The money offered her for a cameo role was exorbitant. Somehow, we had to find a way to get her to accept it. First, we had to get the producer to agree to shoot her sequence in Paris. In this way, she could be brought to the set directly from her apartment without the German press snapping too close at her heels. Secondly, her two scenes had to be filmed back to back. I knew that I could not keep her sober longer than two days. We also had to arrange that her main scene would be staged with her sitting, and her second scene, that required her walking into the set, be cut to only one step into frame. After long negotiations, two contracts were drawn, one my mother saw and finally signed—and the other she never knew existed. Knowing that only the need for money had made my mother agree to make the film, the contract stipulated that she be paid in installments: a large sum, on signing, to hold her locked into the deal; the next payment at the end of the first day of shooting, to ensure that she would not walk off the set; the final payment at the end of the second day, to make certain that she showed up. The private document stipulated that Maria Riva, daughter of Marlene Dietrich, had to be present and by her presence guarantee that Miss Dietrich would be in condition to perform her contractual duties.

So, they made the pilgrimage from Germany to France: the crew, the director, the cameraman, the actors. They built a duplicate of the set already standing on a German soundstage and waited for the great movie star to appear.

She chose a personal friend to design the costume for this film. It was this too personal relationship that I believe interfered with this costume designer's usual good taste. He is much too talented to have designed that hat, that awful patterned veil, that whole ghastly outfit all by himself. If von Sternberg had been there to photograph it, it might have worked. As it was, my mother looked like a female impersonator doing a rather tacky take-off on Dietrich. I arrived in Paris, saw this pathetic get-up that my mother had concocted to hide behind, finished, approved, and ready to shoot, and could do nothing to help her.

Once again I began watering her booze. My job was to keep Dietrich functioning for the next two days. As the first day of shooting dawned, I had grave doubts. She had decided to punish me. After all, I was responsible for forcing her to work, to be seen by a camera, to face a set full of "strangers"—this word was always synonymous with "enemies" to my mother. Worst of all, I had tried to take her scotch away from her!

I was so very sorry for her, but her lifelong refusal to listen to advice, her aversion to investments of all kinds, her extravagance, her romantic childlike belief that money would always be there for her, made it a dire necessity to provide her with the funds to continue living the only life she knew. The Impressionist paintings that she had once owned, then told everyone she gave to her daughter, making of her child a "billionaire," had mostly proved to be fakes, sold to pay the blackmailers who beat a steady path to my door.

It would have served nothing to tell my mother these sad truths. She so needed to believe that she alone had given her daughter life, love, and the means for the pursuit of grateful happiness.

We arrived at the French studio, our star intact. By the second day, my mother had found a breathless young thing and flirted her into smuggling a bottle of brandy into her portable dressing room. Before I found the bottle and could confiscate it, she had consumed half its contents. By the end of the day, she was too drunk to remember the lyrics of "Just a Gigolo." As I had done so often for her later stage performances, with a thick Magic Marker I printed the words out for her on large pieces of white cardboard and held them next to the camera for her to read.

I put her to bed that night. Nerves, exhaustion, and brandy had done their job. On returning home, she had been violently sick. Fearing that she might vomit in her sleep and choke, I stayed the night watching her. Well, we had done it! Pulled it off! She would get paid her full salary for the film. That would take care of the huge bills for a while, at least.

It might have been easier had she lived in New York, but she refused. Her fear of the American press was too deeply ingrained. She never forgot the reporters of the thirties, who had hounded her when von Sternberg's wife named Dietrich in her alienation-of-affection suit, the kidnapping threat, the years of fear of being discovered in the beds of so many lovers. In a way, I was relieved, as Europe regarded her as "holy royalty"—it was much easier to keep her secrets in Paris than in New York.

PARIS

SHE CONTINUED TO FALL. One night, she passed out in her bathroom, clutched the shower curtain as she fell, tore it from its rod—woke the next morning covered in pink plastic. Called me in complete confusion as to how this could have happened, insisting she must have been mugged by her maid who was then "so sorry" she had covered her with the curtain.

Once, on the way down, she hit her head on the edge of a marble table, got a huge shiner that spread down her face, that lasted for weeks—while I feared the phone call that might tell me the blood clot, formed when she hit her head, had traveled to . . . Each time the phone rang, I jumped!

"Sweetheart. It says in the paper that Charles Boyer died. Didn't I do a film with him?"

"Yes—*The Garden of Allah*."

"Oh, him! I thought *he* was dead long ago," and hung up.

In 1979, she passed out in her bedroom, woke, tried to get up and couldn't. Back down those stairs she was carried and x-rayed. She had a hairline fracture above her hip joint. Nothing too

serious, no emergency flights, no dashing am-
bulances. With proper bed care it would heal by
itself in less than four weeks. Refusing to be
hospitalized, she insisted on being returned to
her apartment and put herself to bed for the rest
of her life. She had found the perfect solution.
Now, when she passed out, she would already
be lying down in a soft, safe place. Never once
did the option of giving up drinking instead enter
her mind.

She refused all efforts to help her. Fired
legions of willing and concerned therapists,
would not allow nurses nor trained companions
near her. Only transients, who could be bought
with huge tips to bring her the scotch she craved,
were allowed admittance to her inner sanctum.

Like the organized German that she was,
she assembled the necessities for her existence
and created her own world. Her bed served as
her headquarters. She needed only a very narrow
strip of it on which to sleep in her drugged, unmoving stupor. On her left, her "office"—en-
velopes of all shapes and sizes, stationery, note
pads, string, tape, photo-mailers, postal scales,
sectioned trays of stamps, books, diaries, phone
books, telephone, dozens of reading glasses,
magnifying lenses, files, dictionaries, Kleenex
boxes, rubber bands, paper clips, fan photos,
towels, Handi Wipes, and her trusty six-shooter!
Granted, it was plastic and unlethal, still it made

a big enough bang to scare the hell out of the pigeons that loved to perch and coo outside her bedroom window.

At hand, her ever-ready, long-handled "pincher arms," that she used like a supermarket clerk to reach everything that lay beyond her inner perimeter.

On her right, against the wall, a table unit —its multilevels jammed with hundreds of pill containers, boxes, medicine bottles, jars, tubes, cases of suppositories—her private pharmacy. In front of this, low tables ran the length of the bed. These held second telephone, pencils, pens, markers, scissors by the dozen, dishes, cutlery, pepper mills, hot plate, drinking glasses, thermoses, dishes, cooking pots, frying pan, toothbrushes, plastic bowls, and clocks. Underneath stood her liquor supply, decanted by paid slaves into innocent-looking, tall, green, mineral-water bottles. Next to these, two small, lidded garbage cans, into which she poured her urine, after relieving herself into a Limoges pitcher. No common bedpans for Dietrich! Such an article had the connotation of "invalid," something she loathed. Next to the urine cans stood another receptacle, larger this time, on which perched an old metal casserole that had once belonged in my father's kitchen. Into this, my mother collected her bowel movements.

My mother's insistence on these macabre

toilet maneuvers of hers resulted in constant little accidents. The sheepskins she lay upon and loved, since discovering them in the Sydney hospital, were badly soiled, as was her mattress, her sheets, gray and stained. She refused to allow anyone to touch her, change her bed, wash her. Everything stank. "When Maria comes, she will give me a bath," she loved to tell everyone, but when I arrived, ready to clean her, she found a thousand excuses to get out of it. When I insisted, she would say that she was not dirty enough yet, that the bed had just been "changed" for my arrival and that it wasn't necessary to go through all the trouble of moving everything away from the bed just so I could get close enough to "smear" her with soap. She knew that I was trained in giving bed baths, that I could change an entire bed without the patient having to move. Still, she shrank from being touched.

"Oh! If only I could have a real bath in a tub," she would rhapsodize. When I ordered a special sling chair and handrails to be installed in the bathroom that she had not been in for years, she canceled the orders.

Slowly, her beautiful legs lost their muscles and atrophied. Her unused feet developed a deformity known as drop foot. Her body took on some of the physical characteristics of a concentration camp victim. By now she had convinced herself that her bedridden state was not of her doing and searched medical books for any recognized disease that matched her "symptoms." Although this self-maneuvered return to the womb finally crippled her, its relative safety contributed to her eventual longevity.

I visited her often, while her diaries stated, "I never see Maria." Each time I would note "Maria here"; each time I returned, found it crossed out with her Magic Marker. We played our little games.

"Making order" was her favorite. I would bring drawers to her bed to sort out, discuss, label, then put back—while she made "important lists" so I would know where everything was. Nothing was thrown away. Everything was resorted, repacked, relabeled, to be gone through again the next time I appeared. A Balenciaga raincoat from the fifties was unearthed, originally of heavy rubberized material that, after thirty years, was stiff as a board, when bent snapped like peanut brittle. She examined it very carefully:

"This would be good . . . the worms could never get through *this*!" She was absolutely serious, refused to allow me to throw it out. "No, wrap it, then put it where you will know where to find it—to bury me in."

Throughout her life, my mother often spoke

of her death. Not the actual occurrence but of its aftermath, the "disposal," resting place, and burial of her body. As with everything she dramatized, it could be lyrically romantic, macabre, or filled with her special brand of blackest humor. All were so much a part of the real Dietrich:

"I once found a beautiful little cemetery in the middle of a real French village, with poppy fields and cows, green benches in front of white cottages—just perfect, like a Monet. They even had a very good auberge that served a pot-au-feu almost as good as mine. With a restaurant so close, you could have gone there to eat lunch each time you visited my grave, but they said they had no room and that I wasn't French. The mayoress of the town said that if I bought land in the village, then I could be buried there, but as usual, I had no money, so . . . we will have to find another pretty village with a five-star restaurant that will bury me!"

Or:

"Sweetheart, I figured out how you can get my body out of this apartment after I am dead —without the reporters seeing you: You get one of those big, black, plastic garbage bags and you stuff me into it. You may have to break my arms and legs to fit me all in. Then, you get Peter— he is the strongest of your sons—to sling the bag over his shoulders and take the elevator all the way down to the basement garage. In the meantime, you go to Printemps and buy a big trunk, bring it back in a taxi, then put me in the garbage bag, into it. After that, you can take it to America, or some place. That's up to you."

She was deadly serious, but I just refused to take her ghoulish plan seriously, so attempted to laugh it off, saying: "Mass, what do you propose I do when I am asked to open that trunk in Customs?"

"Customs? Now they never open anything!"

"Maybe they don't with Marlene Dietrich, but with us lesser mortals, they certainly do!"

"Then, all you have to tell them is that you are doing what your mother *told* you to do!"

And then, there was Dietrich's world-famous monologue on her own funeral. She first invented it in the forties, polished and modified it, reassigned roles for new or departed lovers in the fifties and sixties, read other people's versions of it in their autobiographies and damned them to hell for their plagiarism in the seventies; finally, having fewer and fewer listeners, rarely performed it in the eighties. She had many versions, all unique in their own way, all pure Dietrich:

"When I am dead, can you imagine the to-do? . . . The reporters! The photographers! The fans! De Gaulle will proclaim a national holiday. Not a hotel room to be had anywhere in Paris. Of course, Rudi is going to organize everything. He will *love* it! Nellie and Dot Pondel will arrive to get me ready, do the makeup and hair. They are both crying so hard, they can't see, and of course, don't know what to do anyway! All those years they were with me at Paramount, they never had to do anything because I did it all myself! Now, for once, I am not there to do it for them, and they stand sobbing, wondering how they are going to put on the false eyelashes and get the front of my hair right. The back doesn't matter because I am lying down.

"Jean Louis has come all the way from Hollywood and is furious! He thought for once he would get the chance to put me into my foundation for the stage dress—now Rudi tells him that he will not allow his wife to be "seen like that!" and that I am going to wear "a simple black dress from Balenciaga" instead. Rudi says that only because he *knows* how I always wished I could get away with wearing just a little black dress on the stage . . . like Piaf.

"De Gaulle wanted me to be buried next to the Unknown Soldier at the Arc de Triomphe and do the service at the Notre-Dame, but I said "No, I want it at the Madeleine." That is my favorite church in Paris and the chauffeurs can park their limousines in the square next door and go have a coffee at Fauchon while they wait.

"We get one of those army wagons, like the one they had for Jack Kennedy when he was killed, with six black horses to pull the coffin, which is draped in a special tricolor, made by Dior.

"The procession will start at the Place de la Concorde and make its way, slowly, up the Boulevard de la Madeleine—all the way to the church, with the whole Foreign Legion marching to the beat of a single drum. . . . Too bad Cooper is dead, he could wear his costume from *Morocco* and join them. . . . The crowds line the streets, silently weeping. The great dress houses of Paris have closed their doors so that the little shop girls, the fitters, can go to the parade and say their last tearful adieux to 'Madame.' From all over the world, the Queers have arrived. They push through the crowds, trying to get closer to those rugged, handsome Legionnaires. For the grand occasion, they have copied costumes from my films and all look like me in *Shanghai Express* in their feather boas and little veiled hats. . . . From his car, Noël takes one look and wishes he could mingle but knows he has to be on his best behavior—so doesn't stop. He has written a special tribute to 'Marlenah,' which, of course, he will recite at the church himself, but he is annoyed, because when he had dinner with Orson the night before, Orson told him that *he* was going to do a whole scene from *Macbeth* and that Cocteau told him *he* was reciting something too, *very* high class and—in French!

"While I am being marched and mourned

up the avenue, the invited guests start arriving at the church. Rudi stands in his special, newly made by Knize, dark suit, guarding the entrance. On a table in front of him are two boxes filled with carnations—one with white ones, one with red. As each guest enters the church, Rudi gives him, or her, a carnation to wear—*Red* for those who made it, *White* for those who *say* they slept with me but never did. Only he knows!

"Inside, the church is crowded. The Reds on one side, the Whites on the other. They are all looking daggers at each other! You can imagine, everyone trying to see who has *red*, especially the women. . . . By the time Burt starts my overture, everyone is furious, madly jealous of each other, just like they always were when I was alive! Fairbanks arrives in a cutaway, bearing a letter from Buckingham Palace. . . . Remarque never makes it to the church—he is drunk somewhere and forgot the address. . . . Jean, smoking a Gauloise, leans against the side of the church—refuses to go inside. . . . All over Paris church bells begin to peal . . ."

I once suggested that it might be a great touch to have the entire 82nd Airborne Division do a jump, wearing *their* carnations, with General Gavin leading the way. . . . My mother loved the idea so much, she immediately added it to her scenario.

· · ·

BY 1982, my mother's legs were useless. She could no longer stand even if she had wanted to. With her usual fixed determination, she had accomplished what she had set out to do. She now had the perfect excuse to shut herself away from the world. Marlene Dietrich, without her beautiful legs? That was inconceivable . . . such a truth had to be kept hidden inside her bed, behind walls.

She started to cook odd bits of food on top of my father's lamp next to her bed. When that broke, she ordered an old-fashioned electric hot plate from her hardware store. Its plug joined the six others stuck into the various extension cords on the stained carpet next to the urine buckets. My imagination came up with horrific scenarios on that electrical madness of hers. I bought her a fire extinguisher and tried to teach her how to use it, wrote the directions in big black letters and pinned them to her mattress, but, knowing that if there was a fire, she would probably be too drunk to read or remember how to use it, I insisted that she at least learn to push her body down to the foot of the bed and slide herself into the wheelchair I had ordered to be positioned there permanently.

"Mass, in case of a fire, I want you to learn how to get out of here by yourself. As you refuse to have anyone sleep in, you must at least learn to get into the chair, wheel yourself to the front door and get out. You are not paralyzed! You can't just sit here and wait for someone to come up and get you."

"Ridiculous! How could there be a fire?"

"That hot plate next to your bed, that you love so, that you refuse to get rid of, for one."

"This little thing? I heat my sauerkraut all by myself. No one ever brings me anything to eat, so I *have* to cook for myself."

It was one of my mother's favorite fantasies, her being left to starve. I cooked, fans prepared delicacies and sent them over on elegant trays, neighbors were willing to cater the famous star on their floor, her maid fretted that Madame would never allow her to cook, Berlin fans sent her packages of frankfurters that she loved to devour raw; Swedish fans, marinated herring. Her market bills ran to five hundred dollars a week, but Dietrich kept right on convincing everyone, including herself, that she had been abandoned, left to starve—alone!

Despite my mother's withdrawal from the outside world, her expenses remained the same. Now, instead of shoes, she bought Kleenex boxes. Even Howard Hughes would have been impressed by the hundreds stacked high against her bedroom wall. Money had to be found to pay the bills.

I had thought for a long time that as Dietrich was "common property," a term used for those famous enough to warrant losing the protection that normal beings are allowed to enjoy, that anyone not only could, but would, eventually film a documentary of her life. So why not have Dietrich do her own—keep the financial rewards for herself instead of letting others reap the benefits. As her appearing on camera was now impossible, the idea of letting Dietrich narrate her own documentary became an intriguing idea.

It took a long time to convince her, then find the right money, backers willing to go along with the concept of hearing Dietrich's eighty-year-old voice without seeing her eighty-year-old face. Finally, one day in 1982, she allowed herself to be lifted into that wheelchair, and, for the first time in more than three years, was wheeled into her living room and placed in a chair. Under the ruse that broken toes made it impossible for her to move, she remained seated, immobile, while recording a conversation with the director Maximilian Schell that was to serve as the dialogue for her own documentary.

By taping time, she was not as enamored of Schell as she had been in the beginning of negotiations. He had made the mistake of writing her that, to prepare for their auspicious "coming together," he was going off somewhere idyllic— to read Proust.

"What? He goes to read—what?"

"Well, it seems Mr. Schell thinks Proust is the perfect aura to prepare himself for coming to you." I tried to get him out of trouble. I needed him, and her full cooperation was not guaranteed because she had signed a contract that said so. Dietrich considered herself above such legal trifles.

"A Swiss! Typical! That sister of his is the same—a cutsie-poo mennuble. We have made a mistake with him! Proust? To talk to a movie star . . . he has to read *Proust*? What affected mishigas!"

If it hadn't been too late to change him, I'm sure she would have tried. Fearing that I would somehow become involved in their dialogue, that Mr. Schell might be tempted to try and capitalize on having the famous mother *and* her "one and only" so close at hand, I asked my mother's agent to go to Paris and watch her for me while I stayed in Switzerland, played rear guard, and kept my fingers crossed. In order to make as much money on international sales as possible, and as both Schell and Dietrich were trilingual, the deal called for the first three days' conversation to be recorded in English, followed by the same amount of time on subsequent days in French and German. Again, to make certain that my mother cooperated, the contract stipulated that she was to be paid on a daily basis after each recording.

Despite the sincere effort of her agent, my mother was already high and aggressive on the morning of the first day, repeatedly switching back and forth from one language to another. That evening, after receiving the report of her condition, I called and tried, once more, to impress on her that as her largest market was America, the English version must be our main priority. Clear-headed as she always became around ten p.m., before turning to her Fernando Lamas and tranquilizers, she agreed, promising me to speak only in English for the next day's taping.

By eleven o'clock the next morning, all her good resolutions were swept away by the usual tide of scotch. Not only did she lapse into German constantly, she even indulged in rather coarse Berlin dialect, lied, argued, called everything "crap!" When asked about her sister, denied she ever had one. That shook Mr. Schell a bit.

Each day was a new disaster. We never did manage to get on tape what we had planned and hoped for. Maximilian Schell finally left Paris, a nervous wreck, without sufficient material, so he thought, from which to fashion a documentary. Sometimes having nothing, being desperate, can create a climate in which pure inspiration can materialize. Although I never discussed it with Mr. Schell, I believe this is what happened. Finding himself without what he had come to Paris to get, Schell was forced to invent a whole new concept. What this very talented director finally came up with was marvelous. Better than anyone thought possible. New, inventive, far superior to the original format.

Knowing that my mother would be too frightened of having to hear what she had said, of what had been done to her life by "strangers" in an editing room, I flew to Paris, rented a VCR, and, holding her hand, showed her the tape of the rough cut of *Marlene*. My god, how she hated it! She was livid that I dared to think such "junk" was good, and besides, it had been *my* idea—the whole abortion! She ranted and raved, screamed abuse at the TV screen—kept asking me what she was saying:

"What? What? What did she say—that's not *my* voice! That's not *me* talking! I never said that! Vulgar—vulgar! They must have faked my voice . . . that's not me. We have to sue them!" She had become noticeably deaf, but of course refused to admit to this sign of age. She kept complaining that everyone whispered, that the world was full of mumblers, kept the volume on her television set up so high that, in the summer, passersby in the street below would look up at her open windows to see who was shouting at them.

She spent the next six years hiring, firing, and arguing with German lawyers. She was determined to stop the documentary from being shown, later trying to send the producer to jail, or, better still, into "very dark alleys." When her documentary won prizes at film festivals, she relented a bit, suddenly got cozy-chummy with Schell, but it was a "seesaw" relationship whenever she remembered Proust.

Time passed, more and more her bedroom took on the look of a warehouse, everything was by dozens and gross. The Kleenex boxes were joined by containers of glucose, crates of tea, and every liver cleanser sold in Europe and points east. As she could hear well on the phone, those bills ran into thousands. Besides calling me for hours at a time, when she was feeling "mellow" she called fans. This fanatically private aristocrat now babbled her secrets to complete strangers.

As she outlived more and more lovers and pals, she had them framed and hung. I named it "the death wall" and watched fascinated as her conquests were displayed like trophies. After a while, it got pretty crowded up there. Just being dead did not automatically ensure you a place of honor. First, you had to be famous, then dead, to get framed.

In the spring of 1983, my mother decided to acknowledge the hypertension I had suffered from for ten years. My usual flood of mail from

Paris contained a *Newsweek* article on hypertension and—three pounds of salami. This was rapidly followed by—frankfurters, Chinese food high in monosodium glutamate, cheese, and to top it off, a large container of Coumadin, a highly dangerous blood thinner illegally obtained from her druggist, a woman so infatuated that my mother could easily have become the most successful drug dealer in France.

Dietrich played this form of lethal roulette constantly with people. My mother, the postal pusher! When her one-time Swedish Blonde was branded a drug user in the Swedish papers, Dietrich immediately began making secret packages, disguised to hold the amphetamines hidden inside. When I objected, she exclaimed:

"But she is my *friend*! And she'll get it anyway from those two fags she lives with—so why can't I send it to her?"

"Conscience?" I ventured.

"Ridiculous! If it makes her happy—why can't she have what she wants?" and turned back to making her secret bundles. Mme Defarge of friendship. She was unstoppable. Her lethal packages to me were constant. It does give one a funny feeling when one day's post contains a morphine derivative for that "little twinge in your shoulder," cortisone for the "tiny pimple on your chin," handfuls of uppers just in case I might be "tired," downers in case I wanted to "rest" a bit, and for those in-between times? A year's supply of Valium!

When my grown sons, passing through Paris, asked if they could visit her, she always refused, making up ridiculous excuses, either that there were reporters lying in wait for them or she was just on her way to—Japan. Or, "Yes, of course they could come," then when they were announced from the lobby, forcing her concierge to blatantly lie, that "Madame was not at home."

In my family, being embarrassed by Dietrich's behavior was an inherited trait. Sometimes she wrote them scathing letters of personal criticism, then complained bitterly when they did not answer. After all, it was their "duty" to pay her court. When they wrote to her, she sent me their letters along with the fan mail—without comment. When she received pictures of their children, she sent those too, written across the back: "Who are these strange children?" When people would ask her about her grandsons, she would reply: "Maria's children? . . . I never hear from them!"

Although her liver must have been turning to stone, she thrived. Her constitution continually astounded me. One winter, she got bronchitis—called me, her cough deep, rumbling with thick catarrh. I went into my usual spiel about having a doctor look at her, that I knew she would reject, then told her which antibiotic to take from her night-table pharmacy and, passport in hand, waited for the call I was certain would come that my "eighty-something" bedridden mother had been rushed to the hospital with galloping pneumonia. Two days later, she was as right as rain, fit as a fiddle. Others lie in hospitals for just a few weeks and get bedsores—Dietrich was bedridden for more than ten years and got nothing more than itchy skin.

When she heard that David Niven was dying of motor-neuron disease, she decided that here, finally, was the suitable and sufficiently dramatic reason for *her* inability to walk and so convinced herself that she, too, had "Lou Gehrig's disease."

"You know, I have what David Niven has," she announced to everyone, and wrote him about their "mutual" affliction. David, with that infinite humanity of his, took the precious time from his own terrible tragedy to write her, tried to comfort her. Niven died, Dietrich lived on, ruling her world from her private bunker.

Slowly, she alienated the few friends who had hung on to their loyalty, their memory of her, until they too gave up to salvage what was left of their own nerves. She did not miss them. She had her fans, her battalion of infatuated lesbians and gays, and her gofers, the concierges of her building who, for exorbitant tips, fetched, did errands for her between their shifts of duty.

Despite all that liquor and the drugs, during those intervals when she was clearheaded, my mother retained the sharp mind that had enchanted and intrigued the world. Although her opinions reflected her age, her ego, her Teutonic background, her mind never lost its inquisitiveness. Hunched over, peering through her giant magnifying glass, she devoured the newspapers and journals of four countries, cutting out articles on any subject that she deemed worthy of her interest, scrawling her acidic comments along the margins, then sending them on to me—not for my opinion but my "education" and as proof of her "superior intelligence." She had something to say about everything, as always negative, critical, cruel, often ugly.

Stories on AIDS particularly fascinated her. As the majority of her fan mail came to her bed from homosexuals, she developed the theory that she might become contaminated by opening their letters. She sent me a poem she wrote on the subject, saying that I could make a lot of money from it after she was dead:

AIDS

My Mother   She got it
Died of   From
AIDS   The Mails

That's News!	No one
She was hard	But Mails
As nails	And she got
But AIDS	AIDS,
Was harder	My mother did!
Especially	Don't blow
By Mail!	A fuse—
She touched	That's News!

She wrote a lot of what she called "poems" in her last years. Setting down her thoughts always had kept her occupied. Some were satirically funny, some very sad, even frightening, but all, in whatever language, pure Dietrich vintage:

Isn't it strange:
The legs
That made
My rise to glory
Easy, NO?
Because
My downfall!
Into misery:
Queasy, NO.

3 AM
April 9. 85

In later years, Dietrich wrote about herself at the drop of a franc, dollar, or mark. Making up stories around the real love of her life had always enticed her. She would call me, tell me the sum offered, read the questions asked for her to answer:

"Listen to this one: 'Who was the most difficult actor to work with?' Who? What shall I tell them? I make it all up anyway."

"Ray Milland?" I offer.

"Yes—good. Is he dead?"

"Yes."

"Then I can use him—easy! They also want to know who was the nicest one. . . ."

"Michael Wilding?"

"No—nobody knows who *he* is!"

"How about . . . Herbert Marshall?"

"Yes! They know who *he* is and he's dead too. Good. They ask about my stepfather, so I say, 'He was a shadowed figure and was killed in the war.' . . . I write fast—a whole block of paper in one morning. It's all made up, anyway—like when I talk to fans on the telephone —so it's real easy!"

Between writing stories to suit herself and reading the adoring fan mail, her day was filled with the legend of Dietrich. Her diaries, of course, had to remain sad, forlorn, long-suffering, and resigned to desertion—that too was part of the legend.

Her flirtations never stopped. At the age of eighty-five, my mother was given an award by the American Fashion Institute. Although my son David had been asked to accept it in her name, she refused, preferring to find someone who was famous, preferably renowned for their legs. Although she had never met him, she tracked down his private telephone number in New York City and called Mikhail Baryshnikov, asked him to accept the award for her, then proceeded to fall madly in love with him. For weeks after, she would phone me asking for love phrases in Russian so that she could sign off after their many marathon transatlantic phone calls with suitable passionate farewells in his mother tongue.

"Sweetheart, you should hear him! He is so wonderful! So soft, so lyrical, so romantic. But, you know, when I first phoned him I thought I had dialed a wrong number! A strange voice answered with a terrible American twang! But it was him. How is that possible? He is a Russian—how can he allow himself to sound so American? I told him he must get rid of that way of speaking right away. It doesn't suit him. It sounds so low-class! I told him, 'I used to be in love with Nureyev, but now I am in love with you! You are a much better dancer than he is and—you are a real *man*!' He wants to come here to see me. Of course, impossible . . . but it would be nice—after all the years of nothing, I should be nice and tight again 'down there,' don't you think? He would like that. Or just to sleep with him would be . . ." Her voice trailed off as her Fernando Lamas took effect. That was my usual cue to yell down the phone:

"Mass? Mass? Hang up the phone! Hang up—before you forget!"

When, in the summer of '87, her "two hours a day" maid went home to visit her parents in Portugal, my mother became frantic, asking the doormen and their wives to come in especially to empty her pails in the evening. When no one seemed overjoyed by this idea, she called me.

"Wouldn't you think that anyone can pick up a can of pee and throw it down the toilet? What is the big bit? You know, everybody should be *happy* that I *can* pee! Instead of saying 'how wonderful! Madame can pee!' they all behave as though I am asking them to do something unusual. I could be like Chevalier who died . . . remember? Because he *couldn't* pee. So they should all be *happy*! That I *can*, no?"

I had been trying for years to get her to agree to a regular nurse to look after her, but without success. Now I ventured, once again, to suggest that a trained professional could be the answer to all of her many physical discomforts. That made her furious:

"Give a stupid 'stranger' a key? Who has to

be trained? That I have to teach where everything is? And, you know very well how I hate women. No! I have an idea. You know the man who is downstairs, who guards the garage at night? The one I gave a key to already, in case no one else can be reached during the night? He is the one who could come. He could come up every night and pour my pee out for me. He looks older than he is, but he is quite young and very sweet. I don't know why I asked him to come up here the other night but he came and we talked. He sat on the bed and showed me pictures from his wallet. He is a very nice man. He hugged me before he left and I hugged him. I'm sure he would come and empty my pee, if I asked him."

I too was sure that this beguiling garage attendant would appear nightly for his hundred-franc tip and a chance to get to know even better the famous recluse and wondered how much blackmail money I would wind up having to pay him in the not too distant future.

Being bedridden and persistently refusing to allow anyone to live with her, those that served her all had to have keys to be able to get into her apartment. I knew the ones who could be trusted and those who would stop at nothing to make their knowing her secrets a lucrative investment. One of my constant recurring nightmares was that when my mother died, I and the few I trusted would not be able to get to her apartment in time to prevent the vultures from gorging themselves on their publicity feast.

Baryshnikov bit the dust and another took his place—in spades! "He is a Doctor"; always intoned in that turn-of-the-century awe given to those who reached such pinnacles of respect and stature. He started out as just another infatuated fan. Seeing the mighty Dr. on his return address, she picked up the phone, dialed California, and full of booze and self-pity, flirted across the miles, until he caught fire, began writing her love letters, explicit, erotic, and very titillating. As with everything she received, she sent them on to me, proud, gloating a little to show off her ageless seductiveness. I read these tasteless outpourings to know just how far she was allowing this to go, how much she was telling him, and shuddered at the proof of what was developing. They kept on coming, sizzling hot and heavy. I began to wonder if maybe this poor man was one of those sexually aroused by corpses—then discarded this fleeting thought of necrophilia, knowing that like everyone else, he saw her in those frilly panties and garter belt, the eternal Dietrich identity. The references made in his letter to intimate moments involving her and Gabin, Remarque, and others especially worried me—for those were things he could never have known without first being told them.

"Sweetheart, my 'Doctor'—what do you think he wants from me? Something of mine— something, you know that I have worn on my body." She giggles. Eighty-seven-year-old re- cluses are supposed to cackle, not trill deli- ciously, but Dietrich does. "You know what I did? I called Dior and told them I was sending over my concierge to pick up panties—you know, those little itsy-bitsy ones, like chorus girls wear. He came back with a whole selection, but most of them were too big, but one pair was teensy-weensy and cute, so I sort of rubbed it— you know where—then also put perfume on it and sent it to him, express. Of course, you *know* what he is going to do with it when he gets it!" and hung up.

After a year of this running vulgarity, their routine changed. Now it was he who called her, every day on the dot of eight p.m., Paris time, even sending her checks which she endorsed without a moment's hesitation, sent on to her bank for deposit. I had visions of our "doctor" setting up his trusty tape recorder, dialing Mar- lene Dietrich's private number in Paris, letting her talk, ramble on, telling the most intimate times of her long life, then when she hung up, rewinding the cassette, placing the record of his latest conversation with the world's famous re- cluse amongst the others in his locked desk. In the not too distant future, should these juicy recordings in Dietrich's own voice come on the open market, those canceled checks of his, bearing Dietrich's endorsements, could easily be used to claim that he had paid her for recording their conversations and I?— Would spend the rest of *my* days looking for a lawyer who'd be willing to take the case.

I once ventured to suggest that those too, too intimate conversations could become very dangerous.

"What? He is a Doctor!" and hung up, highly offended. An unknown fan had become sacrosanct, untouchable. That he also supplied his lady-love with potent hypnotics had a lot to do with her devotion. He broke the law, the oath of his profession, sending an eighty-eight-year-old alcoholic legally restricted drugs without ever having met her, let alone having examined her, but that, of course, was not considered a yardstick by which to measure his impeccable conduct. His blissfully drugged recipient "trusted" her "pusher."

As time passed, and he reinforced his hold by the regularity of his nightly devotion, he was admitted further and further into her private realm. He was asked to call her accountants with instructions, discussed financial matters with her bank, contacted and gained entrance to famous acquaintances in her name, shopped for her, ferreted information, was given my sons' private phone numbers to contact if he wished, sent me dangerous mind-altering drugs on her instructions, was given my number without my permission—with orders to call me whenever he deemed it necessary.

This reprehensible behavior of hers was not due to extreme old age, senility, nor certifiable alcoholism—this was Dietrich as she always was. She never changed. She was a law unto herself, knew it, lived it, and the world condoned it. Had I been foolish enough to try to protect her, stop her madness by legitimate legal means, any judge would have simply remembered her in those famous panties—and—certified me instead!

FOR THE FOURTH TIME that day, she called: "Sweetheart—you will never guess who called me." Her voice was ever so "springtime young," it reminded me of those "young things picking wild strawberries"!

"Reagan?" (ever since receiving personal birthday greetings from the White House, he was definitely "in"), I asked obediently. I knew this game—"questions and answers" was one of her favorite pastimes.

"No—but I called Nancy. That picture of

her in *Match*, she looks much too thin. I told her she looks *sick*. . . . She was sweet. I now have her private number. You haven't guessed."

"Burt?" Once a year he was overcome by nostalgia and phoned her, usually forgetting the difference in time and catching her just as her Fernando Lamases and Tuinal were taking effect, which made her ever so soft, dreamy, and gentle, which, in turn, charmed Burt anew.

"No, but I saw a picture of that terrible wife of his—she's Jewish!"

"Actually, Carole Bayer Sager is a magnificent lyricist—"

"Can't be. Well, who called?"

"Hepburn?" I knew she wouldn't have called, but my mother would appreciate my thinking she would.

"No, but I wish she would! Then I could tell her—how I love her! What a woman! All those years with Tracy and never a breath of scandal —but that was MGM. There they really protected their people. I hear she shakes all the time now—but still lets herself be seen, even does television! She must be rich—so why show herself like that?— So, who called me?"

"Sinatra?" I was running out of names and just took a stab.

"What? That old drunk? Hasn't got my number—anyway, if he called, I would do the 'maid.' " One of Dietrich's most persistent fantasies was that she could "do" accents, and constantly pretended to be Spanish or French maids who couldn't speak a word of English when answering her phone. She sounded exactly like Marlene Dietrich, trying to disguise her voice, but went right on believing she was another Meryl Streep—whose nose, whenever she saw a picture of her, irritated Dietrich enormously.

"I give up . . ."

"Kirk Douglas!"

"Kirk Douglas?"

"Yes! Out of the blue! How did he get my number? He was sweet. Told me he was writing a book—and I told him how I can't read anymore and we talked. . . . Nice man!"

When that book came out and Mr. Douglas recounted their telephone conversation, I walked into my mother's bunker and found her tearing his picture from his book jacket with a look that could curdle yogurt!

"Oh, there you are! That son-of-a-bitch talked about me in his filthy book, even my Fernando Lamases he mentions on the same page as Reagan! You can't talk about suppositories on the same page as a president! I cabled him. I told that bastard what I think of him!"

·   ·   ·

OVER THE YEARS, my husband knew he lived with a potential bomb in his head, suffered through brain surgery, subsequent stroke, emerged still a whole man through his magnificent courage and incredible will. At the age when boys think of who to ask to the high school prom, my youngest son faced the probability of cancer, endured the agony of major lung surgery, emerged to embrace his young life anew. My mother-in-law entered the long, tortuous road of senility and dementia within our home, et cetera, et cetera—as Yul would have said—and what was I most often asked? "How is your wonderful mother?" The one as healthy as a horse, except for what she alone had chosen to do to herself!

This powerful preoccupation the world has for the famous is a difficult yoke to live under. Those of us who carry it, due to birth, pay a price. Much less of a one, if the fame is earned through heroic or great intellectual achievement, but for those of us less privileged, who know that what is so revered is undeserving of canonization—until we learn that where fame and the power it engenders is concerned, fairness has no place—we scream into the void of nonexceptance and are driven mute by its very repetitive uselessness. Even death does not alter our condition.

Others bury their parents, mourn, for whatever reasons, confront their feelings anew in scattered moments; finding a forgotten letter, an old photograph, entering a newly empty room trigger emotions that with time are allowed to fade, eventually stay buried for good.

Our ghosts can never be laid to rest. They wander through countless laudatory tomes, photographic images, television screens, giant movie screens, their forms magnified a hundredfold— they breathe eternally! Alive forever. This continuous resurrection, this immortality constantly reconfirmed, is a haunting that invades our daily lives as when they lived. There is no escaping them, dead or alive. Dietrich is especially skilled at materializing. Looking for a picture frame anywhere in the world? Whose image will be looking at you from most of the models on display? Fancy card shops are one of her favorite places—there she sits in long racks, in multiple choice, or rolled up, poster size. Another poltergeist specialty is her voice, moaning through "la Vie en rose." It captures you in elevators, pursues you through supermarkets, airports, department stores, ricochets off tiles in fancy ladies' rooms, follows you through hotel lobbies in countries you wouldn't believe. Then there is the "Dietrich" type hat, the "Dietrich" type suit, the "Dietrich" type shoes—the "Dietrich" look. Never is there one day completely free of Marlene Dietrich. What is it like, to have a mother no one knows? Must be nice.

When I am with her, around ten in the evening, she hits a high and wants to "gab." I know I am not allowed to sit on her bed, position a chair near its edge and sit. She flips through the latest French *Vogue*:

"Look at this! They don't know *what* to do anymore! Ugly, ugly, ugly! Remember Travis? Nice man, always listened—had good ideas but, most of all, he listened. We used to work all night, just to get *one* look . . . the Review costume? And that wonderful hat! The hours we worked! But on the first sketches, didn't he have it different?"

"It was blue velvet, with ermine."

"Yes, yes . . . blue . . . not good, like for Jeanette MacDonald, so I made it dark green and—was right! Remember *Shanghai Express*, the cock-feather dress? How we worked and how Travis finally found the right feathers? How beautiful they were! What work! . . . And I made the shoes, like Chanel did years later. What a fake *that* woman was! Did one cut, repeated it a thousand times, and was called 'a great designer'! She was a decorator—not a designer. Like Schiaparelli . . . much *better* than her, but still a decorator. The gloves—did we put white on the inside for *them* or for the ones in *Desire*?"

"The black handbag for the cock-feather dress had a white Art Deco design, so you matched the idea in the gloves."

"Yes! We did a lot of that—as though it was

really *that* important. No one really noticed, but we thought it *had* to be all—perfect. Now, they just throw things on actors and nobody cares. . . . All that work, the hours, the fittings . . .''

She sips her cold tea, swooshing it around her mouth before swallowing. Her tongue probes inside her cheek:

"Here, I lost another tooth—must be a cap? Can't be a real one . . . I used to chew hard lemon candy. Wish I had some of the real sour ones Papi always bought for me in Salzburg. Oh! Remember Salzburg? And how we used to buy out Lanz? . . . All those wonderful dirndls . . . wonder where *they* all are. . . . How we laughed!''

She is unaware she has switched to German. "Tami and I, we used to laugh and Papi scolded us because we always had to then pee! . . . Nice times . . . Remember the cow—Papi got because I told him I *had* to have a farmhouse with a real cow and red geraniums on the windows? He did it all! . . . Another life . . . I *had* to have an Austrian farmhouse with geraniums and a cow . . . then I never saw it—I was so in love with Jaray! The things he put up with!—Did you see that terrible picture of Garbo in the paper? Those bastards . . . they caught her. Did you see her hair? Ugly, ugly, and *long*, so old! Terrible! She used to count every piece of sugar to make sure the maid didn't steal. They never could do a long shot of her because of her big feet."

"I hear she has kidney disease . . . is going to Columbia Presbyterian for dialysis."

"*That* suits her! *That* goes with her character, smelly pee. She'll die of it, like Chevalier. Don't forget, you swore you will never let them take me—to put me in a hospital."

"Yes, Mass . . . I know."

"Remember! You swore on the *heads of your children*!"

She flicks the pages, continues in English, "Everywhere—braids! Big news! I wore braids in *Dishonored* and again in that stupid film, the one with that naked statue. . . ."

"Mass, you know that Brian died?"

"Who?"

"Brian Aherne," I yell. I keep forgetting she can't hear a normal tone.

"Oh? Didn't I make a film with him? Yes —he was in love with me! And came to Paris! A big 'romantic—coming to see me' and sat frozen through the whole dinner because Papi came with us. . . . He was *so* upset at the husband 'knowing' about us, he rushed right back to London. Typically British! . . . He used to write me long boring letters—and you liked him."

She takes another slug of tea, picks up the American *Vogue*. . . . "That Bergman daughter from Rossellini is everywhere! She must be *rich*! With those thick lips of hers, she looks like a

Ubangi! . . . Look at this eye makeup. Clowns! Remember when I wanted dark eyes and put drops in my eyes and got blind as a bat! And Jo just gave them to me with his lights and was angry with me because I hadn't told him that I wanted 'Spanish' eyes? The things we did! And now they write books . . . and think they invented it all. Sweetheart, what was the name of Jack Gilbert's daughter—the one that wrote that terrible book about him and said I slept with her father?"

"Tinker."

"Yes . . . how you remember all those things! And who was the actor who talked to me first on the boat—in *Morocco*?"

"Adolphe Menjou."

"Terrible man . . . didn't he turn out to be a Nazi? Talking of Nazis, Jannings was one. He tried to choke me in *The Blue Angel*. He was furious, because Jo paid so much attention to me."

"I remember when we all looked for your costume through all the trunks and old hat boxes . . ."

"What? You weren't even born!"

"Yes, I was! In the Berlin apartment, with Tami, we all looked for cuffs. And . . ."

"Yes—yes! The cuffs! You *remember* that? I tell the 'Doctor' all the time—'My daughter, she will know, I will ask her, she remembers *everything!' This* you won't remember. One day, the front office ordered a test for *Devil Is a Woman* and Travis got all hysterical because we had nothing designed yet . . ."

"And you made up a terrible costume, even used one of the piano shawls from the Colleen Moore house we rented."

"No, no, no—that *too* you remember? *That* memory you inherited from your father. He remembered everything too. You have Papi's diaries locked up?"

"Yes, Mass."

"I started a file marked 'precious' with rare photographs that I got from fans—important for when you write that book."

That is my cue to hand her the bulging file. I know she wants to show me. The pictures are well known, can be bought from any movie-fan outlet, but she thinks of them as "precious" because they are beautiful.

"Look, here is the beautiful one in the mink hat from *Scarlet Empress* and the banquet dress. Remember that terrible banquet? Me, in all those awful pearls, dying of the heat—and Jo's concentration camp sculptures. Long before we knew they would exist for real. . . . What was the name of the film where I wore that beautiful dress with the little fur cuffs?"

"*Blonde Venus.*"

"Yes . . . and that wonderful hat we made

for the whore scene . . . with the red cherries— same film?"

"Yes, Mass."

The heavy file slips from her hand, she is ready to let go, allow the sleeping pills to do their act of safe oblivion. I turn off the lights and go to my couch in the living room under the wall where Chevalier smirks, de Gaulle preens, Gabin broods, Cocteau poses, Coward mocks, Hemingway looks through you, Fleming sits atop his petri dish. It is three o'clock in the morning.

I have made the beef tea, Irish stew, boiled beef, and gallons of special chicken soup—all ordered and eagerly awaited when sober, that I know she will not eat, that will be given to the maid and doormen the moment I leave.

She wakes. It takes time to emerge from one tunnel, start on the scotch—and enter another. It is her daily journey, when the angry monster takes, once more, center stage and rules our day. As death sits nearer, her fear of being erased by it, overwhelms her. The fury it births invades everything. She hates life for being so fragile, unpredictable, capable of deserting her. How dare it not come into line—obey her command for immortality. Being immortal in the memory of others does not impress her in the least. Control is not ephemeral; control, and its henchman, power, is making people jump to execute one's orders. By renouncing all true friends and family, she faces her private hell alone, un-aided by those who want so much to, and could, help ease her journey. The final rejection of life will not be my mother's death but her own cast-ing out of all true love, and human need; she defies the God she has chosen to reject—to come and do His worst, over her dead body, if He dare!

MY TRAIN WAS LATE, taxis difficult to find on a rainy night. I let myself into her apartment, check if maybe she is still awake. She feels me, sits up, and rejects being taken over by the mul-tiple doses of Tuinal and Serax. My mother can actually do that—command hypnotic drugs to halt their function inside her body. She puts her big pillow behind her back, wants to "talk." I bring my chair.

"Have you *seen* all those weeping pictures in the papers? It is really being overdone! And why wasn't she there to watch her husband race? All this Monaco to-do! It never ends! Now, in-stead of that terrible Stephanie, we are going to get nothing but the Royal Widow bit . . . with all those children . . . and—why was she in Paris? Buying dresses?"

"Mass, Princess Caroline didn't *know* her husband was going to be killed . . ."

"No, no, no—she's playing 'widow' *too*

much. She *must* have a guilty conscience!" She
pretends to look for something on the shelf by
her shoulder, takes a fast slug of scotch from the
shot glass hidden there. "Did you see what that
terrible Bob Hope said in the paper? He isn't
going to the desert in Arabia to entertain the
soldiers—because *he* already has a desert in
Palm Springs? Unbelievable! Terrible man! All
those medals and big awards. For what? Schlepping chorines on generals' planes? Making sure
he got photographed everywhere . . . ever so
brave? Wasn't he once 'low-class English' . . .
like Chaplin?"

I'm trying to keep a straight face—she's in
form tonight!

"Yes, Mass."

"But *now* he's a 'big' American?"

"Yes."

Another fast slug. "Orson is dead, isn't he?"

"Yes, Mass . . ."

"With all that fat . . . no wonder. What was
that film he made about Hearst, that made him
famous?"

"Citizen Kane."

"Yes, that was the one. . . . That terrible
Hearst tried to stop the film. He threatened all
the theater owners so they wouldn't show it.
. . . And I was so in love with Jean at the time,
I paid no attention. Isn't that terrible . . . that
big Hearst scandal and I was so busy making pot-

au-feu, I paid no attention to greatness! I would have gone to bed with him, but he only liked black hair. Oh, I got another one of those 'professor' books. Some American fan sent it. Again, full of 'deep' meanings. What Jo *really* meant with a 'shot,' what I *really* meant with a 'look'! The usual crap. Where do they *get* all these ideas? They all think they have discovered something new. All this 'to-do' about *deep* meanings and Freud. We made a film—then we did another. Now they all think it is *art*. Such stupidity! You get paid to make a film—if it makes money, you get to make another film. If it doesn't, you are suddenly not so la-di-da important. It's a business, not art."

She takes another fast sip. "You do your job—that's what you are here for . . . to do your job! If you can't do it right, you have no right to be paid the big salaries they pay. Does Lendl or that German horse—you know—the one who plays tennis and keeps mooning about her father? Do *they* get paid millions because they play tennis—*badly*? Of course not! But no one writes books about what they *really* meant to say with a forehand, or what *sexual meaning* was in a serve! So why do they always see big meanings in films? Why always with me? The reason I wore tails in *Morocco* was because Jo wanted to hide the legs, and I looked wonderful in them, and the Americans would be shocked! . . . That's why the next one, *Dishonored*, was never talked about—I did nothing shocking, except when I pierce the end of the chiffon scarf onto the tip of the sword. *That* is exciting and that's the only scene they remember and talk about! Meanings . . . meanings. Idiots! Just *work*! You must say *that* when you write your book. Teach them what was important! Today, I got a postcard from a fan, the one from *Scarlet Empress*, I put it in your file, the one in the white dress, with the ostrich feathers and that *beautiful* white wig. How they are all allowed to sell postcards of me and make money, I will never understand. . . . When I was in boarding school in Weimar, I went to a costume ball and wore a white wig. . . . Albert Lasky . . . he was the first who took— what *is* it, that they take?"

"Your virginity?" I venture.

She doesn't hear me, goes right on:

". . . took my 'innocence' away. . . . He was the conductor of the Weimar opera. I went to his house, took off all my clothes, sat on his sofa while he played the piano—but do you think I would take off that wig? . . . Even when we went to bed, I kept it on!"

"Made it more exciting?" I suggest.

"No! Nothing exciting! I just *loved* that wig!"

"But what about that violin teacher?"

"Oh! He was Weimar too. He wasn't so

nice. . . . He took . . . whatever it's called, right there in the music room on the couch."

Her voice, a little sleepy, has slipped into German. "My mother put me in that school. She thought I couldn't get out—we had very strict hours," her face becomes still, thoughtful, her voice lowers, "she was a hard woman." She smooths the top edge of the sheet, as though embarrassed by this implied criticism.

"All day, I have had this song in my head —but I don't remember all the words." She hums a plaintive tune, sings the German words she does remember, a sad little tale of wintertime and swallows . . . calling farewell.

"Once, my mother moved us to where my father was. She would walk us by the hospital, so my father could look down from his barred window and see us. I always thought he had syphilis and it went into his head."

She inspects her thumb. "Split nail—comes from opening all the fan mail."

I hand her the nail file she likes, the one from *Foreign Affair*. "I never felt anything— with any of them. I married Papi because he was beautiful . . . but I never felt—anything. Then . . . I got pregnant . . ." Her sigh is filled with regret.

" 'Fremdgehen,' that means—sleeping with your husband but also sleeping with others." She twists the gold band on her finger. She has begun wearing a wedding ring. I suspect her reason for wearing it. She looks down and remarks: "I thought it looks better—when they find me . . ."

Although she tells me it is her mother's, I know it is not. It is new. Ever an eye on history, Dietrich will be found, the pure lady wife true to her marriage vows, her diary by her side that says: "Have not heard from Maria," "No food," "All alone." She has planned it all. Planned it to the minutest detail, a superbly crafted script that the world will believe. She is the true creator and curator of the Dietrich legend.

Once again, I've come, have tried to get close enough to her to change the dirty sheets, clean her—she screams invectives, her fury out of proportion, raw. I stand there, helpless, and suddenly, I know! I know her game that we have been playing. She wants it! She wants to be found filthy, stench rising—it is her final self-crucifixion: the mother who was left to die alone, neglected by the child she loved too well. A pitiable creature thus discovered would never be branded a whore, especially if she wears—a wedding ring. And such pity floods my soul—for this once glorious creature, who lies in her hoarded filth doing penance, *still* courting beatification.

Her eyes are closing, she is finally willing to let go, allow the pills to take over and finish her day. She slides down, curls against the very edge of the dilapidated mattress, murmurs:

"You're here . . . so I can sleep."

Her legs withered. Her hair, chopped short haphazardly in drunken frenzies with cuticle scissors, painted with dyes—iodized pink between dirty white blotches. Her earlobes have begun to hang low. The teeth, of which she is so proud because they are still "all hers," have blackened and cracked. Her left eye, dulled by a cataract she refuses to have treated. Her once translucent skin is parchment. She exudes an odor of booze and human decay.

Death sits like a Jabba on dirty sheets, and with it all, despite and through the decay, something remains . . . a faint glimmer, perhaps only a memory of what once was . . . *Beauty* . . . so enveloping . . . so enthralling . . . so perfect, that for more than fifty years, all women were judged by its standard, all men desired it.

Her snores are ragged, spittle trails from her furrowed lips. Like a fetus she lies, bony hands cradling a sunken cheek, her matchstick legs tucked high against her frail body, she lies—as though afraid to be born and face yet another day's survival.

I stand looking at this pathetic creature, who calls herself my mother, and feel sorry for both of us.

I make sure the fire extinguisher is by her

side, the hot plate turned off, the water steaming in her thermoses, the pails, bowls, and pitchers ready for the morning. Crawl under the tables, haul out her bottles, take them to the kitchen, pour half their contents down the sink—funny how the smell of scotch turns my stomach—refill the bottles to their original marks with water, shake them, replace them into her hiding place. Even when I am not there with her, she hides her drinking from herself, the final delusion of a doomed alcoholic. I look once more to make sure she is still breathing, I leave—the door ajar as ordered.

The living room where no one lives—grimy drapes swagged in time, carpets threadbare, stained, cartons, packing boxes, files and more files, old suitcases, the big gray elephants of my childhood, all kept, all hoarded throughout the years, lists, lists and more lists hang from brittle Scotch tape amongst the Orders, Citations, Commendations, Awards, Decorations, ornate medals on wide faded ribbons, amongst the framed poster-size images of their once glorious owner—give the scene a sense of sepulchre in waiting.

I stand, looking at the organized deadness of her belongings, wish—oh, for so many things that should, could be different. Next time, I must—I will—try one more time to clean her, wean her off the bottle. Once more— Just once more— I must try . . . it is not right for her to die this way . . . I close the door. I am tired.

The Paris air is fresh and clean—it smells of soft rain and fallen leaves. Across the street, the lights from the Plaza Athénée glisten upside down in the wet pavement. I stand—breathe deep—and, suddenly, I run. Like a child in anticipation, I run. I don't know why I suddenly need to hurry so—but I do. Life and love are waiting and I must get to them. Home! I'm going home.

NOVEMBER 1990.

SCHÖNEBERG 1901   **PARIS 1992**

MORTUARY SHADOWS—silent cold. I stand by the open coffin looking down. Carefully I place the small chamois bag containing her travel charms by her side. She has a long journey before her and might want them. How small she is, this power that controlled my life— Just a child in a white satin shroud—untried vulnerability—and the sorrow comes and I run out into the sunlight.

Dietrich had her funerals. No marching Legionnaires, no color-coded boutonnieres for long discarded lovers—the "husband who knew all" was long dead—as were the many loves. Still, her coffin draped in the flag of France rested before the heroic altar of her favorite, La Madeleine, her opulent wartime decorations displayed by her side and "shopgirls wept for Madame," as did the thousands who came to pay her homage.

Still one wish to fulfill:
"Schöneberg—that's where my mother's grave is— Now, with the wall gone and Berlin normal again, one could go . . ." She leaves the thought suspended, a question half unanswerable.

"Mass," I said without really thinking, "you could, you know, go back. We could do the black wig disguise bit, go by train . . . no one would catch us!"

"NO! A wheelchair on a train? All that way? . . . And then in and out of taxis to go to the cemetery? No! Those sons of bitches would find out and catch us . . . No, too late, FINITO!" Again that tone of longing.

Now she is safe. Shielded in her lead-lined box, no flashbulb can invade her face and now —now finally she can go home.

Before the journey, the tricolor is removed, her coffin redraped with the Stars and Stripes. This one act is for me—a selfish need to show the world, make the statement that Marlene Dietrich was an American citizen, regardless of her romantic attachments.

The coffin has been roped for passage, the Stars and Stripes lashed to its sides. Amidst the luggage of the living, it waits, a unique outline against the setting sun and, for me, it becomes the symbol of all the flag-draped coffins that have sat on lonely tarmacs waiting to be shipped back home—and I weep as they lift hers into the body of the plane.

Schöneberg, sun-dappled peace—in a country not known for it. An idyllic garden, as though conceived for just such a romantic girl's return. My mother sleeps beneath lilies of the valley— I walk the few steps separating her from her mother. I stand by my grandmother's grave and tears choke me. I have so much to tell her, and childhood words are not enough—to say it all— let her know I have brought her child, that was given me so long ago, back to her to love again—perhaps even forgive for the hurting of those who needed her so.

I only whisper: "Be good to her. She needs you to be good to her," and I cry—for all the lost love so unretrievable—and leave them to make their way together.

PHOTOGRAPHIC CREDITS

Lucien Angier: 758 below
Dietrich Archive: All other illustrations
Dietrich Archive/The Kobal Collection: 68, 119, 120, 161 above, 162, 163, 165 above left, 166, 251 below, 252, 256, 257 below, 258 above, 495–497, 591–592, 703–706, 729, 730 below, 674 above, 676 above, 757, 803, 804 above, 885, 931, 932, 933 above and right, 934 above, 955 below, 956, 957 above right and below, 958 below, 979, 980, 1061, 1062, 1099 above, 1101, 1102 above, 1129 below, 1131, 1132, 1207, 1208 above, 1209, 1247–1248, 1265, 1266 above, 1295
Express Newspapers of London/Editorial Enterprises, New York: 1297 below
Milton Greene: 1130, 1345 left
The Kobal Collection: 165 above right
Alexander Liberman: 1210
Life Magazine: 1099 below, 1100 left, 1130
Arnold Newman: 1100 left
Paris-Match: 1294 above right
Photo Giocomelli, Venice: 845
Photo Star, Cannes: 846 below
Photo Werhard, Salzburg: 760 above
UPI/Bettmann Archive: 1100 below, 1345 below
U.S. Army: 997, 1000
U.S. Army Signal Corps: 957 above left, 999 below left and below right, 1029, 1030, 1031 above, 1032
Ginette Vachon: 1346 above